MW01252825

City of Order

Law and Society Series

W. Wesley Pue, General Editor

The Law and Society Series explores law as a socially embedded phenomenon. It is premised on the understanding that the conventional division of law from society creates false dichotomies in thinking, scholarship, educational practice, and social life. Books in the series treat law and society as mutually constitutive and seek to bridge scholarship emerging from interdisciplinary engagement of law with disciplines such as politics, social theory, history, political economy, and gender studies.

A list of titles in the series appears at the end of the book.

City of Order

Crime and Society in Halifax, 1918-35

Michael Boudreau

UBCPress · Vancouver · Toronto

21 20 19 18 17 16 15 14 13 12 5 4 3 2 1

Printed in Canada on FSC-certified ancient-forest-free paper
(100% post-consumer recycled) that is processed chlorine- and acid-free.

Library and Archives Canada Cataloguing in Publication

Boudreau, Michael S. (Michael Scott), 1967-
City of order: crime and society in Halifax, 1918-35 / Michael Boudreau.

(Law and society, ISSN 1496-4953)
Includes bibliographical references and index.
Also issued in electronic format.
ISBN 978-0-7748-2204-6 (bound)

1. Crime – Nova Scotia – Halifax – History – 20th century. 2. Criminal justice, Administration of – Nova Scotia – Halifax – History – 20th century. 3. Sociological jurisprudence – Nova Scotia – Halifax – History – 20th century. 4. Halifax (N.S.) – Social conditions – 20th century. I. Title. II. Series: Law and society series (Vancouver, B.C.)

HV6810.H33B69 2012 364.9716'22509041 C2012-901446-X

Canadä

UBC Press gratefully acknowledges the financial support for our publishing program of the Government of Canada (through the Canada Book Fund), the Canada Council for the Arts, and the British Columbia Arts Council.

This book has been published with the help of a grant from the Canadian Federation for the Humanities and Social Sciences, through the Aid to Scholarly Publications Program, using funds provided by the Social Sciences and Humanities Research Council of Canada.

UBC Press
The University of British Columbia
2029 West Mall
Vancouver, BC V6T 1Z2
www.ubcpress.ca

For two special grandmothers,
Edna Facey and Ida Martin

Contents

Preface

HALIFAX, NOVA SCOTIA, experienced dramatic socio-economic changes during the period from 1918 to 1935. The decline of industrial manufacturing meant growing unemployment, poverty, and out-migration. At the same time, the rise of a service-sector economy sheltered the city from complete economic collapse. New forms of technology, culture, and ideas transformed the daily lives of many residents of Halifax. And while many debated the pros and cons of their "modern" world, most did agree on one thing: modernity had corrupted public morality and unleashed an imposing array of social problems, including crime, upon the city. Some even blamed modernity for the crime that beset Halifax between 1918 and 1935. By examining the incidence of crime and the experiences of some criminals in Halifax during these years, I explore the ways in which this perceived rise in crime, the response of the criminal justice system, and the discussion of order shaped one city's reaction to the challenges of modernity.

Halifax prided itself on being a peaceful, well-ordered city. Crime epitomized the essence of social disorder, and, to counter it, Halifax began to modernize its machinery of order (the police department, courts, and prisons) and to place greater emphasis on the ethos of "crime control." In the process, the rule of law served as a means of regulating the lives of those men, women, and children who broke or who could potentially break the law. Moreover, it helped to entrench the class, gender, and racial inequalities that characterized this city of order.

Most members of the Halifax community opposed crime and the "criminal element," attaching little importance to the reform and rehabilitation of criminals. Only juvenile delinquents received any type of reformatory treatment. In the public discussions that arose about crime and criminals, "traditionalist" and "progressive" paradigms emerged in the attempt to come to grips with the problem of criminality. As the city's law enforcement authorities and concerned citizens battled crime to preserve law and order they constructed an image of the "criminal class." This class, comprised primarily of white, working-class men, provided the police with a convenient target in their efforts to maintain a strict sense of law and order in Halifax.

Women and ethnic minorities who turned to crime also endured harsh opposition from the law and Halifax society. Women, many Halifax citizens believed, could not commit a crime. Paradoxically, however, those who did were perceived as anomalies within society and, hence, were punished severely. Some women attempted to use the criminal law as a source of empowerment, usually against their abusive or neglectful husbands, yet this often met with limited success. Whether as offenders, complainants, or victims, women in Halifax received little equality before the law.

Ethnic minorities bore the brunt of residents' hostility towards crime and disorder. Halifax's dominant white society depicted blacks, Chinese, and "foreigners" as the "other" and relegated them to the margins of civil society. As well, each of these groups was accused of being heavily involved in prostitution and "white slavery," gambling, illegal drugs, and petty crime. In turn, they suffered discrimination at the hands of the criminal justice system.

The "city of order" never fully materialized in interwar Halifax, but those residents who pursued this ideal had a profound impact not only upon the lives of the women, men, and children who were ensnared by the machinery of order but also upon daily life in the city.

Acknowledgments

THE CRIMINAL "UNDERWORLD" of interwar Halifax has fascinated me for perhaps too many years. Along the way it has been my pleasure to incur a number of intellectual debts that I now wish to formally recognize.

Ian McKay at Queen's University was, and remains, a scholarly mentor extraordinaire and, most of all, a friend.

Special mention is also due to the late William G. Godfrey (Mount Allison University), along with George A. Rawlyk and Shirley Spragge (Queen's University). Each, in their own unique way, had a profound influence on me and I continue to miss their wisdom and wit.

My sincere thanks goes to Heather J. MacMillan at Library and Archives Canada; David Saint-Ange of the Correctional Service of Canada Museum (Kingston); Sergeant Don Young of the Halifax Police Museum Archives; Donna Matheson of the Atlantic Institute of Criminology; and the reference staffs of the law library at Queen's University, Dalhousie University Archives and Special Collections, the Legislative Library of Nova Scotia, and, especially, Nova Scotia Archives (NSA). Without their assistance the task of locating and deciphering the mound of archival and statistical material associated with this project would have been nearly impossible. Indeed, Barry Cahill (formally of NSA), John MacLeod, Philip Hartling, and Lois Yorke at NSA were extremely helpful in this regard.

A number of friends lent me a much needed helping hand. At the University of New Brunswick (Saint John) and the University of Ottawa, Greg Marquis and Constance Backhouse, respectively, read the entire manuscript and offered feedback that was vital to improving it. I am also grateful to the UBC Press readers whose incisive comments helped to make this a better book. Jim Morrison (Saint Mary's University), gave me the transcripts from the interviews with two Halifax police officers: these were invaluable sources. At Dalhousie University, Shirley Tillotson discussed with me the history of early twentieth-century Halifax and gave me crucial research leads, as did Suzanne Morton (McGill University). At the Dalhousie Schulich School of Law, Philip Girard helped me unravel the mysteries of the criminal law and the nuances of Canadian legal history; at Acadia University, Barry Moody opened up his files for my perusal; at the University of British Columbia, Tamara Myers enlightened me about the history of policewomen; and at the University of Toronto, Jim Phillips was one of the first scholars to pique my interest in criminal justice history. All of this fine scholarly assistance notwithstanding, I take full responsibility for my work and for whatever "crimes" I may inadvertently have committed.

Randy Schmidt and Holly Keller at UBC Press performed yeoman service in bringing this book to fruition, and Wes Pue, general editor of the Law and Society Series, was unwavering in his support of both myself and this book.

My sincere thanks to *Acadiensis* for allowing me to use, in chapters 2 and 4, some of the material from a previously published article.

At the University of New Brunswick, Bill Parenteau (former editor of *Acadiensis*), Marg Conrad, Linda Kealey, and Greg Kealey have been terrific supporters since my arrival in Fredericton.

I wish to thank St. Thomas University for granting me the McCain Award, which gave me the valuable time that I needed to put the finishing touches on the manuscript. The Senate Research Committee at St. Thomas University also provided generous support to help defray the cost of the index.

Dale Dasset was very helpful in the preparation of the manuscript.

Also at St. Thomas University a number of superb scholars have become close friends and sources of inspiration: Rusty Bitterman, Michael Dawson, Catherine Gidney, Gayle MacDonald, Jean Sauvageau, Peter Toner, Tony Tremblay, and Shaunda Wood.

Finally, words alone cannot convey what Bonnie Huskins has meant to me and to this book, nor can they adequately express my thanks to her; hopefully, my enduring love will suffice. And while this book is not dedicated to Bonnie per se, the spirit of Edna and Ida, to whom it *is* dedicated, lives on in her.

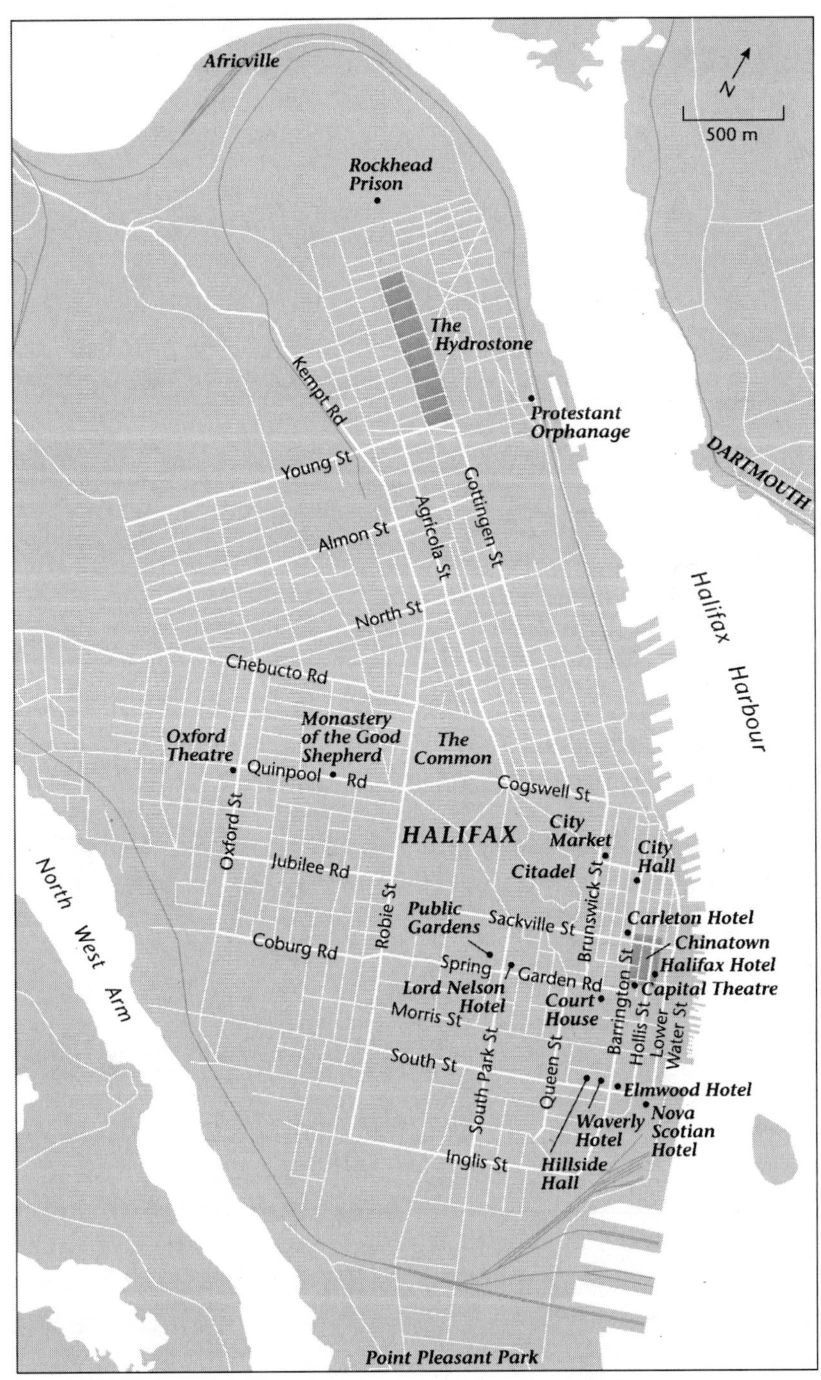

Halifax, ca. 1930

City of Order

Halifax Blues

Junked cars bunch, hunch like rats; laundry,
Lynched, dangles from clotheslines; streetlamps sputter,
Gutter, blow out; gross, bloated cops
Awake and pummel Lysol-scented drunks,
While God grins at scabbed girls who scour the streets
To pass pestilence to legislators.
The harbour crimps like a bent, black cripple;
It limps, drops dead on rocks: each wave's a crutch
That's pitilessly kicked aside. Above,
Grim gulls beat night with wings that beat back rain.
I drag poems from the water's muffled black.
They chomp, wriggle, and thrash on Love's bloody,
Two-pronged hook. I slap them, writhing still,
On paper, and cry beautiful darkness –
The baroque scream of a feeling. Hurt crows
Caw my sorrow better than a thousand white
Doves. I skulk beneath these fainting streetlamps
To disturb taverns, set cops ill at ease.

– George Elliott Clarke, *Lush Dreams, Blue Exile* (1994)

INTRODUCTION

Crime, the Rule of Law, and Society

THE GUNSHOT THAT eventually killed Leslie A. Corkum shattered the silence of what had otherwise been a calm Halloween evening in Halifax in 1922. Corkum, age twenty-six, owned a grocery store on Spring Garden Road in a residential area of the city. As Corkum busily prepared to close up his shop shortly after 11:00 PM, the murderer entered the premises and instructed him to put up his hands. When Corkum refused to do so, thinking the whole affair was simply a hoax (he reportedly said to the bandit, "You are only joking aren't you?"), the gunman shot him in the abdomen, plundered the cash register, and fled into the darkness. Rushed to the Victoria General Hospital for treatment, Corkum died there two days later.[1] Shock and indignation surfaced in the wake of this shooting. A local paper called it one of the "most daring robberies that has ever taken place in the history of this city."[2] Another labelled it a "particularly bold and dastardly" crime that should "bring the authorities sharply to their sense of responsibility as the custodians of law and order in the community."[3] The *Morning Chronicle* then called upon Mayor John Murphy to immediately implement the measures necessary to apprehend the person who had committed this "truly alarming" deed.[4] For his part, the mayor, underlining the extent to which the hold-up was something unprecedented, unsettling, and unconventional – "modern," in short – issued a statement that attempted to offer reassurance to the citizens of Halifax: "An occurrence such as this is new to Halifax. There need be no question in the minds of our citizens as to the steps which have been taken to trail down the perpetrator ... It is only necessary to say nothing is being left undone by the police department to bring the criminal to justice."[5] Even the Attorney General's Office, in an attempt to solve the case, offered a $500 reward for any information leading to the capture of Corkum's assailant.[6] Many in the community wanted this crime solved quickly and a sense of order restored to Halifax.

Sensitive to this public pressure and well aware of its duty to combat crime and protect the public, the Halifax Police Department launched a sweeping investigation. Every available officer and detective took part in gathering evidence, questioning possible witnesses, and locating suspects. The chief of police, Frank Hanrahan, personally supervised the case. He assured concerned citizens: "Every possible clue is being run down and we are leaving nothing undone to capture the man."[7] Taking into consideration the fact that the robbery had occurred in a populated district and a well-lit store, the police believed the man they sought either had to be a "most desperate character or ... completely insane."[8] With this as their guiding assumption, the police initiated a search for the criminal. Initially, the police dragnet failed to haul in the man they wanted. The day after the incident, Chief Detective Kennedy arrested Roland Finlay of Dartmouth, Halifax's twin city across the harbour, on suspicion. Finlay vaguely fit the description Corkum had given to police before he died, and since Finlay had been carrying a loaded gun and could not give a satisfactory account of his actions on the night in question, Kennedy felt justified in detaining him.[9] As the police questioned Finlay, the city continued to exude a feeling of uneasiness over the whole affair. "Probably never before in its history was the city so aroused over a crime," the *Morning Chronicle* declared: "In every quarter of the city yesterday, by citizens of every walk of life, was there the demand that the Police and the authorities spare not the slightest means in their power to run to earth the desperado guilty of Tuesday night's outrage." Although Corkum had been the victim, the *Chronicle* strongly felt that the crime itself affected the entire city, which had to "be protected at all costs."[10] No doubt this uneasy feeling did not subside when, due to insufficient evidence, the police released Finlay after a brief interrogation and fined him twenty dollars for carrying a loaded revolver.[11]

Contrary to public demands, the Halifax police did not bring a speedy end to this case. Despite rounding up a number of suspicious characters, the "Bold Gunman," as the press dubbed him, continued to elude law enforcement officials.[12] Not until January 1923 did the police announce that they had captured and charged Allister Munroe with the shooting death of Leslie Corkum as well as with a series of store robberies throughout the city.[13] Munroe had a reputation as a "bad actor." During their search of Munroe's flat, the police had found a coat allegedly worn by the murderer and a thirty-eight calibre revolver. Now the wheels of justice could begin to turn to guarantee that Munroe answered for his crime.[14] On the surface this appears to be nothing more than an unfortunate, but routine, murder for the Halifax police. Yet, Leslie Corkum's murder exposed the city's vulnerability to crime. For many citizens this shooting represented another flagrant violation of law and order. Moreover, it served as a reminder that lawlessness continued to be an uncomfortable facet of life in Halifax. The Corkum murder, elevated to a *cause célèbre* in the media, also came to symbolize the disorder and moral chaos of modernity itself. Throughout the 1918-35 period, legal authorities, and much of middle-class society in Halifax, engaged in a vigilant pursuit of law and order. They wanted to create a "city of order" in the midst of the storms of modernity that gripped the city during these years. The rule of law and the justice system in Halifax treated the city's "criminal class" (comprised mainly of men), along with the population in general, differently according to their class, gender, and ethnicity. At the same time, however, "criminals" did have one common image in the minds of Halifax's law-abiding citizenry: they were seen as a menace to the city's social order. In her study of sexual crimes in Ontario, Karen Dubinsky cogently argues that crime affected not only the criminals and victims but also the reputation, well-being, and prosperity of the entire community.[15] This was certainly the case for Halifax. From 1918 to 1935, the city's criminal justice system, which underwent a process of modernization, sought to control criminal activity. The implementation of the criminal law was thus dictated in part by those who deemed law and order to be essential to social stability and harmony.

Most residents took pride in Halifax as being a quiet, well-ordered city. As one 1927 article in the *Halifax Chronicle* put it, Halifax "is essentially a conservative city. It has been in business now for more than 175 years and is more or less immune to the hysteria which afflicts younger communities. Its people are steady, solid and reliable ... [and] ... the City of Halifax is ... on a sounder footing than many other cities of Canada that appear to be more flourishing."[16]

Examples of disrespect for law and order, "so much to be deplored," that detracted from the city's reputation did admittedly exist. Nevertheless, as one source notes: "these we are bound to believe were merely episodes and not characteristic occurrences in the life of the community."[17] The same belief in the tranquillity of Halifax held true for Nova Scotia in general. "From its earliest days," one writer asserts, "Nova Scotia has had respect for law and order and although there may be times and happenings which give cause for concern, the exemplary conduct of the thousands of people who [reside in the province] ... is an earnest [example] that Nova Scotians are maintaining the old reputation of their province."[18] That "old reputation" involved a devout adherence to law and order. A 1929 editorial proudly said of Nova Scotia: "This Province, a Province of British laws, customs and traditions, has long prided itself on its law and order. Order is heaven's first law and no state can expect to accomplish very much unless there is a wholesome respect for law. Anything which tends to lawlessness aims a blow at the heart of the state."[19] In agreeing with this statement, many Halifax residents recognized that crime did occur but felt confident that law and order would ultimately prevail. Chief of Police Frank Hanrahan echoed this belief at the beginning of 1923 as part of his department's New Year's resolution to the city. "The police department," Hanrahan declared, "[will] preserve the King's peace in the city ... run down lawbreakers and keep this city as it is today, one of the most peaceful and secure in the dominion of Canada."[20] Hanrahan's reference to the "King's peace" highlights the city's dedication to social order and to a "legal environment" within which the state and the criminal justice system strove to control crime.[21]

A year after Hanrahan's decree, the *Halifax Herald* noted with pride that Halifax was poised to snatch the mantle of "Good" away from Toronto. Since the police had arrested only one drunkard between Christmas Eve and Christmas night, Halifax, the paper believed, could claim the title "Halifax the Good."[22] Yet this confidence in the rule of order, and the willingness to over-read one piece of evidence, suggests the naivety of many citizens regarding the presence of crime in their city. As the *Halifax Herald* remarked four years earlier, following a 1920 daylight attack on a man by a "desperado," general disbelief greeted such events because of the feeling that they rarely occurred. However, as the article lamented, order and safety were not keeping pace with the growth of the city: "In our great regard for our industrial and commercial development and progress, we have not made the same progress in public order and the observance of it as we have in material progress." The paper went on to scold the inhabitants of Halifax for their ignorance of such violence, announcing that the time had come to: "DEPRECATE our smug, complacent attitudes to our development in regard for public order and in the means of protection which safeguard the security of our citizens." The city could not "grow greatly materially" while "neglect[ing] the means of public order and decency." The *Herald* felt that Halifax was in danger of losing its "civic soul."[23]

As Leslie Corkum's killing pointed out to most Halifax residents, order did not occur naturally; rather, a "city of order" had to be constructed and reconstructed on a daily basis. Halifax's citizens found themselves in a rapidly changing city that was becoming more and more modern. They emphasized building a city of order to limit the impact of modernity. To this end, from 1918 to 1935, a campaign arose in Halifax to modernize the city's criminal justice system, or machinery of order (particularly the police department, criminal courts, and penal system), to meet the challenges posed by crime. These challenges were firmly associated with modernity. Characterized by capitalist production and urbanization, modernity made much of North American society a world of "paradox and contradiction."[24] In this specific context, the perception surfaced that the substance of daily life had altered completely. People no longer automatically knew their neighbours or spoke their language; they could not assume a consensus on religion or morality; they lived to a large extent among strangers and worked in impersonal institutions; they shopped in new, massive stores and were influenced by the new arts of the radio broadcaster and the advertiser; and they felt themselves to be part of a society in which the safety of neither person nor property could be assured. Above all, the people of Halifax lived at a time when their world seemed to be changing more quickly than their ability to understand it. The years from 1918 to 1935 proved to be difficult ones, both socially and economically, for Halifax. The city underwent a dramatic and disruptive transformation. Modernity uprooted many of the values and meanings that had been woven into the fabric of Halifax society. The presumption that modernity would lead to the formation of a happier and more secure society did not, in the minds of several contemporaries, become a reality. The idea of a "traditional community" founded upon trust and security seemed to crumble. In its wake came feelings of uncertainty and, for some at least, dread of the social environment.[25] It was through this lens of modernity that many Halifax residents viewed crime. Offences such as the use and sale of drugs (notably opium) and shoplifting could be interpreted as manifestations of a loosening of public morals and a weakening of respect for lawful authority. Similarly, crimes with which Halifax had had long experience, such as prostitution, vagrancy, gambling, and murder, were now characterized as peculiarly "modern."

The response to modernity, like the experience itself, was complex. On the one hand, in the 1920s, many people in Halifax undoubtedly welcomed modernity with enthusiasm. They flocked to modern department stores, attended the cinema, openly discussed sexuality, and felt themselves to be citizens of the world. When it came to the criminal justice system, some of them readily translated the progressive insights of sociology and the new science of criminology – that crime was socially constructed and that its eradication could be achieved through social planning and social reform – into plans to modernize the entire legal framework. At the same time, however, most members of Halifax society, often the same ones who enthusiastically embraced modernity, drew back from what they thought were its consequences. In response to largely media-manufactured "crime waves," they demanded a more punitive and aggressive course of action to defeat the "criminal class," and they usually found a convenient scapegoat in the figure of the "deviant alien." Despite signs of progressive change in this period, evident in the categorization and treatment of juveniles and in a mounting desire to reform prisons, a more basic theme was that of a continuous struggle to uphold "British justice" as the city of order's primary bulwark against the moral and social anarchy unleashed by modernity. Across the landscape of crime, criminal justice, and the discourses generated around them, inertia, traditionalism, and even anti-modernism predominate over any drive for progressive change.

According to Charles Taylor, once a society "no longer has a structure, once social arrangements and modes of actions are no longer grounded in the order of things or the will of God, they are in a sense up for grabs."[26] Halifax's uneasy adjustment from a manufacturing-based economy to one dependent upon the service sector and tourism meant further unemployment, out-migration, and a widening of the gap between rich and poor. It was within this setting that the City of Halifax tried to deal with crime. In some ways modernity made the problem of crime seem more acute than it had been. Indeed, in the eyes of some, Halifax appeared to be on the brink of chaos. Although twentieth-century Halifax was generally a much more orderly city than was nineteenth-century Halifax, the perception was otherwise. To prevent lawlessness and the undermining of social order, most members of the local community actively sought to maintain order. In the process, the rule of law became an important mechanism for criminal justice officials, who undertook a concerted, if not entirely successful, effort to restructure Halifax's patterns of security and surveillance through placing greater emphasis upon "crime control."

By modernizing the city's forces of law and order, many hoped, Halifax would be in a position to cope with, and possibly eradicate, crime.[27]

A social history of crime provides a unique vantage point from which to view the complexities and contradictions of interwar society in Halifax. People lived their lives under the rule of law. Therefore, a study of the history of crime and the legal system that tried to control it will provide some insight into the formation and pattern of individual experience. For many in Halifax, crime came to epitomize the disorder that they felt riddled Nova Scotia's capital. Crime and the social disorder that it produced challenged accepted authority and thus threatened to undermine the socio-economic status quo. Consequently, as the example of Halifax shows, law enforcement and judicial authorities responded to criminal activity by pursuing the ultimate goal of restoring order. The state's reaction to crime is couched in the rhetoric of law and order and the notion of the "common good." This notion forms part of the discourse of order, which requires people to obey the law and to respect the "established order."[28] The ongoing pursuit of law and order by the state, and by those citizens most alarmed by the incidence of crime, is my overarching theme. I choose to examine crime and society in Halifax between the years of 1918 and 1935 for two reasons: (1) Halifax experienced a series of socio-economic changes during these years that heightened many residents' anxiety over crime; and (2) in response to the perceived threat that crime and criminals posed to social order, efforts were made during these years to improve how the criminal justice system dealt with the men, women, and children who could and did commit crimes.

Scholars have yet to reach a consensus regarding the nature and meaning of crime. Noted American law professor Lawrence M. Friedman contends that crime is a legal concept. What renders some forms of conduct criminal and others not "is the fact that some, but not others are against the law." Friedman thus concludes that crimes can be defined as "forbidden acts" that are susceptible to both a legal and a social judgment from the courts and society in general.[29] In Halifax, "forbidden acts" often met with a swift and sometimes harsh response from the criminal justice system in the hope that this would curb the outbreak of crime. To highlight this fact, I provide a multi-dimensional portrait of crime and society in interwar Halifax. It includes not only the incidence of crime but also the experiences of some criminals and the reaction to criminality on the part of the police, the criminal justice system, the law, and civil society. David Sugarman describes the law, whether civil or criminal, as "part of society and economy: it is a social, intellectual, and economic, as well as legal institution."[30] Indeed, the law exists at nearly all levels of society. The rule of law is a framework of authority to which everyone is bound to adhere. In conjunction with the state, the law maintains a social order characterized by domination and opposition.[31] Opposition to the law, primarily in the form of crime, is an important basis of social relations. Whether banded together as an unruly mob or acting on their own as "primitive rebels," men, women, and children have long confronted the law and legal authority. It is this process of committing crimes and restoring order that allows the law to become "an arena for class struggle, within which alternative notions of law [are] fought out." The law thus serves as a way for people to mediate their social and ideological conflicts.[32] What changes, however, is the nature of the crimes and the context within which law and order is threatened and maintained.

In Halifax from 1918 to 1935 modernity furnished the backdrop for the pursuit of order and the battle against crime. Through the criminal law, which is a particular manifestation of the "rule of law," society seeks to affirm and to impose an ideal of "law and order." The criminal justice system dispenses a form of "selective terror" in order to control dangerous behaviour, regulate morality, and keep social order.[33] As Eric Colvin argues, the "rule of law" refers to the regulation of the social order by the legal order.[34] However, the power wielded by the rule of law is not absolute; rather, it rests upon the appearance, not the reality, of "equality before the law." By appearing to be just and to be removed from gross manipulation, the rule of law commands voluntary compliance from most sectors of civil society.[35] The ideal of the rule of law legitimizes the pursuit of actual law and order. Early twentieth-century civil society in Canada required order and stability to function without undue crisis. This order and stability was partly attained through the operation of the justice system and the rule of law, with its theoretical premise of equal treatment for all who come before it. Yet such formal judicial equality also at times perpetuated existing socio-economic inequalities and unequal class, gender, and ethnic relations.[36] It is this contradiction in the rule of law that a study of crime in interwar Halifax reveals. Moreover, the rule of law and the entire machinery of order predicated upon it are two of the central constraints imposed by the state upon civil society. These legal constraints help to construct humans as abstract individuals with formal political and legal rights.[37] The ability of the law and the state to individualize people and to define who is a "criminal," thereby projecting the artificial notion of equality throughout society, is of fundamental importance.[38] The "power to define" what is legal or illegal behaviour is a key component of the rule of law's legitimacy, allowing it to determine the parameters of social acceptance under the rubric of law and order.[39] Much of this comes to light as I describe how, in its efforts to enforce law and order, the machinery of order in Halifax perceived and dealt with crime and criminals.

Legal and criminal justice history has established a firm niche within Canadian historiography and law and society studies generally. In a 1992 article Greg Marquis considers legal history to be "one of the most neglected branches of social history in Canada."[40] However, with the publication of *Law, Society, and the State: Essays in Modern Legal History*, legal history "has ... come of age."[41] Previously, legal history was characterized by somewhat narrowly focused examinations of the law, its development, and the impact that it had upon specific individuals, institutions, or society generally.[42] This concentration, however, tends to ignore the large socio-economic milieu that impinges upon the creation and interpretation of the law. The field of legal history is now marked, in the view of Louis A. Knafla and Susan W.S. Binnie, by an interest in how law and the state are informed by ethnicity, gender, class, and culture. Despite these advances, some legal historians still view crime as an incidental element of the law and have paid it little attention.[43] Yet an appreciation of the world of crime is crucial to an understanding of the way in which the law operates in Canadian society. Similarly, whereas legal history at times minimizes the importance of crime, criminal justice history tries to illustrate its centrality to the definition and functioning of the law. Such themes as criminality, state formation, punishment and incarceration, and police and law enforcement form the contours of this branch of social history.

A brief survey of some of the key studies of crime and society reveals the diversity, along with the strengths and weaknesses, of criminal justice history.[44] The fifth volume in the series *Essays in the History of Canadian Law*, subtitled *Crime and Criminal Justice* and edited by Jim Phillips, Tina Loo, and Susan Lewthwaite, encapsulates many of the current approaches to crime and criminal justice. The book's four sections grapple with questions of ethnicity, gender, state authority, and prisons in relation to the criminal law. Most important, the book underscore how the law detrimentally affected the lives of the socially marginalized (e.g., ethnic minorities and women), while offering a limited source of empowerment to some.[45] Historically, the state has played a central role in the function of the criminal law. Although the rule of law garnered public respect, each contributor to the section entitled "Criminal Justice Institutions and State Authority" notes that this respect did not always trickle down to every segment of society. Thus, what constituted the "law" and "crime" for legal officials often did not do so for members of a specific community. Crime and criminal justice, this section concludes, remained caught up in the interplay of social values and structures.[46] Prisons and reformatories represented a visible reminder of the institutional presence of the state. The chapters in the section entitled "Canadian Prisons in the Nineteenth Century" consider the state's initiatives with regard to reforming male and female prisoners and, hence, preventing crime. In spite of the rhetoric proclaiming their ability to turn inmates into productive members of society, penal institutions failed to solve the problems of crime and rehabilitation. Throughout the nineteenth century, then, punishment displaced rehabilitation in the treatment of convicted offenders.[47] Similar conclusions may be found in much of the literature on prisons and penal reform in Canada.[48] Missing from Phillips et al. is the history of Canadian policing. Initially, police historiography turned to institutional examinations of the Royal Canadian Mounted Police and local forces to depict the role played by the police in the administration of justice. From here scholars branched out to cover policewomen, the policing of strikes, the involvement of the police in settling domestic disputes, and police treatment of minorities.[49] The fact that the police are often empowered to provide working definitions of what counts as a crime in daily life means that to overlook them would be to overlook central players in the struggle over order and disorder in modern society.[50]

The only chronological history of crime in Canada is D. Owen Carrigan's *Crime and Punishment in Canada: A History*. In order to sustain his central contention that the long-standing perception of Canada as a relatively crime-free society is suspect, Carrigan traces the history of crime from the colonial era to roughly 1990.[51] However, he does not delve into the effects of class, gender, and ethnicity on conviction rates and the treatment offenders received at the hands of the criminal justice system. Although *Crime and Punishment in Canada* is an excellent encyclopaedic reference on crime in Canada, its failure to address some of the fundamental questions concerning the nature of crime and the law, and the social and economic influences on their development, weakens its effectiveness and leaves the study of crime in Canada open to further research.[52]

Some historians use the familiar case studies approach to uncovering the world of crime. Usually, these works focus on large cities or towns. The study of urban crime provides a way of uncovering the socio-economic context of Canada's cities. In addition, a community-based model "offers the appropriate scale for blending law and society."[53] Crime, as John W. Fierheller notes, may be utilized as an indicator of social and economic dislocation.[54] A concentration on one city, rather than on several metropolises, also allows for more definitive conclusions to be drawn regarding the incidence of crime and its impact on the administration of justice and the community itself.[55] James Huzel's statistical evaluation of the crime rate in Vancouver during the Depression is one example of this. Huzel illustrates that the onset of this economic crisis contributed to an increase in both the rate and the volume of total property crime. According to Huzel, this surge in property-related crimes in Vancouver was closely connected to the growing poverty and destitution of the 1930s.[56] Huzel's reliance on statistics, while allowing for a detailed description of the presence of crime in Vancouver, does not allow for a complete picture of criminality in this city. The criminals themselves, and the response of the police and the general public to their actions, are not featured in his article. Consequently, few conclusions can be drawn regarding how Vancouver reacted to and dealt with crime in this period.[57]

André Cellard and John C. Weaver provide more nuanced interpretations of crime in urban Canada. Cellard's work on Hull, Quebec, in the twentieth century combines crime statistics and local press coverage of criminal activity. In Cellard's view, Quebec's liberal attitude towards alcohol and Hull's status as a "*ville frontalière*" affected both the crime rate and the actions taken by criminal justice authorities to overcome it.[58] Turning to Hamilton, Ontario, John C. Weaver offers a sweeping treatise on crime from 1816 to 1970. According to Weaver: "the pursuit of order and justice has ... promoted change in the institutions dealing with disorder and crime."[59] In this sense, crime has had a direct effect on the shape of daily life in Canada's cities. Weaver's work is also important because it considers the institutional and social dimensions of crime and punishment. It charts the modernization of Hamilton's mechanisms of law enforcement, from the officer on the beat to the structure of the courts. Each of these combined to make up an increasingly bureaucratic "web of power" that helped to mediate social relations in Hamilton. In addition, Weaver tries to unearth the underlying values that affected law and order in this city. These values, he argues, "have underscored peculiarities about the communities in which they have functioned."[60]

Little has been written on the history of crime in twentieth-century Halifax. Some of the material that has appeared falls into the category of popular history.[61] However, Peter McGahan's overview of crime in Halifax and Saint John, and in the Maritimes generally, deals with the subject in a more scholarly fashion. Relying heavily upon official crime statistics, McGahan outlines the categories of offences committed, arrest and conviction rates, and the profiles of some offenders. While not subjecting his data to close scrutiny, McGahan does conclude that socio-economic underdevelopment in the Maritimes explains the relative stability in the region's crime patterns from the late 1880s to the mid-1900s.[62] McGahan's conclusions, while somewhat generalized, do lay some groundwork for a more focused treatment of crime in these two cities. Much of the academic literature on crime in Halifax concentrates on the nineteenth century. Judith Fingard's *The Dark Side of Life in Victorian Halifax* is the most comprehensive assessment of crime and the law in this period. Tracing the experiences of a core group of recidivists, Fingard depicts the harsh social environment of this "underclass" and the treatment they received from local law enforcement authorities and social reform organizations. Moreover, in following the activities of these individuals, Fingard underscores the prevailing impression of orderliness and concern for the quality of urban life that characterized Victorian Halifax.[63] The challenge posed to the established order by the actions of Halifax's criminal underclass raised the ire of the city's elite and invoked a host of responses whose purpose was to combat deviant behaviour. This dedication to order continued into the twentieth century and profoundly influenced the city's attitudes towards crime and its handling of criminals.

Other accounts of crime in Halifax during the nineteenth century also discuss the criminality of the underclass. Victorian Halifax, B. Jane Price shows, possessed a female criminal class, a caste of women who repeatedly came before the courts for committing petty offences. Many of these women lived in poverty, which, as Price suggests, forced some into a life of crime.[64] Several members of Halifax's middle class viewed the poor and vagrants as threats to social and moral discipline and order. Jim Phillips' work on vagrancy laws and female criminals in the eighteenth and nineteenth centuries in Halifax shows how the criminal justice system tried to curb these chronic problems. Most of those accused of being "vagrants" and criminals came from the ranks of the unemployed and the marginal poor who turned to crime as a means of economic survival. The jailing of vagrants and female criminals, designed to instil in the "lower orders" bourgeois notions of "sobriety, industry, and respectability," served as part of a broader process of social control.[65] This helped to ensure that the law was perceived not only as a harsh (yet necessary) instrument of coercion but also as a legitimate social institution that could display both mercy and impartiality.[66]

The theme of imposing law and order for the sake of social stability in Halifax arises again in the early part of the twentieth century and forms the central topic of this book. I discuss the social construction of criminality, in addition to the class, gender, and ethnic dimensions of crime in Halifax. I also assess the response of the city's machinery of order to criminal activity. As well, I examine the media's and the public's views of crime and of the persons who did, or who could, break the law. The years between 1918 and 1935 were a crucial period in Halifax's socio-economic development and, as such, an intriguing time within which to study crime. This was a time that saw the city plunged into a whirlwind of change and social crisis. Just as soon as Halifax had begun to recover from the effects of the First World War and the devastating explosion of 1917, it confronted an economic collapse in the 1920s, marked by massive factory closures. Unemployment, poverty, and general social dislocation epitomized this period. In these uncertain times, Halifax dealt with what appeared to be a resurgent wave of crime. To overcome the threat that crime represented to public safety and order, the city tried to improve and modernize all of the components of its criminal justice system. The interval between 1930 and 1935, highlighted by the release in 1933 of the *Report of the Royal Commission Concerning Jails* in Nova Scotia signified widespread public disquiet over the measures taken to safeguard the so-called city of order. The royal commission also renewed calls for penal reform and sparked yet another attempt in Halifax to solve the vexing problem of crime and criminal rehabilitation. It is here that one can detect Halifax's movement towards more progressive tactics in its efforts to overcome what some considered to be serious inadequacies in the state's approach to crime and punishment. While the pervasive demand for law and order did not subside in Halifax between 1918 and 1935, the city's strategies for controlling crime did change, however unevenly, to satisfy the demand for order.

Crime and the experience of modernity were closely intertwined in Halifax. Contemporaries often articulated their anxieties about the pace of social and cultural change in the context of numerous "crimes" and "crime waves" confronted in the 1920s and early 1930s. I define "crime" as any event that contravenes the laws of Canada (principally those contained in the Criminal Code) and that was perceived to do so by those entrusted with the power to uphold and enforce the rule of law. I am not unduly preoccupied by some of the familiar doubts expressed about the objectivity of crime statistics, such as those proceeding from the accurate view that what is a crime in one period may not be a crime in another period. The generally accepted meaning of "murder" or "armed robbery" did not undergo any significant changes from 1918 to 1935. However, this is not to say that crime statistics can simply be taken at face value. Clearly, to the degree that they help to draw a general picture of crime and to deflate unduly alarmist notions of Halifax as a uniquely offence-prone city experiencing an unprecedented wave of crime, criminal statistics reflect not only the "realities" of crime but also the efficiency with which crime was detected and prosecuted. They are, nevertheless, to be taken with many grains of salt, and I only use them (primarily in Chapter 1) to furnish a general impression of the extent of crime in Halifax, especially when considered within the overall Canadian context.

In order to explore the world of crime and criminals in interwar Halifax, I divide this book into six chapters. Chapter 1 provides an outline of the socio-economic milieu of Halifax and a statistical overview of crime in the city. Chapter 2 offers a detailed examination of the city's machinery of order, the changes it underwent, and how it worked to sustain social order. Chapter 3 examines the social perceptions of crime and criminals in Halifax. In their attempts to deal with the turmoil wrought by modernity, a core group of Halifax's politicians, judges, lawyers, social reform activists, and journalists expressed their ideas about what caused crime, who was a criminal, and what society should do to resolve the issue of crime. Their commentaries offer a great deal of insight into the nature of Halifax society between 1918 and 1935.

Chapter 4 examines the types of crimes committed in Halifax and also gives a brief profile of the city's "criminal class," assessing how the justice system and the community perceived and treated these individuals. Those who apparently belonged to this coterie of criminals were closely monitored by the police. This chapter also discusses juvenile delinquents.

Youthful law-breakers proved to be a tremendous source of consternation for Halifax's juvenile justice system and the city in general. Chapters 5 and 6 discuss the two groups that generated the most concern over crime and the spread of vice and immorality: women and ethnic minorities. Chapter 5 comments on the perceptions of women in Halifax generally and female criminals specifically, and it shows how the machinery of order dealt with them. Moreover, it provides an explanation not only of how women were victimized by crime but also of how they attempted to use the law as a source of empowerment. It is clear that the criminal justice system in Halifax did its part to reinforce gender ideals and inequalities.

Perhaps more so than any other member of the criminal element in Halifax, ethnic minorities, especially blacks, Chinese, and "foreigners" bore the stigma of being potential threats to law and order. Chapter 6 thus focuses on the criminal activity, both real and imagined, associated with these ethnic communities. This segment of Halifax's criminal underworld encountered the harshest public rebuke and the heaviest discrimination from the machinery of order. By raising the spectre of racial identity, local authorities and those concerned with preserving the socio-economic status quo constructed these alleged criminals as the "other." This relegated them to the margins of society and allowed the criminal justice system to dispense "justice" as it saw fit. The struggle for a state of law and order in Halifax – this modern city of order – can thus be seen as a force affecting the city's people in many powerful and often contradictory ways.

CHAPTER 1

A City of Order in a Time of Turmoil: The Socio-Economic Contours of Interwar Halifax

THE HALIFAX PUBLIC Gardens have long been the city's pride and joy. Portrayed as a "gem of floral and horticultural beauty," the Public Gardens, in the opinion of one promotional brochure, "are the finest on the North American Continent." Occupying roughly seven hectares of land in the heart of the city, the Gardens epitomized the spirit of tranquillity and orderliness many residents enjoyed and hoped to preserve in Halifax. No visit to the city would be complete, the *Halifax Herald* declared, without a visit to the Gardens. The Public Gardens first adorned Halifax's landscape in 1841. They quickly became a "resort for all the wealth and fashion of the time."[1] In design the Public Gardens exuded the splendour and wealth of the Victorian era. Every summer "thousands of distinguished and learned visitors" found a moment of quiet repose in the Public Gardens.[2] They could marvel at the array of blooming annuals and begonias or find some shade under the mulberry, elm, and European beech trees. In one sense everyone, rich or poor, young or old, enjoyed the Gardens. From the day the Gardens opened, children have played there, women's groups have held afternoon teas, and young lovers have walked hand-in-hand along its paths under the moonlight. For the Halifax elite, whether of the 1890s or the 1920s, however, the Gardens have held a special meaning: a testament to the "Victorian sense of peace, order and good government." Nostalgically, the Gardens symbolized all that was safe and decent about Halifax: they were a haven, in other words, from the dirt and disorder of the city.[3]

Yet some in Halifax did not regard this Victorian oasis with the same feelings of reverence and affection. Indeed, the Gardens reveal one of the more striking social characteristics of Halifax – the juxtaposition of wealth and poverty. The Poor Asylum occupied the land near the Gardens until a fire in 1882 destroyed it and took the lives of several inhabitants. The pond in the Gardens also became infamous in the nineteenth century as a place where mothers who could not afford to feed and clothe their new-born babies left the bodies of their dead infants.[4] In the 1920s and 1930s, "vagrants" and other criminal elements frequented the Gardens. In June 1930, for instance, the *Halifax Herald* reported that a thief, or thieves, had burglarized the refreshment stand in the Gardens and made off with a quantity of cigarettes and candy. In fact, as the *Herald* noted, nearly every year this shop had fallen prey to robbers.[5] While many citizens looked upon the Public Gardens as an ideal place to spend a quiet afternoon, a few saw it as simply another spot to pillage. These two opposing images of the Gardens underscore the contradictions that marked the social and economic contours of Halifax during the period from 1918 to 1935. The Public Gardens represented a model of order and an element of continuity in the sea of change that swept over the city during this period as Halifax responded to the many challenges of modernity. The modern world, Agnes Heller contends, is "open-ended, therefore tradition has lost the power of absolute justification."[6] In Halifax, a city that had witnessed a host of socio-economic transformations during the interwar years, residents searched for stability. Many found it within the gates of the Public Gardens. They also sought social order as crime – to some the epitome of the disorder wrought by modernity – appeared to engulf Halifax.

Economic Hope and Despair in Interwar Halifax

Halifax has played an important part in the history of Atlantic Canada and Canada in general. Founded by the British in July 1749, Halifax became the capital of Nova Scotia and soon exerted its political primacy over the province. As the nineteenth century unfolded, Halifax (which was incorporated as a city in 1841), emerged as Nova Scotia's military, administrative, and commercial centre. Halifax also served as a major shipping port for regional, national, and international trade. Dubbed the "Warden of the North,"[7] Halifax has been the focal point for the launching of imperial and Canadian war efforts, notably the first and second world wars. As the largest city in the Maritimes, Halifax (by 1901 its population had reached 40,832) has historically dominated the region's urban landscape.[8] Hope pervaded Halifax and many parts of the Maritimes prior to 1920. In the 1910s, progressivism became the watchword of many middle-class social reformers throughout the region. Progressivism and its supporters searched for policies "designed to restore ... [the] social cohesion whose loss they regarded as a major casualty of modern times." Progressives shared a belief in progress and the need to make the social environment more "efficient, organized, [and] cohesive."[9] In their attempts to organize society along "communitarian" lines, progressives foresaw nothing but advancement for this part of the country.[10] As one source commented in 1912, Halifax's most important asset in the fight to curb the spread of urban blight was the "number of socially minded citizens intent on civic progress."[11] Progressives hoped that the Maritime provinces, with the cities of Halifax and Saint John at the helm, would be the vanguard of progress in Canada. Yet this faith in progressive reform had slowly begun to vanish by the spring of 1920 as many Maritimers faced the dire prospects of economic recession and social dislocation.

If the 1910s contained the final years of abundant hope for Maritime Canada, the 1920s offered anguish and doubt for most. The onset of the 1920s and 1930s ushered in a prevailing doctrine of conservative regionalism.[12] In Halifax, however, hope did not disappear entirely. For some, hope and prosperity continued despite the tough economic times. As David Sutherland explains, career-minded middle-class men and women, enlivened by the ethos of reconstruction following the 1917 explosion, adopted an "activist, interventionist, 'progressive'" outlook on society.[13] They assumed that modernity would lead to the formation of a more secure social order. In essence, these men and women embraced modernity by trying to become "subjects as well as objects of modernization" and by coming to grips with their new environment.[14] As well, the socio-economic transitions produced by modernity fostered a feeling of social alienation and fragmentation in Halifax. In this atmosphere of anxiety, crime assumed a more serious role in the city. In order to overcome this problem and to recapture a lost sense of community, some Haligonians channelled their hope into a concerted effort to restore social order.[15]

The explosion in Halifax harbour on 6 December 1917 had a devastating impact on this port city. In addition to the thousands of people killed and injured, many others had their lives disrupted by the explosion. The industrial rhythm of the city suddenly came to a dramatic halt. A "great many industries were disrupted," the *Labour Gazette* informed its readers, "and thousands of men [were] thrown out of employment." The drydock suffered heavy losses, with its workshops and buildings completely destroyed. All two hundred of its employees found themselves out of work. The Dominion Textile Mills, employer of nearly two hundred workers, burned to the ground, while the Canadian government railways sustained considerable damage. Even the city's tramway system had several of its lines wrecked and its employees seriously hurt, forcing the Tramway Company to hire a few female conductors to keep this vital public service operational.[16] Remarkably, some businesses affected by the blast managed to remain in production. All of the bakeries, except one, continued to provide bread for local residents. "Aerated" water and soft drink establishments, printing and publishing houses, and woodworking plants, after completing minor repairs, reopened within a week to one month of the explosion.[17] The explosion itself also created employment opportunities. Close to fourteen hundred carpenters, glaziers, and unskilled labourers, some of whom came from outside of the city, found jobs in the reconstruction of Halifax's waterfront and a North End that one eye-witness described as looking "like some blackened hill-side which a farmer had burned for fallow in the spring."[18]

The influx of these workers and other relief personnel raised concerns about public safety. A "general disintegration of social institutions and the usual methods of social control – in short, a dissolution of the customary" followed this catastrophe. Moreover, the presence of these men, coupled with relief stations and temporary shelters, "brought about a very unusual commingling of classes," which seemed to be a source of trouble. According to one commentator, looting became rife in the immediate aftermath of the explosion. As a result, the police department hired "special policemen" to cooperate with the military to patrol the city's streets and curb this lawless activity. Detectives and patrolmen worked long hours during those difficult days to guarantee "public peace and order." Their efforts, in the words of one contemporary, were "highly commendable."[19] Halifax slowly began to put its shattered pieces back together. Halifax "became busy as never before," declared sociologist and progressive Samuel Prince, who served as the rector of St. Paul's Anglican Church during these chaotic years. As men and women "worked desperately hard," new homes, stores, piers, and banks "replaced the old as if by magic." Caught in the "spirit of the social age," Halifax enjoyed renewed prosperity from the construction boom. This, in turn, fostered a "fresh faith in the city's future." A "new Halifax," as Prince proudly proclaimed, was about to arise from the ashes of the old.[20]

At the conclusion of the First World War, Halifax appeared ready to tackle whatever challenge lay ahead. Much of this self-confidence originated from the successful rebuilding of the city. Similarly, the prosperity that Halifax witnessed shortly after the war helped to bolster a spirit of progressive optimism. Unlike other urban centres across the country, Halifax, by 1919, did not encounter high levels of unemployment. Similarly, the pulse of industrial productivity could be felt along the Halifax waterfront, generated in large part by the new Imperial Oil refinery, ocean terminals, and shipyards.[21] The completion of the port facilities strengthened Halifax's pre-eminence as the premier port on the Atlantic coast. However, with the decline in manufacturing, the city concentrated on exporting finished products that were manufactured elsewhere, which meant that its economic fortunes were tied directly to the vicissitudes of external economies.[22] Consequently, the city's postwar economy stood on a rather shaky foundation. This fact did not seem to detract from the confidence emulating from the city. The "new" Halifax, as seen in 1920 through the eyes of "One Who Knew It in the Old Days," was a thriving metropolitan centre where people attended the theatre, stores overflowed with merchandise, and businesspeople pumped money into the local economy.[23] In the opinion of this writer, Halifax was now a "city of opportunity ... There is no city where fortune can smile more sweetly ... than in the New Halifax. Truly can it be said of Halifax: Old things have given place to new things."[24] This buoyant view of the city concealed some dire warning signs. On the waterfront, for instance, a plan to build steel ships, encouraged by the government during the war, had faltered by the end of 1920. This caused unemployment to rise and wages to fall.[25] The Halifax shipyard workers responded by launching the biggest strike the city had ever experienced, but the once mighty voice of organized labour fell silent in the face of an employer ready and willing to abandon them and the city itself.[26] As the city, and the region, slowly began to sink into a state of economic dependence on the state and external capital, prospects for the future looked grim indeed.

Much of this despair came as a result of economic dislocation. Over the course of the late nineteenth century to the early decades of the twentieth century, Halifax gradually shifted from an industrial to a service and transportation economy. The National Policy of 1879 had accelerated the industrial growth of Nova Scotia's economy. Traditionally dependent upon the sale of staple commodities during the era of "wood, wind, and sail,"

Nova Scotia had, by the 1880s, made an uneasy adjustment to a more industrialized economy. For Halifax this meant a chance to escape the cycle of boom and bust associated with commercial trade. The 1880s and 1890s became decades of industry and prosperity for the city and province.[27] Manufacturing formed the backbone of Halifax's economy. The main industries in Halifax included sugar, rope, cotton, confectionary, paint, and lamps. In the 1880s these economic sectors employed over four thousand workers and generated over $8 million in revenue.[28] By 1891 Halifax had 348 small-, medium-, and large-scale manufactories, making it a hub of economic activity.[29] These industries paved the way for women to enter the paid labour force, but, as one source noted, their low pay was a "contributing cause of the immorality of the City."[30] The rise of the baking and confectionary industry illustrates the city's advancement to "modern industry" and production. During the 1880s, Halifax residents could purchase an assortment of bread and chocolates from seventeen company and privately owned bakeries. Gradually, Moirs Limited made the switch from small, handicraft production to a factory-style method of baking bread. In the process, Moirs expanded its workforce, intensified the pace of work, secured a larger share of the local market, and drove some independent producers out of business. The long hours and low pay for workers at Moirs characterized many of the trades in Halifax as industrial capitalism transformed the lives of the city's working class.[31]

Similarly, the city's industrial-based economy, much like Nova Scotia's, began to crumble by the 1890s. Nurtured under artificial conditions, notably a protective tariff and an east-west freight rate differential, the city's industries could compete on an equal basis with other companies for the central Canadian market. Once the federal government reduced these subsidies, however, several of Halifax's industries could not maintain their competitive edge. Although manufacturing did not disappear, it could not keep pace with growth outside of the region. As well, the output of durable goods for export began to collapse.[32] Industrial workers were among the first to feel the effects of this downturn. Between 1921 and 1931, the number of workers in manufacturing fell from 2,801 to 2,508. This decrease spelled the further erosion of the skilled trades.[33] In the place of craftspeople, employers hired common labourers who became vulnerable to periodic lay-offs.[34] This meant a reduction in wages and a shortening of the work season. In reaction, carpenters, longshoremen, and other workers in the city waged fifty-four strikes in the 1901 to 1914 period, more than in the half century prior to 1900. These actions marked a "decisive period of class awakening" in Halifax.[35] But their efforts achieved mixed results. Carpenters, for instance, gained some concessions on wages and hours of work, but they could not halt the deindustrialization of Halifax. Only the rise of the service-sector and transportation industries prevented the city's economy from being completely decimated in the 1920s and 1930s. Hotels, public utilities, financial institutions, universities, and the state generally became the driving forces of this new economy. In addition to employing their own staff, these institutions provided jobs for tradespeople and attracted capital to the city. From 1926 to 1927, the building economy revived due to a bevy of construction projects. Carpenters, electricians, plasterers, and painters worked on the new Lord Nelson Hotel, completed in 1928 and funded by the Canadian Pacific Railway, the Canadian National Railways Hotel (built at a cost of $2.5 million), the Capitol Theatre, and the Civic Exhibition. Each of these facilities owed its appearance to Halifax's, indeed to Nova Scotia's, growing reliance on tourism to fuel economic growth. Additions to Dalhousie University, the provincial technical college and court house, and the Victoria General Hospital helped to sustain the building trades' revival and solidified the public service as a dominant component of Halifax's economy.[36]

The Port of Halifax and the shipping trade formed the second plank in Halifax's post-1900 economic platform. Aided by an infusion of government and private funding, the Halifax waterfront managed to weather the storm of economic collapse. In 1929, the National Harbours Board invested several million dollars in renovating the city's port. In 1935, the federal and provincial governments allotted another million dollars worth of materials for waterfront projects.[37] As well, the assessed value of the shipping tonnage handled by the port for the first five years of the 1930s remained above $55,000,000.[38] This justified these expenditures and reconfirmed the importance of sea-based transportation to Halifax's economy. By 1929, then, the city's economy had been restructured and strengthened since the worst days of the postwar crash. Then the Great Depression hit. Construction, valued at over $5.2 million in 1929, fell to one-tenth of that amount in 1933. The salary gains carpenters had made during the building boom disappeared as the economy began to plummet. High wages and job security for many workers across the city vanished throughout most of the late 1920s and 1930s. It would not be until at least 1935, with renewed state funding for commercial building projects, that Halifax exhibited signs of escaping from the clutches of the Depression.[39]

Hard economic times took their toll on the city. As unemployment and poverty rose, many in Halifax reacted by fleeing the city and the province in search of work and a better way of life. This exodus can best be seen in the city's nominal population growth. In 1921, Halifax boasted a population of 58,372, but by 1931 this number had grown by a mere 1.5 percent to 59,275.[40] As a result, Halifax, along with cities such as Saint John and Kingston, all once-important nineteenth-century urban centres, found itself on the decline, eclipsed by Winnipeg and Vancouver. Halifax had now become simply another part of the burgeoning Canadian urban system.[41]

Halifax was a predominately white and Christian (Protestant and Roman Catholic) city. During the 1920s and 1930s, Roman Catholics comprised the largest single denomination in Halifax. Protestants, however, at least in numerical terms, dominated the city's religious milieu. After 1921, the Anglicans, Baptists, Presbyterians, and (after 1925) members of the United Church of Canada, formed the majority of Halifax's Christian followers (Appendix 1, Table A1.1). Although the city possessed other religious denominations, they remained in a distinct minority next to the mainline religions.[42] Ethnically, the English, Irish, Scots, and, to a much lesser degree, francophones, made up 90.5 percent of the city's total population in 1931 (Appendix 1, Table A1.2). The city did have a largely cohesive black population that was centred around its segregated Baptist and Methodist churches. In 1921, Halifax had 940 black residents, but by 1931 this figure had declined to 784 as a result of young people leaving the city to escape racial intolerance and to locate work.[43] Moreover, being the largest urban centre in the region, as well as a port of entry for immigrants, Halifax attracted a variety of ethnic minorities. Chinese, Germans, Italians, Russians, and Scandinavians represented the more prominent immigrant groups in Halifax (Appendix 1, Table A1.3). When combined, these peoples represented 3.4 percent of the city's 1931 population.[44]

As the economic climate worsened in the 1920s and 1930s, poverty became a way of life for many Halifax residents. In 1920, most people in Halifax lived in neighbourhoods in the north, south, and west ends. Outside the downtown, parts of the North End tended to be regarded as a "slum."[45] Covering an area of roughly eight square kilometres, the North End had a high density of industry, working-class housing, and low property values.[46] To some, the North End was a "gloomy" place to live. Neil Macrae, one of the main characters in Hugh MacLennan's classic novel of Halifax, *Barometer Rising*, returned from the war and was struck by the conditions in this section of the city. "This was the disgraceful thing about

Halifax," Macrae thought, "the hurting and humiliating thing about his town, that here, backed by millions of acres of space, there should be slums like these and people dull and docile enough to inhabit them." As he walked through its streets Macrae saw children "ill-dressed and half-dressed ... with dirty faces and blank eyes." The houses "were like cracker boxes standing in rows on a shelf. In some cases the foundations were so cockeyed it looked as though the houses they supported might tip over and sprawl into the street. Their cracked timbers were painted chocolate or cocoa-brown, and these drab colours absorbed all the light that entered the streets, and made them seem even narrower and dirtier and meaner than they actually were." When he passed an open doorway the "interior made him shudder: plastered walls, sticks of furniture that looked like rubbish, everything greasy and hand-touched, sour smells issuing into the streets. In this section of Halifax the noises never ceased all the twenty-four hours of the day." For Macrae, it "was a shock to realize how little he had known of the North End. When he had lived here, he had always avoided the district, and by avoiding it, had contrived to blink at its existence."[47] MacLennan caught some of the grim realities of North End life, but from the vantage point of a man from the upper middle-class South End. Others defined North End problems less impressionistically. As early as the late nineteenth century, the area's substandard housing had been the subject of many exposés in the Halifax press. In 1899, the *Halifax Herald* commented upon the "housing problem" that plagued the city. Surveying the district bounded by Lower Water and Grafton streets as well as the North End, the *Herald* reported: "It is a fact that there are people in Halifax whose homes are bounded by the four walls of a ten-by-twelve room, whose outdoors is the ... dirty street, whose only bit of garden is the tuft of chickenweed that grows up through the grating of the cellar window."[48] Conditions by 1912 had not improved. Bryce M. Stewart, while conducting a brief social survey of Halifax for a "Group of Interested Citizens," discovered "several old structures where there is much overcrowding and where most unsanitary conditions prevail" scattered across the city.[49]

The cry went up for public housing to rectify this situation. County Court Judge W.B. Wallace argued in 1919 that a policy designed to enable working-class men to own their homes would "aid that self-respecting independence which puts a man in the best class of citizens and makes him a staunch upholder of law and order."[50] As is evident from Wallace's statement, some progressives placed a great deal of emphasis on the environmental genesis of crime. A spree of home construction following the First World War, initiated by the federal government as a way of addressing some of the country's social problems, silenced the calls for low-income housing.[51] Yet Halifax did not share equally in this development. Besides the North End Hydrostone, the first public housing project in Canada, Halifax did not engage in a massive publicly financed housing scheme.[52] The bulk of the residential development in the 1920s occurred in Halifax's middle-class districts. From 1925 onwards, an "impressive new city of residences" appeared, west of Robie Street down to the shores of the North-West Arm. A.G. Dalzell, a housing engineer from Toronto, pointed out that Halifax, like many cities that tried to beautify their landscape, chose to protect the better residential areas while allowing sanitary conditions in the poorer neighbourhoods, including the North End, to worsen.[53]

By the 1930s, Halifax became one of the first Canadian centres of organized agitation for affordable housing. On a comparative basis, not many low-income earners in Halifax owned their own homes. In 1931, only 23.6 percent of workers in the provincial capital could be classified as homeowners. Meanwhile, in Toronto, Winnipeg, and Vancouver, home ownership rates among workers exceeded 40 percent. The seasonal nature of Halifax's economy, particularly for dock workers, explains this low percentage. For many, inadequate wages and the high mobility of labour produced a greater demand for rental housing and made the prospects of owning a home remote.[54] That same year (1931), the Halifax Labour Council, supported by a coalition of unions, social workers, and religious leaders, began to lobby for public housing. Their initial success boded well for the future. A survey of the housing situation in Halifax in 1932, followed by the establishment of a provincial housing commission in 1934, put Halifax, and Nova Scotia, at the forefront of social housing policy in Canada. When the civic and provincial governments turned to Ottawa for money, however, the campaign for low-cost housing came to a halt. The Bennett and King administrations resisted the claims that poor families needed subsidized shelter. It would not be until the late 1940s that public housing became a reality.[55] Some working-class families, forced to live in substandard housing, could ill afford this delay. The 1932 housing report, inaugurated by the Social Service Council and supervised by Samuel Prince, uncovered several of Halifax's housing deficiencies.

This report also represented a change in emphasis from a moral imperative to solving housing problems to the modern concern for the physical implications for the city should the crisis be allowed to continue. Moreover, the report was an expression of middle-class fears about the future welfare of the city, not a form of grassroots discontent.[56] This explains the urgent tone of some of Prince's comments. At one point he comments: "[Halifax] is infested with a high percentage ... of tumble-down shacks where whole families eat, sleep, bathe and live in a single room, where cellars reek with filth and vermin ... unfit for human habitation."[57]

The report also contained a more sober assessment of the housing scene in Halifax. It pinpointed overcrowding as a serious health risk to both residents and the city generally. In the process of conducting a "Sanitary Survey" as part of the housing report, A.C. Pettipas, secretary for the Halifax Board of Health, found "several instances" in which "the number of individuals per room reached from 4 to 10." On three streets alone "50 families were quartered upon an average of 3 individuals per room."[58] And not all of these streets and houses were in poor neighbourhoods. Some stood alongside, or close to, the city's downtown businesses on Water Street and the lieutenant-governor's mansion on Barrington Street – a constant and visible reminder that Halifax was a modern city of rich and poor living in a state of uneasy co-existence. Approximately 11,197 men, women, and children, the report concluded, lived in circumstances associated with "bad housing." These included "woefully meagre" bathing and sewer facilities as well as yards and cellars littered with garbage. By living in such homes, the report noted, these people endured physical, mental, and moral hazards.[59] The authors attributed the "doubling up" of friends and relatives in single-family dwellings to the unavailability of proper housing. Adequate lodging for a family of five at a cost of twenty dollars per month, the affordable level of rent calculated by the report, was nearly impossible to find in Halifax.[60] The "Hydrostone" in the North End represented an exception to this rule. Completed in 1921 to replace the homes and businesses destroyed by the explosion, the Hydrostone spread across ten blocks. The project transformed this segment of the city by providing affordable, newly designed housing, paved sidewalks, and improved sewer and water systems. With 328 dwellings, fifteen stores, and three offices, the Hydrostone became home to two thousand people.[61] The opening of new schools and markets gave residents the opportunity to put their lives back together. As one onlooker commented, the Hydrostone soon became a "hard-working wage-earning community."[62] The

Depression hit the Hydrostone hard. Merchants went bankrupt and people were driven from their homes because they could not afford to pay rent. A widow who received a pension of forty dollars a month, plus eight dollars for each of her two small children and ten dollars a week from an older child who worked, spent close to half of her income on rent. By the mid-1930s, 152 houses had been vacated. Tenants appealed to the Halifax Relief Commission, the organization in charge of the reconstruction efforts, to lower their rents, but to no avail.[63] The commission also reimbursed those who lost their homes "on a percentage basis of loss suffered, rather than ascertained need."[64]

Most of the city's blacks also lived in relative poverty. Many resided along Creighton, Maynard, and Gottingen streets as well as in the community of Africville. Residents of Africville lived without water and sewage services even though they paid municipal taxes.[65] This fact is indicative of the prejudice against blacks in Halifax and across Nova Scotia.[66] Another so-called disreputable spot appeared in the city's downtown core. Along Barrington, Brunswick, Grafton, Granville, Jacob, Sackville, and Upper and Lower Water streets could be found numerous shops, cafes, and Chinese laundries, a "red light" district, beggars, and the decrepit buildings that housed gambling "resorts" and liquor "dens."[67] An autobiographical account of life in downtown Halifax between 1934 and 1935 describes the surroundings. According to Harry D. Smith, who as a teenager worked for Clayton and Sons, Wholesale Manufacturers, "smells of poverty dominated the three-storey tenements" around the garment factory. Such slums, he felt, "must surely be the breeding ground of much misery among people ... the people who lived in the midst of it must be made fearful, because of the poverty, the prostitution, the cold and hunger that abounded."[68] "Depression," Smith claimed, hung over this part of the city as he walked to work each morning. To Smith it seemed as if "misery and hopelessness [were] the order of the day" for many in Halifax.[69] These streets and businesses played a central role in the city's criminal activity. All of the crimes did not occur in this one area, but the fact that many did generated the perception among those concerned with law and order that Halifax's "social evils" could be found here and quickly eradicated.

Life for most of those who lived in the economically depressed neighbourhoods of Halifax in the 1920s and early 1930s was bitterly hard. In 1923, the *Morning Chronicle* reported that workers for the Halifax Welfare Bureau had dealt with several families who were living in misery. They suffered from an unemployed and sometimes abusive father, mothers who had to work to support them, and children who either begged or wound up in juvenile court on charges of theft or truancy.[70] The Jost Mission tried to alleviate some of the strains placed on working-class mothers. Founded in 1868 by Halifax businessman and Methodist Edward Jost, the mission provided a nursery and employment service for working mothers. However, with minimal resources at its disposal, the mission could not help all of those in need.[71] Children seemed to suffer the most from the city's unsanitary conditions. Modern medicine did register a victory of sorts in the 1920s when Halifax's infant mortality rate declined, but, from 1924 to 1931, 1,155 children under the age of five years died from illnesses related to poor housing and sanitation.[72] In spite of medical advances, sickness still ended the lives of some impoverished children and their families in the 1930s. For example, in 1933 cholera struck Halifax, and by the end of September the death toll had reached forty-three, most of whom were infants.[73] Anxious parents flooded doctors' offices with calls regarding the health of their babies. People also demanded wider public access to milk.[74] In response, two newspapers established a fund to purchase milk for those parents who did not receive city relief and could not afford to buy an ample supply of fresh milk for their children.[75]

Unemployment, perhaps more than any other factor, caused such poverty to flourish. Halifax's transition to a service-sector and transportation economy left many people out of work. Sixteen percent of the city's wage earners, twenty years of age and over, did not have a job in 1931. The tendency for people to migrate from rural Nova Scotia to the province's capital in the hopes of locating employment and fulfilling the residency requirements for municipal relief, swelled Halifax's ranks of unemployed.[76] Yet, in comparison with the unemployment rate in Nova Scotia (19.3 percent) and Canada (18.3 percent), Halifax managed to withstand some of the shock of deindustrialization (Appendix 1, tables A1.4 to A1.6).[77] For those workers fortunate enough to have kept their jobs, or to have found work in this harsh economic climate, wages failed to match the cost of living. The average Halifax family spent more on food, shelter, fuel, and light from June 1920 to May 1921 than did families in all but three other Canadian cities.[78] In a 1922 letter to the editor of the Halifax *Citizen*, "A STRUGGLER" wrote that, in "Halifax and Dartmouth, there are ... 12,000 working men of 21 years of age and upwards, who are supporting families. Of that number, fully 4000 are earning less than $30 a week. And if said men cannot get a house or flat for $30 and less a month they are going into debt each month, slowly, but nonetheless certainly."[79] Rent was excessively high in Halifax. For instance, in October 1921, a six-room house with modern "conveniences" cost $40 per month, well above the national average of $27. Moreover, a six-room house with "incomplete modern conveniences, or none," fetched between $25 and $35 a month in Halifax while nationally the average rent for similar premises was $19.[80] The price of such staples as beef, eggs, butter, canned vegetables, and wood in Halifax also remained higher than the national average in 1921 and 1931.[81] Only skilled tradespeople could afford these items. Carpenters and electrical workers in 1920 earned a "living wage." Depending upon how many hours they worked a week, they could make a maximum of forty dollars. Painters and "builders' labourers" made at most twenty-nine dollars per week.[82] When the hours of labour fluctuated, which they invariably did, the unskilled could earn as little as twenty dollars a week. Meanwhile, women's annual wages amounted to 50 percent of male earnings in the 1920s and 1930s.[83] Skilled workers also saw their wages ebb and flow throughout much of this period. Carpenters in 1921 earned a yearly salary of $1,006 for forty-two weeks of work, while by 1931 this had fallen to $889 for thirty-eight weeks.[84] This inconsistent pattern of employment meant that workers in Halifax had some of the lowest real incomes in the country.[85]

Unemployment and poor wages forced some people out of their homes. Alderman Minshull, in a report to Halifax City Council in 1933, noted that three hundred families had been evicted by their landlords because of unpaid rent, while another two thousand unemployed tenants waited for the axe to fall.[86] In a letter dated 23 November 1933 and addressed to the premier of Nova Scotia, Angus L. Macdonald, the mayor of Halifax, Albert A. Thompson, stated that the total number of registered unemployed men in Halifax had reached 2,680.[87] And the number of persons with dependants receiving direct relief from the city numbered 10,500. This meant that approximately one in six persons relied on the dole.[88] To alleviate this situation, a cash-strapped city turned once again to make-work projects. Stone-breaking for men and knitting and spinning for women and girls had been classic nineteenth-century responses to the sufferings of the "permanent ... and casual poor."[89] By the time the Depression had set in not much had changed in terms of the city's strategy for dealing with the unemployed. Snow removal in the winter and sewer and road construction in the spring and summer comprised the main elements of Halifax's program of work relief.[90] The city also converted Citadel Hill into a relief camp for unemployed single men. They received twenty cents a day in return for working forty hours during week days and four hours on Saturday morning.[91] Some workers did not sit idly by as the state searched for a solution to the economic crisis. At its meeting in August 1931, the Halifax Trades and Labour Council approved the suggestion made by the United Mine Workers that the provincial Legislature should meet in a special session to "consider unemployment." The council also asked the Nova Scotia government to implement the federal Old Age Pensions Act. In a move that said a great deal about the loss of jobs in the city, the Labour Council decided not to hold any Labour Day celebrations that year "owing to the unemployment situation."[92] Labour also displayed its opposition to the working conditions and poor pay given to relief workers. In March 1934, 150 sympathizers picketed sewer construction sites across the city. On the same evening, 130 men and women staged a noisy parade through the streets, chanting "Don't let us starve."[93]

As one moved out of the North End and away from the downtown district, towards the South End and West End, the city, and those who called it home, seemed oblivious to this economic turmoil. In Ward Two, on the eastern side of the North-West Arm, some of Halifax's elite resided. James Wilson, provincial manager of the Canada Life Insurance Company, lived on Connaught Avenue. On Oxford Street stood the homes of John Calder, owner of J.C. Calder and Company, and "Knock Eyen," the estate of William Payzant of John Payzant and Son, barristers and solicitors. South Street was the site of the North-West Arm Rowing Club and the Armview Boating Club. On Coburg Road were the homes of G.E.E. Nichols, manager of the Montreal Trust Company; J.B. Kenny of McInnes Jenks Lovett Fulton and Kenny, barristers; the "Thornvale" estate of W.M.P. Webster, president of Webster Smith Company Limited; and the St. Mary's Rowing Club.[94] A measure of comfort and leisure certainly characterized this portion of Halifax in the 1920s and 1930s.

The same could be found across the North-West Arm. Fleming Park and the Dingle Tower, land donated to the city in 1908 by railway magnate Sir Sandford Fleming, along with Point Pleasant Park on the adjacent eastern side, complemented the majestic homes and mansions. All of this made the South End the city's premier residential locale and a popular getaway from the stress, destitution, and crime of urban life.[95] One tourist pamphlet described the North-West Arm, circa 1931, as imbued with "natural beauty, bordered with residential properties reflecting [a] happy, comfortable, prosperous home life."[96] This prosperous life was enjoyed by those citizens who patronized the recently opened Capitol Theatre on Barrington Street, purchased automobiles and luxury items from Eaton's Department store, and still paid their bills on time.[97] Noting in 1933 that Halifax had made "marked progress" in the last eight years, the *Halifax Herald* paid homage to the city's achievements. "Historic Halifax," the paper announced, "still has its old forts, its beautiful Point Pleasant Park, its venerable Province House, its star-shaped Citadel and all that of which it is mighty proud. But it has more: modern community development such as hospitals, health centres and playgrounds, modern business methods, modern hotels, modern transportation equipment such as the airport and the new railway station, and increased port facilities."[98] All of these developments, the *Herald* concluded, had made Halifax "a newer, brighter, cleaner ... progressive city, one that ha[d] advanced with the times, yet preserved its traditions."[99]

In an attempt to deal with, or perhaps conceal, the disparities of wealth and the contradictions of modern society, many members of the local middle class developed the ideal of Halifax as a city of order. In April 1930, the *Halifax Herald* published a tourist edition to promote Nova Scotia's beauty and attractions to residents and potential visitors alike. Under the caption, "Halifax Has Distinctive Appeal," the *Herald* described Halifax as a city of order: "[A] peaceful, leisurely city and a city of comparative quiet ... No huge crowds with frenzied mien are rushing to and fro. People walk along leisurely ... There is always time to stop and chat with each other."[100] From the perspective of many elite members of Halifax society, the "city of order" was simultaneously an achievement, a goal for the future, and a rallying cry for the present whenever disorder and crime threatened the propertied and the prosperous of the city. Of course, in so far as Halifax, even in the early nineteenth century, had always been characterized by class divisions, social unrest, and crime, the notion of a "city of order" was largely a romantic ideal. Yet, this ideal did capture what many Haligonians felt they had to lose if the social and economic contradictions unleashed by modernity were not somehow tamed. Every time they expressed surprise that crime had reached their quiet community, middle-class residents of Halifax were confirming how completely, if unconsciously, they had assimilated a vision of a tidy, well-ordered city, innocent of the social turmoil of the modern world. And when they tried to preserve this vision by changing police procedures or creating a juvenile court, their romantic ideal had very real consequences.

"Opportunities for Plunder in Large Cities": A Statistical Profile of Crime in Interwar Halifax

It is important to address the following question: How much was this city of order threatened by crime in the interwar period? A brief statistical analysis of crime in Halifax from 1918 to 1935 provides the context in which to discuss perceptions of crime. Moreover, a comparison of Halifax's crime rate with that of Canada and of Nova Scotia, as well as with the statistical pattern in Saint John and Hamilton, sheds some light on the degree of criminality in Nova Scotia's capital. Saint John and Hamilton were selected as comparisons for their respective similarities and diversities vis-à-vis Halifax. Saint John, a port city with roughly the same population as Halifax and one that underwent similar socio-economic transformations, represents a close parallel, while, for its part, Hamilton was a much larger and more heterogeneous metropolitan centre.[101] Both cities offer a broad perspective from which to assess the representativeness of Halifax in terms of crime in Canada during these years. However, the use of criminal statistics is a problematic endeavour. In the words of J.A. Sharpe, "historians[s] of crime employing quantification must ... be modest in [their] ambitions, cautious in [their] approach, and painstakingly careful in presenting and explaining [their] data to [their] reader[s]."[102] At best, criminal statistics can convey a general sense of crime in a country, province, or city. But they cannot reflect the actual extent of criminal behaviour in society. This is due primarily to the fact that officially published statistics "do not always accurately represent the data from which they are compiled." Moreover, the data are often tainted by contemporary biases and presuppositions about what constituted a crime and who constituted a criminal.[103] An objective and absolute measurement of crime, regardless of the time or place, will forever remain beyond the historian's reach, given the undoubtedly substantial number of crimes that went unreported and/or undetected by legal authorities.[104]

For the purposes of this discussion, the *Statistics of Criminal and Other Offences*, compiled by the Dominion Bureau of Statistics (DBS), serves as the main source of data for crime in Halifax. This statistical profile of crime in the "Warden of the North" relies on the DBS's total number of convictions for indictable and summary offences to gauge national, provincial, and urban crime rates. The weaknesses of this approach are twofold. First, the DBS numbers are susceptible to irregularities in the reporting and collection of data for each judicial district. Consequently, this limits the accuracy of these figures in measuring the amount of crime committed. Second, the number of people charged with, but not convicted of, a crime has not always been factored into DBS assessments of criminality. Those individuals arrested but not prosecuted did not enter into DBS calculations. In the eyes of some, however, those apprehended for breaking the law, whether or not they were convicted, became criminals. One could argue that a realistic estimate of the "amount" of crime would take into account all the reported incidents, not just those that led to the successful prosecution of an offender. The DBS figures fail to consider this social construction of criminality. To compensate for this deficiency, police court and police department statistics for selected years, which include the number of all those charged and brought before the court, are also consulted to assess the perceived incidence of crime in Halifax.

Notwithstanding many alarmed comments from proponents of the city of order, Halifax from 1918 to 1935 was not, comparatively and statistically speaking, a crime-ridden city. As the most densely populated area in Nova Scotia, Halifax naturally accounted for a large percentage of crime in the province. As tables A2.1 and A2.2 (Appendix 2) indicate, in an average year Halifax accounted for 42.1 percent of the convictions for indictable offences and 33.1 percent for summary offences in Nova Scotia. When compared with Canada, however, these percentages shrink to 1.5 percent and 0.8 percent, respectively. Yet, when viewed in terms of the number of convictions for both categories of offences per 1,000 of the population for Halifax, Nova Scotia, and Canada, the conviction rate alters. Tables A2.5 and A2.6 show that Halifax had more convictions per 1,000 citizens than did Nova Scotia or Canada throughout the years 1918 to 1935.[105] Caution must be used when drawing conclusions from these tabulations. Things such as the ability of police forces across the country to detect and apprehend criminals and the effectiveness of local justice systems in securing guilty verdicts also determined the number of convictions recorded. Consequently, these statistics may say more about the nature of law enforcement and the administration of justice in Canada than about crime itself. Nevertheless, it may be argued, on the basis of these figures, that, while Halifax represented a minor component in the grander scheme of crime in Canada, it still had, in proportion to its population, a higher incidence of recorded convictions for criminal offences.

Criminal statistics from Saint John and Hamilton support this contention. From 1918 to 1935 Halifax averaged 352 convictions for indictable and 1,461 convictions for summary offences per year. In Saint John, the yearly average of convictions for indictable and summary offences stood at 128 and 1,321, respectively, while for Hamilton the numbers are 656 and 6,722, respectively (Appendix 2, Tables A2.3 and A2.4). On the basis of the number of convictions per 1,000 population, however, the crime scene looks somewhat different. While Halifax averaged 5.8 convictions per 1,000 population for indictable offences, Saint John averaged 2.7 and Hamilton 4.8. For summary offences, the relevant numbers per 1,000 population are: 24.2, 27.8, and 46.6 (Tables A2.5 to A2.9). Thus, in one sense, Haligonians did have some cause for concern about more serious forms of crime in their city. Although Halifax did not, in comparison to Saint John and Hamilton, witness more minor offences per 1,000 population, it does appear that serious (indictable) crime was more common. This helps to explain the incessant drive for law and order in Halifax. At the same time, it does not lend credence to the belief that Halifax, more than any other city, was being overrun by crime and criminals. Yet, such was not the perception in contemporary Halifax. As the city slipped into a time of economic and social uncertainty, citizens grew increasingly anxious about crime. They also apparently had the statistics to bolster their anxieties. In its fifty-fourth annual report, the DBS observed that, from 1881 to 1929, criminal convictions in Canada "ha[d] practically quadrupled." The report attributed much of this increase to the ill effects of urbanization. "The opportunities for plunder in large cities," the DBS asserts, "continually incite the criminal classes to break in and steal, or to inaugurate financial schemes designed to rob people of their money."[106] Figures from the Halifax police court do demonstrate the plausibility of this stated trend. For the year 1910-11, the police court handled a total of 1,715 cases, 598 of which were for drunkenness. By 1914-15 this number had more than doubled to 3,435, including 1,700 charges of drunkenness, an increase of 1,720 (50.1 percent) cases tried. Following a decrease in the number of cases before the court over the next five years, the figures rose again. In 1919-20, with the return of thousands of soldiers and a brief period of economic prosperity, offenders who appeared before the magistrate totalled 3,204, 1,291 for drunkenness (Table A2.11).[107]

In Halifax, as in most cities, petty crimes dominated judicial proceedings. Tables A2.12 and A2.13 detail the numbers and types of offences handled by the Halifax Police Department for the civic years 1917 to 1922. Out of a total of 12,062 crimes, a select few commanded most of the department's attention. Common assault, creating a disturbance, drunkenness, theft, and violating the Motor Vehicle Act together represented 63.4 percent (7,644) of the department's case load. Available numbers from Saint John and Hamilton disclose a similar pattern. Theft and burglary alone comprised 12.5 percent (224) and 12.9 percent (758) of the offences "known" to the Saint John and Hamilton police in 1920.[108] While Halifax had, in comparison to Saint John, a higher percentage of cases involving homicide, rape, and assault, minor offences predominated in both cities.[109] Serious crime, while overrepresented in Halifax as compared to Saint John, did not overwhelm the forces of law and order in this city.

In comparative terms, the supposed eruption of crime alluded to by the DBS did not besiege either Halifax or the Maritimes generally. According to the DBS, "in the provinces East of Ontario there is a much lower criminality than in the provinces of Ontario and those to the west."[110] Police statistics for 1929, the year the DBS released its assessment of the growth of crime in Canada, underscore this fact. In that year thefts and burglaries "known" to the police totalled 250 and 62 in Halifax, 136 and 15 in Saint John, 1,522 and 176 in Hamilton, and 31,171 and 7,667 in Canada. The number of "known" thefts and burglaries per 1,000 population were: 3.9 and 0.9 for Halifax; 2.9 and 0.3 for Saint John; 10.4 and 1.2 for Hamilton; and 3.1 and 0.8 for Canada.[111] Again, Halifax had either the same number or more of these crimes per capita than either of these cities, or the country in general, but not to any extreme degree. Contrary, then, to the frequently voiced opinion that Halifax had become synonymous with lawlessness in Canada, the statistics paint a picture (admittedly impressionistic) of a city with a fairly average rate of criminal convictions. Yet many middle-class Halifax residents, perhaps seeing in crime a mirror of the modernity they both admired and feared, persisted in making of each new murder and armed robbery a "crime wave" of unprecedented proportions. Little had changed as the Depression descended upon each of these cities. In the six years from 1930 to 1935, the Halifax police recorded an average of 3,908 offences per annum, Saint John recorded 2,402, and Hamilton 12,375 (Table A2.14). In terms of the number of offences known to the police per 1,000 population from 1930 to 1935, Halifax averaged 62.9, Saint John 49.8, and Hamilton 79.6 (Table A2.15).[112] Rather than pinpointing a steady climb in the number of offences throughout these difficult years, these statistics chronicle the erratic nature of reported crime in Halifax over this entire seventeen-year period.

The Halifax police may have faced more crimes on a per capita level than the Saint John police, but this does not mean that the Depression and its economic woes caused an outburst of criminality.[113] Nevertheless, the city's police officers still had their work cut out for them as they and the machinery of order tried to preserve law and order. Halifax, as this chapter outlines, experienced a series of fundamental social and economic changes from 1918 to 1935. Some of these changes further polarized the city between rich and poor and heightened the general sense of insecurity in the provincial capital. Along with this feeling of insecurity came the fear that, as socio-economic conditions worsened, crime, lawlessness, and disorder would consume the city. Even though the statistical evidence does not sustain an impression of a crime-ravaged Halifax, this fear persisted. The forces of law and order would have to be vigilant, many believed, to defeat those determined to commit crimes and wreak havoc on the city's homes and businesses. Crime and disorder could not be allowed to reign in the city. As a consequence, every component of Halifax's criminal justice system would be utilized to solve the problem of crime and to maintain the ideal of the city of order.

CHAPTER 2

The Machinery of Law and Order

FROM "BRAWN TO BRAINS" was how Chief of Police Judson Conrad described the changes that had occurred in the Halifax Police Department over the last forty years. Speaking at a Rotary Club luncheon early in 1935, Conrad told his audience that, at one time, policemen had had to quell "free-for-alls and eject inebriated patrons when closing time came" at the city's bar-rooms. Those were the days, he fondly recalled, when a strong arm and a husky demeanour were the sure signs of a good officer. But Halifax had changed. The North End had been transformed with the construction of the Hydrostone, the West End had become a district of "fine" homes, and the Ocean Terminals had rejuvenated the waterfront. Moreover, new businesses and private residences had to be kept secure and the city's mounting problem of vehicular traffic contained. In order to keep pace with these advancements, Conrad claimed, the department was forced to make the necessary adjustments. According to Conrad, the use of fingerprint technology, two-way radios in patrol cars, and a better organized system of record keeping had increased the efficiency of the department.[1] When the radios arrived in October 1934, the *Halifax Herald* enthused: "Halifax will [now] be placed on a par with the biggest police units on the Continent insofar as the latest police equipment is concerned."[2] In his analysis of modernity, Anthony Giddens focuses on the "surveillance capacities" of capitalist society, whereby the power of the state to regulate civil society is accentuated.[3] It was precisely a progressive intensification of such surveillance that the Halifax police, and many advocates of the city of order, called for in the 1920s and early 1930s.

Within Halifax's machinery of order throughout the 1918 to 1935 period there was a struggle between "traditional" and "progressive" tendencies. New ways of thinking about law enforcement surfaced during these years. At the same time, however, this shift in outlook remained partial and uneven as the city did not abandon those procedures it felt were best suited to controlling crime and maintaining law and order. While this dichotomy of traditional and progressive models for a machinery of order provides somewhat artificial benchmarks, it does allow a way of assessing how Halifax's criminal justice system, on an institutional level, responded to and coped with crime in the interwar years. The essence of the debate between traditional and progressive designs for the machinery of order boiled down to effectiveness. A traditional nineteenth-century system of justice called for stiff penalties as a way to punish the individual, whom society ultimately held responsible for her or his criminal actions. It was also hoped that punishing offenders would deter others from committing crimes.

This classic liberal notion of law and order relied on the police to protect private property and to hold a tight rein over those elements of the population thought to be criminally inclined. It also depended on magistrates to fine and/or imprison offenders and on jails to confine them, with a minimum of attention given to their welfare. Punishment, not rehabilitation, was felt to be the most effective way to make the individual answer for his or her crime. Progressives looked beyond the individual to the social factors that produced crime. They firmly believed that crime, as a socially generated ingredient of modern society, could be contained. To do so, the entire system of justice, including the police, courts, and prisons, would have to be made more rehabilitative and humane. This would mean allotting the necessary funding to train officers of the law in proper police procedures and provide them with the latest technology to apprehend criminals. As well, courts must be better attuned to the socio-economic circumstances that may have prompted someone to break the law and to handle each case accordingly. Jails, meanwhile, should be well kept and segregated on the basis of sex and age and in accordance with the severity of the offence. Prisoners should also be offered practical instruction and employment intended to reform their criminal tendencies and to provide for their reintegration into society. A "modern" machinery of order, in progressives' eyes, need not be guided solely by the need to punish offenders in order to be an effective device for controlling crime and preserving order.[4]

The modernization of the Halifax Police Department, as alluded to by Chief Conrad, belied the fact that the force also remained tied to its nineteenth-century roots. The use of foot patrols and the absence of firearms, for instance, both served as a reminder of the department's humble beginnings. Granted that the creation of uniform constabularies from the 1830s onward in British North America had denoted a "minor revolution in state power," it was a revolution that did not dramatically transform daily life.[5] In the case of Halifax, where the city, after its incorporation in 1841, had established separate night-watches and day-time patrols, with a total number of twenty-four constables, it is doubtful that the disorder and mayhem of the "Upper Streets" (the area occupying the eastern slopes of Citadel Hill) and its brothels and groggeries were ever effectively regulated. Even the consolidation of the two forces in 1864, the hiring later that same decade of a detective and the organization of a "rogues' gallery," along with an increase in the number of police to thirty-seven seemed to fall far short of the progressive ideal of a scientific system of surveillance.[6] These meagre efforts, Chief Conrad explained, would not be enough to contain lawlessness. Instead, some believed, the entire system of criminal justice would have to be overhauled and modernized if Halifax stood any chance of safeguarding social order in the twentieth century. Hence the more elaborate police presence, strengthened and supported by the 1892 Criminal Code, the creation of a juvenile court to handle a new category of criminals, and a limited but renewed interest in penal reform, which culminated in the province's 1933 Royal Commission on jails. All of these changes underscore the image and ideal of Halifax as a city of order – a tightly monitored and progressive city that refused to tolerate any disruption of law and order.

This fundamental shift in attitude towards the administration of justice also contained a hint of irony. In the 1920s and early 1930s, Halifax, from a statistical perspective, did not appear to be any more crime-ridden than most Canadian cities. In fact, the Halifax of the 1850s and 1860s, one could argue, had a much greater problem with crime.[7] However, postwar Halifax, ever mindful of public order, required a more concerted and rationalized regime of law enforcement. Thus shades of the modern regulatory state, which "grew out of public policy concerns about the threat to society at large ... that followed from a modern capitalist economy," had begun to emerge in Halifax as the city tried to grapple with the forces of modernity.[8] In order to keep a close watch on criminals and to ensure that they did not escape justice, Halifax turned to its police and courts. Together, these forces of law and order served as the city's primary instrument in combatting criminality. It is therefore essential to provide an analysis of Halifax's machinery of order: its police force, criminal courts and procedures, and incarceration facilities. This will pave the way for an entry into the city's world of crime and society. Urban justice in Halifax was never completely successful or consistent. It could be extremely harsh to those who committed petty offences and at times rather lenient to those who committed serious crimes. At all times, however, it functioned with a tremendous amount of public support and respect. From the lone officer walking his beat through the streets of Halifax, to the stipendiary magistrate who presided over the daily police court proceedings, to the keeper of the County Jail, these instruments of law and order usually received the deference befitting those representing the British system of justice.[9] This does not mean that the machinery of order itself acted in a rational manner. It, like so many other institutions at the time, did its best to cope with the changes in modern society, while trying to meet the demands of a city determined to have stability. Consequently, the operation of justice was not always smooth.

"Guardians of the Law": The Halifax Police Department

For the 1918 to 1935 period, the Halifax Police Department can best be described as a quasi-professional organization. In many respects, the department made significant advances over its nineteenth-century counterpart. Technology, urbanization, and the influence of social reform movements in the early twentieth century meant that urban police forces became more effective in implementing the law. At the turn of the century, in both Canada and the United States, police operations shifted away from a primitive type of "class control" towards "crime control." This was in line with the trend towards more rationalization, bureaucratization, and professionalization of police work.[10] The new emphasis on "crime control" marked the transition of Halifax to a modern city of order. The "modern" city could not exist, some have suggested, without order. However, the process of professionalizing the police unfolded in a slow and uneven fashion. Modern methods of fighting crime often did not supersede, but only supplemented, more traditional approaches. As John C. Weaver notes for the Hamilton police force, Victorian administrators fought to make it a professional body "though never quite succeeding."[11] By no means on the cutting edge of police procedures, the Halifax force nevertheless possessed some of the rudiments of a professional law enforcement agency.

The size of the department fluctuated almost on a yearly basis. For instance, in 1923 it had eighty personnel, while in 1935 this number had fallen to seventy-two. In terms of the city's population, the police had one officer for every 752 residents in 1923, a ratio that widened to one officer for every 884 residents in 1935. In comparison, the Hamilton Police Department had 125 officers in 1923 and 154 in 1935. This converts into a ratio of one policeman to every 979 Hamiltonians in 1923 and one to 1,038 in 1935.[12] Both departments also had fairly successful conviction rates. In 1923, 57.9 percent and 84.6 percent of the cases prosecuted in Halifax and Hamilton, respectively, ended in convictions. For 1935, the rates were 78 percent and 87.1 percent, respectively.[13] While these percentages do suggest that the Halifax and Hamilton police proved effective in turning arrests into convictions, they may also speak to the efficiency of these cities' police courts and the fact that many defendants simply pleaded guilty to such minor offences as drunkenness. (As Appendix 2, Table A2.11, reveals, 42.4 percent of the cases tried before the Halifax Police Court from 1910 to 1920 were for drunkenness.) In spite of this success, the reduction in personnel in the Halifax force hampered it's ability to secure the safety of the local citizenry. Fiscal restraint proved to be the source of these cut-backs. In 1929, the refusal of the Police Commission and the city's Finance Committee to grant an appropriation to the department to hire six additional men and three special officers to fill in for patrolmen on vacation evoked a rather bitter plea from Chief Palmer for assistance: "I have 14 less men then my predecessor had ... We have 13 men to cover 21 beats – every one of them long beats. There are seven square miles of city that require protection – 128 miles of streets. It is an impossible task."[14] Even though Mayor Gastonguay supported Palmer's request, citing the difficulty the police had enforcing the law in light of the increased number of people and automobiles in the city, the Finance Committee held firm in its decision. While the city may have wanted an effective police force, it seemed reluctant at times to put forward the money to attain this objective.

From 1918 to 1935, only three chiefs stood at the helm of the Halifax Police Department. The first, Frank Hanrahan, resigned in 1924 after thirty-two years of service. He had joined the force in 1892 and had served as a patrolman until 1906, when he became a detective. In 1918 city council appointed him chief.[15] His successor, William Palmer, occupied the position of deputy-chief under Hanrahan before being promoted to the senior position. Palmer guided the force through many of its changes and personally tackled a few of the city's more serious crimes. In 1933, citing ill health as the cause of his retirement, Palmer bid farewell to a department he had served for thirty-two years, collected his pension, and watched as his deputy-chief, Judson Conrad, assumed the mantle of chief of police.[16] Elevated to the rank of sergeant in 1919, Conrad advanced to the position of deputy-chief in 1929 and remained chief when 1935 came to a close. The chief conducted most of his work at police headquarters, located at thirty-four Duke Street in downtown Halifax. The station itself was quite modest. As one retired officer remembered, in 1933 the police station was "just fairly ordinary, four or five rooms," without "any particular equipment."[17]

The chiefs presided over a cohesively structured department. They answered directly to the Police Commission for their actions and those of the department in general. The Police Commission consisted of the mayor as chairperson, two aldermen, and the chief of police. The commission heard cases against delinquent officers, reviewed the department's expenditures and yearly budgets, and screened applicants to the force.[18] Below the chief the chain of command consisted, in 1923, of a deputy-chief, chief detective, city marshal, inspector, detective, sergeant, and patrolman. By 1931, the ranks of inspector and detective had been combined, and the position of traffic officer had appeared.[19] Usually the department had six detectives and six sergeants, with patrolmen comprising the bulk of the force. The department was organized according to a rigid division of labour. Detectives conducted most of the serious criminal investigations, such as those involving murder, while the sergeants assisted when needed. The latter also oversaw the administrative details of the department. Much of the responsibility for enforcing the law fell to the patrolmen. They had the arduous tasks of keeping watch over the city both night and day, arresting those they found breaking the law, preventing others from doing so, providing assistance to people victimized by crime, and generally representing the force to the public at large. The son of a former officer who joined the force in 1920 remarked: "most of the men on the beat did a lot of the [department's] work in those days."[20] This hierarchical structure was an indication of the force's efforts to function as a professional unit. As well, reflecting the ethnic and religious make-up of Halifax, all of these men were white, British, and Protestant or Roman Catholic. In 1923, Roman Catholics represented over half (53.8 percent) of the officers (forty-three), while Protestants accounted for the remaining 46.2 percent (thirty-seven) of the staff. (A denominational breakdown of the Protestant members appears in Appendix 2, Table A2.17.) This relatively even religious split characterized the Halifax Police Department for the majority of the interwar years.[21]

The addition of two policewomen represented another phase in the modernization of the Halifax Police Department. In the early years of the twentieth century, cities such as Vancouver, Calgary, Toronto, Montreal, and Halifax hired policewomen.[22] Policewomen, it was felt, could help to prevent crime through social service intervention and by dealing directly with female suspects.[23] In Halifax, Bessie Egan and the felicitously named May Virtue served as social welfare and morality agents. Bessie Egan joined the Halifax Police Department in 1917 and May Virtue in 1918. Their presence is perhaps the most vivid indication of the police force's attempt to adapt to modern society. Egan quickly "proved herself ... efficient in this branch of welfare work." A "willing and efficient worker," with "tact [and an] exceedingly kind heart," Egan enjoyed the admiration of many in Halifax's social reform community.[24] As members of the department's "morality squad," Virtue and Egan "look[ed] after the bad girls" of Halifax. They assisted in raids on bawdy houses and liquor dens and arrested any women found on these premises.[25] Virtue and Egan also acted as matrons for women taken into custody, escorting them to jail and then to their preliminary hearings. In a letter dated 28 January 1916, from R.H. Murray (K.C.), secretary of the Nova Scotia Society for the Prevention of Cruelty, to Mrs. Stead of the Halifax Local Council of Women, Murray outlined the tasks he envisioned for the city's policewomen. They "could be in attendance at the Police Court from day to day to see whether any women were arraigned for offences," Murray wrote, and "then get in touch with the offender and advise the magistrate as to the proper course to adopt" for sentencing. "In the case of the vagrant class and the helpless needing shelter," Murray continued, they "could also be a better officer to appeal to than the ordinary policeman." Murray believed that Halifax's troubles with "girls under the age of 16 years and irresponsible women soliciting on the streets" could "also be handled by the officer[s] in question."[26]

True to form, Virtue and Egan searched the city for young women or families who needed social assistance. During the course of her rounds in 1923, May Virtue discovered a fifteen-month-old baby on the verge of death, attended by a young girl in a small attic room on Water Street. Since the father had deserted his "little brood," their mother worked during the day to support her children. Virtue promptly reported their condition to the mayor, who instructed her to do whatever she felt was necessary to help this family.[27] Virtue and Egan also dispensed moral guidance to the young, errant women whom they encountered while on duty. In 1927, during one of the department's periodic "clean ups" of the city, Virtue and Egan hauled in Violet Betch and Dorothy Brigley, whom they had found wandering the streets late one Saturday night. Unable to provide a satisfactory account of themselves, these women were charged by Virtue and Egan with vagrancy.[28] May Virtue responded to a complaint in October 1931 from a husband at twenty-five Maynard Street who accused his wife of "drinking out nights." To remedy the situation, Virtue sternly warned this woman against indulging in alcohol and then continued on her rounds.[29] In Halifax, Virtue and Egan played a central role in the police department's attempts to control vice, and they provided a maternal face for the city of order.

In certain circumstances, the department could also appoint "special police" to help it patrol the city and to maintain social order. Under the Halifax City Charter, the Police Commission, whenever it was "of [the] opinion that the regular constables [were] not sufficient for the preservation of the peace and for the protection of persons and the security of property in the City," could hire "such number of special constables as it [thought] fit to hold office during the pleasure of the committee."[30] Given a badge and a baton, each special constable could "exercise and enjoy all such powers, authorities, immunities, indemnities, privileges and protection, and be liable to all such duties, responsibilities and penalties, as any constable duly appointed has by virtue of any law or statute within his constablewick."[31] In keeping with this mandate, in 1925 the Police Commission made Roy Yeadon (a shoemaker), Charles White (a barber), and Richard MacKinnon (an ex-soldier and farmer) special officers for the summer months to help the regular force cope with the influx of tourists.[32] On another occasion, Vincent O'Brien took up duty at the Halifax Forum as a special officer for the winter of 1932, mainly to prevent juveniles from vandalizing the building.[33] The working-class background of these special officers underlines the important fact that most Halifax police officers occupied the uncomfortable position of enforcing the law against workers and destitute individuals while they themselves were members of the working class. Besides being a source of much needed seasonal employment for some men, the position of special police allowed the department to extend its authority over the city to an extent that its limited resources would not otherwise have allowed.

While trying to control crime in a modern city, the Halifax police often found themselves in a difficult position. On the one hand, the department had a broad mandate to fulfill. The chief of police and the men and women under his command were responsible for "the peace, quiet and good order of the City."[34] On the other hand, it lacked the modern equipment this mandate involved. To perform this task the force had to rely on four patrol cars, one patrol wagon, and two motorcycles.[35] The department issued each officer a uniform, a badge, and a baton, but not a revolver: police officials remained hostile to the idea of arming officers. Those police who did carry a gun usually owned it themselves.[36] The social conditions of a modern city, however, soon made the need for more modern police methods imperative. Following the shooting death of a policeman in 1924, the public demanded that all officers be given a standard service revolver. One newspaper decried the fact that, in this instance, the officers who had tried to apprehend the assailant had been an "ill-organized, ill-equipped squad of individuals, pitifully unprepared to cope with such a desperate situation."[37] During a meeting of the Police Commission, held on 22 October 1924, Alderman O'Toole made an impassioned plea for the arming of police officers. "I want to see the night duty men armed," O'Toole declared. "If our men were armed" he argued, "there might not be so much breaking [in] at night time. If crooks knew that our men carried arms they would think twice about breaking into a place." Yet Police Chief Palmer felt that several members of his force could not be trusted with firearms.[38] As a result, the commission adopted Palmer's recommendation and refused to grant guns to patrolmen.

Most Halifax police officers received inadequate training and pay. In 1929, Alderman Robertson complained that police officers carried out their duties without the proper instruction. Another report indicated that new recruits did study a manual before starting work but that no means existed to test them on their knowledge of this material.[39] To silence the critics, the mayor informed city council that, for every new officer, the chief personally outlined his responsibilities prior to sending him out on patrol.[40] Some patrolmen, however, did not consider this to be enough guidance. According to Inspector O'Brien: "It wasn't very fair to us because we were not lawyers ... just a grade nine or ten education and that was it. So it was all up to us to decide what was right and wrong." Patrolmen

Police officers pose for a photograph taken at the Grande Parade in 1914. With their motorcycles proudly displayed they represent the modern police force. However, this photo was taken before Halifax's first policewomen, May Virtue and Bessie Egan, were hired. [Cox Bros. Co., photographer, 10 July 1914; Nova Scotia Archives, R.V. Harris Collection, 1992-415, no. 5]

had to decide on the spot, O'Brien remarked, whether or not to place a suspect in custody. If they did, then another officer at the station, usually with a similar background, had to determine whether the suspect should be charged and under which section of the Criminal Code. While O'Brien felt that taking someone in was a fairly easy decision to make, officers still had to "worry about the criminal's rights."[41]

In terms of payment for their services, patrolmen's wages did not match the professional stature sought by the department. In 1918, they earned between $750 and $850 per year depending on seniority.[42] Next to their superior officers and some skilled workers, patrolmen were underpaid. That same year (1918), sergeants made $1,000 to $1,100 and detectives $1,150 to $1,400. On another level, policewoman May Virtue's annual salary of $600 placed her well below her male counterparts.[43] Police officers' poor incomes solidified their position as members of the city's working class. So too did their place of residence. Using the 1923 roster as a sample case, fifty-seven, or 71.2 percent, of the officers rented or owned their own homes; seventeen, or 21.3 percent, boarded (four did so with their co-workers), while the accommodations of six could not be determined. In terms of location within the city, thirty-eight (47.5 percent) lived in the predominately working-class North End, while another sixteen (20 percent) lived in and around the downtown core. The remaining nineteen (23.7 percent), including Chief Hanrahan and Chief Detective Kennedy, resided in the more affluent South End.[44] This physical separation accentuated some of the workplace and social divisions between patrolmen and their commanders. Officers' low pay forced some to quit. "Unless the city officials wake up and realize that the men on the police force cannot live on their present salaries," said one disgruntled patrolman in 1918, "there will not be one married man on the city force by Christmas." Citing the long hours on patrol, which "is by no means child's play," and insufficient wages, several officers resigned before the end of 1918. Even as late as 1924, four men left the force to join the staff of the Canadian National Railways, probably as part of the CNR police, due to the higher pay offered by the company.[45] Chief Hanrahan tried to lobby for a substantial pay increase to attract "a class of men worthy of the city, fit for the duties of law enforcement and capable of coping with growing responsibilities," but with little success.[46]

City Hall's unwillingness to grant officers a satisfactory raise in pay lowered morale on the force. In 1924, the *Morning Chronicle* reported that "discontent [and] dissatisfaction" over the city's "cutting" policy, designed to reduce the size of the force while effectively ending some patrolmen's chances for promotion, swirled throughout the ranks of the department.[47] This helped to spark renewed interest in unionization. In 1915, thirty-nine officers made a tentative attempt to unionize policemen when they signed a petition asking for more money. "We feel that the salaries we now receive," the petition read, "are not in keeping with the duties we have to perform, and we know that with the ever increasing cost of the necessities of life our salaries are not sufficient to provide us with the means of living comfortably and at the same time keep from debts."[48] Twelve years later, at the start of 1927, a group of officers met to discuss the formation of a police association. With organizational help from the secretary-treasurer of the Painters' Union, those in attendance laid the groundwork for the Halifax force to join the Police Officers' Mutual and Protective Association. It was noted that, while the police could not strike, or side with any other faction in a labour dispute due to their role as "guardians" of law and order, they could still help in "labor's great struggle for its emancipation through education along constructive and constitutional lines."[49]

Disharmony among the rank and file and inadequate resources made the job of protecting certain areas of the city difficult. The lack of a police presence in the North End generated considerable discussion among residents there in 1921. "Adequate police protection is badly needed by the taxpayers in the north and northwest sections of the city," Alderman Hubley told the press.[50] Public opinion held the police to be a competent and efficient force. But many citizens also felt that officers had too much ground to cover on their "beats," which nullified their ability to protect all of the homes and businesses in a district.[51] Three years later, in 1924, a second break-in in the city's South End elicited another outcry over the inadequacy of police surveillance. Burglaries, the *Morning Chronicle* argued, occurred more often where a police officer appeared infrequently. The officer in this part of the city had to patrol an area extending from Grafton Street west to the North-West Arm and from Quinpool Road south to Inglis Street (a total of eleven kilometres), a beat large enough for three men. As a result, break-ins could easily be made even though an officer was on duty.[52]

The Halifax Police Department confronted a severe challenge when it came to protecting the city from crime. A closer look at the department's method of patrolling Halifax's streets suggests a rather archaic approach to crime control. As of 1926 the force operated on a daily three-platoon system in which officers worked eight-hour shifts. Previously, they had worked only on a two-platoon system forcing them to work longer hours and cover more territory on foot.[53] Under this new format, patrolmen walked their assigned beats for an eight-hour period. They started their shift at a designated "standing point" and then walked the entire length of their beats. Regulations required that officers do this in roughly fifty minutes, returning to their standing point, where they remained for ten minutes before setting out again. This gave their superiors an opportunity to contact them should an emergency arise in a particular section of their beat.[54] In 1932, Chief Palmer tried to improve his department's services by placing his detectives on a twenty-four-hour schedule, ensuring that at least one detective would be on duty in police headquarters at all times.[55]

The forces of law and order, it was now hoped, would be better able to combat lawlessness and to maintain order in Halifax. In reality, however, this system of police surveillance was seriously flawed. Both citizens and the police themselves vociferously denounced the beat system for being too difficult and, in some cases, too dangerous to work.

Sergeant O'Halloran, testifying before a Police Commission inquiry in 1927 into charges of police ineptitude, stated that the districts set out for officers, especially in the wake of recent personnel shortages, tended to be exceedingly large. This, in O'Halloran's eyes, made proper law enforcement nearly impossible. Sergeant Eisenhaur, who also appeared before the commission, concurred with O'Halloran's assertions and reiterated that the sergeant on duty could not possibly check up on all of his officers on a given night, due to the length of their beats and his administrative responsibilities at headquarters.[56] But despite the difficulties involved, patrolmen did provide a public presence for the police force in the city. Officers rotated their beats periodically, but not before they had established a close rapport with local residents and merchants.[57] The officer on the beat became a familiar and welcome sight for most citizens of Halifax. Personal knowledge of an area and its inhabitants, gained through talking with residents on a daily basis, allowed police officers to determine potential trouble spots and identify would-be criminals. Moreover, officers relied to a great extent on individual property holders and those middle-class residents connected to the phone service to do most of the reporting of crime.

The advent of the patrol car made the police more mobile in their pursuit of criminals. Late in 1921, the police department purchased a new patrol car. This "motorized ... model," as the *Halifax Herald* called it, replaced the horse-drawn wagon first introduced in 1905. Now, instead of "always getting there sometime" when called to a crime scene, patrolmen could respond immediately to any incident. By 1935, the department had four patrol cars, leaving it somewhat behind the advances made by other urban forces in Canada.[58] Constable Alfred Kinsman, who on the night of 29 June 1934 drove patrol car number two around the city, symbolized the more modern look of the department. The sights and sounds he encountered that evening provide a glimpse of the criminal activity in Halifax and the daily routine of most police officers. It also demonstrates that most patrolmen could only handle a small number of usually minor offences while on duty. Shortly after Kinsman went on duty at 4:15 PM, he instructed a boy not to ride his bicycle on the sidewalk. At 5:30 PM he checked in with the chief of police and half an hour later he stopped Frank Romans for speeding on Kempt Road. Around nine o'clock he spoke to a group of boys playing ball on the boulevard at Seymour and Morris streets. From 10:20 PM until 11:00 PM he inspected ten vacant houses to ensure that none had been broken into, and for his last act of the evening he ordered a gang of "young fellows" away from the corner at North and Windsor streets. At midnight his shift ended.[59] Officers on the beat and the gradual use of patrol cars, a mixture of nineteenth- and twentieth-century crime control practices, represented the transitional phase in which the Halifax Police Department found itself prior to 1935.

The Halifax police received a bit of assistance in combatting crime in 1930 when the province introduced provincial policing. The Conservative government of E.N. Rhodes created the Nova Scotia Police in the wake of a 1929 plebiscite that brought an end to prohibition. The force, according to John Phyne, helped the state secure control over the liquor trade by enforcing the newly created Nova Scotia Liquor Control Act (NSLCA).[60] With one hundred men across the province, the Nova Scotia Police, as their commissioner, F.A. Blake, noted, tried to "carry the benefits of constant police protection and surveillance beyond town limits into the country districts."[61] "A" District of the Nova Scotia Police, with a staff of one sergeant, two corporals, sixteen constables, and five special constables, was responsible for Halifax City and County. Although their duties included the enforcement of all provincial statutes of a criminal nature, Criminal Code provisions, and a few select federal statutes, infractions of the NSLCA accounted for over 50 percent of the force's work in the province during its first year of operation.[62] In Halifax this meant that the local police force could shift some of its focus away from liquor offences and concentrate more on other forms of crime. As the province's economic climate grew dimmer in the mid-1930s, the Nova Scotia Police fell victim to budgetary constraints. In April 1932, the Royal Canadian Mounted Police (RCMP) replaced the provincial force and assumed most of its duties throughout Nova Scotia.[63] The majority of the RCMP's efforts went into the protracted battle against bootleggers. The Nova Scotia Police and the RCMP represented another modern instrument through which the city and the state could express their determination to impose the rule of law and to maintain social order in Halifax.

The "guardians of the law" in Halifax enjoyed a great deal of public respect. Much of this esteem originated from the view that police officers, especially the patrolmen people saw every day, stood as the city's first line of defence in the battle against crime. In 1922, a local newspaper carried an article entitled "Policeman's Lot Not a Happy One." The story tried to evoke widespread support for the patrolmen who braved the cold of winter to keep a constant vigil over the city's streets and neighbourhoods.[64] An editorial in the *Halifax Herald* in 1932 concerning the conduct of police officers on duty asserted: "[The] average officer is a pretty good man [and while the *Herald*] has never sought to condone the deliberate actions of officers who have failed in their duty ... we have tried to remember that the great majority of police officers attempt to do their duty as they see it, and where most of them make mistakes the errors are not wilful."[65] Other Halifax residents shared this faith in the police. Percy Blanchard wrote to the editor of the *Halifax Herald* that, although the police may have had difficulty solving some crimes, the "police of Halifax [were] probably as fine a body of men as [would] be found in any City." If problems plagued the force, Blanchard contended, the citizens of Halifax should place the blame not on the officers themselves but, rather, on the politicians who oversaw the force.[66] At a time when many citizens felt crime to be "on every hand," people looked to the police as one of the primary sources of order. The desire on the part of many people in Halifax and the media to praise and defend the police department coincided with a general pattern across the country, which showed that, as an institution, the Canadian police commanded considerable public admiration.[67]

"Clearing Houses of Human Misery": Courts in Halifax

Just as the police department indicates both the drive to modernize and the continuing hold of old forms and traditions, so too did the courts in Halifax. Here, however, inertia far outweighed progressive innovation in the interwar years. Beginning in the late nineteenth century, the judicial system in Halifax, much like the police department, developed into a more professional organization. However, this did not mean that the ad hoc nature of justice, evident in the early nineteenth-century practices of the justices of the peace, disappeared completely.[68] A brief account of the various criminal courts, their jurisdictions, and procedures highlights this claim. To capture this system in action, I discuss the case of Allister Munroe, who stood trial for the murder of storekeeper Leslie Corkum (the details of which are outlined in the Introduction), along with the experiences of a few individuals charged with minor infractions, in order to reveal the wide array of disputes that the courts dealt with on a routine basis. Clearly, the struggle for law and order in Halifax was played out in the courtroom as well as on the street.

In January 1923, the police charged Allister Munroe with murder, shop-breaking, and theft. Munroe's arrest came after a taxi driver identified him as the person he had seen in the vicinity of the October 1922 shooting. The evidence presented by the Crown at Munroe's preliminary hearing did not bode well for the prisoner. Charles Larsen, a labourer, testified that he had talked to Munroe on two separate occasions shortly before Corkum's death. According to Larsen, Munroe claimed he "was busted" and needed some money. The next time they spoke, Larsen noted: "[Munroe] was talking about a place on Spring Garden Road, Corkum's. He said [he] wanted me to go with him. I said no ... Munroe had a black jack and showed me a gun."[69] Following these statements, Jacob Cramp, a friend of Munroe's, told the court that, after a story about the shooting appeared in the newspaper, he had had a conversation with Munroe. "As near as I can remember," Cramp said, "Munroe ... told me he was the man that fired the shot." Munroe then apparently told Cramp how the revolver accidentally discharged while Corkum was raising his hands and how he had had no intention of shooting him.[70]

Stipendiary Magistrate Fielding committed Munroe to stand trial before the Nova Scotia Supreme Court for the shooting death of Leslie Corkum. The trial was scheduled to begin in April 1923. As "Witnesses ... and spectators" gathered for the opening day of the proceedings, the *Halifax Herald* commented:

> Crimes of violence are not foreign to Halifax. Murder trials have been conducted in the none too remote past. But few happenings have attracted such widespread interest as the killing of Leslie Corkum last Halloween. The mystery attending the crime, the apparent baffling of the investigators, the tracing of the alleged murderer, the divided condition of public opinion concerning his guilt, the untold stories which may lurk in the shades behind the scenes, these elements have moved the public profoundly.[71]

All eyes, it seemed, would be glued to the events in this courtroom. Munroe's trial did not last long. On 6 April, just three days after it started, the jury filed into the courtroom after an hour and five minutes of deliberation. As the foreman read aloud the verdict of "not guilty," someone in the back of the room shouted "Hurrah" and general pandemonium broke out among the spectators before the sheriff could restore order.[72] During the trial, the defence had suggested that Munroe had been framed, and Munroe's lawyer skilfully convinced the jury to acquit him. Afterwards, in an interview with the *Halifax Herald*, Munroe was emphatic in his innocence: "I am certain that I was framed and I hope the people of Halifax know that I was framed." When asked how the police could have made such a mistake, Munroe referred to his criminal record as a likely motive for his arrest: "I've done lots of things in my life, and it was these things that helped them to get it on me the way they did."[73] Munro's acquittal meant that the death of Leslie Corkum remained another of Halifax's unsolved murders.

The Halifax Police Court marked the first stopping point for the majority of those, like Allister Munroe, who broke the law. A general belief in Halifax, dating back to 1792, that crime had out-stripped the capacity of the justices of the peace to cope with it, had led to the creation of the police court in 1815.[74] The police court essentially widened the public's access to criminal courts. Occupying the bottom rung in the judicial hierarchy, the police court, located in City Hall, dealt with most criminal matters in the city other than indictable offences.[75] Police courts in several British North American cities became important state institutions. They meted out punitive justice to repeat offenders and served as "clearing houses of human misery." By the mid-point of the nineteenth century, stipendiary magistrates took control of the police court and bestowed an air of professionalism to the proceedings.[76] However, the volume of cases handled by the court (for 1919-20 alone the Halifax police court tried 3,204 cases [Appendix 2, Table A2.11]), combined with the small number of barristers available to defend accused persons, compromised the court's impartiality and fairness. The police court also functioned as an arena of popular justice for many members of Halifax's working class, women, and ethnic minorities. They used this court to bring forward charges against friends, relatives, spouses, or strangers in the hopes of settling their grievances.[77] In all these respects, "justice" in the police court was close to the people, and it was administered with efficiency and a modicum of fairness.

The stipendiary magistrate presided over the police court. The title "stipendiary magistrate" derived from the method of payment for this position. In Halifax, stipendiary magistrates received a regular stipend, or salary. In 1867, Henry Pryor, a barrister, became Halifax's first stipendiary magistrate. The creation of the office of stipendiary magistrate followed a pattern of progression in Canada from the justice of the peace to the Mayor's Court to stipendiary magistrate.[78] Appointed by the Governor-in-Council (i.e., Cabinet), each magistrate swore an oath of office and held tenure during good behaviour. Magistrates had to exhibit such qualities as "punctuality," a "kindly disposition," and a "modest amount of knowledge of the elementary principles of law."[79] In keeping with the belief that the state should maintain the "Peace, Order, and good Government of Canada," the position of police magistrate, when it first appeared, "was perceived as an administrative tool in carrying out that task."[80] Those men who occupied the post of stipendiary magistrate in Halifax from 1918 to 1935 conducted themselves, and their court, with a measure of professionalism. G.H. Fielding, who was appointed to the position in 1894 and who retired in 1924, regularly sought to "temper justice with mercy" in most of the cases brought before his court.[81] Fielding's replacement, Andrew Cluney, much admired by lawyers and the general public alike, combined professionalism and human kindness on the bench. This made him, in the opinion of the *Halifax Herald*, "at once the inflexible guardian of justice and the friend of the unfortunate who were brought before him." He was, as the *Herald* believed, an "ideal" magistrate who, after his death in September 1929, would be hard to replace.[82] Although these men did not leave written accounts of their lives and work, it may be concluded from the press coverage that they dominated court room activities and played an influential role in the administration of criminal justice in Halifax.

For most offenders, the first stage in their legal battle began when they appeared before the stipendiary magistrate. The Nova Scotia Summary Convictions Act laid out the procedures and rules for the province's courts. Once a complainant laid an "information," or charge, before the magistrate, a warrant, or summons, would be issued either for the accused's arrest or requesting her or his appearance in court. A magistrate could also lay a complaint against a person for an alleged criminal act. If the defendant appeared before the court, and the complainant did not, the Summary Convictions Act gave the magistrate the authority to dismiss the complaint or, "if he [thought] fit," to adjourn the case to another day.[83] If the defendant "show[ed] no sufficient cause why he should not be convicted, or why an order should not be made against him ... the justice ... [would] convict him or make an order against him accordingly." But if the defendant disputed the information that had been laid before the court, then the magistrate convened a preliminary hearing.[84] During the preliminary hearing for indictable offences, the magistrate heard the Crown's evidence against the accused and allowed the defence counsel, or the defendant, depending on whether or not she or he had retained counsel, to cross-examine those witnesses called by the Crown.[85] In the majority of cases heard in the police court, the defendants did not have legal representation. Only in serious criminal matters (notably murder) or where a person could afford legal counsel did the accused have the advantage of a lawyer at her or his side. The benefit of legal aid did not exist as an option for an accused during these years of the Halifax legal profession. After the Crown had delivered its evidence to the court, the defendant or defence lawyer had the option to present evidence and call witnesses in answer to the charge. The accused did not, however, have to enter a plea. Before deciding what to do, the accused could have the depositions read back to her or him and then the magistrate would issue the following caution:

> Having heard the evidence, do you wish to say anything in answer to the charge? You are not bound to say anything, but whatever you do say will be taken down in writing and may be given in evidence against you at your trial. You must clearly understand that you have nothing to hope from any promise or favour and nothing to fear from any threat which may have been held out to you to induce you to make any admission or confession of guilt, but whatever you now say may be given in evidence against you at your trial notwithstanding such promise or threat.[86]

The tendency was for defendants to remain silent in the face of their accusers in most criminal cases, whether serious or minor. Often ignorant of the law and the punishments associated with their crimes, without the advice of counsel, and quite likely intimidated by the entire process, many offenders stood at the mercy of the criminal justice system. After considering all of the evidence presented before him, the stipendiary magistrate would decide whether or not a "prima facie" case had been established against the accused. If he ruled in favour of the Crown the defendant would be committed to stand trial before the County Court or the Supreme Court; if not, the defendant would be released. The magistrate then had to determine whether the accused should be granted bail. If denied bail, as was Allister Munroe, due to the seriousness of his alleged offence, the police brought the prisoner to the Halifax County Jail to await the commencement of his/her trial.[87] For less serious indictable offences, – namely, those punishable by under five years imprisonment – the magistrate could let the accused "go at large" upon his/her own recognizance.[88] In many situations the granting or denial of bail boiled down to whether or not the magistrate felt that the person in question could be trusted to return for his/her court appearance once released.

The Supreme Court of Nova Scotia served as the province's highest court for both civil and criminal cases.[89] The Supreme Court's jurisdiction in criminal cases extended only to indictable offences – those crimes deemed serious in nature (murder, obstructing a peace officer, perjury, manslaughter, rape, and procuring an abortion) and that usually carried a jail term of five years or more.[90] The Supreme Court also heard criminal appeals from anyone "who [thought] himself aggrieved by a conviction."[91] Not every criminal case was tried in the Supreme Court. For most indictable offences, the accused could elect to be tried under the provisions of the Speedy Trials of Indictable Offences section of the Criminal Code.[92] This part of the Code stipulated that an accused had to appear before the County Court judge, without a jury, to be tried. However, the accused had to consent to be tried by judge alone. As one lawyer noted at the time, the Speedy Trials option "ha[d] greatly lightened the burden of the Supreme Court," thus allowing it to concentrate on more pressing criminal issues.[93] In 1874, the Nova Scotia Legislature instituted a system of county courts for the province, which began operating in 1876. Divided into seven districts (Halifax being District Number One), each County Court had one presiding judge who had at least seven years of experience as a barrister before his appointment to the bench. In 1889, the Halifax County Court inherited the authority to hear those criminal cases within the ambit of the Speedy Trials provisions.[94]

For those committed to stand trial in the Supreme Court, the Grand Jury held out the final hope of a reprieve. If the accused chose the Speedy Trials route, then she or he waived the right to have her/his case presented before the Grand Jury. Similarly, since the Grand Jury only dealt with more serious, indictable offences, it was not a factor in many of the cases that came before the Police Court. Created to ensure that an individual was accused and tried only with due cause, the Grand Jury encountered criticism from some contemporaries who thought of it as a "fifth wheel to the legal coach." Others supported it as an important element of

British jurisprudence, which protected personal liberties. Nevertheless, as the nineteenth century progressed, many lawyers, and other members of the criminal justice system, criticized the Grand Jury – and juries generally – as unprofessional anachronistic bodies that did little to advance law and order.[95] The Grand Jury was structured on clearly defined principles of class and gender. Only those people who had resided in Nova Scotia for at least twelve months and who were assessed for real or personal property at $400, or real and personal property combined at $600, could sit on the Grand Jury. In Halifax, however, the property qualification was $4,000. Moreover, only men could occupy the twelve available positions on the Grand Jury.[96] As one American commentator noted in 1934, Canadian juries tended to be "high-calibered," comprised only of "real citizens in active life."[97] The Grand Jury decided whether or not a charge or indictment, referred to as a "true bill," would be found against an accused. It thus served as a jury of presentment or accusation.[98] To guide them in this task, a Supreme Court justice advised the members of the Grand Jury with regard to the law and the facts as they related to the specific charge. The members of the Grand Jury then retired and considered only the evidence presented by the Crown in the lower court and any new evidence against the accused uncovered by the Crown in the interim. They then had to determine whether the prisoner should stand trial for the alleged crime.[99] R. Blake Brown has documented that grand juries in Halifax, between 1867 and 1888, found true bills in the "vast majority" of cases, which essentially reduced the Grand Jury to a symbolic, if not redundant, part of the criminal justice system.[100] After a true bill had been found against an accused, her or his case went to the Supreme Court. Here the accused faced a judge and a jury of his or her peers, described as a "petit jury." The petit jury heard evidence from the Crown and the defence and received instructions from the judge as to how the law applied to the particular case at hand. The onus then fell upon it to find the accused guilty or innocent of the charge.[101]

In a majority of the cases heard before Halifax courts, such elaborate and lengthy procedures were not necessary. Most of the crimes committed in Halifax in these years were classified as "summary," or non-indictable, offences – those crimes punishable by a small fine, a prison term of two years less a day, or both.[102] They could be dispensed with quickly in the police court. As Tables A2.1 and A2.2 (Appendix 2) show, from 1918 to 1935, the total number of convictions for summary offences in Halifax (26,304) far outweighed the total convictions for indictable offences (6,356). In terms of percentages, 80.5 percent of the sentences handed out by Halifax courts in these years were for summary offences, while only 19.5 percent were for indictable offences. Some non-indictable offences, depending on their severity, did advance to the Halifax County Court. But for many criminals, the police court served as the main forum for their dealings with the law. Stipendiary magistrates dispensed a form of summary justice designed to handle the constant flow of cases, not to address the problem of crime or to provide any sort of reformative measures to reduce criminal activity. For the most part, magistrates rendered stiff judgements, according to the guidelines of the criminal law and their own personal standard of morality, on those who passed through their court. To some the Halifax Police Court was home to the characteristic elements of the city's "criminal class." The reporter who covered the police court for the *Morning Chronicle*, in a style reminiscent of the Victorian era, described those who frequented this courtroom as "the army of the great unwashed," who "daily jam[med] into the Police Court lured by morbid curiosity, and by a desire ... to escape any work that might happen to be going begging ... apparently unaffected by the strong smell of creosote or some other fumigatory substance used to overpower the stench which [was] peculiarly a part of the Police Court atmosphere."[103] Magistrate Barnhill recommended that the courtroom be moved to another part of the court house, where "respectable" people would be able to give evidence in cheerful surroundings.[104]

For some of the "great unwashed," November 1926 was another typical month in the police court. Stipendiary Magistrate Cluney tried a total of 322 cases during this month. They included 61 indictable offences (18.9 percent), 57 for drunkenness (17.7 percent), 45 for infractions of city ordinances (13.9 percent), 44 for violations against the Nova Scotia Temperance Act (13.7 percent), 40 for assault (12.4 percent), 18 for non-support of wives and dependants (5.6 percent), 15 for vagrancy (4.6 percent), 10 for breaching the Customs and Inland Revenue Act (3.1 percent), 6 for assault causing grievous bodily harm (1.9 percent), 3 for driving a motor vehicle while under the influence of liquor (0.9 percent), and 23 miscellaneous charges (7.1 percent).[105] Among these cases was Charles Houseman, arrested by the police in his home for inflicting a "severe pounding" on his wife. Charged with creating a disturbance, the magistrate released Houseman for six months on his own recognizance on the condition that he behave himself.[106] James Shea, convicted of "indecent conduct," received a fine of twenty-five dollars or, in default, sixty days in the City Prison. Walter Wisell fared a bit better when he went before the magistrate for assaulting a shoemaker. His friends swore that the alleged assault had never occurred and the complainant could not produce any witnesses to support his claim. Under the circumstances, the magistrate had no choice but to dismiss the case.[107]

Due to the plethora of cases and offenders constantly shuffling through the police court, an emphasis had to be placed on speed and efficiency. Consequently, the administration of justice in Halifax could be haphazard and arbitrary. "Swift justice," the *Herald* reported, had been meted out by Magistrate MacLeod to Henry Kane, "colored." Alfred Sheldon had accused Kane of stealing goods from his store. The court then issued a warrant for his arrest at 3:30 PM. Exactly one hour later, at 4:30 PM, Kane's trial took place, during which he pleaded guilty to the charge.[108] The quick turnover in cases could adversely affect the defendant. Unable to afford legal representation and lacking access to any system of legal aid, most people who stood before the magistrate accused of a crime defended themselves, with little knowledge of the law at their disposal. In April 1921, a young man by the name of Mills pleaded not guilty to a charge of assault. Magistrate Fielding, upon learning that a representative of the Crown was not present, said to Mills, "I don't know that there is anything that can be done unless you oblige us by pleading guilty." Before Fielding could say another word, Mills surprised everyone in attendance when he replied, "Alright, I plead guilty." Fielding then granted Mills a conditional release. Later Fielding commented that this had been the first time in his tenure as police court magistrate that a prisoner had changed his plea from not-guilty to guilty to facilitate court proceedings.[109]

"A Child Saving Station": The Halifax Juvenile Court

Juvenile offenders travelled a different road through the city's criminal justice system. Juveniles, those girls and boys under the age of sixteen when taken into custody by the police for a criminal offence, did not stand before the police court but, rather, the Halifax Juvenile Court. Established in February 1911 following the 1910 proclamation in Nova Scotia of the federal Juvenile Delinquents Act, 1908, the Halifax Juvenile Court led the fight to "save" juveniles from a life of crime.[110] As one of the first locations for a juvenile court in Nova Scotia, and indeed in Canada, Halifax apparently suffered from a serious problem with juvenile delinquency.[111] Overseeing the administration of juvenile justice in Halifax during the years from 1918 to 1935 were four judges: W.B. Wallace (1918-19), Dr. James Johnson Hunt (1919-25), Ernest Blois (1925-33), and W.W. Walsh (1933-35).[112] In the minds of many, the juvenile court, whether in Halifax or elsewhere in Canada, must be a "child saving station," a place where children would be shown guidance so that they could become "citizen[s] saved to the state." The court should also be an "intelligent instrument for the defense and protection of the unfortunate victim, rather than a tool of retribution and destruction." And perhaps most important, the juvenile court should not be a "place to punish children, but help and protect them from themselves and others."[113] This emphasis upon "maternal justice" became a hallmark of juvenile courts in Canada and an extension of state authority into the lives of mainly poor, working-class children and families. Besides a judge, the Halifax Juvenile Court also employed a probation officer. Probation was another form of social regulation for many children in Halifax. The city's probation officer, J.E. Hudson, spent much of his time keeping a close watch over young offenders who had been released on probation. In addition, Hudson, like many probation officers, could influence the outcome of a case. Before a case came before the court, the probation officer investigated the relevant details and then, bearing in mind the best interests of the child in question, recommended to the judge how the case should be handled. In other words, the probation officer could help to determine whether or not the court would give an accused a suspended sentence, place her/him on probation, impose a fine, or sentence her/him to a reformatory.[114] The Halifax Juvenile Court also worked closely with the Children's Aid Society of Halifax, the police department, and local reformatories (discussed later in this chapter) to curb the growth of juvenile crime and to ensure the reformation of delinquents.

The Halifax Juvenile Court stood as a testament to a more modern approach to juvenile crime – an approach that in Nova Scotia had first appeared in 1890 with the passage of an Act to Provide for the Reform of Juvenile Offenders. As part of this legislation, any boy under the age of sixteen who was found guilty of breaking the law could be sentenced to a reformatory rather than to a jail.[115] The arrival of juvenile courts in North America has been heralded as one of the notable innovations of the Progressive era. Some of its supporters considered the juvenile court to be an instrument of "social betterment" not only for children but also for society as a whole.[116] Similarly, the entire juvenile justice system, Tamara Myers contends, was considered to be an improvement over adult courts because it was intended to operate on the principle of treatment rather than punishment.[117] The Reverend C.L. Ball saw the need for a specialized procedure for treating juvenile offenders. Writing in the *Halifax Herald*, Ball said that lumping juvenile and adult criminals together only "tend[ed] to confirm the criminal in crime." "We should not treat a juvenile," Ball argued, "as we would an adult offender." To remedy the situation Ball proposed that "severity of punishment" should be reduced and that more supervision should be applied to children through probation. Only by regulating their lives, it seemed to Ball, could children who ran afoul of the law be "saved ... as good citizens."[118]

The architects of the juvenile court in Halifax no doubt felt the same way. The Nova Scotia Society for the Prevention of Cruelty had spearheaded the drive for a juvenile court to protect the interests of children. The society also felt that parents should shoulder more of the blame for their children's delinquent ways.[119] In this sense, it was hoped that the juvenile court would hold parents more accountable for neglecting their children or for any part that they may have played in contributing to their children's delinquency. The federal and provincial governments tried to meet their demands, but they also realized that a juvenile court would not be an ultimate panacea for the problem. Commenting in 1918 on the recently tabled report of the superintendent of neglected and delinquent children, the province's attorney general, Orlando Daniels, insisted:

> [A juvenile court] is not a complete remedy, or cure-all, for crime. It is not, and cannot be, a substitute for parental care, moral and religious training and good environment ... It is not really a court for deciding cases, but rather a bureau of practical justice, and a "clearing house" where conditions of juvenile delinquents are adjusted. It is not so much a method of investigation with a view to the punishment of a delinquent act as a remedy for conditions from which the delinquent act probably arose.[120]

The government created the juvenile court, Daniels continued, because "every child [who has broken the law] has a right to a fair chance to become an honest, useful citizen." Bearing this in mind, Daniels concluded: "the business of the court is to search out the underlying causes of juvenile delinquency and to supply preventive measures."[121] Hence the prevention of juvenile crime and delinquency became a cornerstone of Halifax's, and Canada's, newly created juvenile justice system.

The Halifax Juvenile Court, in accordance with the Juvenile Delinquents Act, dealt with wayward children by classifying them into two categories: "neglected" and "delinquent." Neglected children included those whose parents had failed to provide or care for them and who had suffered accordingly. If uncared for, court officials believed, these children would soon become delinquents. In cases where the court found parents guilty of neglecting their children, or contributing to their delinquency, the judge could impose a fine of up to $500 or confine the child in a reformatory for one year. As Judge Wallace commented, "I have had occasion to enforce a fine more than once with good effect."[122] Delinquents, on the other hand, were those juveniles found guilty of deeds that would be deemed criminal if the perpetrators had been sixteen years of age or over. Some of these acts included truancy ("the forerunner of many greater offences," according to Judge Blois), petty theft, damage to property, and mischief.[123] Judges had the discretion to suspend a child's sentence if they felt it to be in her or his best interests. This, judges hoped, would give youthful offenders an opportunity to forsake their deviant ways. If, however, they considered the conditions in a child's home to be a hindrance to his/her reform, the judge could send him/her to a reformatory.[124] The average length of stay for children in a reformatory tended to be two years, but some did receive indefinite sentences. As one commentator said about Judge Hunt, he imposed sentences "not as punishment, but as an aid towards building up character."[125] It was anticipated that juvenile court judges would embody masculine virtues of honesty and moral character and thus serve as role models for young boys. Indeed, character building was considered to be one way to reform wayward boys.[126] The Halifax Juvenile Court, and its judges, represented one attempt on the part of judicial officials and the state to rehabilitate a segment of the city's criminal element. Some feared that, as soon as juveniles became adults, all chances of "rescuing" them would vanish and the criminal justice system would have to deal with these older law breakers more harshly.

"A School for Crime": Prisons and Reformatories

The primary method of dealing with adult criminals in Canada was incarceration. Halifax's penal institutions were filthy and wretched places, where inmates wallowed in the monotony of a few menial tasks and overwhelming boredom. They had improved little since their creation in the mid-nineteenth century, when the focus was primarily on the punishment of prisoners.[127] For much of the early decades of the twentieth century, the drive to improve Halifax's prisons had enjoyed little success. Dissatisfaction with the penal situation would culminate in 1933 with the release of the *Report of the Royal Commission Concerning Jails,* which called for sweeping changes to the province's system of incarceration.[128] The government, however, implemented few of its recommendations and Halifax's jails continued to operate as outdated and ineffective institutions. The movement for penal reform in Halifax exposed the hopes and limitations of progressivism. Those men and women committed to making Halifax's penal regime more efficient and attuned to rehabilitation, in essence more modern, fought an uphill battle. They asserted that prisons did nothing to improve the lives of inmates and instead made them more prone to continue a life of crime after their release. They stressed that with the proper facilities and training, prisoners' criminal habits could be broken and crime thus controlled. Nonetheless, most of those concerned with law and order in Halifax viewed prisons as nothing more than places to confine those people who had committed crimes. This coincided with their firm belief that "criminals" were not intent on changing their ways. Once imprisoned, so the argument went, little could be done to help criminals, other than to ensure that they no longer posed a threat to social order.[129]

The city lockup, or police lockup, served as the main weapon in this effort to secure order by incarcerating criminals. Situated in the basement of City Hall, with a cell capacity of fifteen, the lockup was an overnight detention centre for those arrested, but not always formally charged, with a crime. Vagrants, drunks, and unemployed transients often spent a night, or a weekend, in these cells as part of the police department's efforts to rid the city's streets of undesirables.[130] The commissioners who inspected the lockup as part of their investigations in 1932 found it "to be in an unbelievably filthy condition and ... unquestionably one of the worst and most disreputable places of detention" they had viewed. Moreover, due to an absence of seating and sleeping accommodations in many of the cells, male prisoners had to stand or lie on the "cold cement floor like animals in a stable. That they did so was evident from the human excreta still lying unremoved on the floor."[131] Some of the men and women in the lockup awaited trial in police court, while others had simply fallen into the police dragnet. The commissioners concluded that they could "find no words adequate to condemn the use of pens of this character for the detention of men and women, however guilty they may be, while to the innocent, such confinement [was] grossly unjust." As a result of these conditions, the commissioners called for the closure of the City Lockup "as it [was] wholly unfit even for temporary detention."[132] The Halifax County Jail was no better. Built in 1865 and located on Spring Garden Road adjacent to the court house, the County Jail housed those awaiting (or on) trial in the police, county, and supreme courts as well as those convicted of minor offences. Under the supervision of a jailor (who for the years from 1918 to 1935 was Malcolm Mitchell) and a matron, the County Jail had eighteen single and four double cells in a poorly ventilated, dark, and overcrowded building. Often two or more prisoners slept in one cell, and when the County Jail reached capacity some had to sleep in the corridors. The County Jail also lacked "adequate accommodation for religious services ... [had] no satisfactory facilities for caring for the sick ... and the section for women prisoners [was] inadequate." As well, the "toilets [were] of the crudest type and located in ill-lighted closets ... There appeared to be no strict enforcement of cleanliness, with the result that towels, pillows and bed-clothing were not satisfactorily clean."[133]

The state of the County Jail aroused a bit of public controversy. One of the most scathing attacks on the jail came in 1924 from the pen of Reverend Harold Roe. Roe, a Methodist minister, wrote a column for the *Evening Mail* under the nom de plume "Vigilant." As a leader in the city's moral and social reform movements, Roe regularly visited the jail.[134] Like most penal reformers, Roe viewed Halifax's outmoded jails as part of the dire consequences of modernity. In "The Promenade of the Dammed," Roe exposed the city's complacency with regard to conditions in the County Jail. "Right in the heart of this fine old British City," Roe wrote, "stands a building which is a veritable House of Shame. It is supposed to be a place of correction, it is instead a prolific source of corruption ... You have walked Barrington street and revelled in the summer glory of the Public Gardens, but what do you know of the Promenade of the Dammed ... in the County Jail?"[135] Roe also pinpointed what he considered to be the most vexing and perennial problem in the County Jail – namely, the lack of prisoner segregation. Young men and women who had not yet been convicted of a crime, or who had been jailed for a minor offence,

Roe argued, mixed with "hardened" criminals, making the jail a "breeding place of vicious habits." Moreover, the jail's brutal surroundings, Roe insisted, ignited the "fires of revenge" within the prisoners and made first-time offenders more apt to commit another criminal act once freed.[136]

Roe's article elicited a quick response. Two days later, the province's attorney general, W.J. O'Hearn, instructed the Grand Jury to visit the County Jail and to deliver a report based on its findings. As the *Halifax Herald* commented in light of O'Hearn's decision, "It has been common knowledge for years past that the County Jail is not an institution that is a credit to this city."[137] Yet not everyone endorsed Roe's allegations. Dr. W.D. Forrest, county health officer and surgeon for the County Jail, maintained that "most of the statements [were] grossly exaggerated and in many instances absolutely untrue," that they were intended to discredit the jail in the eyes of the public.[138] The Grand Jury's report, however, disagreed. The jury recommended that prisoners awaiting trial be separated from those already sentenced. The report denounced confining prisoners afflicted with venereal or other infectious diseases with healthy inmates. It also deplored the enforced idleness of prisoners and their lack of exercise as one of the "greatest curses" of the County Jail. To rectify this, it suggested that prisoners be allowed outside for one or two hours a day and that employment be provided to those capable of working. In this vein, the Grand Jury soundly rebuked the jail as "wholly inadequate" for the care of prisoners and urged the government to build a centrally located prison farm for all convicted criminals serving sentences of two years or less, where they would be given regular work "under proper control and uplifting discipline."[139] The province and the city now had a blueprint for overhauling the antiquated County Jail.

Yet, years later, little had been done to resolve the situation. In 1927, the Grand Jury filed another report on the County Jail, this time praising it as a suitable place for those awaiting trial but once again expressing deep disappointment over its continued use as a prison for convicted criminals.[140] Even Dr. Forrest, in his annual report of jail conditions in 1929, lamented the fact that idleness still characterized prisoners' daily routine. "No provision is made," Forrest noted, "for giving a prisoner any exercise whatsoever, whether he is confined for a day or a year. This is certainly the refinement of cruelty."[141] Overcrowding among the prisoners was a further problem. The annual report of the County Jail for the year ending September 1931 revealed that the number of incarcerations had increased by 189 over the previous year. From 1 October 1930 until 30 September 1931, the County Jail admitted a total of 899 prisoners (848 men and 51 women), forcing "the sleeping at times of two in one cell on stone floors."[142] R.H. Murray, whose career as Crown prosecutor and as leader of the Nova Scotia Society for the Prevention of Cruelty had given him credentials as a progressive on questions of crime, put it graphically: overcrowding in the airless cells caused "shocking immorality." In general, Murray concluded, this led to the contamination of those who had to serve time in this environment.[143] A prison farm, first proposed by the Grand Jury in 1924 and endorsed thereafter by penal reformers as an excellent venue for the rehabilitation of prisoners, became one of many schemes to fall by the wayside.

The debate over the efficiency of the County Jail continued to rage into the early 1930s. In particular, the 1933 *Report of the Royal Commission Concerning Jails* in Nova Scotia soundly condemned the general administration of the County Jail. The commissioners denounced the fact that the County Jail was not segregated on any basis: "Youths in their teens are mixed with older offenders, the diseased with the healthy, and those awaiting trial with convicted prisoners." The commissioners accused the "authorities" who ran the County Jail of exhibiting "little concern or responsibility for the reformation of the prisoner, by [not] furnishing ... either occupational, educational or other elevating influences." They concluded that the majority of the prisoners in the County Jail should be transferred elsewhere and that a more centralized institution (a proposed "Provincial Reformatory of Nova Scotia") should be erected to house prisoners who had been sentenced to a term of one month or less.[144] (The full text of the commissioners' findings and recommendations for Halifax's lockups and prisons is reproduced in Appendix 3.) Other opponents, including the Halifax Prisoners' Welfare Association and some local clergy, described the jail as a "school for crime" and a "disgrace to the people of Halifax." Defenders, such as Dr. Forrest, dismissed these groups as "loquacious interlopers" and countered that prisoners at the County Jail "[were] better housed and fed and more comfortable than [were] many in homes in this city and county today."[145] Ultimately, the city's, and the province's, limited financial resources remained one of the major stumbling blocks to the modernization of Halifax's entire machinery of order. Clearly, penal reform did not attract widespread support in Halifax.[146]

The city's main institute of correction was the City Prison, known to contemporaries as "Rockhead." The Halifax City Prison, constructed in

1860 in a non-residential area of the North End, struck an imposing figure on the city's landscape. In 1923, McLeod's Slaughter House, the Hospital for Infectious Diseases, and the Rockhead Military Hospital all huddled nearby, creating a sombre aura of imprisonment, infection, and death.[147] From 1918 to 1935, George Grant served as governor of the City Prison and his wife Martha Grant acted as matron. Together they oversaw the daily administration of the prison and its inhabitants. The structure itself had eighty-two vault-like cells (seventy-one for men and eleven for women) in a series of corridors enclosed by "dungeon doors with small grated apertures for light and air." In general the prison (in the words of the 1933 royal commission) was "entirely unsuited ... for the housing of its population of often a hundred or more human beings."[148] Prisoners sentenced to the City Prison had committed any number of criminal acts. Similar to the County Jail, the City Prison only kept those convicted felons serving terms of less than two years. Following this guideline, the magistrate would then determine in which facility offenders would be confined. As a rule, most "petty" criminals went to the City Prison. They stayed for one or two months on such charges as vagrancy, robbery, breaking and entering, and liquor law violations. Drunkenness was the most prevalent form of crime for the men who ended up in the City Prison. For the "ordinary common drunk," interred for a few days, little could be expected in the way of reformation, prison officials felt, "except to sober and clean him up and send him on his way with the hope that he [would] not return too quickly."[149] A 1920 Canadian National Committee for Mental Hygiene survey of the province's institutions, which was designed to care for people who suffered from mental disorder as well as inmates of jails, reformatories, and almshouses, concluded that the male prisoners in the City Prison belonged, for the most part, to the "labouring class" and that, as a group, "might be considered of dull normal intelligence with a considerable number falling into the definitely mentally deficient category."[150]

The City Prison was segregated according to sex. Men comprised the bulk of the population. Female prisoners had their own ward separate from the men, where roughly seven to ten women served their sentences. Otherwise, prisoners mingled freely among themselves. The Prison Committee, which included the governor and city aldermen, felt this situation must be rectified. First offenders, the committee warned, should be separated from "drunks," "hardened" criminals, and men of "poorer mentality." Moreover, the convict sentenced to more than one month should be so classified and "placed as far as possible with men of equal standards, persuaded to use his leisure time to good advantage, treated as far as possible with courtesy and firmness, teaching him if possible to respect himself and assuring him that there is still room in the world for him to make good."[151] This emphasis on the need to reform prisoners in the City Prison set it apart from the County Jail. Idleness among inmates did not become a serious problem in the City Prison. While there, regulations required that all those men not ill or infirm would "be kept at work" in the carpentry and shoe shops, cookhouse, stone shed, and on the prison's small farm. This belief in the redemptive value of labour harkened back to the mid-nineteenth century, when many were convinced that "labour, instruction, and moral reformation ... would bring about wholesale rehabilitation of offenders."[152] Their production either went towards maintaining the prison itself or belonged to the City of Halifax, which had jurisdiction over Rockhead.[153] Women worked in the kitchen, cleaned the cells and corridors, and served as domestics for the prison matron.[154] Despite its age and the fact that some of the work, in the words of the Prison Committee, tended to be "degrading to most prisoners," the Nova Scotia Penal inspector felt that Rockhead "[was] the nearest approach [the city had] to a penal institution conducted according to modern ideas."[155] Halifax, at least in the view of some officials, had attained a certain level of sophistication in its handling of prisoners. Yet, at the same time, the authors of the province's Royal Commission on Jails declared: "[the City Prison] is not and cannot be made completely satisfactory for the requirements and purposes of a modern correctional institution."[156]

Such outmoded facilities, many thought, did not represent the type of environment suitable for juvenile delinquents. In accordance with the prevailing attitude towards young offenders, reformatories in Halifax tried to advance the lives of the girls and boys placed in their charge. In attempting to do so, reformatories played an important role in Halifax's machinery of order. Adhering to the belief that children – boys in particular – should be taught a trade and receive food "suitable for a growing boy" and fresh air while under institutional care, Halifax's juvenile reformatories set out to turn delinquents into respectable and productive citizens. The juvenile justice system in Canada, according to Joan Sangster, was charged with the task of remoulding children's values. Children who had broken the law had apparently rejected parental guidance and formal schooling, along with respect for private property and social order. Similarly, delinquent girls lacked sexual and moral decency.[157] This process of remoulding children was gendered. As "citizens-in-waiting," boys needed to learn respect for familial and community authority, private property, and a work ethic. As one writer in 1929 emphasized: "If anything permanent is to be done for [the] average man, it must be done before he is a man. The chances of success lie in working with the boy, not the man."[158] Girls, however, had to be taught how to be decent, moral wives and mothers. And, in general, juvenile delinquents required protection, discipline, and self-control.[159] Juvenile court judges had this formula firmly in mind when they sent the young people brought before them to the city's industrial schools and reformatories.

During the seventeen-year time span covered in this book, four institutions handled commitments from the Halifax Juvenile Court. While the juvenile court and the penological philosophy underlying these reformatories were rather new, the system itself still relied on traditional agencies (such as the church) and methods (notably segregation) to achieve its ends. They were not, therefore, fully modern. Clinging to their nineteenth-century roots, all were organized according to religious affiliation and gender. The Halifax Industrial School and Saint Patrick's Home cared for Protestant and Roman Catholic boys, respectively; the Monastery of the Good Shepherd housed Roman Catholic girls; and Protestant girls had to travel to the Maritime Home for Girls located in Truro, roughly one hundred kilometres northeast of Halifax. Private organizations managed the two Protestant homes, while the Christian Brothers operated St. Patrick's, and the Sisters of the Good Shepherd tended to the monastery. Each underwent a regular state inspection and received per capita grants from the provincial treasury and the municipalities involved for each child committed by the juvenile court.[160] All of these institutions dedicated their efforts to reclaiming for society the wayward children who had been placed in their care.

The Halifax Industrial School epitomized this initiative. Founded in 1863 by a "number of public spirited citizens," the Industrial School was described by one of its superintendents, H.O. Eaman:

> not [as] a place of punishment nor a prison in any sense of the term, but a training school where boys because of circumstances, usually over which they had no control, have become a community problem, receive the instruction and training best adapted to mould and perpetuate good character, establish habits of industry, and impart

> knowledge that will fit them to take their places in the community when their course of training is completed.[161]

Eaman and his successor, Reverend Wilson, former pastor of the Central Baptist Church, along with their colleagues, hoped to accomplish this task by combining classroom instruction in the "general precepts of the Christian religion, the power and goodness of God, and lessons of morality and virtue" with training in printing, carpentry, farming, and some basic academic subjects.[162] The boys who were sent to the Industrial School often came from poor and undisciplined homes. In the words of the superintendent: "[The boys] come from homes very near to the poverty line, from homes where parental rule has lost its authority. There has been no authoritive [sic] rule in their lives and they have drifted into trouble." The purpose of the Industrial School, the superintendent concluded: "is to correct if possible these early defects."[163] Some of these boys quickly settled down and adjusted to their new life in the school, but the "majority who [were] sent [there were] little *rebels* and refuse[d] for a time to recognize any authority." "Our business," Wilson asserted, "[was] to help these boys to become good citizens" for the benefit of themselves and society and to help maintain social order.[164] St. Patrick's Home for Catholic boys functioned along lines similar to that of the Industrial School. Opened by the Roman Catholic Church in 1885, St. Patrick's cared for delinquents committed either by the juvenile court or the boys' parents.[165] The boys attended school for five hours a day and received manual training and "physical instruction." While not ideal homes, they still provided delinquent boys with a degree of comfort that most would not have received in any of Halifax's adult prisons.[166] Moreover, these reformatories demonstrate, despite their drawbacks, the importance those in the juvenile justice system placed upon diverting children away from a life of crime.

Those Roman Catholic girls who strayed to the wrong side of the law underwent their reformatory treatment in the Monastery of the Good Shepherd. Built in 1892, the monastery was established by the Sisters of the Good Shepherd in 1890. Trained in rescue work and offering "experienced and sympathetic supervision," the Sisters opened their doors to "lost" girls, many of whom had been found guilty of minor offences. All of the monastery's inmates underwent a strict regimen of educational and practical instruction. Academic lessons continued up to Grade 6, while industrial classes gave every girl the opportunity to learn a host of gender-specific tasks: sewing, knitting, crocheting, dress-making, and domestic science.[167] The education and training that these girls received would not provide most of them with the necessary means, upon their release, to escape a life of poverty or prescribed gender roles. Protestants in the Maritimes responded to the need to reform their own delinquent girls with the Maritime Home for Girls. Built in Truro in 1914, the home cared for and educated those Protestant girls between the ages of seven and sixteen years who were deemed to be "incorrigible or delinquent."[168] The home provided girls with moral discipline and practical instruction in most "branches of household science" to ensure that they became "worthy" members of society.[169] Despite one estimate that 50 percent of the girls were "definitely mentally abnormal," the Canadian National Committee for Mental Hygiene, which surveyed the home in 1920, found them to be "happy and industrious." "There can be no doubt," the committee added, "that girls leave this institution very much better than when they entered, and it is a model for similar organizations of its kind in Canada."[170] Thus, in Halifax, juvenile delinquents did have recourse to a system of reform that was not available to adult criminals sentenced to the city's jails and prisons. Children, it seems, warranted specialized care. But those beyond the age of childhood innocence who had committed crimes, so many concluded, did not deserve the same treatment.

As the tide of penal and criminal justice reform ebbed and flowed in Halifax, one organization, the Prisoners' Welfare Association (PWA), held firm in its commitment to helping convicted criminals cope with their situation. Organized in the early 1920s by the Halifax Social Services Council, the PWA devoted itself to promoting the general welfare of prisoners during and after their release from custody.[171] The PWA also served as a representative of the Canadian Prisoners' Welfare Association (CPWA). Founded in Montreal at the beginning of the 1920s, the CPWA represented one of the first efforts on the part of a private organization in Canada to deal effectively with the "welfare of prisoners and their dependents."[172] Both associations formed a part of Canada's burgeoning social reform movement of the 1920s. Although the PWA in Halifax lacked a strong organizational base, it did benefit from a rather prestigious membership. In 1933, Charles Mercer became the association's president. Mercer, a professor of modern languages at Dalhousie University, was an ardent advocate of penal reform. In 1934, with John Kidman, he also co-authored a report on the province's county jails.[173] Another prominent member of the PWA was Dr. Samuel Prince. His social activism led him to the presidency of the Nova Scotia Society for Mental Hygiene and the Halifax Council of Social Agencies as well as to a position on the board of the Halifax Industrial School. During his ministry at St. Paul's Anglican Church, Prince supported the cause of prison reform by serving as one of the commissioners on Nova Scotia's 1933 Royal Commission Concerning Jails and by acting on the board of directors for the John Howard Society of Nova Scotia and the CPWA.[174] J.E. Hudson served as the PWA's secretary-treasurer. He was also assistant to the director of child welfare, a probation officer, and a judge of the Halifax Juvenile Court.[175] Women too gave their time and effort to the PWA. Miss Hoebrecker occupied the post of first vice-president in 1931, while Mrs. Hagen, Mrs. George Maling, and Miss Ogden formed part of the association's executive.[176] Together these men and women tried to help those prisoners released from the city's jails secure a fresh start in life. As was noted in 1928, the PWA was "doing ... good work in extending a helping hand to released prisoners and in trying to make useful citizens out of those who are disposed to reform."[177]

In spite of the efforts launched by the PWA, by 1935 little had changed within the walls of Halifax's lockups. A 1937 federal royal commission, initiated the previous year to investigate Canada's prisons, denounced Nova Scotia's jails and thus sounded a familiar refrain to the members of the PWA. Jails in the Maritime provinces, Mr. Justice Archambault, the commission's chairman noted, remained "entirely inadequate and ... the manner in which prisoners [were] treated in those jails [could] only result in degrading them morally and physically."[178] The commissioners found that overcrowding and unsanitary conditions persisted in most prisons. The lack of employment opportunities and the concomitant idleness also continued to plague Halifax's jails. Recalling the province's own royal commission in 1933, the federal report called for the construction of a central prison farm that would help the region to eradicate the many "evils" of the existing system.[179] The persistence of these problems suggests Halifax's lack of commitment to the rehabilitation of criminals. To capture and penalize, rather than to reform, the offender remained the central purpose of Halifax's machinery of order.

Conclusion

The contours of urban justice in Halifax reveal that the city and the province invested a great deal of effort to ensure the maintenance of law and order. The police department, court system, jails, and reformatories all functioned, with varying degrees of success, to control crime. However creaky and inadequate, the machinery of order commanded respect from most Halifax residents. The fact that these institutions formed part of the British system of jurisprudence and criminal justice helped them to foster a sense of legitimacy. Moreover, as the next chapter explores more closely, the social construction of criminality in Halifax produced a distinct set of perceptions and images of "crime" and the "criminal" that predisposed many citizens to accept the machinery of order, whatever its manifest defects. From 1918 to 1935, Halifax's machinery of order was characterized by both change and continuity. The desire to modernize the forces of law and order never waned. But this penchant for advancement did not give way to a streamlined, professional, and rational system of law enforcement. The police department purchased patrol cars, used fingerprint technology to apprehend criminals, and tried to provide its officers with better training. An outmoded "beat" system to patrol the streets also hampered the department's efficiency, giving it, like others in Canada, the "appearance of an emerging professionalism" but one that ultimately "lacked ... substance."[180]

The criminal justice system, with a police court and stipendiary magistrate at the helm, tried to instil some decorum into the day-to-day workings of British justice. Under the weight of a heavy case docket and without the advantage of legal-aid lawyers, the police court was often forced to dispense a kind of nineteenth-century-style speedy justice unbecoming to a modern institution. Juvenile justice, however, reaped the heralded benefits of modernity. A juvenile court and three regimented reformatories gave the care and attention many felt were needed to rescue children from a life of crime and thus, it was hoped, to benefit society. But the same could not be said for Halifax's adult criminals and the jails that housed them. The city's prisons, while in theory the object of debate and reform along modern lines, in practice did not change in any ways that might have helped them rehabilitate offenders. Thus, the transition from a traditional machinery of order to a more "progressive" model was incomplete. Halifax may have fully embraced some of the tenets of modernity, but when it came to dealing with crime and enforcing law and order, many believed that punishment, not rehabilitation, was the most effective way to handle most criminals.

CHAPTER 3

The Social Perceptions of Crime and Criminals

The criminal produces an impression, partly moral and partly tragic ... and in this way renders a "service" by arousing the moral and aesthetic feelings of the public ... The criminal breaks the monotony and everyday security of bourgeois life.

– Karl Marx, *Theories of Surplus Value*

A ONE-NIGHT SPREE of robberies in December 1918 brought the effects of modernity into clear focus for many Halifax residents. The *Halifax Herald* reported that William Duggan, Albert Thoms, Melburn Trefrey, and James O'Donnell faced prosecution for thefts in various parts of the city. Duggan, a one-armed man of "Indian blood," was arraigned on two counts of theft; Thoms, an escapee from the City Prison, had robbed a man on Market Street; Trefrey had stolen a sum of money from a boarding house; and O'Donnell had made off with sixty dollars from his employer's safe. In light of this criminal activity the *Herald* sarcastically announced: "Halifax Is Rapidly Developing into a 'Modern' City."[1] The *Herald*'s words convey the confusion and ambiguity felt by some members of Halifax society towards modernity. The city went through a series of profound social and economic changes in the 1920s and early 1930s, which produced a mixture of optimism, despair, and uncertainty about the nature of society. Part of this uncertainty originated from the perceived perils of modernity, especially crime, that had begun to manifest themselves in Nova Scotia's capital. In response, a discussion arose about the prevalence of crime, seen in the debate about "crime waves," the causes of criminality, and the nature of the criminal. Beneath this assessment of crime lay a commentary on modernity itself. Most if not all forms of modernist thought, Marshall Berman notes, are pronouncements about and protests against the process of modernization.[2] So it was in Halifax that the fear expressed about crime and criminals revealed the belief among some that this city did not need everything that modernity had to offer.

An array of discourses surfaced in Halifax as to the sources of and solutions to crime. Some focused on the mental and moral defects of the criminal, while others blamed a harsh social upbringing and environment for an individual's descent into a world of crime. Most also added the inadequacies of the city's, and the province's, penal system and lack of rehabilitation to the list of reasons for the outbreak of criminal activities. Moreover, each group held firm to its line of reasoning that, if the aspect it emphasized were to be reformed, crime could be controlled. These commentators used their stand on crime to attack the evils of modern society and call for the maintenance of social order and the restoration of a "better day."[3] From among this disparate collection of arguments, a consensus did emerge on one point concerning the origins of crime: the individual ultimately played some role in the execution of her or his actions and, consequently, would have to answer directly for her/his criminal wrong-doing. So in the minds of these observers, the supremacy of the rule of law remained beyond reproach.

But for some, society should also be compelled to undertake a host of socio-economic reforms to help prevent the repetition of crime. Social perceptions of crime and criminals in Halifax also spawned a discourse of order. Sustained by a cohort of intellectuals and officialdom (mainly judges, police officials, politicians, penal reform advocates, clergymen, journalists, and university professors), this discourse helped to legitimize the city's machinery of order and worked in tandem with it to control crime. Those most concerned with crime tried to establish a plausible framework within which they could understand the phenomenon, which they articulated in terms of an underlying "social order." Often blending "modern" and "anti-modern" attitudes towards crime and society, they developed an entropic myth of decline and fall, in which modern crime was juxtaposed with an idealized, orderly past.[4] These arguments point to a partial and halting transition from "traditionalist" to "progressive" notions of criminal law enforcement in Halifax. While these may be artificial paradigms, as heuristic devices they do provide a way to measure many responses to crime and criminals in interwar Halifax. This chapter describes those commentators who spoke out on the causes of crime and the steps necessary to control it, the image of the criminal, the purpose of law enforcement, and the importance of social order to Halifax. In most cases, these two models did not converge, but in the writings of some, a mingling of traditionalist and progressive ideals concerning law and order can be detected.

The Discourses of Crime and Order

With regard to crime and punishment in Halifax, the traditional liberal paradigm focused primarily on the individual. According to this line of thinking, crime originated as a matter of individual choice and moral and spiritual weakness. Idle hands and alcohol, as the illustration on the next page shows, led to temptation and crime. Only work and religious values could "save" the individual from a life of crime. It followed, then, that a "traditional" discussion of crime looked to the personality and choices of the individual when constructing an image of the criminal. Thus, the raison d'être of the machinery of order must be to apprehend and punish the individual criminal. To this end, traditionalists supported increased surveillance and stricter enforcement of the law. In this regard, the rights of the accused were secondary to the importance of securing private property and maintaining order. Similarly, "crime waves" were to be met with a fierce and systematic attempt to reimpose social order. At the same time (and especially in the context of an economically troubled city), most traditionalists did not anticipate the need to dramatically increase expenditures on the machinery of order. In their eyes, there was no fundamental reason to tamper with a system that, over the years, had worked effectively. A few minor adjustments might be in order, but a wholesale change of the criminal justice system was not necessary to preserve the "city of order." Traditionalists often yearned for an older, more peaceful time. Safety, it seems, could only be found in the comfort of the past. Hence traditional rhetoric about crime tended to be either panic-stricken or nostalgic; the city of order had to be constantly constructed and reconstructed in the face of the turmoil produced by modernity.

Progressives, on the other hand, considered crime to be socially generated. It could be explained, they thought, in terms of the environment or rapid social disruption. Heredity could also be a factor, but even in these situations the individual could not be held solely responsible. Since society, in their opinion, was a social organism, the rise of criminality was to be explained socially, not individually. Crime, in other words, was an inevitable consequence of social and economic change. In keeping with this reasoning, progressives held out hope for reforming criminals. People did

WORK, THE SOLUTION!

"Work, The Solution!" This cartoon captures the belief, held by many Halifax residents, that crime occurred as a result of individual choice and moral and spiritual weakness. [*Halifax Herald*, 12 January 1921]

not enter a life of crime voluntarily or because of some innate wickedness. On the contrary, they turn to crime for a number of other reasons: economic desperation, the absence of proper parental guidance, or a corrupting social influence. The lawless acts of one did not necessarily condemn others of their ilk to follow their example. The fact that human nature was essentially good meant that one could work with most criminals, especially juvenile delinquents, to "salvage" them for the benefit of society. To accomplish this objective, the machinery of order had to be proactive, not reactive. Its primary aim should be to rehabilitate, not punish, the offender. Subsequently, the criminal justice system had to alter its orientation: no longer could it be simply punitive. The control of crime required scientific techniques. More specifically, as a means of rehabilitation, the entire penal system would have to be overhauled, whatever the costs involved. To progressives, the city of order was a reflection of all that modernity had to offer. Throughout progressive discourse there is an almost urgent demand for new approaches and institutions to respond to the fact that society is not an aggregation of individuals but, rather, an organic process.[5] It was with this in mind that progressives devised and actively sought social order.

Social order is systemic to the rule of law. Order has been defined as a "set of values that structured social relations." It is "constituted and reconstituted ... through a set of concrete rituals or institutionalized practices ... that reflect particular understandings of the world and particular historical circumstances."[6] As Tina Loo and Lorna R. McLean suggest, the law can be understood as "one means of ordering society, of creating and enforcing certain relationships among people and between people and governments."[7] In Halifax the machinery of order served as a bulwark for an ordered society; those agitating for its progressive extension were mainly members of the middle class. To comprehend how citizens of Halifax dealt with crime and criminals, it is necessary to explain how they saw these aspects of their world.[8] Thus an examination of the social perceptions of, and attitudes towards, criminal acts and their perpetrators in Halifax demonstrates how Haligonians viewed crime in their city and those who broke, or could potentially break, the law. Socially constructed images of criminals have often reflected anxieties about the actions of certain individuals who appeared to be uncontrollable. Moreover, in the late nineteenth and early twentieth centuries, "crime" became a metaphor for social disorder, and criminal and penal policy fostered a means of achieving an ethos of respectability.[9] Such was the case in interwar Halifax. Many people in this city held crime and criminals in contempt. Emotional responses to criminal acts varied, depending on the severity of the deed (robbery, for example, did not evoke as harsh a rebuke as did murder), but scorn remained the overriding attitude towards criminality.

Notions of class, gender, and ethnicity also shaped the way in which the police, courts, and concerned citizens understood the problem of crime and criminals. As such, certain images emerged about the poor, women, and "foreigners" that influenced how they were treated by the criminal justice system.[10] While one single stereotype of the criminal did not exist in Halifax, expectations about who might commit a crime or be lured into a life of injustice – notably young unemployed men, single young women, neglected children, or the Chinese – informed public perceptions of criminals. As well, many residents saw crime as a means of disrupting and defying Halifax's settled, safe way of life. As a result, victims and onlookers alike demanded swift action on the part of the police and the justice system to quash any threat to law and order. The ability of the justice system to wield such power derived in part from the respect it commanded in Halifax and across Nova Scotia. The source of most of this admiration lay in the strong ties Canadian criminal law (embodied in the Criminal Code of Canada) forged with British institutions and ideals of justice. Canada had adopted many legal traditions from Great Britain, including the separation of the judiciary from the political process, the presumption of innocence, and an accused's right to a fair trial. Consequently, a profound concern to defend the tradition of "British justice" can be discerned in interwar Halifax. Similarly, popular culture upheld the superiority of British justice and liberty: crime and disorder were "anti-British."[11] Many of Halifax's residents would accept without reservation this emphatic warning from the *Halifax Chronicle*: "For the future well being of this Province, lawlessness cannot be allowed to spread, be it cured as it will."[12] A majority of the people who resided in Halifax viewed crime and criminals through the lens of order and British justice. The identity, magnitude, and character of crime depended on the prevailing "cultural conceptualizations" in a given historical setting.[13] In Halifax these included a desire for order and the sanctity of British justice. British justice had a dual role to fulfill in the ongoing maintenance of order. At its liberal core, British justice sought to protect the rights and safety of the individual. At the same time, it had to be seen as operating in the "public interest" in order to guarantee the legitimacy of the criminal justice system and the rule of law.[14] Similarly, key figures in the legal and social reform communities of Halifax, as well as the press, constructed the "other" against which such justice was defined. Phrases such as "social evil" and "underworld" appeared to describe the genesis and geography of crime. Crime and criminals were such because the criminal law, which enjoyed enormous popular legitimacy, was empowered to label people and their behaviour and actions as "criminal."[15] Residents took comfort in the fact that all those who committed crimes would be duly punished, which would hopefully deter others from embarking on a life of crime and thus ensure public safety and social order. But they did not see the need to initiate new programs for crime prevention.

Social Panic and Crime Waves

From 1918 to 1935, Halifax went through periodic phases of fear and panic over crime. Throughout much of North America in the 1920s, the belief that crime had recently become a serious social problem with which the legal system could no longer properly deal gained acceptance.[16] Mrs. Donald Shaw, in a series of letters to the *Halifax Herald* in 1920, provided evidence of this siege mentality. The "civilized world," Shaw began, "seem[ed] to [be] passing through a wave of disorder and lawlessness" in which all the rules and morals of the past were being rent asunder. Crime, especially among juveniles, "[was] assuming paralysing proportions." Since the end of the First World War, in Shaw's view, "there ha[d] certainly swept over the face of civilization an extraordinary wave of irresponsibility, an obstinate and determined refusal to take life seriously." Then in an attack on modern life as crime-inducing, Shaw argued that "a restless craving for perpetual movement and a positive orgy of spending ha[d] engulfed us, and beneath it all [lay] the reeking cesspits of Sin and Vice sucking down into them every day more and more lives that might otherwise be good and useful ones."[17] The media in Halifax played a significant part in the construction of perceived crime waves in the 1920s and early 1930s. As Chris McCormick notes, crime waves are often "social constructions, accounts created by journalists, [and] fed by competition and coherence of opinion among newspapers." The depiction of crime in the news can affect public perceptions of safety and danger and influence their response to this perceived threat.[18] Steven Chermak goes even further when he argues that the media's presentation of criminality has "little to do with the realities or complexities of crime."[19] The *Halifax Herald*, the city's main daily newspaper, had a penchant for sensationalism. Under the ownership of William Dennis, the *Herald* became even more "impulsive," with an "exclamatory and repetitive" editorial style and an aggressive news policy. Its rival, the *Chronicle*, while often more measured than the *Herald*, would still slant a story, as did the *Herald*, according to its political persuasion.[20] When it came to covering crime stories, both papers, but especially the *Herald*, helped to manufacture a virtual frenzy concerning the magnitude of crime in Halifax. And although one can never measure a newspaper's impact on public opinion with certainty, it is unlikely the highly popular daily press of the day was far removed from its audience.

Social anxiety about crime also led to some direct public action. "Owing to a feel[ing] of unrest prevailing in the city ... and because of the necessarily restricted size of the regular police force," Halifax Mayor Arthur Hawkins declared in June 1918: "it has been deemed advisable to call upon the business men and other citizens to come to the aid of the city and to volunteer their services to act as special citizen constables."[21] Hawkins hoped that a force of special constables could be raised to restore a "sense of security" to the city. Almost a week later, nearly one hundred men had enlisted, including such figures as Dougald MacGillivrary, manager of the Canadian Bank of Commerce and president of the Board of Trade, along with other "well known citizens." Many of those who volunteered hailed from "suburban districts" and felt that areas around the North-West Arm, and other reputable areas, needed protection.[22] This enthusiastic response came in the midst of an apparent rash of criminal activity. The *Herald* reported an increase in burglaries and hold-ups, evident in the same-day robberies at the American Book and Shoe Store on Barrington Street and the Recorder Office on Granville Street, both in the heart of the city's commercial sector and very near to the police station. Moreover, a riot in May 1918, in which a hoard of returned soldiers and civilians looted and attempted to burn down City Hall, left many residents feeling unsafe in their own city (see Chapter 4). As a consequence of these events, Halifax, in the *Herald*'s view, had begun to earn an "unenviable name" for itself in the Maritimes.[23] Thus "it [was] high time the citizens of Halifax," the author insisted, "REALIZED what was GOING ON and took action ... to see that ratepayers and business houses [were] given adequate protection."[24]

This mood of alarm was sustained the following year. In October 1919, Frank Genoe died following a heated argument and fight with three other men: Victor Tomarelli, Peter Kovacish, and Rogers Stephens soon confessed to the killing. The reporter covering the case, with a mixture of outrage and hopelessness, described it as: "one of the most diabolical crimes in the history of our city ... smacking of the 'Black Hand' in its intensity and ferocity, sending a thrill of horror thru the most phlegmatic and causing to rise uppermost in the minds of most self-respecting people, the query: 'WHAT ARE WE COMING TO?'"[25] Implicit in this article is the assumption that Halifax had always been a safe city in which to live. Residents had often read about crimes in other cities but generally acknowledged "THAT IS NEW YORK. NOTHING LIKE THAT COULD

HAPPEN IN HALIFAX." This may have once been true, but now, the author lamented: "Anything is liable to happen in Halifax ... In short, Halifax is growing, and we are paying the price of the honor of becoming cosmopolitan."[26] Other writers brought out the connection between crime and the city's economic crisis. As an editorial in the *Morning Chronicle* on the "Costs of Crime" argued: "Crime is not only a moral offence, it is the direct or indirect cause of great economic loss, not only through the losses suffered by the victims of the crime, but in the cost of detection, prevention and prosecution of criminal offences."[27] These costs, the editorial continued, justified some expenditure for preventive research to reduce crime. This theme of modernizing the city's approach to crime appeared again in 1934, when the *Herald* told its readers that the one thing they and the state should remember was that, "while crime must be put down and punished wherever it shows itself, the possibilities of preventive action should be enlarged."[28]

The 1922 killing of Leslie Corkum, the incident with which I open this book, unleashed a storm of alarmist rhetoric. In an article entitled "Time for Action," the *Morning Chronicle* viewed this murder as the last straw. For the past several months a succession of unsolved robberies had plagued shop-keepers across the city, and now an owner had died in the course of yet another robbery. According to the *Chronicle,* it was now up to Mayor John Murphy, as chairman of the Police Commission: "to put into operation, without a moment's delay, the most vigorous measures to clean up this menacing crime situation and round up the dangerous characters who are abroad ... The citizens will demand of Mayor Murphy that no time be lost in running down the criminal."[29] The demand for prompt action to bring Corkum's assailant to justice underscores the bouts of panic over crime in Halifax and the desire for law and order. Nova Scotia's 1933 *Royal Commission Concerning Jails* captured this sentiment when the commissioners, two of whom hailed from Halifax, insisted: "All are agreed [that crime must be combatted] for civilization is impossible without order and security."[30]

The nervousness expressed in Halifax regarding crime also manifested itself in a debate about crime waves. This debate fuelled concerns about criminality and helped to shape public perceptions of crime and criminals. It also exposed some of the tensions between traditional and progressive ideals relating to crime and punishment in interwar Halifax. In 1920, the *Halifax Herald* sounded one of the first notes of trepidation about a crime wave in Halifax. Referring to the frequency of burglaries in the city, the *Herald* reported in December: "The public ... feels that the abnormal number of crimes of this nature is out of all proportion to the size of this city and cannot be contemplated with any degree of satisfaction."[31] One way to halt the spread of break-ins, the *Herald* argued, was to hire more policemen to patrol the city's streets. If not, businesspeople especially would continue to suffer. According to the *Herald,* "[they and the] ratepayers of Halifax have a right to expect ADEQUATE PROTECTION from the police." Similarly, these proprietors: "whose contribution to the maintenance of the city is much larger financially than that of the average citizen, should be able to feel that [their] premises are as safe during the ... evenings as in the daytime."[32] The situation seemed to go from bad to worse with the start of a new year. After a report of at least two more hold-ups along with the capture of two burglars, the *Herald,* on 15 February 1921, urgently demanded that this "Lawlessness ... Be Conquered." "The present situation in Halifax with regard to undetected crime and its growing frequency," the article stated, "clearly indicates that unless PROMPT, EFFICIENT and EFFECTIVE measures are taken the epidemic stage, the crime wave, will speedily be reached." A "growing feeling of impatience amongst the citizens" was also reported, while many insisted that "something must be done, and done speedily, to arrest the alarming increase of undetected crime in this city."[33] In a defiant tone, the *Herald* declared itself against crime and in favour of order:

> Halifax wants no crime wave. Citizens demand action and reasonably expect protection. Let the cost be what it may Halifax refuses to be victimized by thugs, burglars and hold-up men. Lawlessness must be crushed and conquered. There must be no unchecked crime wave here. There is more than one thing operating in Halifax, and the taxpayers will look to the police to round up all the "hold up" experts.[34]

The police department tried its best to address the public's concerns about uncontrolled criminality. However, with its meagre resources and limited personnel, it could neither prevent nor solve every crime. So instead, police officials tried to calm the situation by reassuring citizens that they had things under control. Chief of Police Hanrahan, in his 1918 annual report, commended the work of his detectives, who, with the assistance of patrolmen, "ha[d] spared no pains nor industry in attempting to detect and punish all violators of the law coming within the immediate jurisdiction of their department."[35] As the public's demand for action against "thugs" mounted in 1921, Hanrahan, rather defensively, commented: "[crime] has been checked somewhat this year and offenders brought to justice."[36]

Besides the press, others joined the chorus of comments about crime waves. Dr. H.L. Stewart, professor of philosophy at Dalhousie University, wrote an essay for the *Halifax Herald* on: "THE WAVE OF CRIME THAT HAS SWEPT THROUGH NOVA SCOTIA." According to Stewart, because of three murders in different areas of the province, "WITHIN THE LAST FEW MONTHS THERE HAS BEEN A SORT OF CRIME WAVE IN NOVA SCOTIA [AND IT IS] SWELLING MORE OR LESS ALL OVER THE WORLD."[37] Stewart attributed this outbreak of crime to a reversion to the primal instincts inherent in all men. As he succinctly put it: "Scratch The Man and You Find the Gorilla."[38] The "chief cause" of this behaviour, Stewart posited, "seems to lie in the temporary breakdown of those restraints by which crime is normally inhibited." In a critique of modernity, Stewart described how: "[in] times earlier and quieter than those in which we live, life was far more sacred, law was far more effective, [and] far less apology was made for anarchic individualism." A return to these far-off times, with the aid of the church, the school, the courts, and the government, Stewart believed, would solve the problem of crime waves.[39] The crime wave that Stewart explored on a somewhat abstract level, the newspapers were more inclined to treat as a thrilling story. In late August 1931, the Quinpool Road branch of the Royal Bank of Canada was the scene of an early morning hold-up perpetrated by two "daring gunmen" who struck the manager, locked the staff in the vault, and made off with more than $16,000 in "loot." This robbery, "one of the most daring crimes in Halifax for many years," capped off a year that had seen the "crime wave" reach new proportions. The press played up the bravado of the robbers. In an interview with the *Herald*, a bank-teller said: "I was scared stiff ... When I looked into the muzzle of that gun, I did what I was told."[40] Within a matter of days the police had launched the "most intensive man-hunt Nova Scotia ha[d] ever known" for these "desperadoes." Soon hundreds of people, their interest in the case aroused to a "keen pitch," came forward with information they hoped would lead the police to the culprits. Their efforts finally paid off when in October one of the "most sensational chapters in the criminal history of Halifax was brought to a dramatic climax" with the arrest of three young men.[41] The Royal Bank robbery left some people in Halifax questioning their city's perceived insulation from crime. As the *Herald* noted: "[Halifax] should be one of the last places on the continent in which bandits could operate and successfully escape. But up to the present the responsible public bodies in Halifax have not recognized the seriousness of the situation."[42] Until the police had captured the perpetrators of these crimes and placed them behind bars, the paper felt, "lawlessness [was] not likely to abate."

The province took some steps to facilitate the process of controlling crime. In November 1931, no doubt with the Royal Bank incident fresh in its mind, but also making its own comment on a key element of modern culture, the Nova Scotia Board of Censors banned all but one of the "gangster" films that were scheduled to be shown in theatres across the province in 1932.[43] The furore surrounding the bank robbery and the feeling of vulnerability within the city helped to mould traditionalist attitudes towards criminality and to generate the perception of a crime wave.[44] In their thinking about criminality, some people in Halifax developed a specific set of causes and a distinct image of offenders. In so doing, they devised what Jim Phillips calls a "social meaning of crime," an assortment of ideas about how crime could be defined, prevented, and punished.[45] Moreover, it may be argued that this social meaning of crime was shaped, in part, by the growing presence in people's lives of the media and other cultural depictions of crime and vice (e.g., films). The move to ban American "gangster" films is indicative of the perceived negative effect that cultural images and portrayals of crime could have upon many people's feelings of personal and community safety. Similarly, in evaluating the social meaning of crime in Halifax it is apparent that many residents felt that crime consisted of any reprehensible act that breached the city's sense of order and that originated with the unsavoury and unfortunate elements of society. Often drawing on nostalgia for the image of a more peaceful age, these people developed a sharp contrast between the crime-ridden present and the peaceful past.

Some of the most outspoken public figures in Halifax regarding the causes of crime were judges. Judge Wallace of the Halifax County Court, who was in some ways a progressive, delivered a series of public lectures on the causes and prevention of crime. A barrister for sixteen years, and a judge of the Halifax Juvenile Court (1918-19), Wallace was considered by some to be an "honorable, conscientious and reliable" judge.[46] Wallace dedicated a portion of his time to investigating and trying to solve the housing crisis in Nova Scotia. His 1919 pamphlet, *The Housing Problem in Nova Scotia: An Evil, Its Growth, and Its Remedy*, combined environmental theories and an evangelical sense of purpose in its call for social reform. "I maintain," Wallace declared, "that there is often a very close connection between bad housing conditions and moral delinquency."[47] In 1923, speaking before a gathering of social reform experts, Wallace asserted that a "lack of self-control" produced much of the crime currently plaguing society. This absence of self-control resulted from the inadequate training young people received in matters of restraint and self-denial.[48] In 1924, Wallace elaborated upon these ideas in a speech to the Halifax Rotary Club. A person's "will," Wallace repeated, was the main source of crime. He also listed a number of contributory factors: a desire to "keep up with the Jones [sic]," "the moral character of the home," poverty, heredity, and non-enforcement of the law. Wallace then expanded upon a few of these points. The "moral character of the home," he felt, "ha[d] far more influence in forming a boy's or a girl's impressions of what constitutes right and wrong than schools or sermons." If the surroundings at home posed a menace to morality, then a child would be adversely affected and thus never taught the "binding forces of moral law."[49] "Poverty" on the other hand, Wallace continued, "may be a secondary cause of crime ... but [it was] blamed too much." Anyone who worked closely with the poor, as Wallace apparently did, knew that "virtue" exists among them. It was a tribute, in Wallace's opinion, to the poor's "rugged honesty" that their dreadful conditions did not weaken their morals. If an impoverished home contained what Wallace described as the "old fashioned virtues of honor and self control," it would be a better place than a mansion in which "spiritual poverty ... prevail[ed]." For, as Wallace concluded, revealing his more traditionalist views: "One great factor which ultimately leads to crime ... is the lack of any religious training."[50] Only by a return to religious and moral values, Wallace felt, could the descent into criminality be stopped.

In his third "interesting and instructive" talk, Wallace touched upon the administration of justice as a contributor to the increase in crime. Previously, Wallace had argued: "The punishment of crime by the state is not an end, but a means ... The chief purposes of legal punishment are to satisfy justice and to repair the moral order which has been violated. Other purposes are to protect society, to deter others from wrong doing and to reform the offender."[51] Two years later, in 1926, addressing an assemblage of five hundred attending a Sunday afternoon meeting of the Halifax YMCA, Wallace blamed the rise in crime on the laxity in the prosecution and conviction of offenders. This came from a "universal outburst of soft-heartedness" that was extended to lawbreakers, something

Wallace deemed to be a "spurious pity."[52] Wallace did not deny that mercy was a virtue, but it ceased to be so when its exercise destroyed or disrupted the "good order and justice" of the community.[53] "Books tell us ... that crime is more a result of environment," Wallace contended, "but I think that assuming sanity we must regard offenders as personally responsible" for their actions. The justice system must therefore be reformed to halt repeat offenders and to protect people from these "incorrigible criminals." Wallace did admit that "some of these poor unfortunates should be protected against themselves."[54] Once again, Wallace's thinking seemed to oscillate between progressive and traditionalist notions about the origins of crime and the aim of the machinery of order.

Mr. Justice Joseph Chisholm, a former mayor of Halifax (1909-1), who became a judge in 1916 and chief justice of the Nova Scotia Supreme Court in 1931, had a more traditional analysis of the "crime wave" than did Wallace. Striking a note of frenzied anti-modernism, Chisholm argued that, when compared to thirty years before, the 1924 calendar of the criminal trial session of the Supreme Court revealed itself to be: "symptomatic of a state of disorder and a disregard for law which does not augur well for the community. One of the contributing causes ... is [that] the persons who take up a life of crime think they can pursue the calling without danger of discovery or punishment. Our duty in [these] circumstances is to apply the corrective and punitive provisions of the law with fairness and courage."[55] The next day, an editorial in the *Halifax Herald* emphasized the duty of every citizen to reflect upon Justice Chisholm's observations and to act accordingly: "Conditions in general in this province have not been satisfactory. During the last few years there have been violations of law of a major character, but the offenders have managed to escape detection."[56] "The root of the trouble," in the view of the editor, "lies in the inefficiency of the men whose duty it is to trace crime to its source. And this inefficiency must be charged to the higher-up authority that tolerates it." In light of this, the paper hoped that "responsible heads of administration" would take heed of Chisholm's warnings: "[for] it is to them that the public must look for protection and safeguarding."[57]

A quite different, and more progressive, slant on this question was taken by Dr. Samuel Prince of the Department of Sociology at King's College. Unlike Chisholm, Prince believed strongly that rehabilitation rather than punishment could best serve the cause of crime control and prevention. He too denounced the side effects of modernity, including poor housing and the slums, which he associated with "physical, emotional and spiritual disabilities, delinquency, truancy, social and physical degeneration."[58] Yet Prince also combined an anti-modern critique with a "progressive" emphasis on environment. In a sermon at St. Stephen's Anglican Church in New York, where he served as summer rector for forty years, Prince spoke out against what he saw as a "current evil" of modern society: the "worship of speed." "The deity of speed and bigness has succeeded in laying a firm hold on most of humanity," Prince told his congregation: "We travel fast, we marry fast, we divorce fast ... and amuse ourselves fast. We talk big, see big, plan big, build big, and as a whole do everything better on a never-before-dreamed-of scale."[59] While an obvious opponent of the pace of modern life, Prince embraced progressive ideas and tactics when it came to reforming criminals. He kept in close touch with the police in Halifax and did everything he could to familiarize himself with the difficulties faced by some of the city's poor and criminally inclined. Once referred to as the "greatest crusader for the good of the common people we have ever had in Halifax," Prince argued that social problems could not be solved until their root causes had been identified and cured.[60] Prince, in a collection of lectures on how sociology was applicable to the problem of delinquency and crime, claimed: "Crime ... is the Gibraltar of social problems. Against it the waves of social effort have beat in vain. We have made conspicuous progress in other realms of human welfare, but in this we confess but little progress ... Other questions are doubtless important but no people can long survive with crime in the ascendant."[61] As a man who had dedicated much of his life to social work, Prince naturally looked to social factors both as the source of crime and as its panacea.[62] Feeble-mindedness, economic depression, family disintegration, and illiteracy, Prince maintained, all contributed to the emergence of crime. Although Prince insisted that a "true social policy puts first the protection of society and after that the reformation of the offender," he still recognized the need for child welfare programs, public health reform, and moral training to usher in a "better day." This "better day" would come, Prince believed: "when the rebellious social laggard we call the criminal has been breeded [sic] out of the human family."[63]

Advocates of prison reform in Halifax formed another prominent group intrigued by the sources of crime. Their views amounted to a mixture of those put forth by Wallace, Chisholm, and Prince. One recurring theme in their arguments was the detrimental effect the city's jails had upon inmates, particularly the impressionable "young offender." Crown

Prosecutor Murray made the case to the Halifax Commercial Club for improving the conditions in local jails. The County Jail, in particular, he described as a "school for crime," from which prisoners graduated well versed in the measures needed to commit more serious offences.[64] A few years later, in 1934, Murray continued his condemnation of the County Jail. As Murray, who was now County Court judge, told the Social Service Council: "throwing men in this kind of jail will never reform them." According to him: "[the] environment in such places has been one of the main causes of crime in this province."[65] Even Judge Wallace had labelled the County Jail a "veritable school for crime," where many offenders were "grossly wronged" by the treatment they received within its walls.[66] On at least one issue – the segregation of prisoners – both sides of the debate over crime could agree. Whatever the apparent impact of current penological theory on those in Halifax who spoke out on criminal justice, they had little impression on correctional and policing practices. J.B. Feilding, chairman of the Prisoners' Welfare Association of Halifax and guest speaker at the 1924 annual meeting of the Union of Nova Scotia Municipalities in Dartmouth, informed the delegates that crime begat crime: next to war, crime constituted one of the most wasteful elements in the world. Crime, he argued, always began the same way: "the doing of something which we call wrong for the lack of something useful or more congenial to do."[67] When a person becomes "morally sick, we clap him into a gaol" and forget about him. However, as Feilding complained, this did nothing to solve the problem; in fact, it only exacerbated it. Feilding asserted that Halifax's jails released men and women back into the community in far worse condition than they were in when they entered. While behind bars, the first-time offender developed a desire to exact revenge on society and learned "more ways of getting a living easily, and ... satisfying his already weakened emotions than he ever thought existed."[68] Feilding exhorted those assembled to take immediate action to resolve this crisis. "This is not a political issue," he declared, "but a social problem, which, unless taken up now, will at no distant date become a serious charge on both our public and private finances."[69] As a way to prevent crime, Feilding urged the union to form a "Prisoners' Friend Association." The association could assist "convicted prisoners in gaol" and render "friendly help to discharged prisoners on re-entering free life." These measures, Feilding believed, would create the "greatest asset in any country ... a law-abiding, healthy citizenship."[70] Such statements characterized the essence of progressive discourse regarding the sources of crime and the best way to cope with it. Unlike traditionalists, who looked to the individual as *the* cause of crime, progressives, in an attempt to understand both crime and the criminal, adopted a more holistic perspective.

Thieves and Vagrants: Public Images of Criminals

The mainly negative connotations associated with the origins of crime coincided with public perceptions of and attitudes towards criminals in Halifax. Judging from the available evidence, most people in this city looked upon criminals with scorn. The recurrent figure of the "thief" highlights this sense of animosity. Usually described in the press as "unkempt" and darkly clad, these "contemptible" men preyed upon unsuspecting victims throughout the city. The objects of their greed ranged from women's purses to church collections. In 1926, the robbery at St. Mary's Cathedral of a basket containing Christmas contributions to the St. Vincent de Paul Society "proved the fact," the *Herald* professed, "that the meanest man in the world is not confined to fiction but is a disgusting reality right here in ... Halifax."[71] A similar comment appeared in 1932 after a six-year-old girl, while on her way to her grandmother's house, was accosted by a man who grabbed $2.50 from her purse and fled. The police searched in vain for the "world's meanest thief" who had "turned up in Halifax."[72] Violent crimes also generated a certain image of the villain. In the aftermath of Allister Munroe's arrest for the murder of Leslie Corkum, the police officers in charge of the investigation informed the newspapers that, in their opinion, whoever shot Corkum had to be a "desperate thug, rendered desperate through drink or drugs or want of money, or possibly a combination of all three."[73] Similarly, in 1931, following a hold-up at a drugstore by two men brandishing revolvers, a general feeling of dissatisfaction arose over the police department's reluctance to investigate reports of unknown men seen loitering in the area prior to the robbery. Their inaction, the *Herald* asserted: "[gave the] thugs every opportunity to escape the law and at the same time will help to chalk up just another crime to the long list already on police records."[74]

The image of the criminal was often connected to mental imbalance. As one account explained, someone is a "wrong-doer ... because either through heredity, misfortune or environment, he suffers a mental, moral, physical or industrial lack."[75] In contrast to this ethical judgment of criminals, J.B. Feilding categorized the majority of inmates in Halifax's jails as "moral wraps [sic] ... They are persons of low intelligence, with ... an entire lack of control of their emotions." Since most were "callous" and had "no real love for man," religious instruction was needed to help them realize their own sense of self-worth.[76] The abnormality and moral degeneracy characteristic of criminals meant that they should be kept separate from the rest of society. In his essay on crime waves, professor R.D. Liddy explains that 30 percent of all criminals exhibit signs of mental deficiency. As a result, they tend to become, in Liddy's view, habitually "crooked," with rarely any inclination to reform. The most important remedy for this class of mentally deficient criminals, or the "feebleminded," Liddy suggests, is segregation and sterilization.[77] Liddy's views form that part of modern psychiatric thinking that holds the "mental degenerate" responsible for much of society's crime, poverty, and immorality.[78] While most people in Halifax probably did not support such drastic measures as the compulsory sterilization of the "unfit," they did evince a sense of unease over the presence of a group of criminally inclined individuals in their city.

Nowhere does the public's perception of and attitude towards criminals come more clearly into focus than over the issue of vagrancy. Although vagrancy did not produce as much outrage as did murder, its ubiquity in Halifax meant that it represented a constant and visible reminder for most residents of the problem of crime. In his study of vagrancy laws in late nineteenth-century Halifax, Jim Phillips reveals how members of the city's middle class perceived vagrants as a threat to social discipline. As well, the vagrancy situation raised calls for the improvement of law and order in Halifax.[79] Both Phillips and Richard Quinney note how vagrancy laws singled out a type of person – notably someone poor – rather than a particular form of conduct as criminal. In essence, these laws served as a way of regulating the activity of an undesirable portion of society.[80] In Halifax, during the early stages of the twentieth century, not much had changed with respect to the perception and treatment of vagrants. In a brief discussion of vagrancy, the men who examined Nova Scotia's penal system in 1933 conceded that some vagrants could be classified as "thriftless wanderers" and victims of misfortune but that vagrancy was the "one substantial rendezvous [sic] of the criminal class."[81] In a move to curtail the activities of these "thriftless wanderers," Chief of Police Palmer declared in 1925 that the soliciting of alms on Halifax's streets would no longer be tolerated. The "mendicants" would be duly warned, and if they persisted, Palmer had ordered his officers to deal with them accordingly. "It [vagrancy] is giving Halifax a black eye," Palmer informed the press, and he would not rest until every beggar had been removed from public view "once and for all."[82]

The law regarding vagrancy contained ten provisions that defined "the vagrant" more vividly than her or his actual "crime." A few examples illustrate this point. As Section 238 of the 1924 Criminal Code states: "Everyone is a loose, idle or disorderly person or vagrant" who, "not having any visible means of subsistence is found wandering abroad ... or lives without employment"; who, "being able to work and thereby .... to maintain himself and family, wilfully refuses or neglects to do so"; "who causes a disturbance in or near any street ... by screaming, swearing or singing, or by being drunk"; or "being a common prostitute or night walker, wanders in the fields, public streets or highways ... and does not give a satisfactory account of herself."[83] The class and gender biases of these definitions, in addition to their breadth, demonstrate how this law created both a crime and an image for the accused. The vagrancy law directly affected the lives of many people in Halifax, especially after 1929, when unemployment and poverty worsened in Nova Scotia, and when many local residents as well as those who flocked to Halifax from across the province in search of work and/or public relief were, almost by definition, guilty of vagrancy. One report intimated that the imprisonment of young men for this crime had "multiplied greatly." The situation was particularly acute in urban centres, where a "considerable number" of men had been arrested for the first time. In "a large number of cases," however, "the man concerned [was] simply the victim of unemployment."[84] During the period from 1930 to 1935, Nova Scotia registered a total of 1,225 (1,120 men and 105 women) convictions for vagrancy. For the same years, the Halifax Police Department gave shelter, usually for one night, to 3,377 people, some of whom were undoubtedly arrested as, or considered to be, vagrants.[85] A few may have welcomed a night in jail. One resident recalled: "[It] was customary among some vagrants ... [to] arrange to be arrested ... to enjoy the thought of not having to spend money on winter fuel and warm clothing. Although the local jail was far from resembling the 'Ritz,' it had advantages to those who thought seriously about being arrested for vagrancy, loitering or disturbing the peace."[86]

John Mullins and Gregory McGuire may have had this strategy in mind. Found by the police, begging on the city's streets, Mullins and McGuire spent a cold 1933 February evening in the lockup.[87] Police departments in major North American cities often sheltered "tramps" as a way of monitoring a group they felt to be potential trouble-makers.[88] But others did not get off so easily. In October 1932, William Mosher, from Hants County, received a two-month sentence in the City Prison for vagrancy. The following month, Magistrate Barnhill ordered Edward Peterson to leave the city within twenty-four hours, his punishment for being a vagrant. However, he did not comply. The police discovered him later in front of St. Paul's Church soliciting alms. This time Barnhill lost his patience with Peterson and sent him to the City Prison for three months.[89] The jailing of vagrants in 1932 caused a stir within some segments of Halifax society. The PWA condemned as a "blot on the City and the Church" the habit of throwing men in jail for vagrancy "because they [were] unable to obtain work."[90] The Halifax Trades and Labour Council added its voice to the protest. At its monthly session, the council decided to petition the attorney general of Canada to amend the vagrancy law. It thought that it was a disgrace that so many unemployed men went to jail as vagrants through no fault of their own.[91] Defenders of these actions responded quickly to such criticisms. Magistrate Barnhill, speaking as someone who had sentenced some of the men in question, declared: "We are merely carrying out the provisions of the *Criminal Code* when we send vagrants to prison." He pointed out that the law did not permit the city to provide relief for non-residents. If taken into custody, "outsiders" were given the opportunity to leave Halifax. If they chose not to exercise this option, Barnhill emphasized, they surely could not be permitted to roam the city's streets. His remarks were indicative of the widespread fear in Halifax of vagrants as a source of social disruption.

Conclusion

The question of vagrancy in Halifax, at least in the early 1930s, conveys some of the tensions surrounding public opinion of criminals. It also points to the traditional/progressive dichotomy concerning the debate about crime and punishment. An apparent consensus within the city's middle class, along with the police and the courts, held that those suspected and convicted of being vagrants, men and women who appeared to be out of keeping with prevailing social mores and ideas of respectability, deserved the full punishment of the law. Yet it was this very notion of respectability that encouraged the PWA and the Halifax Trades and Labour Council to demand a halt to the imprisonment of unemployed men for vagrancy. The problems of modern society, they felt, should not be blamed upon the poor and powerless.[92] Vagrancy was thus one law and order issue around which one can discern clear divisions of opinion based on class.

Commentaries on crime and criminals in Halifax tended for the most part to be couched in an aura of indignation and hostility. Law-abiding citizens agreed that crime could not be permitted to destroy the orderly nature of their city. While they found it difficult at times to understand how and why crime occurred, they remained determined to remove it from their midst. This determination generated a proclivity on the part of those most concerned with preserving social order to see crime as being pervasive in Halifax. Those who enjoyed social and economic power seemed to feel most threatened by the outbreak of crime. Newspapers so intensified the fear of disorder that, over and over again, contemporaries expressed their dread of an impending, or actual, "crime wave." Whatever their perspective on crime, none could escape the fact that this modern city of order still experienced bouts of lawlessness.

Ideas surfaced from several quarters regarding what hereditary and societal factors produced criminals and why they broke the law. Men such as Wallace and Prince, and others who spoke out on crime, its causes and remedies, felt a profound sense of loss with the coming of modernity. They were a part of this new world, indeed some even embraced modern theories, but at the same time they felt detached from its values. In their minds, the world they hoped to preserve, one marked by law and order and respectability, was under siege. As an identifiable product of modernity, and a serious social problem, crime became the main focus of their attention. Only by speaking out on crime could these men devise a way for Halifax to control it. In the process, an image of the criminal as a deviant, or pariah, was socially constructed in Halifax. This did not amount so much to a cohesive interpretation of who or what constituted a criminal as it did to a general perception of offenders. As a result, most of those individuals arrested and/or convicted of a crime encountered public condemnation and the full force of the criminal justice system. Moreover, the perception of the criminal as a social outcast meant that the poor, some women, and members of ethnic minorities would automatically become suspects once a crime had been reported. This only served to reinforce the accepted vision of criminals. As this chapter demonstrates, not everyone in Halifax looked with disfavour on criminals. Some, like the PWA, attempted to help those who were arrested, imprisoned, and eventually released. Yet, such dissenting voices were seldom heard above the din made by those who denounced criminals and their actions. While progressive Halifax tried to proclaim itself to be a modern city of order, there was much that remained traditional in the city's dominant perceptions of crime and criminals.

CHAPTER 4

"Miscreants" and "Desperadoes": Halifax's "Criminal Class"

LATE ONE SATURDAY night in 1925, four drunken soldiers went on a rampage in the Frisco Cafe on the corner of Sackville and Argyle streets. The soldiers caused considerable damage to the cafe and attacked one of its Chinese proprietors. Officer Michael Lawless arrived on the scene in time to prevent these trouble-makers from doing any further harm. Almost single-handedly Lawless "battled, subdued and finally locked up [the] four soldiers who had started on the war path." Thus it appeared that, according to the *Halifax Herald*, Lawless had lost none of his "old time fighting proclivities with the passing of the years," for "despite his name his first thought [was] for the preservation of law and order."[1]

Sergeant Michael O'Halloran also had a memorable career dealing with "thugs" in Halifax. At the conclusion of his twenty-sixth year with the Halifax Police Department, O'Halloran recalled how criminals, drunks, and "wrong-doers" tended to be pugnacious and invariably resisted arrest by using their fists or a weapon. For eight years, O'Halloran had walked the Albemarle Street beat, reportedly one of the toughest assignments on the force. Indeed, it was in a house on this street that O'Halloran arrested Allister Munroe, alleged murderer of Leslie Corkum.[2] Another officer, Vincent O'Brien, remembered that most people in Halifax respected policemen. O'Brien, who joined the force in 1933, noted: "[When I] went to a disturbance ... usually the sight of a uniform itself was enough to quiet things down ... I think that the uniform itself meant a lot to people in those days."[3] Contrary to legend, there was little camaraderie or mutual respect between police officers and criminals. As O'Brien remarked, "I think the general public felt that we were a necessary evil and the criminal[s], well, they disliked us through fear." The feeling seemed to be mutual. "I think we instinctively had a dislike for criminals," O'Brien asserted: "When we caught them, I think we felt good about it."[4] For the most part, Halifax's policemen and policewomen took pride in their work. They accepted the task of maintaining order, if the experiences of Lawless, O'Halloran, and O'Brien are any indication, with fortitude and resolve. And they were seen, and often saw themselves, as confronting a "criminal class." Reportedly most of the city's criminal element lurked in the downtown core. If the police needed information on a crime, or wanted to question and/or arrest a suspect, they often turned to this area first. During a Police Commission investigation into the conduct of a patrolman, Bessie Heighton, convicted of illegally selling alcohol, described the district of Upper and Lower Water streets as the "toughest spot in the city."[5] The police kept a watchful eye over events in downtown Halifax. Besides being a hive of activity for the illicit liquor trade and prostitution, this neighbourhood could also be potentially dangerous. At a meeting of the Police Commission in 1929, Alderman O'Toole declared: "The way things are getting in Halifax, it seems to me that the police can hardly compete with the toughs on the streets at night, and we have in the city today, lots of young women who are going to be bad, walking the streets at night."[6]

The "toughs" and delinquents referred to by the police and politicians did not form a faceless part of the city's population. They had distinct identities and lives. Yet when they broke the law, Halifax's criminal justice system, in its efforts to apprehend and punish them, treated these individuals strictly as abstractly defined "criminals." Those who fit this bill ranged from Hilda Simon, found guilty of stealing merchandise valued at fourteen dollars from Eaton's on Barrington Street in 1930,[7] to a fifteen-year-old boy who for two weeks in mid-August 1922 had masqueraded as a representative of the Salvation Army and solicited donations.[8] These two very different people, and many other cases, were placed within the same grid of assumptions and categories. Although all of these many individuals engaged in different crimes for a myriad of reasons, together they represented a part of Halifax's socially defined criminal class. Here I examine this criminal class, the crimes that they committed, and the treatment accorded them by the police, the courts, and the community generally. I also discuss how their criminal activity was a product of the city's socio-economic inequalities, along with the fact that the administration of justice in Halifax, a city bent on preserving law and order, entrenched these imbalances. Moreover, those deemed to be members of this criminal class never seemed to escape either the stigma of being a "criminal" or the suspicion that accompanied it. For some, this fact shaped the conduct of their daily lives.

The concept of "criminal class" is ambiguous. Halifax did not really possess a well-defined criminal class in the interwar period or at any other time in its history. Because the actual number of "criminal acts" can never be known (all that is available to us is the official record of arrests and convictions), it is impossible to compile a reliable dataset representing all those in Halifax who carried out acts in violation of the Criminal Code. Consequently, any conception of a criminal class as an actual existing group with a collective identity must be treated with great caution. Yet the notion of a criminal class, if seen as a cultural construct – as a way of summarizing how reputable contemporaries regarded their city and the people whose activities were threatening to undermine its orderly existence – is useful and important. As I show in this chapter, many Halifax residents believed that within their city there existed an identifiable group of individuals, bent on a life of crime, who lived in a particular area and who shared certain other attributes. Tracking this perception through time provides a significant clue as to how Halifax's machinery of order dealt with criminals and the nature of crime in the city. Most Haligonians seemed to agree that members of a criminal class could be distinguished from the rest of the population by their poverty, their sinister appearance and gruff demeanour, at times by their ethnic "otherness," and by their obvious disregard for law and order. Here was a class that grew, as the *Herald* put it, "like a noxious weed."[9] I first set out the classic instances in which this "noxious weed" was observed and controlled – notably cases of "mob violence," of armed robbers and "desperadoes," and of repeat offenders. I then turn to more troubling instances of observation and control – specifically, those involving returned soldiers and juvenile delinquents, thus showing that one need be neither sinister nor gruff to be a criminal in interwar Halifax.

In one sense, the idea of a criminal class was a comforting notion for those middle-class members of Halifax society most troubled by crime. It provided them with a means of explaining the genesis of crime and confirming to themselves that lawlessness remained the preserve of a "class" of social outcasts.[10] At the same time, when groups such as returned soldiers and juveniles committed crimes, and thus appeared to be a part of the criminal class, contemporaries responded in disbelief. Veterans and children, so many in Halifax wanted to believe, could not belong to such a cohort of wrong-doers. But if Halifax did have a criminal class, then many ordinary ex-soldiers and juvenile delinquents were central components of it. Thus empirical evidence, which suggested that many people caught at the wrong time or in the wrong place might be criminals, could be deeply alarming since it indicated that the boundaries of crime could not be artificially and neatly circumscribed by the concept of a criminal class. The majority of those arrested and convicted of crimes in Halifax shared a few related characteristics. Most were male, young, poor and/or working class, and of British ethnic origin. People fitting these criteria, therefore, are my main focus. Numerically, men dominated known criminal activity. For example, from 1917 to 1922, the Halifax police arrested a total of 11,165 male offenders and only 749 female offenders. This meant that, on average, men accounted for 92.4 percent and women 7.6 percent of the arrests made annually by police officers in Halifax (Appendix 2, Tables A2.18 and A2.19). Statistics, however, do not attest to the presence of a criminal class. From the standpoint of many of those who lived in Halifax in the 1920s and early 1930s, the phrase "criminal class" implied a specific set of people ("hardened criminals") who were determined to thwart law and order and to disrupt the city's social order. For the purposes of this analysis, the term "criminal class" is used to highlight the experiences of some of these individuals. As well, it underlines how Halifax's machinery of order and many of its residents tended to view some law-breakers as a coherent body of criminals.

Juvenile delinquents are also discussed as a part of this so-called criminal class.[11] Children who broke the law represented a serious dilemma for legal authorities and social reformers. Some of them believed that Halifax had a "juvenile delinquent class" lurking in their midst. But officials were quick to distance this delinquent class from the more general criminal class. To have equated juveniles with adult criminals would have made the problem of juvenile delinquency, in the outlook of those dedicated to their reformation, more serious. Not wanting to condone their actions by handing down a lenient sentence, judges at the same time wanted to direct youths away from the "hardened" criminal element. As a compromise, most delinquents received some form of punishment (which included being placed on probation) and rehabilitative care. Within the context of the general fear of crime in Halifax, juvenile crime acquired an added significance. This was due mainly to the widespread belief, in Halifax and elsewhere, that children represented the future of society. And if too many boys and girls became delinquents, it was believed, the possibility of their turning to a life of crime as they grew older increased, which placed the progress and stability of society in jeopardy.[12] Most of those who were generally concerned with crime and the implementation of justice and order considered youthful offenders to be worthy of reform. There thus emerged in Halifax signs of a gradual, but important, transition from traditional to more modern ways of classifying and dealing with children who had committed crimes.

A Criminal Class in Halifax

Before embarking upon an exploration of Halifax's alleged criminal class, a brief explanation of this term is in order. The identification of a criminal class remains a problematic task. Scholars have offered numerous definitions and descriptions of this collection of law-breakers. The phrase itself, as Victor Bailey notes, entered criminological discourse in England in 1851. To many Victorians, the criminal class became synonymous with the "dangerous classes," a group of people deserving of nothing but judicial severity, below the moral and social standards of the honest working poor.[13] Bailey outlines two prevailing images of the criminal class: one a "group of rational, calculating, 'habitual criminals'" and the second an "irrational, degenerate 'race,' marked by distinct physical and mental traits."[14] Similar perceptions appeared in the United States and Paris. Eric H. Monkkonen argues that nineteenth-century observers of crime often lumped criminals in with poor people and labelled them the "dangerous classes." Members of these classes appeared as the "product of accident, ignorance, and vice" who formed the "great masses of destitute, miserable, and criminal persons."[15] The Paris bourgeoisie, Louis Chevalier contends, believed the "proletariat" to be a separate "race" who could be held responsible for much of the crime and social disorder of early nineteenth-century Parisian society.[16] In Victorian Halifax, "underclass" became a common expression to depict the city's poor and those inclined to criminal activity.[17] In John Phyne's words, the underclass included all the people who "combined poor employment opportunities with involvement in crime for social survival."[18] These accounts capture some of the traits assigned to Halifax's criminal class during the interwar period. Many of those who supposedly belonged to this class lived on the socio-economic margins of society. Similarly, when taken into custody they received little sympathy for their plight. Their crimes and the criminals themselves were felt to be a threat to social order, which demanded a quick and sometimes harsh response from the courts. Yet criminals in Halifax did not represent a class in the sense that they articulated a common identity or shared a common relationship to the means of production.[19] In most respects, they were a "class" by external ascription – due mainly to the categories and actions applied to them by police officers, judges, jailers, journalists, and many ordinary citizens.[20] It was at this level, where the poor, the disorderly, and the criminal were interpenetrating categories, that the phrase "criminal class" was used to describe a certain social reality.

The term "criminal class" did not appear frequently in public pronouncements about crime in Halifax. However, the image of a core body of "undesirables" prepared to live their lives on the wrong side of the law persisted. Consequently, their activities came under close scrutiny from the police and local newspapers, the latter of which provided readers with daily, and often lurid, accounts of Police Court proceedings, thereby placing the criminal class in a continuous state of opposition to the rule of law. As well, some magistrates tended to base their verdicts and sentences upon a defendant's criminal record or class status. Men who stood before the magistrate with prior arrests or convictions, who were unemployed and deemed to be of dubious character, often left the courtroom poorer or jail-bound.[21] As Jennifer S. Davis shows for mid-Victorian London, media reports of these trials only reinforced the public's belief that the poor perpetrated much of the crime in Halifax.[22] This tendency to see the poor as criminal helped to construct a criminal class in Nova Scotia's capital. Similarly, it furnished those determined to maintain law and order in Halifax with a vulnerable assortment of characters as a focus for their efforts to combat crime.

"Mob Rule" in Halifax

Many citizens of Halifax realized, in the wake of the 1918 and 1919 riots that engulfed the city, that their campaign against crime was going to be a protracted struggle. These melees challenged the city's social order and threatened to dispel the fragile sense of hope for its reconstruction.[23] This section concentrates on the 1918 riot and on the ways in which each riot prompted an outraged response.[24] Above all, the riots demonstrated just how much middle-class Haligonians cherished order and how they and the police placed the blame for these lawless acts upon a distinct group of misfits who formed a part of the criminal class. On Saturday night, 25 May 1918, "Mob Rule" gripped downtown Halifax. The whole affair had started rather innocently. Police officer James Eisenhaur responded to a call from Woolworth's "five, ten, and fifteen cent" store on Barrington Street. Apparently James Smith, an enlisted sailor from Newfoundland whose ship had recently docked, had refused to pay for a bar of soap he had picked up from this store. Eisenhaur arrived and escorted Smith out of Woolworth's. Moments later, Smith, who was intoxicated, began to hurl profanities at Eisenhaur. In the meantime, a group of Smith's compatriots had assembled and began to jeer the policeman. A scuffle followed until both Eisenhaur and a second policeman, Thomas McDonald, finally restrained Smith and brought him to the police lockup.[25] Smith's arrest triggered a chain reaction of events that ended in violence and destruction. Angered by the arrest of a fellow comrade, a band of soldiers and sailors, many of whom had spent the night drinking, pursued Smith and his captors to the police station in City Hall, gathering supporters along the way. Soon downtown Halifax became the scene of the "wildest disorder that Halifax ha[d] witnessed in the memory of its citizens."[26]

Determined to secure his release, or merely caught up in the frenzy of the moment, the crowd, estimated at between three and four thousand strong, began to throw rocks and bottles at the building. Huddled inside, a small group of officers refused to yield to the crowd's demands. Soon, according to one observer, "The thing seemed ... to grow until it got to its height."[27] Some members of the crowd stormed the building, battering down the door leading into the front chamber, while others crawled through broken windows. Once inside they ransacked the premises; some headed straight for the police court and began to destroy the furniture and throw law books outside. Their escapade resulted in nearly $5,000 worth of damage.[28] James Smith, meanwhile, the initial cause of this outburst, continued to languish in his cell, apparently forgotten in the heat of battle. To quell the protesters the city called in the army. The police department was at a loss to prevent such an explosion of violence as its lack of personnel and resources hampered its efforts. In the opinion of one report, which captured in the word "mob" the reified and demonized "other" that many people in Halifax constructed as soon as the city came under threat, "the police were at the mercy of the mob because they were not sufficient to cope with it." Finally, with the help of one hundred soldiers with fixed bayonets, the throng began to disperse.[29] Their actions had reminded many citizens of Halifax that, as residents of a port city, they lived under the ever-present danger of military-induced mob violence.

Outrage and calls for stiffer measures of law enforcement surfaced as the city began to clean up the debris left from the 1918 riot. The disorder witnessed on Saturday night was, in the words of the *Morning Chronicle:* "one of the most deplorable events in the history of our City. Halifax has always been proud of her reputation as a law-abiding community," a reputation now tarnished by this riot.[30] While the police may have shown a lack of discretion in some of the arrests they had made, according to the *Chronicle:* "that was no excuse, much less justification, for the recourse to mob rule and the outbreak of lawlessness which ensued." "Law and order must be observed," the editorial concluded, "[and] the safety and security of citizens and their property must be ensured against riotous conduct." To this end the paper insisted that the police force be strengthened immediately in order to maintain the "honor of Halifax."[31] The *Halifax Herald* echoed this plea for law and order. In its view, the entire episode had been directed at the police department, the "custodians" of the city's peace. As a result, "the law which punishes all who obstruct them in the performance of their duty ... is one which the whole community ... MUST BE MADE TO RESPECT."[32] Ironically, however, the man who precipitated the entire incident, James Smith, escaped virtually unscathed. A few days after things had calmed down, Smith appeared before the police court. Convened in the corridor of the police station while the chambers underwent repairs, the court, after listening to Smith plead guilty to public drunkenness and using abusive language, fined him two and three dollars for each offence, respectively.[33]

On the nights of 18 and 19 February 1919, the streets of Halifax belonged once again to riotous crowds. These disturbances also involved soldiers and civilians. Unlike the previous riot, however, the 1919 affrays had a racist undertone. The rioters unleashed a wave of destructiveness on some of the city's Chinese-owned businesses. On the first night, two men descended upon the Crown Cafe, a Chinese establishment on Gottingen Street. While there they destroyed tables, chairs, and windows before proceeding to their next destination. As they began their march from Gottingen Street to Barrington Street, several people, including returned soldiers, joined their ranks. Five more Chinese restaurants fell victim to this group's rampage. The damage amounted to roughly $2000. One newspaper reported that every one of the city's sixty-eight police officers had tried in vain to contain the "mob."[34] Only with the assistance of military and naval police did the authorities subdue the crowd. Despite the loss suffered by the proprietors and the numbers of participants who had taken part, the police made only three arrests.[35] Before residents had had a chance to absorb the shock of these attacks, an "outbreak of lawlessness and mob rule" paralyzed the city the next night. From 10:30 PM until midnight on 19 February, thousands of citizens and soldiers took over the streets of downtown Halifax. Disgruntled ex-servicemen had served as the spark that ignited this riot. Controller John Murphy, a witness at the inquiry into the 1918 and 1919 riots, testified: "[A] very small circle of returned men felt they had some grievances [and] ... were able to create some following and the situation developed. I don't think it was prearranged in any way."[36] In a demonstration similar to that of the 1918 riot, soldiers and civilians gathered in front of the police station to demand that a solider who had been arrested be set free. When the authorities refused to comply, the crowd dispersed. But it quickly regrouped at a shoe store owned by Joanna Patton, a "respected resident of the North End." Mistaking her for what Mayor Hawkins referred to as a "foreigner," the "upholders of Freedom and Justice" broke the front window and door and ransacked the store.[37] "For ten minutes shoes rained on Gottingen street," the *Halifax Herald* announced, before the looters moved on, driven by "no desire save to smash, to break and destroy," until brought under control by a military show of force.[38]

In the aftermath, nine retail stores had been wrecked at an estimated cost of $20,000, while a dozen people went to hospital with "more or less serious injuries," along with "hundreds of others with cut faces, torn clothing, and bleeding scalps." Eight rioters found themselves behind bars.[39] Conditions in Halifax, the *Herald* asserted days after the second 1919 riot, "ha[d] reached a serious state" and, as such, "no consideration [could] be shown by the authorities to either civilians or others who take part in riots."[40] Halifax, it seems, had had enough. This mood of defiance led to a demand for martial law. The city, in the opinion of many, could not be held at the mercy of "gangs of hoodlums." If politicians and the police could not cope with the situation, then it was "time that they asked the military authorities to step in, and take charge." According to the *Herald:* "Placing the city under martial law would give Halifax a black eye, but its reputation cannot be more seriously assailed than by permitting a repetition of Tuesday's and last night's happenings."[41] Civic leaders concurred and took the necessary steps to ensure the city's safety. They stopped short, however, of invoking martial law.[42] The next evening

Halifax was calm as two hundred soldiers and sailors joined forces with the police to patrol the downtown core. With these men well armed to protect themselves and the lives and property of most citizens, the *Herald* confidently believed: "[the] law in [the] future is going to take its course, Halifax is going to be made a safe city for people to live in."[43] This confidence, steeped in a desire for a return to social order, came at the expense of troops guarding the streets of peacetime Halifax.

The views expressed regarding the cause of and individuals behind these riots explain the rationale for such extreme measures. The riots also underscore the fact that not everyone was comfortable with the socio-economic status quo in Halifax, particularly returning veterans who looked forward to a smooth transition to civilian life. When this did not materialize, due to delays in demobilization and in the remittance of back wages, the frustration of some quickly turned to violence.[44] It did so in part because, as E.P. Thompson holds for riots in general, a few of those involved sensed that they possessed a degree of power to aid their cause.[45] Whatever legitimate complaints the rioters may or may not have had, most concerned citizens in Halifax did not want to give these people credence; rather, they viewed most of them with contempt. By labelling them a "mob," authorities and citizens alike were able to interpret the events and those involved as, in the words of George Rude, the "'passive' instrument[s] of outside agents ... 'demagogues' or 'foreigners,'" provoked by motives of "loot, lucre, free drinks, bloodlust, or ... the need to satisfy some lurking criminal instinct."[46] In March 1919, Chief Justice Robert Harris of the Supreme Court of Nova Scotia, in an address to the Grand Jury, which was investigating the cause of the riots, spoke of the need to remain steadfast in the pursuit of law and order. "Good order and tranquillity are essential to the general welfare of the community and its citizens," Harris insisted. If people were allowed to break the law with impunity, then all respect for it would vanish, he continued. This is because: "every man becomes a law unto himself and the community in which such conditions are allowed to prevail soon becomes no place for any respectable citizen to live." Harris implored the grand jurors to approach the task before them with diligence: "[for] there are many signs of a spirit of lawlessness which bodes ill for the public safety and happiness of the people of this City unless there is a proper and fearless administration of the laws of the land."[47] The rioters had thus undermined the city's aura of law and order and struck fear into the hearts of some officials.

The Grand Jury did not entirely share Harris's sense of panic, however. In its final report, issued in the spring of 1919, it found that the riot of 1918 "was primarily due to the resentment of military and naval men against one of their number being arrested by the Civilian police; augmented ... by the ... sympathy of a Halifax crowd for a 'sailor' in trouble, and not to the premeditated design of any group or groups of people." With regard to the two confrontations of 1919, the Grand Jury could find no clear-cut reason for their occurrence. It did, however, rule out alcohol as a probable cause. "[S]o far as we can learn," the Grand Jury stated, "there was very little evidence of drunkenness that night or the following night." Despite their rather dismissive tone, the jurors did suggest, at least for the remainder of 1919, that, "while conditions may be more or less disturbed," a "close affiliation" be kept between the military and civilian police to "'nip in the bud' any threatened uprisings."[48] Many other residents of Halifax shared their apprehensions. The riots produced a number of responses from Haligonians. Most expressed fear, anger, and a certain amount of surprise that such pandemonium could happen not once, but three times in less than two years. Even though these riots fit the characteristic form of others in North America and Europe, with "small beginnings ... triggered by a chance word or act of provocation ... [that] assume[ed] a dimension and momentum that no one ... could have planned or expected," a fact acknowledged by the Grand Jury, they still made an indelible mark on the city.[49]

Lewis Bevis: A "Desperado" and a "Cowardly Assassin"

In the years that followed the riots, Halifax's criminal class, and the crimes that it committed, assumed various roles in the Halifax drama of law and order. As a result of a chequered criminal record, culminating in the murder of Halifax police officer Charles Fulton in 1924, Lewis Marshall Bevis became the city's consummate "desperado" and the embodiment of the criminal class. Bevis, who was twenty-five at the time of the shooting and a former serviceman, had spent much of his life on the wrong side of the law. From escaping detention in industrial school, to breaking and entering, and uttering threats to his mother, Bevis was no stranger to the Halifax police. He later told authorities that, as a child, his father had forced him to break into vacant summer cottages. If he had refused, Bevis recalled: "I would be unmercifully beaten."[50] Bevis's final brush with the law proved to be his most serious. For a progressive, Lewis

Bevis was an excellent example of the damage done by a pernicious social upbringing, while for a traditionalist he was simply a force for evil. In July 1924, however, both would probably have agreed that Bevis, who, along with his three-member "bandit gang," was "terrorizing the city and suburbs," had to be captured and placed behind "steel bars." The saga began when the police learned that Bevis and his cohorts had held up the driver of a Fry's bakery truck and made off with six dollars. Earlier the gang had stolen a few items, including the gun used in the hold-up, from a home near the Dingle Tower (North-West Arm). The police followed Bevis's trail into the surrounding woods only to be met by gunfire, which wounded one officer. Eventually they caught up with Bevis's three companions, but he eluded them.[51]

With Bevis still at large the police search intensified. Every available member of the Halifax police force joined the manhunt. One newspaper dubbed it the "most desperate man-hunt in the history of the city and province."[52] Bevis managed to slip past his pursuers and made it to the West End of the city. When the police arrived there later, "scenes the like[s] of which had never before been enacted in this peaceful community" unfolded. The smell of gunpowder filled the air as the police unleashed a torrent of gunfire in their attempt to halt Bevis. At one point the police had Bevis trapped behind a house on Preston Street, but he "took a chance with death and won" as he dodged a hail of bullets and resumed his "course to liberty." The police then pursued Bevis across the playground at the St. Thomas Aquinas School on Le Marchant Street. Halfway across the playground Bevis turned and fired at officer Fulton, who was closest to him at the time. As one eye-witness recalled: "As the shot was fired, Fulton made as though he fell or tripped and Bevis went back toward him. Bevis had a gun in his hand and went right back to him and shot him in the head."[53] Bevis then fled the scene but finally surrendered to the police at the Camp Hill Cemetery.

A combination of sorrow and outrage greeted the death of officer Fulton and Bevis's arrest. The *Halifax Herald* tried to share with its readers some of the grief felt by Fulton's widow. "As the sun sank slowly below the horizon last evening, leaving a trail of glorious colour that gave place to a silvery moon of exquisite loveliness," the *Herald* moaned, "in the heart of one Halifax woman there was nothing but desolation and ... despair." Then, seething with hostility, the paper stressed that, while Fulton's body awaited burial, Bevis, "the creature who had brought such sorrow[,] was still alive and unrepentant in the city jail." Fulton, a "sturdy, right-thinking young man of good old Presbyterian faith," who had served with honour in the war, was "as fine [a] Canadian as his murderer was the opposite."[54] The imagery spoke for itself. Fulton, the respectable, middle-class citizen, who distinguished himself protecting others as a soldier and police officer, had been killed by Bevis, an evil, emotionless, dehumanized criminal. In this heated atmosphere of sorrow and revenge, it was easy to overlook the fact that Bevis had served his country in the war. Public commentary, in addition to assessing the personal impact of Bevis's actions, also addressed the dire effects this event had had on the entire city. An editorial in the *Morning Chronicle* declared: "Halifax has been so long and singularly free from crimes of violence that the occurrence of acts of banditry within the city limits and in the heart of its residential district has profoundly moved the community." The shooting by this "desperado," the *Chronicle* continued, had reminded those responsible for the care of law and order that, within the city, there existed "vicious elements" who must be closely watched. Another lesson to be taken from this crime ("by far the most sensational in the modern history of the city"), was the need to properly arm the police force so that it could deal with criminals and protect the public in such emergencies.[55]

During his appearance in police court the local press cast Bevis in a sinister light. At his preliminary hearing, where he pleaded not guilty to the charge of murder, Bevis bore a "rough appearance accentuated by four or five days growth of beard." One paper even claimed that this "cowardly assassin" had told the police: "I am not sorry for what I've done ... I'm going to swing for it any way ... I am sorry I killed a man who I had nothing against, but what's the use of squealing about it."[56] Bevis's defiant attitude seemed to irritate some of the officials close to him. Malcolm Mitchell, jailor for the Halifax County Jail where Bevis was held, commented: "Bevis is unrepentant ... He is not sorry for what he has done [and] he ... regards himself as somewhat of a hero. The fact that a murder charge has been preferred against him does not seem to bother him at all."[57] In one sense, the press and criminal justice officials tried to construct an image of Bevis not only as evil but also as wholly "other," a being devoid of feelings and any respect for law and order.

Bevis's indictment paved the way for his trial in the Supreme Court. During these proceedings the defence and the Crown each conveyed their own assessment of the case and Bevis's character. In his closing statement to the jury, defence counsel J.W. Madden of Sydney argued that, under the circumstances, Bevis had had every right to fear for his life. With scores of police and citizens chasing after him shouting "Shoot him!" and gunfire all around, his natural instinct had been to flee. And so, Madden contended, Bevis had shot Fulton in self-defence. If Bevis had not defended himself then the police would have gunned him down. Madden also turned to Bevis's wartime record to underscore the difficulties he had had adjusting to life in a peacetime environment. As a soldier in the First World War, Madden noted, Bevis had been trained to kill, and when the war ended "he was told to go back home and be a good boy, resume the golden rule and forget all the nightmare he had lived through." Yet, the business of killing, Madden stressed, "was hard to learn and harder to unlearn, it can't be done."[58] Madden, it seems, tried to rely on progressive notions of social causation and psychology to defend his client's actions. The Crown, on the other hand, couched its summation to the jury in the more traditionalist rhetoric of law and order. As W.J. O'Hearn, Nova Scotia's attorney general, asserted, society gave police officers the right to shoot at fugitives if they posed a threat to public safety and if the officers deemed it necessary to ensure the criminal's capture. Similarly, criminals must be brought to justice "in order that society may exist [and] in order that we may have law and order in the land." Bevis, in O'Hearn's opinion, as "an ex-convict, a crook, [and] a gunman," had known what he was doing when he failed to surrender and shot Fulton. O'Hearn then begged the jury to weigh its decision carefully since a verdict of not guilty would send a message to "every burglar and gunman that if he gets in a close fix and is about to be captured by an officer of society then you say to the gunman 'shoot your way to liberty; shoot to kill.'"[59]

Some members of the jury, however, apparently did not take O'Hearn's warning seriously. After twelve hours of deliberation, the members of the jury filed back into the courtroom and announced that they could not reach a unanimous decision. At this, the "breathless hush among the spectators relaxed" and Bevis "settled back a little as a man who had passed through a grim ordeal." Although Bevis "still [stood] in the shadow of the gallows ... he ha[d] another chance for his life."[60] In November 1924, a second jury, on the basis of new evidence and similar defence and Crown arguments, found Bevis guilty of murder. Breathing a sigh of relief, the *Herald* welcomed the verdict, stating: "No individual facing a capital charge in this province ever had a fairer trial ... Bevis was defended by one of the most eloquent and resourceful criminal lawyers we have ever had in

Nova Scotia." The paper felt that an acquittal "would have served notice on the lawless element in this province that they could commit crimes of violence and then shoot their way out." In the mind of the *Herald's* editor one fact stood out above all the rest, namely:

> The career of Lewis Bevis ... was bound to end in tragedy. From his cradle he lived in an atmosphere of crime; of defiance of the law; of preying on Society ... wherever the blame may be placed, it is clear as day that something must be done to correct such conditions; for men of the Lewis Bevis type grow to maturity in an environment where crime thrives like a noxious weed. And Society has in this regard a duty equally as clear as the duty which compelled a verdict of guilty against Bevis by a jury of his peers.[61]

Lewis Bevis, a born criminal and a convicted murderer, no longer posed a threat to social order in Halifax. The task that lay ahead, as indicated by this editorial, was to ensure that the "Lewis Bevis type" never jeopardized "Society" or challenged law and order again.

The Supreme Court sentenced Bevis to hang for the murder of Officer Fulton. After Madden's appeal to the Supreme Court of Nova Scotia for a retrial failed, Bevis could do nothing but await his fate.[62] In the interim, however, a few voices spoke out in support of him. The Roman Catholic archbishop of Halifax, the Anglican archbishop of Nova Scotia (Bevis belonged to the Church of England), the Great War Veterans' Association, and J.M. Weeks, manager of the *Citizen* (a Halifax labour paper), all sent Ernest Lapointe, the federal minister of justice, telegrams pleading for clemency for Bevis. Each appeal underlined the jury's recommendation for mercy and Bevis's troubled childhood as grounds for commuting his sentence to life imprisonment. In the progressive words of the archbishops, Bevis's "heredity and boyhood environment almost inevitably led to [a] career of crime."[63] Not surprisingly, no letters of support, or requests for clemency, came from any member of Halifax's criminal justice system. Few within this community – and, it may be argued, among respectable middle-class society – felt a sense of remorse over the pending death of Lewis Bevis. He had broken the law and placed the lives of many orderly citizens in peril; therefore, he should pay what the law deemed to be the appropriate price for his actions. Thus, in their eyes, the machinery of order had fulfilled its intended role – namely, to administer the ultimate form of punishment to Lewis Bevis: death.

Once Lapointe had dismissed the requests for a commutation of Bevis's sentence his execution proceeded on schedule. In the early hours of Wednesday morning, 11 February 1925, a small group of officials gathered to witness Bevis's hanging. Lewis Bevis faced his death with "remarkable coolness." He mounted the scaffold with a firm step, smoked a cigarette, and then uttered his last words: "Good-bye, boys."[64] Justice had apparently been done, yet a sense of uneasiness about the affair lingered. In considering the execution, the *Halifax Herald*, a strong supporter of a proposal to relocate all such spectacles to Dorchester Penitentiary, commented: "Such events as these, amid the peaceful and ordered routine of the towns and cities of the country, have a very certain effect upon many classes of people, particularly women and children. They leave in the memory scars that time can never quite remove." The *Herald* acknowledged that capital punishment was the law and that the law must be carried out: "but in this advanced age the law should be so amended as to provide for some more desirable method of carrying out the dictates of the law."[65] Ironically, some Halifax residents felt uncomfortable with the fact that, in the process of maintaining order – in this instance by executing Bevis – the city's criminal justice system had also disrupted it. As the twentieth century progressed, more and more critiques of hanging as inhumane and barbaric could be heard. In response, the state attempted to restore Canadians' faith in the ability of officials to administer capital punishment fairly and in a humane manner. It knew that, without that faith, as Carolyn Strange surmises, public fear that hanging was brutal and uncivilized would continue to grow.[66]

Halifax's "Usual Suspects": Recidivists and Returned Soldiers

The riots and the Lewis Bevis case were not the only serious criminal disruptions of order in the provincial capital from 1918 to 1935. Nor do they present a complete picture of the city's criminal class. They do, however, epitomize the opposition to crime in Halifax and the city's determination to secure order. The tendency to express anger and resentment towards criminals, and to view most of those who broke the law as members of a criminal class and thus as inherently inclined towards criminality, accompanied many reported crimes in Halifax. Nowhere was this more evident then in regard to recidivists, those individuals who repeatedly found themselves charged with a host of minor crimes, from public intoxication to vagrancy. Lewis Bevis fit neatly into this category of criminals. As Michael B. Katz et al. note, late nineteenth-century commentators understood one of the key characteristics of the criminal class to be its members' engagement in a variety of illegal activities.[67] This belief remained widespread in early twentieth-century Halifax. Recidivism did not suddenly become a serious problem in Halifax at the turn of the century. On the contrary, it had been a scourge for the city's law enforcement authorities and social reformers throughout much of the mid- to late nineteenth century. Judith Fingard traces the lives of a core group of recidivists in Halifax: alcoholics, the chronically unemployed, and prostitutes, some of whom, she argues, were driven by a basic survival instinct to steal food and clothing. The identities of these people became known to the police, and many aspects of their daily lives fell under the watchful presence of a patrolman. As a result, a select group of suspects – a criminal class – appeared for the police to question and/or arrest at their discretion.[68]

Harry O'Bellerio, better known as "Spanish Harry," was one of the more infamous "usual suspects" in Halifax during the 1918 to 1935 period. In 1927, O'Bellerio came into conflict with the law on four separate occasions. O'Bellerio had lived in Halifax for a few years prior to 1927 and worked sporadically as a taxi driver. In January the police arrested him for "unlawfully and wilfully" assaulting John Hayes. At his preliminary hearing the police called O'Bellerio a "bad influence" and an "undesirable" citizen, which led Magistrate Cluney to suggest that, in the best interests of the city, O'Bellerio should be expelled from the community. Instead, following his conviction, the Halifax County Court sentenced him to two months at hard labour in the City Prison.[69] But breaking stones at Rockhead did not seem to reform O'Bellerio. In August one newspaper reported that Spanish Harry, a "well known local character," who within the last three months had been in the "toils" twice, once on a charge of resisting arrest and once for assaulting a Chinese resident, was again "given [a] free ride in the police patrol [car]." This time the police caught O'Bellerio trying to steal hogs. In addition to this offence, a jury in the Halifax County Supreme Court found O'Bellerio guilty of assaulting a police officer who had tried to take him into custody while in an Upper Water Street "resort." Spanish Harry "skipped gleefully out of the box," a reporter noted, when the Supreme Court ordered him to spend three months in the County Jail. O'Bellerio then "covertly winked at [the] spectators as if to indicate his pleasure with the sentence."[70]

Spanish Harry neatly fit the perception that many in the city's criminal justice system and the general public had of criminals. In their eyes these people drifted in and out of jobs, dressed poorly, possessed a low moral character (usually as a result of their penchant for alcohol), committed a myriad of petty crimes, and harboured an overall disrespect for the law. They constituted a permanent class of undesirables.[71] But they did not always, so the police believed, take part in the more "daring" crimes. On the same day the police apprehended O'Bellerio for attempted theft, two men accosted a woman standing at a street corner and made off with her handbag. Immediately the *Halifax Herald* insinuated that O'Bellerio must be considered the prime suspect. Detective McIsaac, however, dismissed the notion. In his mind criminals like O'Bellerio did not commit such infractions. As McIsaac told the press: "After a thorough inquiry into the ... hold-up, I have no clues which would lead me or my co-workers to believe O'Bellerio had anything to do with it. It is not at all the type of crime these men would commit."[72] This segment of Halifax's criminal class, while certainly to be counted on to commit a number of summary offences, could be ruled out, perhaps after a brief investigation, as the main suspects in most cases involving serious criminal acts. The criminal justice system in Halifax tried to cope with what seemed to be a criminal class that was perpetrating much of the city's crime. On the one hand, men like Lewis Bevis could not be permitted to flagrantly violate law and order; on the other hand, the likes of Spanish Harry did not warrant the total force of the law. They and their comparatively minor antics could be kept in check without sentencing them to lengthy prison terms or death sentences. While the machinery of order dealt with these members of the criminal class as it saw fit, another group, returned soldiers, who seemed to be no different than Lewis Bevis or Spanish Harry in terms of their backgrounds or criminal misdeeds, posed a particular challenge to the image that many in Halifax had of the "criminal."

Most Halifax residents were not prepared to see returned soldiers as belonging, in any way, to the criminal class. Shortly after the destructive riots in downtown Halifax in 1919, the *Halifax Herald* claimed that this recklessness had been the "work of Hoodlums," not decorated veterans.[73] Patriotic Haligonians, it seems, did not want to concede the fact that servicemen could be lawless. Nevertheless, after their return from the war, some ex-soldiers in Halifax drifted into lives of crime. The early postwar years proved to be difficult ones for many of Canada's veterans. Dim job prospects and a general lack of state-funded pension and rehabilitation programs left many feeling disillusioned.[74] In Halifax, as the disembarkation point for Canada's soldiers returning from overseas, these problems became acute. The Nova Scotia Returned Soldier Commission, established in 1915 to care for discharged soldiers, admitted in 1919: "[the] re-establishment of our soldiers is not as complete and satisfactory as had been hoped for and expected." The commission also found that, despite the formation of the Employment Service of Canada, "a large number of men still appl[ied] to [its] office for employment." Of the 7,114 soldiers the commission dealt with in February 1919, 1,640 (23.1 percent) were unemployed, while 2240 (31.5 percent) were enrolled in vocational training or hospitalized. The remaining 3,234 had found jobs, many of which proved to be low-paying, unskilled positions.[75] Those who could not find work had to resort to drastic measures to survive. In 1920, the Halifax YMCA reported that many returned soldiers came to its office on a daily basis looking for work. These men had begun to saturate the job market to such an extent that, when a job advertisement did appear, dozens of them applied. In some cases their wives had to work in order to pay the family's bills. According to YMCA social secretary H.G. Pope, something would have to be done for these men before the arrival of winter; otherwise, their suffering would worsen.[76] As a result of these conditions, many ex-soldiers in Halifax and across Canada grew dissatisfied with the poor treatment that they were receiving, especially in light of their wartime sacrifices. In Halifax at least, this dissatisfaction quickly reached the point of overt discontent and hostility. The riots were the ultimate expression of this discontent. However, other forms of criminal activity involving returned soldiers soon came to the public's attention.

Robbery was one of the more common crimes that soldiers committed. In August 1918, the police captured two unidentified returned servicemen after they had beaten and robbed three people in one evening. A few weeks later, John O'Connor was indicted for stealing fifty dollars. Then, in April 1920, the police uncovered a series of thefts from the Department of Soldiers' Civil Re-Establishment. They arrested two former soldiers, Harry Umiah and Charles Doyle, for these acts.[77] The poverty that plagued some former soldiers had reduced them to charity cases, while forcing a few to commit crimes to support themselves and their families. The difficulty some ex-soldiers had in returning to civilian life seemingly precipitated their crimes. The police seized George Shrum in December 1919 as he left the Victoria General Hospital, where he had been recovering from a self-inflicted gunshot wound, and charged him with the attempted murder of his wife. As the couple had been out on a leisurely walk on the night of 13 October 1919, Shrum had suddenly hauled out a revolver and shot his wife in the head and then shot himself in the arm. Shrum and his wife had been married for seventeen years and they had six children. When he came home from overseas service, Shrum discovered that his wife had given birth to another child, which he denied fathering. When Shrum heard the "talk" among his neighbours, he asked his wife to leave the house, which she did. He then met with her on the night in question under the pretence of seeking a reconciliation.[78] Shrum pleaded not guilty to the charge, and with the aid of an astute defence lawyer, John J. Power (K.C.), he was acquitted of attempted murder. Power argued that Shrum's wife, a "paramour" who wanted to rid herself of her husband and be with the father of her new-born baby, was to blame for the shooting. While the court agreed with most of the defence counsel's arguments, it still convicted Shrum of inflicting grievous bodily harm upon his wife.[79]

Halifax's returned soldiers seemed to break the law somewhat reluctantly. The difficulties of adjusting to life as a civilian in a modern city, combined with the unexpected hardships of unemployment and familial problems, drove some to acts of desperation.[80] This is not to excuse their actions but only to contextualize the incidence of crime among this group of people who, no less "criminal" than Spanish Harry, seemed to fall beyond the boundaries of Halifax's imagined criminal class. In response to their illegal activities, Halifax's machinery of order did not dwell upon the need for criminal rehabilitation. Most criminals, according to much contemporary thinking, stood little chance of changing their ways. Thus, there seemed to be little need, or will, to invest time and money in implementing "modern" ideas and procedures to reform them.

Halifax's "Juvenile Delinquent Class"

There was, however, one exception to this pessimistic rule of acceptance: juvenile delinquency. Juvenile delinquents evoked a reformative response from Canada's criminal justice system. In certain respects, delinquents posed a more critical problem for the maintenance of law and order then did adult criminals. In the minds of some, criminal tendencies started with the young. To prevent the spread of juvenile crime, progressives believed, would be to stem the tide of adult criminality. Across Canada and the United States, late nineteenth- and early twentieth-century progressives looked to poverty and inadequate parental care as the primary causes of delinquency. In conjunction with the state, these "child savers" instituted a host of measures, including child labour laws, compulsory school attendance, and training for mothers in the proper care of their children, designed to improve the lives of the nation's youth.[81] All of these initiatives implied a new degree of state regulation over the lives of mainly poor, working-class children and their families. The "invention" of juvenile delinquency to cope with the legal dimensions of children who broke the law extended this regulation. By passing laws to prevent crime and render the administration of justice more efficient, the state criminalized much of the behaviour characteristic of poor urban youth. As a result, juvenile delinquency was "legislated into existence," imposing a strategy of power, or a "morality of domination," upon children and their families.[82]

The Juvenile Delinquents Act, 1908, entrenched a new category of crime in twentieth-century Canada. This act, which also mandated the creation of juvenile courts in each province, provided a blueprint for the treatment of delinquents – one that envisioned them as distinct from adult offenders and as people who should receive care and training rather than harsh punishment. As the act states: "the care and custody and discipline of a juvenile delinquent shall approximate as nearly as may be that which should be given by its parents and that as far as practicable every juvenile delinquent shall be treated, not as a criminal, but as a mis-directed, misguided child and one needing aid, encouragement, help and assistance."[83] The goal of proponents of child welfare was the defence of society. They wanted to ensure that children would not grow up to become paupers, drunkards, or criminals. By so doing, they hoped to improve not only their world but also the world that their children would inherit. For those children who did come into contact with the law, the Juvenile Delinquents Act, with its emphasis on the rehabilitation of the child in a family-like environment, provided what many felt would be the best remedy for "problem children."[84]

The act also signalled the emergence of a new conception of the "child" in child welfare and criminal justice discourse. As Deborah Gorham argues, "the development of the idea of childhood was a feature of the rise of modern society."[85] The Juvenile Delinquents Act recognized a degree of legal autonomy for children as separate from adults. As one contemporary legal scholar in 1924 said of the act's outlook towards children: "children are children even when they break the law, and should be treated as such, and not as adult criminals. [A] child ... should be held incapable of committing a crime strictly so called." Children, in other words, practised their own brand of criminality. In the matter of rehabilitation and detention, the act's decree that "no child ... shall be held in confinement in any county or other jail or other place in which adults are or may be imprisoned, but shall be detained in a detention home or shelter used exclusively for children," gave legal sanction to the distinct needs of children. By defining a "child" as a boy or girl under the age of sixteen, the act acknowledged that these early childhood years marked a particular stage in a person's development. These years were a window of opportunity for the criminal justice system to steer delinquents away from a life of crime.[86] To achieve this end, juvenile justice officials relied upon a two-tiered institutional structure. The juvenile court owed its creation to modern notions of judicial practice that emphasized dealing with juveniles as separate from adult offenders. Reformatories were seen as part of a progressive initiative to reform delinquents, and they placed a nineteenth-century emphasis on denominational and gender segregation. In this sense, the state and reformatories continued to serve as moral guardians for children.

In spite of the reform impetus of the Juvenile Delinquents Act and its modern ideas about delinquency and the child, it never eliminated juvenile crime. The struggle Halifax's juvenile justice system waged with delinquent crime in the years from 1918 to 1935 underscores this fact. A comment made in 1912, one year after the opening of the Halifax Juvenile Court, indicates what progressives were up against in the battle against juvenile delinquency. Bryce Stewart, who in that year had conducted a preliminary social survey of the city, remarked: "Much of our juvenile delinquency can be traced to community apathy with regard to such matters as the employment of children in street trades, the sale of trashy literature, the presence of children upon the streets at night, lack of training in sex hygiene, and failure to provide recreational facilities. The number of older persons contributing to juvenile delinquency in Halifax is quite alarming."[87] From this collection of social ills sprang what P.F. Moriarty, a member of the Halifax Prisoners' Welfare Association, called the "juvenile delinquent class."[88] Halifax's chief of police made similar references to juvenile delinquents. In his 1921-22 annual report, Frank Hanrahan found juvenile crime to be a "difficult problem to handle at the present time," especially with regards to break-and-enters in homes and stores throughout Halifax. "Every effort," Hanrahan assured his superiors, "has been made by this Department to control criminals of this class and age";

nonetheless, a number of boys and girls had appeared before the juvenile court during the past year. "It would seem necessary therefore," Hanrahan continued, "that some system be devised whereby youths of this class could be given more personal attention and more earnest efforts made by the Government to redeem such youths before they have been able definitely to enter upon a career of crime."[89]

Halifax's juvenile justice system pursued this goal with mixed results. Between 1930 and 1935, for example, the Halifax Juvenile Court handled an average of 140 cases annually. In half of these cases (50.3 percent), the court convicted the offenders, while 42.2 percent of the cases were adjourned and the remaining 7.5 percent dismissed (Appendix 2, Table A2.20). Punishments often ranged from a sentence in a reformatory to probation and possibly a fine. However, these sanctions were meant to keep children out of jails and provide them with proper guidance to escape a life of depravity and criminality. The high percentage of adjournments is open to interpretation. It does seem to indicate that the juvenile court did not function as efficiently as local officials had hoped it would. As well, the court may have been forced to adjourn cases because of the inability of the police to gather sufficient evidence against the accused. In addition, adjournments may have allowed the court time to probe the backgrounds of both the children and their parents to strengthen the case against them and/or to determine a suitable sentence or an alternative course of action. The state, in other words, tried to monitor the lives of some parents and their children beyond the scope of the courtroom.[90] The sex composition of the juvenile delinquent class in Halifax mirrored that of known adult criminals. Boys far outnumbered girls in the crimes reportedly committed by juveniles. From 1930 to 1935, 90.6 percent of the total number of delinquents who appeared before the juvenile court were boys (Table A2.20). Much like their older counterparts, juveniles engaged in a host of major and minor crimes. In 1922, for example, the Halifax Juvenile Court registered eighty-one convictions for major offences and fifty-nine for minor infractions. Theft and "house-breaking" comprised the bulk of the major offences, while the minor offences ranged from truancy, trespassing, and shouting in public to coasting on the street.[91] Although these minor offences were at times depicted as examples of boyhood exuberance, the fact that the law classified them as illegal attests to the state's desire to regulate the lives of mainly poor, working-class children.

This need for regulation and close supervision of children surfaced in particular around the question of truancy. In the words of Juvenile Court judge Hunt: "[truant children] soon become delinquent and delinquents often become criminals." Thus every effort had to be made, Hunt asserted in 1920, "to fasten on the minds of our boys the advantages of a clean life and high ideals."[92] Included among these "high ideals" was the importance of staying in school. Yet convincing every school-aged child in Halifax of the virtues of attending school on a regular basis proved to be an impossible task.[93] The truant officer's annual reports document the never-ending war he and the juvenile court waged against children who failed to go to class. The figures for the number of children apprehended for truancy fluctuated from a high of 301 in 1919 to a low of 40 in 1924. Overall, for the years 1918 to 1935, an average of 121 children were reported annually for truancy.[94] According to government officials, the truancy law in Halifax was "carried out very efficiently." "Persistent" or "habitual" truants were tried before the juvenile court and most were given a suspended sentence for their first offence, along with a card, which their teachers had to sign, indicating that they had attended class. Each child had to report to the truant officer every Saturday and show him his or her signed card, but if his/her truancy persisted, then the "truant" was committed to a reformatory.[95] Officials attributed truancy to poverty, "street trades," and lack of parental guidance. Truant Officer Anderson noted in 1921 that a "great many" children did not attend class, particularly during the winter, because they did not own adequate clothing and boots. The parents of these children, most of whom Anderson believed to be unemployed, could not afford to properly clothe their children and thus kept them at home. That same year, Anderson granted permits to fifty-one boys and fourteen girls, all over the age of fourteen, to leave school for part of the year to work to supplement their families' incomes. He repeated the practice the next year and then stopped, no doubt in response to pressure from juvenile justice officials to keep children in school.[96] This underlines the hardships some families endured during the early 1920s in Halifax.[97] It also raised doubts about the effectiveness of imposing fines upon parents as a way to combat truancy.

Family poverty meant that some children turned to the streets to earn a living. In 1923 the *Halifax Herald* declared that too many children could be seen begging on the city's streets. By giving to these children, the *Herald* claimed: "[People made it] very profitable for our younger citizens to become expert in lying and probably stealing ... Surely conditions are not so bad in Halifax that our babies are forced to beg! ... There can be no doubt that by encouraging these children ... we are giving them the very worst training for good citizenship."[98] Selling newspapers in downtown Halifax also kept children away from school. According to Judge Blois (who succeeded Judge Hunt upon his death in 1925), newspaper selling tended to be the most common cause of truancy. One twelve-year-old boy sold papers before and after school and then worked in a bowling alley until midnight. He eventually came before the juvenile court for neglecting his school work. "Such boys [in] street trades," decried Judge Hunt, are "exposed to undue temptation, their work interferes with their school studies and they are brought into contact with undesirable adults at an age when they are not able to withstand such evil influences."[99] As was the case in other cities, officials in Halifax felt that boys who worked in, or roamed, the streets were often the unsuspecting victims of "bad company" who usually led them astray.[100]

To overcome the dilemma of truancy and its concomitant ills, judicial and state officials called for the punishment of parents and the strict supervision of children. In 1919, and again in 1922, the court summoned a number of parents to explain why they had allowed their children to remain at home. Most could not provide the court with a satisfactory answer and were thus handed fines of five and ten dollars.[101] Some parents told the court that they did not have the money to purchase new clothes and boots for their children to wear, but sometimes judges expressed little sympathy for their plight. In one case, a woman could only send her son to school after she had borrowed a pair of boots for him to wear. She was fined five dollars for allowing her son to loiter on the streets during school hours; however, the boy did not have to attend classes until he received a new pair of boots.[102] In addition to punishing parents to help prevent truancy, the city also tried to closely monitor the activities of children; specifically, section 927 of the Compulsory Attendance at School Act gave a truant officer the power to arrest, without warrant, any "truant or absentee child found wandering about the streets, or other places of resort."[103] Halifax City Council, as well, took aim at "street trades" involving children after receiving numerous complaints about minors selling newspapers in downtown Halifax. In January 1932, council drafted a set of amendments to Ordinance 21, Petty Trades, designed to keep children off the streets. They read, in part: "No newspaper shall be sold on any street of the City ... by any person under the age of twelve years after the hour of eight o'clock in the evening."[104] Similar restrictions were put in place in some American cities. By 1915, thirty states had outlawed boys' selling newspapers and engaging in other street trades.[105] Reformers and the juvenile justice system in Halifax seemed determined not only to eliminate truancy but also to ensure, by limiting their activities on city streets, that children did not succumb to the temptations of immorality and crime.

But their efforts did not always prove successful. The outbreak of more serious crimes among the city's youth sparked fears of successive juvenile crime waves. In May 1923, the police commented on the exceptional number of juvenile misdemeanours occurring in the city. The police spent much of their time answering complaints from irate citizens about their lawns being torn up, flower pots destroyed, and windows broken. The *Herald* attributed some of this vandalism to the arrival of spring, when youthful spirits, pent up during the winter, sought release: "Parents who desire to protect either the morals or safety of their children, will do well to see that they are not allowed to play or roam promiscuously about the streets."[106] It seemed to many residents that juvenile crime, from breaking windows to theft, had not subsided in Halifax. In sentencing two fifteen-year-old boys to indefinite periods in a reformatory, Juvenile Court Judge Hunt characterized them as two of the most desperate young criminals he had ever dealt with during his career on the bench. The boys reportedly had taken great delight in telling the court of the several robberies they had staged. Had they not been apprehended, the *Morning Chronicle* insisted, their spree of crime would have continued unabated.[107] Within a twenty-four-hour time span in September 1924, the police brought an "unprecedented" number of young boys, some under the age of ten, to the police station for questioning in relation to various unsolved crimes in the city. Two brothers admitted to stealing two dollars from a hardware store and two mouth-organs from a bookstore. Another boy, arrested for nabbing a woman's purse, received a two-year sentence in the Halifax Industrial School. In light of this criminal activity, Halifax, in the words of the *Herald*, was "in the midst of a juvenile crime wave."[108]

This juvenile crime wave resulted in a vigorous debate regarding the best course of action to take in order to solve the problem of juvenile delinquency in Halifax. As a means of addressing this crime wave, some reformers and criminal justice officials turned to modern arguments and schemes for dealing with wayward children. But, at the same time, they also stressed the loss of such traditional values as religious faith and biblical teachings as a factor in the perceived proliferation of juvenile delinquency. Most agreed on a distinct set of origins for juvenile delinquency: "1) Complete lack of parental control and discipline. 2) Neglect which is the result of extreme poverty, obliging both father and mother to go out to work and leave the children all day to do as they like. 3) Poor and squalid living in the streets with their evil lures[, and] 4) Lack of Religious Training."[109] The vital importance of children to society, Judge Hunt insisted, meant that if parents could not care for them then the community and the state had a responsibility to do so. Following from this, Hunt favoured the construction of supervised playgrounds as the "best means of keeping down juvenile delinquencies" and the opening of a juvenile library as a "powerful factor in promoting their welfare."[110] The *Halifax Herald*, while endorsing this general assessment of the causes of juvenile delinquency, laid much of the blame on parents. The *Herald* attributed the "lamentable looseness in the behaviour of an increasing number of young people" to the "inefficiency of home training." It continued: "Parental authority has become very much weakened. Children are allowed to ramble about the streets day and night. If they have any inclination to mischief they are likely to find congenial companions, and the steps from stealing fruit ... and other not very serious offences to house-breaking are easily made." The *Herald* concluded that the large number of people near the age of twenty in Canadian penitentiaries was "evidence of the rapid progress which youngsters [could] make in crime."[111] The *Herald*'s belief that children would grow up to be criminals if something was not done to guarantee their wholesome upbringing was shared by many within Canada's juvenile justice system.[112]

This environmental view of juvenile delinquency found favour among other social activists. For former Juvenile Court Judge Wallace, "juvenile delinquents [were] not born, but made." Delinquency could be traced, he stressed, to "defective home conditions involving ... shameful carelessness or moral obtuseness of a parent." Many child welfare advocates, guided as they were by Christian principles and some of whom had embraced the social gospel ethos of improving peoples' spiritual and material lives, argued that city life seduced young people into crime and immoral behaviour. In Wallace's opinion, only religious instruction could guarantee the proper development of a child, for without "training of the will ... to direct the will towards good, and away from evil, then the education of the [child would be] a failure."[113] While not all of the suggestions for stemming juvenile crime and reforming youthful offenders came to fruition in Halifax, leniency rather than corporal punishment did become a common element of judicial practice. A 1934 editorial summed up this situation: "It has been noted with much satisfaction that there is a growing tendency among our [juvenile court] judges ... to be lenient with youthful first offenders, and that the brand of a conviction or sentence is not to be lightly imposed ... We think in many cases, perhaps in most cases, that this treatment will have better effect than a sentence, or even a remand."[114] Children who were "neglected" or "delinquent" could be and deserved to be reformed and to have their lives renewed for their sake and for the advancement of society. This was the view held by many middle-class social reformers and courts in Halifax, and it had a practical impact on the actual treatment of delinquents.

Conclusion

Halifax's criminal class constantly challenged the city's social order and self-perception. As John C. Schneider explains for nineteenth-century Detroit, the significance of crime lies not just in its incidence but also in such considerations as its locations and its targets.[115] The looting of City Hall by a "mob," the murder of a police officer, and the constant presence of men like Spanish Harry and his ilk outraged many people in Halifax and stiffened their resolve to combat crime within their city. In the process, they constructed various images of the criminal, from the "thug" and "desperado" to the "miscreant." These men had to be dealt with to the fullest extent of the law, so many believed, if Halifax were to retain its aura of law and order. Moreover, crime had to be kept away from the city's respectable areas. To allow criminals the opportunity to commit their deeds in middle-class neighbourhoods and the business district would, it was thought, alter the very fabric of social life in Halifax. Hence the public anger and panic surrounding the riots of 1918 and 1919 and concerning the apparent spread of crime generally.

In the minds of citizens and law enforcement officials alike, at least two types of criminals existed in Halifax. Men such as Lewis Bevis formed the most dangerous element of the criminal class. They lived a life of crime from their youth and would stop at nothing to continue their criminal ways and avoid capture. But Bevis also reveals the contradiction in residents' attitudes towards criminals and the existence of a criminal class. The inability of the first jury to convict him underscores the reluctance of some people to see veterans as hardened criminals and to condemn an accused to death. Yet, ultimately, the image of Bevis as a "desperado," and thus as a member of some criminal class, sealed his fate. On another level were men such as Spanish Harry, who made a career of committing minor crimes. They revealed to contemporaries that crime could supposedly be traced to a particular group of undesirables. Returned soldiers, however, complicated this idea of a distinct criminal class. While they did not prove to be a ubiquitous source of crime in Halifax, their brushes with the law highlight how some individuals chose crime as a response to the poverty and social turmoil that gripped the city. Since most Halifax residents did not regard former servicemen who broke the law either as "miscreants" who had brought chaos to their city or as members of the criminal class, they were confronted with the dilemma of determining the boundary between "hardened criminals" and the "ordinary citizen." One thing, however, did remain certain. The criminal justice system and those citizens most concerned with law and order believed that the Lewis Bevises and the Spanish Harrys were beyond any hope of reform. Once they had chosen the path of crime, little could be done to turn them around. As a result, Halifax's machinery of order did little more than arrest, prosecute, and, where applicable, imprison the city's criminal element in the name of justice and social order.

Juvenile delinquents were another matter. This was the one law-and-order issue around which a progressive consensus seemingly prevailed. Crime among adults, many believed, originated in their childhood years. Thus, preventing juvenile delinquents from becoming professional criminals would deal a decisive blow against the proliferation of crime in the city. Making sure children stayed in school by attacking truancy and passing laws designed to regulate children's public lives was one plank in Halifax's reform platform for juvenile delinquents. The juvenile court also served as the conduit for the administration of delinquents. By sentencing children to local reformatories, giving them a reprimand, or placing them on probation, the juvenile court and its judges acted as a paternalistic overseer of Halifax's wayward children.[116] The importance of children to the future development of the nation also prompted the move in Halifax to suggest ways of reforming delinquents, the hope being to put a stop to juvenile crime and to turn young criminals into productive members of society. The city's attitude towards the juvenile delinquent class, and the children who belonged to it, often through no fault of their own, does suggest a sense of optimism about the redeemable nature of some criminals in interwar Halifax. This approach to the problem of juvenile delinquency was a clear indication that Halifax had embraced most facets of Canada's modern juvenile justice system. It also underscores the fact that Halifax was at the forefront, along with other Canadian cities in the interwar period, of efforts to regulate and criminalize the lives of primarily poor, working-class children and their families.

CHAPTER 5

Women, Crime, and the Law

MARIE THIBEAULT, A "pretty" twenty-one-year-old waitress, worked the late shift at the Radio Cafe on Sackville Street. On 28 September 1932, she left the restaurant shortly after midnight and headed home. As she walked along Grafton Street in the midst of a heavy rain storm, she was violently attacked. Acting upon a tip, the police discovered her body huddled against a garage. They took her to the police station, but when she failed to regain consciousness they rushed her to the Victoria General Hospital. The doctors, however, could do little to save Thibeault. She died soon after her arrival as a result of a fractured skull and brain haemorrhage. Speaking to reporters afterwards, Chief Inspector Fox said of Thibeault's death that "it look[ed] very much like foul play."[1] Marie Thibeault's murder sent shock waves through the City of Halifax. The brutality of the crime stood as a grim reminder to citizens of the dangers some Halifax women faced. While the police remained baffled as to the cause of her death, one newspaper wondered whether Thibeault had been "slain by a shadowy midnight assassin?" Eventually the police concluded that someone had bludgeoned Thibeault to death, but the murderer was never found.[2] The public horror that greeted Thibeault's killing also reveals some of the societal attitudes towards crime and women in Halifax. Thibeault's demise represented another scar that crime had left upon the city. The *Halifax Mail* called the Thibeault case "one of the most puzzling and baffling mysteries Halifax ha[d] experienced in several years."[3] This statement highlights the feeling of dread many people experienced with regard to crime. In a modern city of order, it was thought, women and children should not be exposed to random acts of violence. When such incidents occurred, the press shrouded them in a cloak of mystery, partly due to their unexplainable nature and, perhaps more important, partly because many people in Halifax had trouble accepting the fact that murder and crime existed in their city.

Citizens' concern over crime also translated into worry about young women. Marie Thibeault was single and worked outside of the home. She and her counterparts in Halifax, and across Canada, symbolized something new, or modern, in society: women who exerted a measure of socio-economic independence. In Toronto, as Carolyn Strange shows, single women who performed non-domestic waged work and lived away from home "captured Torontonians' ambivalence about the social and moral consequences of industrialization and urbanization."[4] Working "girls" in Halifax, and elsewhere, also signified the perils of modern city life in that they were considered to be both the victims and the sources of crime and immorality. This, in turn, bred public suspicion of these women. One of the first things the police did in their investigation into Marie Thibeault's death was to examine her personal background. "We have checked on the girl," detectives informed the media, and "she seems to have been straight, honest and reliable, with a good character."[5] The police could now rule out the possibility that the attack had been motivated by lust or jealousy. In other words, Thibeault could not be held responsible for her own death. Of course, these specific comments underlined the general sense of women as authors of their own misfortune, whether as victims or as perpetrators.

In addition to being victims of crime, women in Halifax broke the law in a number of ways. One of the most commonly reported crimes committed by women was shoplifting. The "genus" shoplifter usually surfaced during the Christmas season. According to one account from December 1922, shoplifters reaped a rich harvest from numerous stores across the city. Concealed by the hustle and bustle of the holiday crowds, shoplifters made off with everything from knick-knacks to expensive dresses. Women, it was argued, shoplifted because "the female of the species ha[d] always proved a particular adept in this kind of enterprise."[6] Women committed only a small portion of the known crimes in Halifax from 1918 to 1935. Using the years 1917 to 1922 as a representative sample demonstrates this point. The annual reports of the Halifax Police Department provide a first-hand account of the incidence of crime in this city. During this five-year time span (which ran from 1 May 1917 to 30 April 1922), the police apprehended approximately 150 women per year for an assortment of crimes. This amounted to an average of 7.6 percent of the total number of offenders for these years. Men, on the other hand, represented an average of 92.4 percent, or 2,233 arrests per year, for these same five years (Appendix 2, Tables A2.18 and A2.19). Prison statistics for a later period attest to the continuity of this trend. Among the 5,241 committals to the Halifax City Prison from 1929 to 1936, only 325, or 6.2 percent, were women. Figures for women committed to the Halifax County Jail are comparable: 244 and 4.8 percent.[7] In both institutions, which absorbed the bulk of those sentenced to jail by the city's courts, men comprised the majority of the prison population. The apparently low rate of crime among women in early twentieth-century Halifax remains consistent with patterns across Canada and in eighteenth- and nineteenth-century Halifax.[8] Men, not women, did most of the known law-breaking in Nova Scotia's capital.

Nonetheless, whether murdered on the street or stealing from a department store, women in Halifax could be found on both ends of the spectrum of crime. As the victims of crime, specifically murder, sexual and physical assault, and robbery, women found interwar Halifax a dangerous world. In this light, little had apparently changed from eighteenth-century Halifax, described by Jim Phillips as "a very dangerous place for women, a society in which they were victimized by male violence at a high rate."[9] As the perpetrators of crime, women found themselves at the mercy of a society and a justice system determined to preserve law and order. The fact that they were women, those considered the least likely to break the law, only compounded the problem for all concerned. Women's encounters with the law in Halifax underscored the socio-economic inequalities they endured, and, in the crimes that women committed, a subtle response to their subordination may be detected.[10] Moreover, the struggle some women waged for social power may be gleaned from their attempts to use the criminal justice system to their own advantage. By examining the interaction between women, crime, and the law in Halifax from 1918 to 1935, I show the experiences of women as criminals, victims, and plaintiffs. In so doing, I reveal how gender structured the response of the police and the courts towards female criminality and women generally.

"Men Commit Crimes, Women Commit Sins": Images of the Female Criminal

Respectable women, many Nova Scotians (and, indeed, Canadians) felt, did not pursue criminal activity of any sort. Only men, it was believed, could be inherently criminal. Prescribed gender roles for women lent credence to the perception of women as generally sinless. In her study of a working-class suburb in Halifax during the 1920s, Suzanne Morton chronicles how most women bore the responsibility of being good wives, mothers, and daughters. By strictly adhering to these roles, women could cultivate social and community respectability.[11] This sense of respectability, combined with the infrequency of women's being arrested for crime, reinforced the feeling that women, for the most part, posed no threat to law and order. Yet this conclusion had a paradoxical implication: once she had abandoned (and usually not deliberately) her "respectability," a woman was, in the eyes of a patriarchal society, truly lost. Although it took a woman years to earn a respectable image, it could be relinquished by one "unfeminine or unrespectable" deed.[12] This could assume numerous forms: frequenting disreputable cafes and dance halls, neglecting one's children, or being placed under arrest. The ethnic or racial identity of women also complicated the process of attaining respectability. Black women especially fought a never-ending and often unsuccessful battle for equality and respectability in Halifax.[13] In addition, as soon as a woman ran into trouble with the law, she stood little chance of escaping the stigma of being a criminal. Thus, the police and magistrates in Halifax considered certain women to be a possible source of criminality. In their minds, men committed crime but women committed sins, which meant that specific women, those who challenged established social and moral values, could be "bad."[14]

Women had a strong numerical presence in Halifax. In 1921 and 1931, women comprised close to 52 percent of the city's population.[15] This prevalence of women resulted from the deaths of many of their husbands, fathers, and brothers during the war and the out-migration of males in the interwar period.[16] Women in Halifax began to live a more public life in the 1920s – specifically, greater numbers of women started to work outside the home. Over the course of the 1920s, the percentage of women in Halifax's paid labour force increased from 25.5 percent in 1921 to 26.9 percent by 1931. Although small, this increase nevertheless points to the growing public presence of women.[17] Modernity provided the opportunities for women to enter the labour market. The "clerical sector" in particular (stenographers, secretaries, and telephone/telegraphic operators), opened up new avenues for women. Further, as regional and national retail outlets such as Eaton's expanded into Halifax, women began to work as clerks selling clothing and consumer goods. Attracted by the chance to earn money and its accompanying "independence," young women from rural Nova Scotia moved to small towns and to cities such as Halifax to work and live unattached from their families. This new trend in early twentieth-century Nova Scotia made women an increasingly important, although underpaid, part of the province's economy.[18] By labouring beyond the confines of the home, women became more visible in Halifax. In stores, restaurants, and laundries, women were recognized publicly for the jobs that they had traditionally performed in the family home. This visibility created problems for women with regard to attitudes towards female crime and their personal safety. The slightest criminal and/or moral transgression elicited a quick response from the forces of law and order; and, in the course of living their public lives, women (like Marie Thibeault) exposed themselves to the dangers of Halifax's streets. Women, therefore, lived under the threat and the reality of violence both inside and outside of the home.[19]

"Women's Crimes": Shoplifting and Vagrancy

Women in Halifax resorted to crime partly out of economic necessity. Poor wages, job insecurity, and the need to support a family, sometimes without the aid of a male breadwinner, made life a daily struggle for many women. The city's dismal economy only made matters worse. In 1933, the Welfare Council of Halifax-Dartmouth, after surveying 508 unemployed women, reported that older women especially were "on the verge of starvation." Some lived with aging parents, while others found it difficult to pay their rent.[20] Delegates attending a general meeting of the Women's Federal Labour Union in Halifax heard similar findings. "Girls," reports declared, could not locate a room for under three dollars, and wages for women fluctuated and did not keep pace with the cost of living. Waitresses earned from five to seven dollars a week, while some factory employees made seven dollars. School girls who worked on the weekends in department stores took home a scant $1.60 per day.[21] This resulted in many women, both young and old, searching for alternative ways to make ends meet.

Before the emergence of the welfare state, working-class women in Halifax often used their homes to generate an income. Older women and widows converted their homes into boarding houses or rented a room out to a boarder. Married women with children would care for their neighbours' youngsters if their mothers worked, engaged in dressmaking, or ran small-scale grocery and confectionary stores from their homes.[22] Besides these legal pursuits, some women turned to illegal methods to either support themselves or supplement their families' income. The covert sale of alcohol from their homes or flats proved that crime formed part of some women's underground economy. In April 1920, the police caught two women serving a bottle of rum to a group of men at 77 Brunswick Street. Annie O'Brien received a $200 fine following her conviction for selling liquor. In March 1933, Edith Bevis was arrested on a warrant charging her with keeping liquor for sale. Bevis's capture came amid the police department's efforts to clean up the city's liquor "dives."[23]

Shoplifting from Eaton's, Halifax's largest retail store, was one way some women obtained household and personal items for themselves and their families. A few women even stockpiled this merchandise, possibly for resale in the city's underground economy. In 1929, the police apprehended two women for stealing a quantity of ladies' garments valued at over $100. A plain-clothes officer discovered the stolen goods after he searched the home of a Mrs. James. Her colleague, Estella McKenzie, was also taken into custody.[24] In Canada and the United States, shoplifting heralded the rise of consumerism. Consumerism targeted women and was centred primarily around the department store. In this environment, the department store emerged as a "site ... of pleasure and social life" and a new social space for women. By the early part of the twentieth century, shopping had become a major part of most women's lives. With the growth of a national market in the 1920s and the expansion of Eaton's and other retail chains, a "culture of consumption" had secured its grip on Canada.[25] The female shoplifter exposed to public view the moral crisis caused by this modern consumer revolution. In most cities, including Halifax, many people regarded female shoplifters as "irresponsible, more childlike than adult, unable to resist monetary temptation and ready to succumb to the 'lust of possession.'" These women were either middle class and "respectable" (stealing to attain the material trappings of their social position) or poor and working class (turning to shoplifting as a "budget-stretching device"). Moreover, shoplifting was often depicted in newspapers in Halifax and elsewhere as "quintessentially feminine."[26] And the courts showed such women little leniency. In September 1931, policewoman May Virtue looked on as two women who had shoplifted from Eaton's answered for their crime. Sarah Hart (age seventy-three) and Lena Larder each received a one-year suspended sentence. Two years later, in October 1933, a woman under Virtue's supervision went to jail for one week on the same charge.[27] To halt such thefts Eaton's hired a "lady detective," a practice that was followed by other department stores and that denoted a "recognition and acceptance of the fact that many customers could not be trusted."[28]

Poverty also worked in tandem with the law to create female lawbreakers. Vagrancy laws, as Joan Sangster points out, could be used by the police and magistrates to address the problem of women who transgressed their roles as respectable and orderly citizens.[29] In essence, the criminal justice system in Halifax relied on the multiple definitions of vagrancy in the Criminal Code to regulate female morality. The paternalistic nature of the city's courts can also be seen in the prosecutions for vagrancy. According to B. Jane Price, in the second half of the nineteenth century, Halifax's legal system operated more on the basis of paternalism than proceduralism. This meant that magistrates handled offences according to a woman's actions and, hence, moral character rather than paying strict attention to the actual law that had been broken.[30] This practice also predominated in the early decades of the twentieth century as Halifax's machinery of order attempted to curb women's immoral activities and keep the destitute among them off the streets. In this way, the Halifax police maintained a constant lookout for women who roamed the city. Dressing improperly and associating with the wrong crowd landed two young women in police court on a charge of vagrancy. The fact that both were "nattily" attired, replete with military riding breeches, which displayed a "much greater amount of silk hosiery than is customarily shown by the female sex," brought them to the authorities' attention. Inspector McIsaac believed that the women were "street-walkers" who lacked a legitimate means of support. Being unable to provide a satisfactory account of their actions, the women were arrested by McIsaac. Both "girls," McIsaac claimed, had bad reputations, being drunkards and frequenters of Chinese cafes.[31] In the eyes of the law, these women, remanded into custody by Magistrate Archibald, epitomized the 1924 Criminal Code definition of vagrancy: "loose, idle or disorderly person[s]."[32]

Generally, women of "bad character," and those without steady employment, became classified as vagrants. Ada Casey, seventeen, received six months in the City Prison for vagrancy. Policewoman Bessie Egan told the court that Casey had spent most of her youth either in reformatories or houses of ill-fame.[33] Female drifters also caught the eye of the police. In 1925, Kathleen Grove and Henrietta Ripley were arrested following several complaints to the police about a number of young women seen sleeping in the Public Gardens. Grove went to jail for six months and Ripley for three.[34] A year later, Mary and Edith Wamboldt, who for weeks had wandered aimlessly about the city without a place to live, spent two years in the Maritime Home for Girls as a result of their vagrancy. As Amanda Glasbeek demonstrates in her study of the Toronto Women's Court, arresting women for vagrancy indicates that the criminal justice system engaged in a "direct contest over their very presence in public places."[35] Vagrancy laws allowed Halifax's female police officers to serve as surrogate parents to wayward "girls." May Virtue told Hilda Carmichael that if she did not find work, and if her mother complained about her misbehaviour again, she would have no choice but to charge her with vagrancy.[36] In other words, Virtue took it upon herself to ensure that if Hilda's mother could not control her young daughter, then she would take the necessary steps to do so. Thus, the criminal justice system attempted, however feebly, to restore the shattered remains of the contemporary family. Peggy McDonald and Edith Urquhart, both seventeen, were subjected to the court's paternalistic nature during their sentencing for vagrancy. The presiding magistrate turned Urquhart over to the custody of her mother and arranged for McDonald to be sent home to Sydney. The magistrate also warned Urquhart that, unless she changed her ways, he would put her in jail.[37]

The perception of female vagrants as outcasts held true for black women in trouble with the law, regardless of their crime. The majority of black women in Halifax were poor and confined to jobs in domestic service, laundry, and sewing. They also endured the dual burdens of racism and sexism, which effectively eliminated any hope they had of being recognized and treated as respectable members of the community. That a few of them broke the law only made matters worse.[38] The press, the criminal courts, and much of white society in Halifax depicted black women as quaint and unfeminine, further proof, in addition to their supposed criminality, of their "otherness." Similarly, the press often identified non-whites who had been arrested by their race: "dusky maidens," "colored ladies," or "negresses." This practice furthered the process of racializing criminality and criminals. In 1918, police officer MacAdam arrested two "negro" women, with "latent vaudeville talents," for creating a disturbance in a public place. Once he locked them in the "Ritz-Carleton" for women at the police station, they apparently entertained the policemen on duty with hymns and jazz songs.[39]

Halifax's "Girl Problem": Prostitution

For poor and desperate women in Halifax, prostitution was another potential source of income. Some chose to sell their sexual services of their own accord; others were forced to do so by their husbands or male partners. In either case, economic circumstances propelled many women into a life of prostitution.[40] From a statistical standpoint, prostitution does not appear to have been a major crime in Halifax. Using the available figures from the annual police reports, from 1917 to 1922 the department laid 159 prostitution-related charges. This amounted to 1.3 percent of the overall crimes recorded by the police department during this period.[41] While this percentage is small, it, like most criminal statistics, fails to take into account the number of prostitution offences that went unreported and undetected. Nor does it convey the frustration and opposition many in Halifax felt towards the existence of prostitutes and brothels in their city. Regardless of the statistics or the motives, prostitution was the most visible reminder to Halifax residents that women could and did commit crimes. Moreover, prostitution represented for many a breach of public morality as well as a threat to the family and social stability. In many ways, prostitution was the most painful and unavoidable blemish on the city of order. Hence the need to control it, for to do so, as Philippa Levine argues, "meant controlling women, because women, defined by their sexuality, threatened disorder and unruliness." As a result, prostitutes, despite whatever degree of agency they demonstrated, still "experienced ... acute marginality, powerlessness, exploitation and social isolation."[42]

Prostitutes and bawdy houses had long dotted the landscape of downtown Halifax. Most North American and European cities in the Victorian era possessed one or more notorious districts where prostitutes lived and plied their trade. To many contemporaries, prostitution was an urban menace, a "gritty" metaphor for the disorder and contagion of the city.[43] In mid- to late nineteenth-century Halifax, the downtown area bounded by Albemarle, Barrack, and City streets contained many of Halifax's "sins and sorrows." An 1862 pamphlet on the city's darker side of life described prostitution as the "woe-curse of Halifax." Young and old, black and white, mothers, sisters, and daughters, "fallen women" all, engaged in this "horrid commerce." Often within sight of the police station, churches, and schools, the prostitution trade, fuelled by the demands of the city's military presence, contributed to Halifax's vice.[44] In the 1920s and 1930s, little had changed when it came to the presence of prostitutes in the city. However, the nature of the trade did undergo a subtle transformation. After the turn of the century, prostitution in Halifax gradually became less oriented towards brothels and more oriented towards "street-walking."[45] These "street-walkers" proved to be a source of consternation for respectable Halifax society. The dawn of the twentieth century in Halifax witnessed the growth of a new intolerance of prostitution. Previously, this "vice" had been tacitly accepted by some as a necessary aspect of military and port life. The removal of the British garrison in 1906, which altered the tone of the "rough" streets, and the mounting pressure to reform Halifax along more progressive lines, meant that whatever tolerance for prostitution that had earlier existed largely evaporated. In its place, prostitution became, in the minds of many reformers, a significant modern moral and social crisis. To them, prostitutes defied both respectability and women's proper role as mother and nurturer.

Before the outbreak of the First World War, the Halifax Civic Reform League led the fight against prostitution. As Christmas festivities drew near in 1907, A.M. Bell, R.H. Murray, and P.F. Moriarty, accompanied by Reverend Donaldson and Reverend Aikens, all of whom were adherents of the social gospel, met with the mayor and demanded that he take action to rid Halifax of its "Houses of Ill-Repute." As one delegate said to the press: "Every adult knows that in Halifax we have what is variously known as 'the red light district' [and] 'the local tenderloin' ... Yet on they go. Why? Because of official acquiescence in the brazen defiance of the law." Publicity, the league thought, would guarantee that the mayor and the Police Commission would enforce the law and suppress these "dives."[46] Their complaints brought a quick response. The next day the chief of police notified the league that his department would do all it could to protect children from being corrupted by prostitution and would shut down as many "houses of ill-repute" as possible.[47] However, the battle to rid Halifax of prostitutes proved to be a protracted one indeed. In 1912, the *Evening Mail* bitterly remarked: "[The] vice district exists. It has been known to exist for years and has laughed at 'the reformers' for many years. Why should it not do so, with perfectly indifferent, utterly inert police commissions to act as 'buffers' between it and reform." The paper then added: "THE VICE DISTRICT ... IS IN THE HEART OF THE CITY[,] within a stone's throw of ... St. Mary's boys' and girls' school, St. Mary's cathedral ... and practically at the doors of respectable poor people whose poverty obliges them to live in some locality where they can get cheap rent."[48] A few of these "respectable poor" joined the anti-vice crusade. In a petition to city council, the "workingmen" of this district demanded that politicians take immediate action to "protect [their] families from these terrible influences which [were] daily growing."[49] Residents jammed the council chambers to hear civic politicians announce that "keepers" and "inmates" of "bawdy houses" would be told to cease their "nefarious traffic" at once or face the wrath of the law.[50] Judging by the postwar outrage over prostitution, however, the council's ultimatum did not produce the desired results.

A 1918 letter to the *Halifax Herald* written by W.L. Tuttle, a shoe retailer, continued the opposition against Halifax's "red light districts." Referring to the disruptive antics of a group of returned soldiers who had visited several of the city's brothels, Tuttle wondered: "Does this kind of business still have to be tolerated in a city of churches and reform associations?" "All decent citizens," he continued, "are looking to our mayor ... to root out this business for good." To do otherwise, Tuttle implied, would be to imperil the future of the "new Halifax."[51] The *Herald* joined Tuttle in denouncing prostitution. Calling it a "great ... social evil ... fraught with danger to the entire community welfare of this city," the *Herald* decried the failure of police authorities to alert citizens to the dangers posed by this menace. Whether residents realized it or not, declared the *Herald:* "[Prostitution] is rampant in this city, and a disease foul as leprosy and far more insidious than tuberculosis ... is permitted to stalk UNHINDERED in our midst. To tolerate it in so complacent a manner is a terrible wrong to our youth of both sexes. To raise no protest is shameful. To permit it to continue is shameful."[52]

The panic associated with prostitution also gave rise to anger over the "girl problem." Both issues symbolized the complexities and the fears of modern society. The young women who milled about Barrington and Gottingen streets in the evenings after work, the *Herald* believed, while not necessarily "bad," were "heedless, careless ... and ignorant of the harm they [were] doing [to] themselves." They lived in a world where all around them was the "careless gesture, the pert remark, and the silly giggle of the 'pick-up' ... the walk, the inviting dark doorway, and the 'date.'" Such a lifestyle, the paper argued, would mean that these women "[WOULD] LOSE THE ESSENTIAL QUALITIES OF WOMANLINESS THAT COMMAND EVERY MAN'S RESPECT. IN SOME CASES, THE GIRL [WOULD] GO DOWN AND OUT, AND THE END [WOULD] BE RUIN, SORROW AND MISERY."[53] Those men and a few women who ruled Halifax's "segregated colony of vice" would lure these unsuspecting women into prostitution.[54] The chances of this happening only seemed to multiply in the aftermath of the war. In the wake of the 1917 explosion, Halifax had a "large number of girls rendered practically homeless and thrown on their own responsibility." Knowledge of this fact, the ever sensationalist *Herald* predicted, "ha[d] probably convinced the 'procurers' for the 'white slavers' to look upon Halifax as a likely field for their nefarious practices." In light of this, the *Herald* issued a dire warning to its female readers: "Girls would be wise to be careful regarding strangers, both men and women, accept NO invitations and advancements made by persons unknown to you ... This is a very grave menace indeed. To fall into the clutches of these human vultures is a fate too terrible to contemplate."[55] Young women needed to be protected from this ever lurking, if rather over-embellished, danger.[56]

Halifax seemed determined to prevent women from becoming prostitutes. This proactive emphasis upon prevention broke somewhat with the nineteenth-century reactive tradition of rescuing "fallen women." Between 1854 and 1900, nine homes had appeared for women who had fallen prey to sin and corruption. Inspired by evangelical Christianity, these homes tried to "save" and reform deviant women.[57] The Refuge for Fallen Women, located in the heart of the "tenderloin district," had worked with the "most pitiable and wretched class of the population" until their "character and position were regained."[58] In the context of the city's new twentieth-century atmosphere of intolerance towards prostitution, such options for women dwindled. Similarly, the drive to halt the spread of prostitution meant that once a woman had chosen this practice there were few sympathizers who would help her out of her plight. A majority of social reformers across Canada scorned prostitutes. In 1922, Emily F. Murphy, an Edmonton police court magistrate, wrote: "[Prostitutes are] corrupting the manhood of the country ... Until we loose the strangle hold of the prostitute on our populace, we can never hope to make any marked progress in staying [the] abominable evils [of narcotics and social disease].[59] Yet such reformers signally failed to improve prostitutes' lives (if they intended to do so) by their inability to provide these women with real alternatives.[60] Without such alternatives, prostitutes would have little or no choice but to continue serving the sexual demands of men in order to make a living. Improved wages for female workers, so "ONE OUT OF WORK" argued, would drastically reduce the number of prostitutes in Halifax. Writing to the working-class Halifax *Citizen* in April 1927, this woman explained how she had applied for a kitchen job in a local restaurant. The position paid six dollars for a twelve-hour day, seven days a week. "Do you think that is a fair wage for anyone?" she asked: "We read in the daily papers about the police making a crusade against girls walking our streets at night. Perhaps some of those poor unfortunate girls were unable to work 84 hours a week for $6." Defiantly, she concluded: "GIVE THEM A CHANCE TO WORK AT A FAIR WAGE AND DECENT HOURS AND CONDITIONS AND NINETY PERCENT OF OUR NIGHT WALKERS WOULD DISAPPEAR."[61]

In Halifax the problem of dealing with the prostitution trade rested solely with the police and the criminal justice system. These institutions alone, however, could not provide a solution to the prostitution quagmire; instead, the status quo of exploitation and criminal prosecution prevailed. The Halifax Police Department and police court magistrates officially abhorred, yet unofficially accepted, prostitution. The police in particular did not possess the resources to stamp it out. The best that it could hope to do, it seemed, was to limit bawdy houses and street-walking to a clearly defined area of the city. By so doing, the police could launch periodic raids and make the necessary arrests and thus present the appearance of maintaining public order.[62] This meant that prostitutes, and not their customers, endured the burden of police crackdowns. The Criminal Code provisions for prostitution and "bawdy houses" made clamping down on these women easy. The broad definitions of these offences gave police officers a great deal of discretion when it came to laying charges. Section 225 of the 1924 Criminal Code defined a "common bawdy house" as a "house, room, set of rooms or place of any kind kept for purposes of prostitution, or for the practice of acts of indecency, or occupied or resorted to by one or more persons for such purposes." Along such streets as Lower and Upper Water, Gottingen, Granville, and Grafton, police officers could enter a number of homes on the presumption that they were being "kept for the purposes of prostitution." The Criminal Code described prostitution as an "act or practice of a woman offering and giving her body to promiscuous and indiscriminate sexual intercourse with men."[63] From a legal standpoint, the onus of guilt fell entirely on the woman. The law prohibiting vagrancy could also be used to define a woman as a prostitute. Vagrancy, as Tamara Myers has shown in the case of Montreal, provided an option for police officers to take suspected prostitutes into custody. If the police believed, but could not prove, that a woman was a prostitute, they could arrest her for vagrancy. Subsection (i) of section 238 states that everyone was a vagrant who, "being a common prostitute or night walker, wanders in the ... public streets or highways, lanes or places of public meeting or gathering of people, and does not give a satisfactory account of herself." Again, the assumption is that only a woman could commit this crime.[64]

Emma Major was one such woman. On the night of 18 September 1934, she allegedly approached plain-clothes officer Harry Langille and said, "How is everything going?" "All-right," Langille replied. She then asked, "Do you want to come to my room?" Langille wondered what for, and Major responded: "Cut your fooling; you know what for ... Do you want to get screwed?" Langille said yes, and the two went off together towards her room. On their way they passed the Three Ess Taxi office. Langille, knowing that the taxi stand had a phone, showed Major his "shield," placed her under arrest, and called for the patrol wagon to take her away.[65] Major pleaded not guilty to soliciting, and a trial ensued. The outcome of this case rested solely on Major's reputation and on whose version of events Magistrate Barnhill believed. Langille, who had been "detailed" to the vicinity of Hollis and Sackville streets (where women supposedly solicited), described Major as a "common prostitute" who had initiated the entire sequence of events. Defence Counsel G.R. Ramey (Esq.) countered that one solicitation was "not enough to warrant conviction and [did] not make a woman a prostitute." Major testified that Langille had spoken to her first and had demanded that she come with him. He "dragged [her] on the street and made [her] arms all black and blue," Major claimed in her own defence.[66] But Barnhill rejected Major's story and found that Langille had caught her in the act of soliciting "for the purpose of immoral intercourse with her in return for the payment of money therefor by him." "Finding, as I do," Barnhill concluded, "that the evidence of the Officer is to be believed in this matter, I think that the evidence amply justifies me in convicting the accused." He then sentenced her to one month in the Halifax City Prison.[67] The city's desire to curb prostitution, coupled with the fact that Major had been accused in 1925 of "unlawfully keep[ing] a disorderly house," no doubt placed her at a disadvantage and strongly influenced Barnhill's decision.[68]

As they had done in the past, and as they continued to do when they apprehended Emma Major, the Halifax police kept close tabs on the city's brothel district. Setting their sights on three alleged "disorderly houses," Chief Detective Kennedy and three officers apprehended six "ladies" for being "proprietresses" and inmates. Massile Morris, Blance Gavell, Lina

Leblanc, Lina Loy, Louise Devalle, and Gracienne Faugarait all went to the lockup that evening. However, two men found on the premises did not face any charges.[69] In the city's efforts to control prostitution, and in the eyes of the law, the men who paid for this service did not share the same burden of guilt as did the women themselves.[70] Occasionally, however, men did not escape the grasp of the law. The police charged Louis Cox, owner of the Temperance Hotel, for keeping a bawdy house. The charge came in the wake of the conviction of John Gallano, the hotel's manager, for violating the Nova Scotia Temperance Act and operating a bawdy house. Gallano opted for the three-month prison term rather than pay the $203.15 fine that the court had imposed. Even though Nora Westhaver and Christina McInnis testified against Gallano, they went to jail for two months as neither could pay the fifty-dollar fine for being inmates.[71]

Social, as well as criminal, implications followed in the wake of an arrest for prostitution. Violet Squires came to Halifax in June 1917 from Saint John's, Newfoundland. She arrived with a Mrs. Feeder, who took Squires to the home of Mamie Barrett (alias Mamie Wade) on Grafton Street. Barrett told Squires that, by staying in her house, she could earn more money than she could if she worked as a servant. The police eventually arrested Barrett for procuring Squires to have "unlawful carnal connection with men."[72] Justice Russell of the Supreme Court lashed out at Barrett, calling her procuring charge a "grave offence ... one of the darkest kind of crimes known to law." As a witness for the Crown, eighteen-year-old Squires explained to the court how she had received payment every night from different men and then gave a portion of it to Mamie Barrett. After working a few weeks for Barrett, Squires contracted a venereal disease, which rendered her, in the words of one doctor, "Damaged Goods." Squires had escaped from the Barrett home and found work as a domestic. But within a matter of days, the same doctor revealed to her employer "what sort of girl she was," resulting in her dismissal.[73] Newspapers, while supporting the police in their efforts to round up prostitutes, paid little attention to the difficulties endured by these women. The hardships faced by prostitutes in Halifax, and the socioeconomic conditions that forced many of them to practise this lifestyle, were ignored and thus left unresolved by those concerned with the problem.[74] As long as the police kept a close watch on prostitutes' activities, and the courts doled out the appropriate penalties, the hope was that this form of criminal activity, if it could not be eliminated, could at least be controlled.

"Illegal Operations" and "Concealment of Birth": Abortion and Infanticide

Abortion and infanticide proved to be equally vexing but less visible "women's crimes" for the law and Halifax society. Both, but especially abortion, gave women a degree of control over their sexuality, which many saw as a threat to the moral and social order. In the 1920s, when sexuality and the "erotic" began to be expressed more publicly through the medium of popular culture and consumerism, abortion raised some fundamental questions about the distribution of social power between men and women.[75] Ironically, when placed alongside such issues as prostitution and prohibition, abortion did not cause much concern for the social reform movement in Canada. Nor did a public campaign either for greater access to abortion or for its decriminalization emerge.[76] Much of this lack of organizational fervour had to do with the low incidence of reported abortions. Only when the mother died and evidence existed to lay a charge – either a death-bed confession or the testimony of a male partner – did this "crime" come to light.[77] This did not, however, stop the police from arresting women and men on the charge of performing an "illegal operation." In so doing, the state intervened in the private lives of citizens in an effort to prevent and/or punish violations of the sexual and moral codes of marriage and maternity. And once an abortion trial began, it attracted a tremendous amount of publicity and public interest.[78] This certainly proved to be the case in Halifax when, in 1926, and again in 1932, Amelia Murray was convicted and sentenced to lengthy jail terms for conducting an "illegal operation."

From 1918 to 1935, only four "abortion and attempt to procure abortion" charges came before criminal courts in Nova Scotia. Two of these charges were brought against Annie and George Hadley in Cape Breton in 1924. It was alleged that the Hadleys had "unlawfully administered" to Emily Badger, "a woman who was then with child, drugs for the purpose of procuring a miscarriage." Following a trial in March 1925, Annie and George Hadley were acquitted.[79] Amelia Murray accounted for the other two charges and, hence, the only two convictions for abortion in Nova Scotia during these years.[80] The number of actual abortions, however, exceeded the number of charges laid. For the years that statistics are available, 1921 to 1935, roughly 104 abortion-related deaths were reported in the province. Twelve of these, or 11.5 percent, occurred in Halifax.[81] These statistics must be closely scrutinized. Of the 104 abortion-related deaths, the number of "abortions" was thirty-four. The figure of 104 also includes forty-five abortions with and without "septic conditions and ectopic gestation," five "self-induced" abortions, and twenty "other" deaths associated with childbirth. The "other" and "Accidents of Pregnancy" categories probably included some "spontaneous abortions" or miscarriages and premature births. In Halifax, the twelve abortions were only recorded for the 1930 to 1935 period and consisted of one "abortion" and eleven abortions with and without "septic conditions and ectopic gestation." The city did not register any "self-induced abortions" during these six years. While the official number of criminal, or "illegal abortions," may not have been high, the point remains that some women in Nova Scotia did procure abortions, either by themselves or with the help of others, and thus broke the law.

The low detection rate for abortions underlines the hidden nature of this crime. It also suggests that, faced with grave difficulties in obtaining evidence, the province's police forces either chose to ignore, or could not effectively detect, abortion. On a national level, Angus and Arlene Tigar McLaren estimate that, between 1926 and 1947, four to six thousand Canadian women died as a result of bungled abortions.[82] While the apparent Halifax number was much lower, the existence of two successful criminal prosecutions does provide a glimpse into the treatment accorded this phenomenon by the courts and local society. Although the state had outlawed abortion, some women still turned to it as a means of controlling their fertility. Due to its illegality and social stigma, abortion always took place under a veil of secrecy. Married and single women, usually working class, turned to abortionists to help rid them of an unwanted and perhaps illegitimate birth and the problems it entailed. With limited access to safe and reliable forms of contraceptives, whose advertisement and sale were illegal, abortion became a last resort for desperate women. Complications often arose as a result of this procedure, causing everything from a mild infection to death.[83] Twenty-four-year-old Flossie Joyce met the latter fate in 1926. Joyce, a machine operator at the Stanfield Mills in Truro, went to Halifax in May to obtain an abortion. Upon arrival Joyce and her friend Anna Gates retained the services of Amelia Murray. After Murray conducted the procedure, she prescribed a treatment for

Joyce to follow. While recuperating, medical problems arose, forcing Joyce to the Victoria General Hospital, where she died on 13 June.[84] Gates, formerly a public health nurse at the Halifax Infirmary, witnessed the operation and alerted the authorities shortly after Joyce's death.

The Attorney General's Office had received complaints from "professional men" (physicians) demanding an investigation into Murray's activities.[85] By 1918, the modern medical "expert" in Canada had monopolized the practice of medicine. This achievement came after doctors struggled tirelessly throughout the nineteenth century to secure their position as professional caregivers. But not all of them felt that the fight had ended. Abortionists and midwives continued to be a thorn in the side of many doctors (the vast majority of whom were men), who tried to discredit their competitors' services. On the eve of the Second World War, midwifery in the Maritimes had become "virtually non-existent." Midwives in the region could not withstand the challenge of doctors who had, to their advantage, "masculinity, a professional style ... and the virtues of efficient hospital care, modernity in fact."[86] Doctors had the power, in other words, to usurp the role of midwives. Abortionists, however, were a more elusive foe. Not every doctor opposed abortion, but most did feel strongly that laypeople should not perform this procedure. Dr. Cannon of Hamilton, writing in the *Canadian Medical Association Journal* in 1922, argues: "[The] abortionist does not make adequate preparation of the parts, the hands, or the contrivances. The work must, perforce, be done secretly, which presages the fact that the operation is undertaken without assistants or proper preparation."[87] In Cannon's mind, abortionists "flourish and enjoy a certain immunity owing to the apathy of the public toward their crime." The "medical profession," Cannon stresses, "has ... a duty in this connection." He asserts that, "while the violation of the confidence of patients is not to be considered, it is possible by discreet communications to the local officers of justice to rid the community of the obnoxious person."[88] So when news of Flossie Joyce's death surfaced, doctors of Cannon's ilk promptly called for swift action. The Attorney General's Office, which had been monitoring Murray's actions for some time, obliged.[89] The decision to prosecute Murray lent credence to the rumours, which were "extremely difficult to verify," that places did exist in Halifax where women could pay for abortions. Some reports claimed that young girls from the country came to the city and stayed in boarding houses whose keepers colluded with those "unscrupulous" individuals who carried out this operation. If the keepers did not oblige, the homes of midwives, so it was said, provided another location for this crime.[90] In this context of innuendo and accusations, it is not surprising that physicians in Halifax, and other parts of Nova Scotia, followed Murray's case with keen interest.[91]

These forces and those determined to control female criminality in Halifax sided against Amelia Murray. In the course of their investigation into Joyce's death the police searched Murray's home. In her bedroom they found several instruments allegedly used in the operation. They later arrested Murray and charged her with unlawfully using a "catheter and certain other instruments ... with the intent to procure the miscarriage of Flossie Joyce," contrary to section 303 of the Criminal Code, an offence which carried a maximum penalty of life imprisonment.[92] Thus, the Canadian criminal justice system considered abortion to be a serious crime. From the outset, Murray denied the allegations and staunchly declared her innocence. Her protests, however, fell on deaf ears. Two contrasting portraits of Joyce and Murray quickly emerged in the press. Joyce's death caused tremendous sorrow in her home town of Oxford. She had lived the "perfectly normal life of a healthy girl," attending public school and then working for the local woollen mill before moving to Truro. A high-school graduate, a Baptist, and the daughter of well-respected parents, Flossie Joyce's life had ended when she was in her prime.[93] Murray, on the other hand, conformed to the profile of those abortionists and midwives charged in Canada at this time. Fifty-one, married for fifteen years, a mother of three grown children, an "abstainer," and a "practical nurse,"[94] Murray had spent most of her life in Halifax. Midwives tended to be older married women who worked in the abortion field part-time to earn extra income for their families.[95]

The magistrate, following a preliminary hearing, decided that there was sufficient evidence to charge Murray with the murder of Flossie Joyce. The Crown did not, however, move forward with the count of performing an illegal operation. It may have surmised that, without Joyce's testimony, the case did not rest on a solid foundation. This brought to a close the first chapter in this "sordid story," which had shocked the entire community. The Grand Jury reversed the magistrate's decision a few months later by finding "no bill" on the murder charge but a "true bill" against this "elderly woman" for performing an abortion. All of these proceedings had begun to take their toll on Murray. Although she still denied any involvement in Joyce's murder, police officials reported that she had become less light-hearted and more sullen as her Supreme Court trial approached.[96] Recreating the courtroom drama of this case has proven to be difficult. The trial transcripts, along with the medical report on Flossie Joyce, are not extant, and, at counsels' request, Supreme Court justice Mellish cleared the courtroom of all reporters.[97] According to the Crown prosecutor, "this step [was] taken in the interest of public morality." All that remains is an image of Murray, "rather pathetic looking," responding to the charge with the words: "I am not guilty."[98] The jury found Murray guilty of performing an abortion but with a "strong recommendation for mercy." Mellish, taking this into consideration, sentenced Murray to three years and two months in Dorchester Penitentiary.[99]

Five years later, the police arrested Murray again for the same crime. In 1932, twenty-eight-year-old Cydella Whalen, from East Dover, Nova Scotia, worked at the School for the Blind in Halifax. Her suitor, Howard Thomas Raftus, contacted Murray at Whalen's behest and asked if she could help her "out of her trouble." Murray allegedly said yes and conducted the procedure for a ten-dollar fee. Murray seems to have been Whalen's only option. Whalen told the court that she had never taken any pills or used any instruments on herself to get "rid" of the child. After Whalen returned to East Dover her health quickly deteriorated. A doctor was called from Halifax, and he immediately admitted her to the Victoria General Hospital and informed the attorney general of the situation. Fortunately, after spending ninety-nine days in the hospital, Whalen recovered.[100] When the police arrived at her home with an arrest warrant for conducting an "illegal operation," Murray replied: "I am innocent." She then asked: "Is the girl dead?" The police did not charge Raftus as an accomplice.[101] Given the fact that Whalen had not died, the court granted Murray bail at $5,000 following her indictment. The trial, held in March 1933, ended in a hung jury, and it was not until October that a second jury, after three hours of deliberation, found Murray guilty. Murray was sent to Dorchester for five years, and she served the full sentence.[102] By imposing a fairly stiff penalty upon Amelia Murray, the Supreme Court tried to make an example of her in order to convey its abhorrence of this crime. As Angus McLaren notes, abortion trials functioned in defence of the social and sexual status quo.[103] Women such as Flossie Joyce and Cydella Whalen should not have been trying to terminate their pregnancies, and Amelia Murray should not have been offering such services to young women. Amelia Murray's trials reveal that criminal justice officials in Halifax viewed abortion as a social *and* as a moral crime. Indeed, in the United States, abortion was considered by many to be the "ultimate crime of womanhood."[104] The function of the law in these cases was to regulate the lives of both the perpetrators and the victims of this crime. Moreover, these cases indicate that the law against abortion was used primarily against poor and working-class women.

The lives of those women who committed infanticide also came under close scrutiny. Although the actual number of infant deaths in Halifax from infanticide cannot be accurately determined, it does appear, at least on the basis of press coverage, that this method of birth control was more prominent than abortion.[105] The same held true in much of Canada throughout the nineteenth century. A majority of the women accused of infanticide were young, single, and worked as domestic servants. Often unaware of birth control methods, or sexually assaulted by their male employers or co-workers, these women tried to conceal and then terminate their pregnancies to avoid dismissal and the social backlash that accompanied an illegitimate birth. In general, Canadians did not regard infanticide as a heinous crime but, rather, as an understandable, albeit morally corrupt, response to the problem of an unwanted pregnancy. As a result, juries, especially in cases involving domestics, rarely convicted a woman on a charge of murder or manslaughter in an infanticide case, preferring instead to find them guilty of "concealment of birth," which carried a lesser penalty.[106] Prior to 1948, a conviction for infanticide carried an automatic sentence of death. It is for this reason, as well, that juries across the country were reluctant to convict mothers of this crime.[107] Many of Halifax's residents shared this lenient attitude towards women who committed infanticide. Mary Ellen Wright notes that, from 1850 to 1875 in Halifax, only ten women (six of whom were black) and one man went to trial for this offence, with each receiving minor sentences.[108] This pattern continued into the twentieth century as women still suffered from poverty and the burdens of child care. Added to this was the indignity of being arrested and charged with the death of their child and the fear of how the justice system might make them answer for their crime.

In 1924, Hilda Reynolds cracked under the pressure of a police interrogation and admitted to murdering her child. A twenty-one-year-old native of Fox Island, Nova Scotia, Reynolds had come to Halifax in August shortly after she had killed her baby. Rather than leave the infant's body behind she wrapped it in a blanket, placed it in a trunk, and took it with her. When she arrived in Halifax, she found work in a local hotel and hid the body in the basement. Someone eventually found it, no doubt drawn to investigate the smell coming from the decomposing corpse, and notified the police. Initially they charged Reynolds with concealment of birth, but after several "grillings" in the police station, Reynolds, "broken hearted" and in a near state of "hysteria," confessed to smothering the child.[109] About a week later, Beatrice Thomas, a black woman, placed her deceased infant in a clump of bushes on Barrington Street. She lived alone in an attic room on Upper Water Street, and her husband had gone to Chicago and left her and their young daughter in a "destitute condition." On the night her second child was born, Thomas, who had suffered a great deal of pain and sickness, panicked. "The child was live born," Thomas said in her official statement to the police: "I put a rag in its mouth to stop it from crying and so as the people downstairs would not know ... After I put the rag in its mouth it died ... The reason I put the rag in the baby's mouth was so as I would not have to support it." Indicted for murder and "concealment of birth," the Supreme Court acquitted Thomas of the more serious charge but convicted her of concealment.[110]

Mary Murray, a domestic servant, also tried to hide her newborn's body to save both her reputation and her job. At an inquiry into the death of the "male infant of Mary Murray," held on 31 August 1934, Murray recalled how she had felt scared and confused after she gave birth. She did not know whether the baby was alive or dead, so she decided to take it outside and dispose of it because she "didn't want to give too much trouble to ... Mrs. [Walsh]," her employer. Ashamed that she was uncertain as to who had fathered the child, Murray did not seek help from Mrs. Walsh when she went into labour, nor did she want anyone to discover what had happened. A police officer later found the baby's body in the backseat of a car parked in the Walsh's shed.[111]

Sometimes the police did not have a suspect to prosecute in cases of infanticide. In at least two reported instances, in January 1925 and June 1929, residents found the dead bodies of infants in an alley on Granville Street and in the Camp Hill Cemetery. Both babies had died at birth, but the police could not locate the parents or determine who had abandoned the bodies.[112] Whether the police caught the perpetrators or not, infanticide produced two victims: the child and its mother. Each bore the hardships of poverty – the child fatally, the mother perhaps no less painfully (bearing as she did the knowledge that she had taken her child's life and that society would stigmatize her). In one sense, Halifax society and the criminal justice system showed some mercy to those mothers accused of infanticide. Yet, at the same time, by arresting them and thereby publicizing their actions, and by offering little physical and emotional support, they condemned these women and the lives they had led.

"It Is Not Safe for a Woman or Girl to Go out on the Streets of Halifax at Night": Violence against Women and Their Response

Murder and attempted murder on the part of women – like prostitution, abortion, and infanticide – also raised alarms about the extent of female criminality in Halifax. Late one night in July 1928, Luigi Caliacco, a labourer, came home intoxicated and in a foul mood. A "family squabble" soon broke out during which Luigi beat his wife Reta. In the midst of this skirmish, Luigi pulled out a .32 calibre revolver and threatened to kill Reta. Reta managed to wrest the gun from Luigi, at which point he "made at her" and she shot him in the stomach. Neighbours heard the shot and called the police. While all of this took place, their seven-year-old daughter screamed hysterically "but was helpless" to stop them. The police arrested Reta for attempted murder and whisked Luigi to the hospital, where he lay "hovering between life and death."[113] In October, Reta came before the Supreme Court to answer to a charge of inflicting grievous bodily harm upon her husband. Since Luigi had recovered from his wound, the Crown settled for this charge rather than attempted murder. After considering the evidence the jury sympathized with Reta. The day after the shooting a front-page photo of Reta appeared in one newspaper, her head cut and covered with blood, with an explanation that she had fired the shot only after Luigi had attacked her. The court also learned from Luigi that once he had been shot he had picked up the gun and struck his wife over the head several times before he collapsed.[114] In light of this and the fact that all Luigi could remember from that night was his drinking, the jury found Reta Caliacco innocent. In defence of her honour and for the danger Luigi posed to Reta and their child, not guilty seemed to be the only just verdict. Justice had been served and society would not benefit, it was thought, by sending Reta Caliacco to jail and thus further weakening the family's stability.[115]

Annie Florence Gormley received the same verdict following her trial in 1931 for the killing of Gorden Lister. Gormley and Lister lived together, apparently as husband and wife, in a rooming house. Gormley claimed that Lister, a labourer, had come home one November night in 1930 "very drunk." In order to convince him to stop drinking Gormley had told Lister that she would make him something to eat. Lister, it seems, had agreed to help prepare the meal but then had suddenly decided to leave. As he went out the kitchen door, Gormley said she "heard a little shuffle in the hall, like somebody falling." She then rushed to one of her neighbours and asked him to phone the doctor because her "husband had met with an accident." Lister later died in the hospital from knife wounds to his heart and lung.[116] Gormley told the police that she and Lister had not quarrelled and that Lister had fallen on the knife he was using to peel potatoes. But testimony from two witnesses did not corroborate Gormley's version of events. According to John Farrell, a seaman who walked by the rooming house on the night in question, someone yelled from inside: "You go and fuck yourself!" Farrell admitted that he did not know if it had been a man or a woman who had uttered these words. Catherine Carroll, who lived in the same building, explained that she had heard Gormley accuse Lister of making advances towards Carroll and called him "a son of a bitch."[117] Dr. Woodbury, the city's medical examiner, felt that the wounds sustained by Lister could not have resulted from his falling on the knife. Despite this damaging circumstantial evidence, the jury acquitted Gormley of murder. Afterwards, Gormley said of the verdict: "It is a big relief."[118] The jury's decision seemed to tell women that they had the right to protect themselves if threatened by their husbands.

While a few women in Halifax physically injured men, more suffered from the violent acts of a handful of men. As a consequence, some women faced the threat of assault either in their homes or on the city's streets. Halifax's inadequate system of street lighting exacerbated this problem. Near the end of December 1920, "Moral depravity could not descend further," after a "degenerate man prowling around garbed as a woman" accosted a young telephone operator on Almon Street as she made her way home from the theatre. This was one of several recent arrests of "degenerates" who were frightening women on dark streets. The *Halifax Herald* quoted one citizen as saying: "It is not safe for a woman or girl to go out on the streets of Halifax at night." A spree of attacks on women prompted another person to comment: "Most of this would not happen if we had sufficient lighting ... A few plain clothes men might also do some good. The police force is undermanned, and this, with no lights in some places where there is considerable traffic, invites trouble. Something should be done to protect the women and girls of this city."[119]

Physical and sexual assault directly shaped the lives of some Halifax women. Friendly gestures could turn into a nightmare. In 1922, as a young woman walked home one night from the circus on the Halifax Common, she met an acquaintance, Scott Hurgson. He offered her a ride and she accepted. Instead of driving her directly home, however, Hurgson stopped near a park. A patrolman heard her screams and intervened before an "outrage" happened. Officer Parks found the woman in a semi-delirious state, with her clothes torn and her body badly bruised. Hurgson denied that he had taken part in this "violent and cowardly attack." The jury did not agree and convicted him of indecent assault, or what the *Morning Chronicle* described as "attempted criminal assault."[120]

Another threat to women's public safety came from strangers. For many small communities and cities across the country the "stranger" became a popular symbol of the danger inherent in modern society.[121] Emma LeClair found this out when she suffered a "brutal beating in broad daylight" one winter afternoon in 1931. She had been the latest victim of a "mysterious man" who had "waylaid members of the feminine sex" in various parts of the city. LeClair's attacker had come up behind her as she walked along Bayers Road, struck her, and then tried to strangle her. LeClair fought off her attacker and escaped with a partially closed eye, a torn ear and lips, and a swollen face. LeClair was proud of her resistance. "I'm glad it was I," she said: "He might easily have killed some other weaker girl." Despite questioning a number of "suspicious characters," the police failed to capture the man who had unleashed this "brutal attack."[122]

While unknown assailants attacked women in interwar Halifax, many more women suffered physical abuse from their husbands. Men beat their spouses for a host of reasons: their perceived infidelity, failure to perform a household duty, or out of sheer rage after a bout of drinking. Many women endured the violence without making a formal complaint. Others, however, either left their husbands or took them to court. In so doing, they made a firm stand against their husbands' violent actions.[123] They also ran the risk that the court would not punish their spouses; or, if it did, that this would deprive them and their children of a source of income.[124] Yet some women took this gamble. As Kathryn Harvey stresses, a woman's decision to charge her husband "was a rational calculation based on very limited choices," which women made "out of a desire to exercise some control over their domestic lives."[125] One average day in the Halifax police court reveals the myriad of outcomes in wife abuse cases. In November 1922, Magistrate Fielding faced three "wife beaters." One man "evidently settled things satisfactorily with his better half" and was discharged. While they may have "settled things," the wife may also have had second thoughts about her chances of winning or about the consequences if she did win. The second man, a soldier, had already been convicted by Fielding and was awaiting sentencing. Fielding decided to remand him for a second time and granted him bail in the interim. For this man's wife, knowing that he could return home at any time may well have caused her some anguish. A "sad tale of domestic infelicity" unfolded during the third trial. A woman claimed that her husband had beaten and threatened to murder her. The husband blamed their troubles on his in-laws. Things had been fine until her brother "butted in[to]" their affairs. Under questioning from the magistrate, the husband admitted shoving his wife off their bed. For Fielding, this was enough to prove guilt, and he asked the wife what she wanted done with her husband. She requested that he be forced "to keep the peace," but Fielding suggested that two months in Rockhead prison best suited his crime. The accused's wife rejected this option, probably because his incarceration would have left her without the means to pay the family's bills. Fielding finally decided to adjourn the case and give the couple a chance to "get together and begin their life all over again."[126]

When women did want to punish their spouses for abusing them, however, the courts did not always cooperate.[127] The early twentieth-century legal system in Nova Scotia placed a great deal of emphasis on marital stability, even, in some cases, in the face of spousal abuse. By essentially discounting the seriousness of male violence, the law, in the words of James Snell, "was helping to maintain male authority in the family and was implicitly condoning the use of violence there."[128] Women in Nova Scotia did have recourse to cruelty as grounds for divorce. As the 1920s progressed, the definition of cruelty expanded to include sexual conduct considered outside the realm of "normal" sex and that was enacted "coercively." Nevertheless, this did not prevent husbands from sexually or physically assaulting their partners, nor did it significantly increase the degree of punishment for these men.[129] As Terry L. Chapman suggests for Alberta: "Since the family unit had to be preserved, there were no provisions for its breakdown. Reconciliation was the ultimate goal [of the courts]." As a result of this need to stabilize the family in the midst of the social disruptions fostered by modernity, judges imposed "token" sentences rather than maximum sentences on husbands convicted of abuse.[130]

Women found guilty of vagrancy and shoplifting, as outlined above, received the same (or harsher) penalties as did men who physically harmed their wives. James Sullivan, convicted of assaulting his wife, went to the City Prison for thirty days. Initially the magistrate felt content in binding Sullivan over to keep the peace. His wife, however, protested vehemently and demanded that he be sent to jail. She told the magistrate that, a year previously, Sullivan had brutally attacked her and had not gone to jail. He had not learned his lesson because when he arrived home last night, the "good wife" recalled, "he looked around to find something to hit [her] with ... but he could not find anything so he used his fists."[131] When sentencing husbands convicted of assaulting their wives, magistrates did not want to break up the family. In 1928, Mrs. McKinnon charged her husband, Dougal McKinnon, a former magistrate in Cape Breton, with assault. McKinnon pleaded not guilty but, on the advice of counsel, he admitted to striking his wife. Mrs. McKinnon testified that her husband had done something she had not condoned, and when she had raised the matter with him he became incensed and struck her on her face and arms. After hearing the evidence, the magistrate turned to McKinnon and sternly remarked, "If I took my own view of this matter I would send you to prison for sixty days." But when he considered that a jail term would mean that McKinnon's wife and children would suffer financially in his absence, the magistrate relented, censured McKinnon and ordered him to keep the peace.[132] The magistrate's decision "left unchallenged the sexual hierarchy that continued to undergird and define the marital unit," and by not sending him to jail on the assumption that Mrs. McKinnon could not survive without her husband's wage, the court tacitly acknowledged its failure to assist women who were trapped in abusive marriages.[133]

Women who tried to use the criminal law to punish their husbands for desertion and non-support did enjoy some success. Desertion, the "Poor Man's Divorce," was relatively common in 1920s Halifax. In 1920, Judge Hunt noted with a sense of alarm that the desertion of wives and children "[was] becoming ... frequent ... The problem [was] one of the gravest [the judiciary was] called upon to face." Feeling the pinch of a sluggish economy, some men left their families for work outside the province. Sometimes husbands and wives arranged these temporary separations, only to have the husbands disappear for good.[134] This usually resulted in the collapse of the family unit. Besides turning to friends and family, deserted women had only the criminal courts to turn to. Nova Scotia did not have legislation that forced a delinquent husband to provide his family with a reasonable measure of support. Even if a magistrate ordered a husband to provide financial support for his wife and children, the court could not guarantee that he would do so since, as Hunt fumed, it was "common knowledge among this call of men that very little, if anything, [could] be done to them and they simply laugh[ed] at the whole matter. As they [were] generally earning good wages they [could] afford to hire a good lawyer to defend them, while the woman [could not]."[135] In spite of this, the criminal justice system in Halifax, in an effort to rebuild the family, would usually find in a wife's favour. For the women themselves, a combination of revenge, necessity, and a desire to assert their sense of equality within the home influenced their decision to go to court.[136]

For the second time, David Dunbrack appeared before Magistrate Cluney to answer to the charge of neglecting to provide for his wife and five children. Mrs. Dunbrack accused her husband of not supporting his family and of spreading lies about her with the intention of having her fired. "I can keep up and work if I am not bothered but this worry is breaking me down and I can't stand it," she told Cluney: "If he will leave me alone I will do the best I can." Dunbrack, who denied the allegation that he had been a nuisance to his wife, said to her request to have him jailed: "Well, lock me up." She quickly fired back: "I wish they would for six or seven months, until I can get out of the city. I can't stand all of this trouble." The court apparently accepted her plea as Dunbrack later appealed a six-month jail sentence.[137] A man's failure to provide for his family also prompted moral censure from the court. Magistrate Cluney accepted policewoman May Virtue's assessment of Arthur Creelman as a "worthless character" and sentenced him to three months with hard labour in the City Prison for failing to provide for his wife and family. Creelman admitted that he had not cared for his family and agreed to support two of his children if the state placed them in an institution, but he felt that his wife could care for herself. Creelman's actions grew out of his dissatisfaction with his wife's habit of staying out late at night. Virtue rebuffed these accusations and assured Cluney that Mrs. Creelman was a decent woman who looked after her children to the best of her ability. Cluney thus gave Mrs. Creelman the benefit of the doubt.[138]

In Halifax, husbands rarely conceded their guilt when formally accused of non-support. In 1926, John Foran adamantly opposed the idea of supporting his wife. He believed that his wife, who had laid the charge against him, had been unfaithful and did not deserve his money. The magistrate rejected Foran's claims of infidelity but still offered him a chance to provide for his wife. Foran refused and grinned when the magistrate sent him to prison for three months.[139] Arthur Marshall, a twenty-four-year-old truck driver, when asked by Magistrate Barnhill what he intended to do about his wife's welfare, answered: "I'd rather do 50 years than take her back." Barnhill subsequently jailed Marshall for eight days.[140] In other cases, however, the risk that women ran by taking their husbands to court for non-support did not pay off. For instance, in two months in 1923 the Halifax City Court dismissed, discharged, or handed down a suspended sentence to five men charged with "neglect to provide."[141] And even a legal victory could result in some women experiencing a practical defeat. Unless the court ordered their husbands to pay them support, which some did not do, women still faced the problem of making ends meet. The criminal law, while allowing some women a chance to punish their husbands and gain the support that they and their children needed, also perpetuated women's and children's socio-economic inequality.

Conclusion

Some women in Halifax from 1918 to 1935 broke the law and tried to use it as a source of empowerment. Even though many people could hardly conceive of it, women did engage in criminal activity. In the case of shoplifting and prostitution, they did so partly out of economic necessity. For crimes such as vagrancy, the law itself had as much to do with defining their criminality as did their actions.[142] Women were often caught in a dilemma when it came to the detection of crime. Most residents and criminal justice officials saw women as unlikely to commit a crime of any nature. However, once women did commit a crime and, in so doing, stepped beyond the bounds of respectable behaviour, they usually faced a criminal justice system that was determined to prevent these "moral menace[s]" from undermining social order.[143] All of this meant that gender played an influential role in determining Haligonians' perception of and reaction to crime. Police officers paid close attention to some women, especially prostitutes, whom they believed might cause trouble; and police court magistrates and senior judges had few reservations about imposing harsh penalties on female offenders. This contrasted with the comparatively lenient sentences given husbands convicted of abusing their wives. In most cases, the courts dealt sternly with women – not to save them from their criminal ways but (as with Amelia Murray) to make an example of them and to regulate their social and moral behaviour. In instances in which the courts acquitted women of serious crimes, notably murder and infanticide, they failed to address and possibly alleviate the abuse and physical and emotional hardships (such as those that led Reta Caliacco to shoot her husband and Beatrice Thomas to murder her infant).

Women in Halifax turned to the law in an attempt to exert a modicum of social power. By taking their husbands to court for desertion or assault, women could exact a measure of justice and revenge. When a husband had blatantly neglected his duty as the family breadwinner, magistrates felt justified in placing him behind bars. Yet victory was not always guaranteed. By appealing to the criminal law, these women entered a system that generally did not see or treat women as equal to men. Hence, the court would refuse to find in a woman's favour if hope remained for a reconciliation. Winning could also be a Pyrrhic victory for women. A husband behind bars did not bring home a paycheque, nor did he receive treatment for his abusive tendencies. Women and children thus had to fend for themselves and cope with the scars of spousal abuse. The machinery of order in Halifax also failed to protect women from the dangers of the city's streets. The threat of sexual and physical assault, at times resulting in death, faced young women in particular on a daily basis. The police did capture some of these male offenders, and the courts meted out justice accordingly. But the law governing rape usually resulted in the women themselves being blamed, or at least held partially responsible, for their victimization.[144] Similarly, the unsolved attacks and deaths, including that of Marie Thibeault (whom the police deemed to be a respectable woman), speak to the difficulties that the police department and the criminal justice system had in preserving law and order in Halifax. It also reveals that hostility towards women was an integral part of daily life in this city.

CHAPTER 6

The Ethnic Dimensions of Crime and Criminals

THE INTERWAR PERIOD, with the social and economic tensions that accompanied it, proved to be a difficult time for ethnic minorities in Halifax and throughout the Maritimes. Trapped on the margins of the region's economy, ethnic minorities faced discrimination and hostility from some whites who felt threatened, socially and economically, by their presence.[1] Halifax has long been a city with a diversity of ethnic groups, but in the interwar period local "alien" communities represented a greater than usual cultural challenge to white society. Halifax residents were thus forced to wrestle with the question of ethnicity under modern conditions. One of the central experiences associated with modernity is that of living with "strangers" – people of different cultures and values, who, in the eyes of many members of the dominant culture, cannot be trusted. Given the desire on the part of most citizens of Halifax to maintain law and order, those individuals who committed crimes fell into disrepute. This was especially the case for those criminals of non-British or non-French origin. By focusing on some of the crimes committed by blacks, Chinese, and "foreigners" in Halifax from 1918 to 1935 and on the treatment accorded them by the police, courts, and the media, I demonstrate that these minorities endured the wrath of a justice system and a public opinion firmly committed to preserving social order. Moreover, their penalties were determined as much by their ethnic identity as by the severity of their crimes.

Halifax's Ethnic Composition

While by no means teeming with minorities, Halifax did have visible ethnic communities. As a port city and, after 1881, an official point of entry for immigrants arriving in Canada, Halifax was anything but isolated from "foreign" cultures.[2] An episode from the police court highlights this fact. On 25 February 1924, the *Morning Chronicle* reported that a "Strange Gathering" had taken place in the magistrate's chambers. Many corners of the globe had representatives on hand for the proceedings. A South African faced a charge of violating the Temperance Act, and an Australian and a Russian had each been arrested for public drunkenness. The paper concluded its coverage of this "cosmopolitan" docket by stressing: "that justice was meted out to all it is needless to mention."[3] This scene captures some of the ethnic flavour of early twentieth-century Halifax. Compared to the city's dominant British population, however, the number of people from foreign backgrounds remained small. In 1921, those individuals designated as "English," "Irish," and "Scotch" comprised 86 percent of Halifax's total population of 58,372; in 1931, this percentage had fallen slightly to 84.3 percent.[4] In comparison, in 1921, blacks and Chinese in Halifax represented 1.6 percent and 0.2 percent of the city's population, respectively.[5] For the Chinese, this amounted to a tiny fraction of their numbers within Canada.[6] The Dutch, Germans, Italians, Jews, and Russians were prominent among the non-British and non-francophone groups who made up the remaining 12.2 percent of the population in 1921. In Halifax in the 1920s and early 1930s, most white residents used the phrase "foreigner" to refer, often in a derogatory fashion, to these groups specifically and to all those considered to be neither British nor French generally.

Much of the criminality associated with these enclaves was tied to men. One reason for this was the low number of women within some of these groups in Halifax. Among the Chinese, for example, in 1921, only one woman appears in the census returns alongside 140 men. Of these men, the majority (130) were twenty-one years of age or over.[7] This pattern is consistent with Chinese settlement across Canada. Chinese immigrants prior to 1923 tended to be young married men who had left their wives and families at home. Driven from their homeland by poor economic conditions and an unstable political climate, many Chinese men came to Canada as contract labourers. Others worked as independent miners, servants, and merchants. They hoped to earn enough money in Canada to support their families and eventually return home or bring their wives and children to this country. Yet, as a result of the Chinese Immigration Act, 1923, most Asians could not legally enter Canada, causing a "married-bachelor society" to emerge among those Chinese men already in the country.[8] Another cause of the low incidence of reported criminality for ethnic women is the perception that men were the main perpetrators of crime; however, some foreign women, notably Gypsies, did become known to the machinery of order. This tendency to perceive the criminal as male shaped the surveillance practices of the police, the administration of criminal justice, and the nature of news coverage devoted to crime in Halifax.

Although Halifax's population could scarcely be characterized as either racially or ethnically heterogeneous, the city did contain some vibrant and close-knit communities. Frustrated in their attempts to secure a measure of respectability and acceptance within white Halifax society, black leaders at the turn of the century began to advocate "separatism" from whites as a means of fostering racial pride and unity.[9] This meant that family and community ties for blacks became increasingly important as sources of social and economic survival. Their churches, in particular, played a significant role in the lives of many blacks in Halifax, lending "a sense of dignity and sanctification as well as an outlet for collective activity both secular and religious."[10]

For the city's Chinese residents, associations such as the Chinese Freemasons Society, Nationalist League, and Chinese Club provided meeting places to consolidate friendships and organize cultural activities.[11] For instance, on 1 January 1927, one hundred Chinese Freemasons gathered to celebrate the new year with a fireworks display.[12] And the Chinese in Halifax, building on ties forged through the networks developed in their voluntary organizations, tried as best they could to defend their interests and protect their members. This was demonstrated in May 1921, when, following a raid on a Chinese tea shop, "which created much excitement among the Chinese population of the city," the police arrested five Chinese men for illegal possession of opium. In response, several of their friends hastened to the police station where they paid the $500 bail set for each prisoner with money raised from within the community.[13] Despite this solidarity, their small numbers and ethnic identity meant that minorities did not attain any substantial degree of socio-economic power in Halifax. Consequently, they were susceptible to hostility and discrimination from many sectors of white society.

Racialization and the Construction of the Criminal "Other"

Blacks, Chinese, and foreigners waged an ongoing battle against racial and ethnic discrimination in Halifax. One way to highlight this is to explore their dealings with Halifax's criminal justice system. In most cases, racial animosity manifested itself not in violent acts but in subtler forms of rejection, one of which was ethnic stereotyping. In the city's efforts to combat crime and maintain the socio-economic status quo through an adherence to law and order, police officers, the police court magistrate, and many residents associated particular criminal acts with specific minority groups. Blacks and Chinese were thought to be engaged in prostitution and the "white slave trade." The Chinese also apparently spent most of their time gambling and smoking opium.[14] And, along with blacks and the Chinese, the foreign element, perceived as prone to violence, could be counted on to break a gamut of laws, from public intoxication to theft. Underlying these assumptions about the criminal intent of these visible and not so visible minorities was the belief that they posed a threat to the city of order. The public fear associated with ethnic stereotypes had much to do with the socially constructed "racial" identities conferred upon minorities. Precisely because race is given meaning "through the agency of human beings and social contexts, and is not a biological or natural category," it continues to be a potent ideology.[15]

In Halifax between 1918 and 1935, a process of "racialization" flourished. Essentially, racialization denotes a willingness on the part of a hegemonic class to identify skin colour, language, birth place, and cultural practices as markers of distinction – in other words, to depict those who do not belong to the racial majority as the "other."[16] For the blacks, Chinese, and foreigners of Halifax, this meant that they would be accorded marginal status within the city. This marginalization manifested itself, in part, in the tendency by members of the majority ethnic group to equate the "other" with criminality. Many citizens in Halifax perceived these "aliens" as more likely than members of their own ethnic group to inhabit the city's criminal underworld. Although not seen as the only members of this clique, minorities joined the prostitutes, vagrants, and "miscreants" in the imagined criminal underworld. Thus, as was the case in other Canadian cities, the inclination to blame the prevalence of prostitution, gambling, and vice generally on racial minorities surfaced in Halifax.[17] This provided the police with a specific group of suspects to apprehend and allowed magistrates to pass the sentences they deemed fit to restore public safety. It also reinforced the view that crime and criminals epitomized everything that law-abiding citizens believed to be reprehensible and incompatible with a traditional, ordered way of life in Nova Scotia's capital.[18]

The opposition to ethnic minorities in Halifax did occasionally break into open hostility. Both blacks and Chinese suffered physical abuse and damage to their property. Sometimes a specific incident, or the rumour of an incident, triggered an attack. Around eleven o'clock on a Saturday night in 1918, a group of young boys, soldiers, and sailors, acting on a rumour that a "negro" had attacked a white child, forcibly dragged the alleged culprit from a shop on Cogswell Street where he had fled for protection.[19] It seems that they intended to impose their own brand of justice on this supposed criminal. While some members of the mob searched for a rope with which to hang their prisoner from a nearby tree, six police officers fought their way through the crowd and rescued the besieged black man. He emerged from the throng badly "maltreated[,] having been trampled under foot and battered by the fists of the rioters." After piling into a patrol car the police and the victim sped away "to the accompaniment of a barrage of all sorts of missiles." Although the attack appeared to have its basis in a particular incident and to be focused on a specific individual, it is significant that the rumoured assault was never confirmed and that no arrest was made.[20]

The Chinese regularly felt the sting of racial intolerance. The most glaring example of this occurred during the city's "race riot" of 1919. Six Chinese restaurants sustained severe damage following a rampage by a group of returned soldiers and civilians on the night of 18 February 1919.[21] The reaction to this devastation illustrates the city's abhorrence of lawlessness as well as the seemingly contradictory views that many in Halifax had of the Chinese. "The race riots and raids on the Chinese restaurants in Halifax Tuesday night," the *Halifax Herald* declared, "were most flagrant violations of justice and law and an utter disgrace to the capital of Nova Scotia."[22] Yet even in condemning the rioters, while absolving the victims of blame, criminal justice authorities and other commentators sought their explanations for the riot in the otherness of the Chinese. The Chinese residents of Halifax, noted one observer, were "perhaps the least public spirited of all the large foreign element in Halifax; that they live[d] cheaply, contributing a minimum of the money they earn[ed] ... to the prosperity of the community [was] admitted; but except for these national failings, the Chinese [were] a law abiding, thrifty and peaceful people." Therefore, he concluded, there was "not the phantom of an excuse for the lawless excesses of [that] Tuesday night."[23] Chief of Police Frank Hanrahan agreed with this assessment of the Chinese character. During a Grand

Jury investigation into the 1919 riot, Hanrahan, in testifying as to the cause, stated flatly that the "Chinamen [were] not troublesome" and thus did not provoke the attack.[24] In the minds of many Halifax residents, this perception of the Chinese as docile, coupled with their "national failings," conjured up an image of the Chinese as inferior, which, in turn, relegated them to the social and cultural periphery of the city. This attitude was perhaps reinforced by the city's reluctance to compensate the financial losses incurred by those Chinese merchants affected by the riot.[25]

Other examples of violence towards the Chinese following the February 1919 incident abound. In that same year, a customer who had paid his bill at the Crown Cafe suddenly pulled out a knife and slashed the Chinese proprietor across the forehead.[26] Chinese-owned stores also continued to be targeted. Late in 1921, a gang of "hoodlums" paraded through the city's North End, "making a specialty" of wrecking Chinese laundries. This spree of vandalism upon "Celestials, all of whom [were] of a very quiet disposition," resulted in hundreds of dollars in damage.[27] The dismissive use of "Celestial" to describe the Chinese helped to entrench their other-worldly image. Meanwhile, the beating of two members of the "Chinese race" in 1928 evoked memories of the "incipient race riots" of 1919. These men had walked by George Burns speaking to one another in Chinese. Burns took offence to the sound and struck each of them before help could arrive.[28] So while outrage in the press greeted these attacks, the fact that they occurred also suggests that some white residents believed that, as Madge Pon asserts, "beneath the veneer of the smiling, harmless Chinaman lurked an evil so deep and so incomprehensible that assimilation was impossible."[29] The failure of the authorities either to prosecute the offenders or to provide compensation to the victims in these incidents underscores the difficulties faced by many black and Chinese Haligonians who routinely dealt with daily discrimination. The fact that both of these groups were victims of crime was often ignored or forgotten by much of Halifax's white population, which tended to perceive both groups as potential criminals. This meant that it was the victims' activities, rather than those of their tormentors, that were closely monitored by the police in their attempts to curb crime. The source of this stigmatization may be traced to the separate identities constructed for ethnic minorities by Halifax's white majority. Blacks, Chinese, and foreigners who committed crimes, or who were considered as suspects, were cast in a sinister light: their ethnicity and criminality were inextricably linked in the press.

Black "Deviance" and Crime

The social and cultural geography of Halifax contributed to this categorization of racial "others." Africville, while physically a part of Halifax, remained a social appendage of, and a so-called "national blot" on, the city. During the 1920s and 1930s, this "segregated black settlement," located on the northern extremity of the Halifax peninsula, was known as a place where blacks and some whites could go for "boot-leg booze and fun," notably prostitution. It became, in essence, a potent symbol of black "deviance."[30] In 1919, some of the area's ratepayers tried to combat Africville's negative image by petitioning city council for improved police protection. And, unlike police authorities, who assumed that all of the troubles in Africville came from within the black community itself, the petitioners identified the troublemakers as outsiders. As the petition's preamble states:

> That a police officer seldom or never visits this district, except with a warrant or subpoena; That conditions which now prevail here are worse than at any time heretofore; That there are many persons, strangers in our midst, living openly in a state of debauchery, which must corrupt the minds of the youth; That there is nightly confusion, carousal and dissipation, which disturb the peaceful night; That these carousal[s] have been the centres for spreading infection through the village; That we believe, if this disgraceful state of affairs continue[s], there will be some grave crime or crimes committed.

The petitioners concluded, echoing a progressive refrain, that if the council would come forward with assistance: "the evil influences now at work may be greatly reduced [and] then shall we be better able to train the young in the way of good citizenship and place the village on a better plane of Social Welfare."[31] Municipal politicians and the police gave this request a lukewarm response. The Police Commission recommended: "[The] residents of Africville district [should] form their own Police Dept. and any one they appoint to act as a policeman the Mayor [should] swear in as a Special Constable, as the City Dept. have no spare men to send such a distance." Besides, as the commission dryly noted: "In the event of any serious trouble being reported the Chief is always in a position to send a squad to this district."[32] Despite one alderman's assertion – "now is the time to do justice to the colored residents [of Africville]" – the city made no effort to extend a police presence to this portion of Halifax. Civic and law enforcement officials would respond to crime in Africville, but they would not try to prevent its outbreak.[33] By making this decision, they implicitly placed Africville on the margins of the law. As well, this practice further isolated the community and helped to convey a picture of Africville as both crime-ridden and "outside the bounds of legitimate society" while portraying blacks as lawless.[34] During the entire interwar period Africville was seen by many whites, and most "respectable" black residents of the North End suburbs, as a raucous and potentially dangerous area of Halifax. And, as Jennifer J. Nelson posits, racialized groups such as the black residents of Africville were "seen not only to live within defiled spaces, but to embody those spaces."[35]

The issue of alleged "white slavery" (i.e., pimping) also exemplifies the supposedly inherent deviance of blacks. Black men, so some believed, had brought this scourge to Halifax. If Mariana Valverde is correct in insisting that "many people believed white slavery was a serious social problem," despite the fact that there was little hard evidence to prove its existence, then Halifax certainly shared in the panic.[36] In 1919, detectives felt that "white slavers" had commenced operations in Halifax. They had suspected for some time that "girls" from Montreal, and other "Upper Canadian" cities, had been brought to Halifax for immoral purposes.[37] The arrest of Granville Hutchings, "colored," for what the *Morning Chronicle* called "White Slavery," or procuring an "attractive" white "girl" who had been living with him to become a "common prostitute," seemed to lend credence to these claims.[38] Hutchings' lifestyle had aroused the suspicions of the police. Since his arrival in Halifax in November 1918, Hutchings had not held a job, but he was always dressed well and never wanted for money. At his preliminary hearing on a charge of "being a male person unlawfully liv[ing] wholly or in part on the earnings of prostitution," a "colored" woman, Clare Hardy, testified that Hutchings rented a room in her house at 153 Maynard Street and that men would often visit the premises late at night. One evening she saw the woman who stayed with Hutchings return with two men and soon after she heard the woman scream. Upon investigating, the witness found that Hutchings had struck the woman because she had not come back that night with a "hand down."[39]

Gertrude Forge, whose earnings the police accused Hutchings of receiving, then took the stand. This twenty-five-year-old woman admitted that men came to see her and that on several occasions she had given money to Hutchings, adding that he did not keep the money for himself but instead paid the rent and bought her things. Forge said that she had come to Halifax from Montreal, at her own expense, after Hutchings had promised to marry her. But, as she noted: "since I have been in Halifax he has never made any effort to carry his promise out."[40] At the conclusion of Forge's testimony, Hutchings, "a smart looking young colored man," spoke in his own defence. An embalmer by trade, Hutchings explained that he had worked on the railway until he had recently lost his job. Expressing nothing but good intentions towards Forge, Hutchings said he hoped to marry her once he obtained a divorce from his wife in the United States. The money he took from Forge, Hutchings claimed, went to support her and he had enough money saved to care for himself. He then denied striking Forge. Her bruises, Hutchings assured the court, resulted from an accidental fall down a flight of stairs and a burn from a stove. The magistrate did not believe a word of what Hutchings said and committed him to stand trial. The jury subsequently found him guilty of living off the avails of prostitution.[41]

While perhaps a symbolic victory for the champions of moral and social purity in Halifax, this outcome was of little practical benefit to the victim. Gertrude Forge remained caught in the trap of prostitution, with no recognition of the hardships she endured.[42] The hearing itself, and much of the crusade against the alleged existence of white slavery in Halifax, was not intended to address, or solve, the problem of prostitution and its inherent exploitation of women like Forge.[43] It also demonstrated how the criminal justice system in Halifax singled out some black men as the cause of social evil. As Karen Dubinsky suggests, many contemporaries saw the period from the 1880s through to the 1920s as one of sexual danger, and some were inclined to focus narrowly on the foreigner and outsider as its cause.[44] Blacks represented the "bogeymen" in Halifax's battle against the efforts of the "other" to lure young white women into a life of prostitution. The fact that Hutchings associated with white women made him a perfect candidate for prosecution. The same held true for John Keeling, a "colored street-corner inspirational preacher and vendor of newspapers who [was] a landmark on the main streets of Halifax," whom the police charged with keeping a disorderly house. The police also arrested two white women for being "inmates" of this house.[45] While these cases cannot be considered representative of all the charges laid against men and women, both white and black, for engaging in the business of prostitution, certainly there was an assumption in Halifax that black men were most likely to commit this offence. Similarly, the surveillance of Granville Hutchings, who seemed to have had too much money for an unemployed black man, indicates how the Halifax Police Department conducted its investigative work with a distinct core of suspected, or suspicious, characters in mind – a core constructed, at least in part, according to racist assumptions.

The image of blacks as criminally inclined appeared vividly around the issues of violence and murder. The near fatal stabbing of young William Walsh by an unknown "colored slasher" is a case in point. Walsh, accompanied by his elder brother Edward and his six-year-old sister Olive, went for a walk on Citadel Hill on New Year's Day, 1929. As they were walking, a man approached them and cut Walsh across the stomach. When the children's mother arrived to escort them home, Walsh said to her in a weak voice: "Mummy, a colored man stabbed me." His mother rushed Walsh home, treated him, and then brought him to the hospital. Soon after, word began to spread about this "fiendish ... crime," which aroused the entire neighbourhood in which Walsh lived. A crowd of "determined men" quickly began combing the city looking for the man who had committed this "brutal assault."[46] Detectives told the press: "[A] short, fat, freckled negro is the man we want ... There is undoubtedly a bad man at large." With this in mind officers rounded up a number of suspects, none of whom proved to be the "Negro Knifer," and eventually no one answered for this crime.[47] Nevertheless, this affair is indicative of some police officers' attitudes towards blacks. The investigating officers felt confident that once they arrested the "Negro Knifer" they could attribute a series of other unsolved crimes to him. Similarly, those close to Walsh and his family, along with the police, were convinced that only a black man endowed with a violent and lawless character could willingly harm a defenceless child. This attitude also surfaced during the trial of Daniel P. Sampson, who was convicted and sentenced to death for the 1933 murder of two white boys, Edward and Bramwell Heffernan. After a number of appeals for clemency, which cited his "low mental capacity," had failed, Sampson was executed on 7 March 1935 at the Halifax County Jail. Daniel P. Sampson was the last person to be executed in Halifax.[48]

The trial of Louis Jones for the shooting death of his wife Alice provides further evidence of racism in Halifax society and the criminal justice system. Alice Jones and her friend Mary Howe took a cab on the night of 12 September 1927 en route to a bean supper and dance at Africville. Along the way they stopped at Alice's boarding house so she could change her clothes. As she emerged from the taxi, her estranged husband Louis appeared and started to berate her. Within a few minutes, as Arthur Wyse, who accompanied Louis Jones on that night, later recalled, a shot rang out and Alice Jones screamed, "My God, I am shot!" Her death, however, did not come immediately. According to Wyse: "Mr. Jones lifted the woman up by the shoulder and the woman staggered behind the taxi, dragging Jones with her; she tried to make the steps again and she fell and Jones fired a second shot ... Mr. Jones picked the woman up by the shoulder and the woman made a step up towards the door and fell; Mr. Jones then fired the third shot." Wyse then concluded, "I didn't see the woman move any more."[49] Soon after the shooting the search for Louis Jones began. Twenty police officers mounted what the *Halifax Herald* described as one of Halifax's most intense manhunts. They scoured the city, keenly aware that somewhere there lurked a man "who they had reason to fear, would not stop at murder."[50] Their persistence paid off. Within a few hours Jones was captured by the police in Africville. From the beginning, the Halifax newspapers portrayed Jones in an unfavourable light. A part-time longshoreman, bootlegger, poker player, and "hanger-on" in billiard parlours, Jones had lived a marginal life. He also had a lengthy police record. In his home town of Saint John, Jones' first contact with the law had come at the age of fourteen, when he had stolen an overcoat. From then on he committed a string of crimes, ranging from using profane language to threatening his mother with a knife and assaulting his wife. The latter incident occurred only weeks before he murdered her. The *Herald* seemed justified in labelling Jones a "dangerous man."[51] Even during Louis Jones' trial, the press did not dwell on Alice Jones' death. To them it was simply the culmination of Louis Jones' life of crime and nothing more.

During the Supreme Court trial, Louis Jones' lawyer, John F. Mahoney, tried to convince the jury that Jones, in a fit of jealous rage over his wife's infidelity, shot her.[52] Mahoney, in a November 1927 letter to M.F. Gallagher, chief of the Remissions Branch in the federal Department of Justice, alluded to the morally suspect character of Alice Jones and the racial dimensions of this case. In seeking a stay of execution for his client, Mahoney outlined how Alice Jones' boarding house had a reputation as a "dive" and observed that, in spite of her husband's record, Alice had still been Louis Jones' wife. "They had their troubles it is true," Mahoney noted, "but what else are we to expect between people of this class."[53] As if to lend support to this argument, the *Herald* described the Jones' home as a scene of abuse and a "liquor den for some notorious characters."[54] Alice's apparent social impropriety, compounded by her racial identity, seemed to make her responsible for her own death. This case had more to do with the need to rid Halifax of a "half white" killer, and thus to preserve law and order, than with ensuring that women who were assaulted or murdered received justice.[55] In his charge to the jury, Mr. Justice Robert Graham noted bluntly, "I see absolutely nothing in the evidence to justify a verdict of not guilty."[56] The jury agreed and found Jones guilty, with a unanimous recommendation that his death sentence be commuted to life imprisonment. The jury made this decision in light of his wife's dubious character, which lent some extenuating circumstances to the crime, effectively rendering her murder a "crime of passion."[57] As Kimberley White notes about this case, the jury's recommendation of mercy, which was rejected by the judge and the federal minister of justice who allowed Jones' execution to proceed, may have been the result of a belief that, even though Jones was guilty, his "questionable character," a product of his racial background, meant that perhaps he was not entirely responsible for his crime.[58]

On the surface a classic case of the way domestic violence was perceived and dealt with by the media and the criminal justice system during this era, its racist undertones throw into graphic relief the clear image of blacks as the other – a group to be treated differently not only by the general public but also by the law. Even Jones' own lawyer relied upon racist stereotypes. In writing to Gallagher to request that the death sentence be commuted to life imprisonment, Mahoney stated: "I want you to take into consideration the general character of the half white. I admit that it is not up to standard, but they are usually people of very strong passions and feelings, possessing a good deal of the white mans [sic] vanity and pride, without the mental qualities to off-set them."[59] Mahoney also pointed out that this case, and Jones' fate, no longer commanded a great deal of public concern. In Mahoney's view: "It is a row between a husband and a wife; and at this moment there is hardly anybody in Halifax who would bother noticing the fact if the sentence were commuted to life imprisonment. So far as the public is concerned: 'This is just another nigger.'"[60] Mahoney's letter also disclosed a disturbing fact about the personal views of the jury's foreman. The jury had issued its appeal for mercy, Mahoney admitted, even though the foreman, Daniel Chisholm, a lumber broker in Halifax: "dislikes niggers because they are niggers. I did not know this at the time he went on the jury; but he has a decided feeling towards all niggers as is the case with most whites here."[61] When this argument failed to persuade federal authorities, Mahoney, in December 1927, exercised his final option – a letter to Ernest Lapointe, minister of justice. This time Mahoney stressed the futility of executing Jones: "I do not believe the hanging of this man can be regarded as having a deterrent effect. His crime was so absolutely without purpose or motive. As one of the dregs of humanity, I feel he merits special consideration and mercy. I always feel we can well afford to deal a bit generously with the ignorant victim of passion when we come to consider that his mental world is one of which we are ignorant."[62] Mahoney's words, however, fell on deaf ears. Louis Nathan Jones, thirty years of age, was hanged in the courtyard of the Halifax County Jail on 19 January 1928.[63] Justice and order, at least in the minds of some, had been served with the execution of Jones. This case highlights the inequality and discrimination faced by many blacks in Halifax. Victimized by her husband, even in death Alice Jones bore the moral judgment of a white jury that had deemed her character to be "bad," thereby in one sense absolving Louis Jones of her murder. Louis Jones also found himself placed in a socially constructed category that depicted blacks as "niggers," poor, of low mental capacity, and capable of committing a plethora of crimes, including murder. Even the black community, politically and socially disempowered, could raise little public protest over the murder of Alice Jones or the handling of the case and its outcome.

"John Chinaman," Racism, and Crime

The Chinese in Halifax also lived under an aura of opposition and suspicion. Ignorance bred many of these feelings towards the city's Chinese residents. An article by "Observer" in the *Maritime Merchant* of 1918, "a prominent Halifax periodical," dealt with this issue. The common perception of "John Chinaman," the author noted, "is that he is making all kinds of money in his little laundry, spending very little of it here, and sending the most of it home to China. Nobody wants a Chinaman for a neighbor. Nobody associates with a Chinaman."[64] As a consequence of this anxiety about the presence of John Chinaman in their midst, "Observer" suggested that a "great gulf ... between the oriental and the occidental" had formed, preventing the latter from getting to know the former. Rather than leading a privileged life, the writer believed "John" to be "a stranger in a strange land, with nobody to take a sympathetic interest in him."[65] This was certainly the case for most of the Chinese in Halifax and in the rest of Canada. Misunderstandings about Chinese culture and lifestyles contributed to the process of racialization in Halifax. As well, recognition of the socio-cultural differences between whites and the Chinese, as highlighted by "Observer," helped to produce a relationship of dominance that favoured white society over Chinese.[66] From this emerged a vision of Chinese men spreading the twin evils of opium use and gambling, the former of which enslaved young white women.

The social and geographic organization of the Chinese community in Halifax lent credence to this image. A "Chinatown" on the scale of those in Vancouver and Montreal did not develop in Halifax during this period. Nevertheless, as one contemporary recalled, a small Chinatown did appear in the downtown core by the 1920s. Chuck Lee, one of the "pioneers of the Halifax Chinese community," recalled that his father opened a grocery store at 33 Granville Street. Another, owned by Man Wo, stood on the corner of Granville and Salter streets, and in between them the Lee Society and the Chinese Freemasons had their offices. A walk along the adjacent streets of Grafton, Hollis, and Sackville in the 1920s would reveal Chinese cafes, laundries, and corner stores. Many of these businesses doubled as the owners' residences.[67] This compact neighbourhood proved to be both beneficial and detrimental to its inhabitants. The existence of a mini-Chinatown was useful because it provided a home, contact with friends, and a source of income. In a city crippled by economic depression, and in which "racial prejudices were rampant," work in a Chinese restaurant or laundry kept many Chinese immigrants from destitution.[68] As a result, the Chinese forged a feeling of ethnic consciousness that gave them a sense of collective strength. On the other hand, Chinatown was harmful to its residents because their cohesion kept them separated from the rest of the city and denied them, along with blacks, social equality.[69] It also furnished white Halifax, and the police in particular, with an area to pinpoint as a source of crime. As Kay Anderson notes in her study of racial discourse in Canada, white society pictured the Chinese as consummate gamblers and their communities as centres of lawlessness, where evil lured white women into prostitution and debauchery. Chinatowns became everything that white society did not perceive itself to be and thus confirmed the "otherness" of the Chinese.[70]

In Halifax, the Chinese community endured repeated attacks in the city's war against crime and immorality. Preparations for battle began as early as 1918. In July, various social and commercial organizations convened a meeting to form a committee to wipe out immorality. Committee chairman Dr. W.H. Hattie, the provincial health officer, outlined the targets of their campaign: "Open violation of the Lord's Day Act, Chinese Restaurant Cubby Holes of Unsavoury Reputation and Alien-Owned 'Cabarets,' the Resorts of the 'Underworld' and other Features of 'Modernity' Now so Rampant in Halifax." These establishments, by providing men and women with a public venue in which to socialize outside the conjugal family and home, represented symbols of modernity that many in Halifax feared and distrusted. At a time when most Canadians were making sacrifices for the war effort, the committee asserted, "alien" businesses should not be allowed to open on Sundays. In the words of their spokesman: "The majority of ice cream parlours and restaurants which most openly disregard the Sunday closing regulations are operated by aliens; and it is in alien establishments which one finds the greater number of the various devices for gambling by machinery which are now so common in Halifax and which are operated in ... defiance of a dozen or more statutes, municipal, provincial, and federal."[71] From the perspective of the committee, the Halifax Chinese community could be equated with these alien businesses, which were fronts for gambling and opium dens as well as moral traps for young women. In tackling the problem of vice, the Halifax Police Department reinforced the image of the Chinese as a threat to decency. The police launched a series of raids on Chinese laundries, cafes, and homes in order to seize opium, break up gambling rings, and rescue "girls" from the clutches of evil. In so doing, they helped to solidify the belief that the Chinese, not whites, could be blamed for the spread of vice – notably drugs.

Opium smoking had not become a real concern to Canadians until the dawn of the twentieth century. Police raids on Chinese "dens of infamy" raised public awareness of the presence of opium in Canada. Similarly, it was only when the "heathen Chinee" became associated with opium and its sale to whites, even though some "respectable" Canadians had used opium without legal censure, that the state ciminalized its use. The Opium and Drug Act, 1911, helped to establish the image of the Chinese as one of the main causes of drug addiction and its concomitant social problems: white slavery, gambling, and immorality.[72] In Halifax, public opinion connected the use of opium and the illicit drug trade to a "certain class" of Chinese. The *Halifax Herald* described the drug traffic as "insidious in its ramifications and persistent in its schemes for circumventing justice." Here was an evil that clearly had to be stopped.[73] Emily Murphy, arguably the most prominent crusader against the drug trade in Canada in the early 1920s, was a staunch opponent of drugs, especially opium. In her 1922 exposé of drug abuse in Canada, *The Black Candle*, Murphy describes the inside of a Chinese opium den. "In smoking," she begins, "the Chinaman reclines on a mattress on the floor, having beside him a pan which contains the opium 'lay-out.' The cracks of the windows and doors are packed with wet cloths that the odor of the smoke may not escape." "For the same reason," she continues, "the keyhole of the door is plugged, thus preventing its being locked with a key. The door is secured with a butcher knife driven into the door-jamb. [Then the] available furniture is piled against the door to guard against surprises."[74] Murphy also attributed the successful operation of the "Drug Ring" to "Occidental ingenuity and Oriental craftiness." While the Chinese are "patient, polite, and persevering," their role in the drug trade led Murphy to suspect that they wanted to "injure the bright-browed races of the world."[75]

Legal authorities in Halifax shared her alarm, and their crackdown on opium users yielded some quick results. During 1922 the police made a succession of raids on "opium dens," seizing a quantity of the drug and laying criminal charges on each occasion. Within these dens, according to the *Halifax Herald:* "Social evil flourishes ... Our young girls must be had in mind in dealing drastically with the men or women who sell or have the drug in their possession."[76] The *Herald* also declared that opium smuggling, mainly from Montreal and the United States via Saint John, had become a widespread evil in Halifax.[77] The Chinese, in the *Herald*'s view, controlled most of the opium coming into the city: "[thus] these people must be taught that British law does not permit them to corrupt themselves and their fellows physically and morally."[78] In 1922, in each of the twelve convictions registered by the Halifax Police Court for offences against the Opium and Narcotic Drug Act, the magistrate levied fines of up to $200.[79] These twelve convictions, eleven for "Breach of opium and drug act" and one for "Smoking opium," comprised the total convictions for drug offences in the entire province of Nova Scotia in 1922. All but two of the twelve men convicted were Chinese, a trend consistent with the rest of Canada.[80] After peaking at 1,858 in 1921 and 1922, the number of convictions under the revised Opium and Narcotic Drug Act steadily declined across Canada, reaching a low of 446 in 1930. However, the percentage of Chinese as a percentage of the total number of convictions remained above 60 percent in both Halifax and the country generally.[81] In Halifax at least, "these people" certainly did receive a lesson about the expediency of British law and justice.

Despite the apparent success of the police in reducing the incidence of opium use, public fear in Halifax continued to rise. Two editorials, one appearing in February and the other in April 1929, underscored this concern. In discussing Parliament's consideration of amendments to the Drug Act, the *Halifax Chronicle* commented: "dope traffic ... has become an evil of widespread proportions." The *Chronicle* also described those who distributed narcotics as "men of the lowest type, who are utterly unconcerned as to the harm they do."[82] The *Halifax Herald* elaborated upon this theme and went one step further by identifying the purchasers. The main market for the growing quantity of "contraband" in Halifax, the *Herald* argued, could be found among the city's Chinese population. The "drug ring" itself, however, had managed to elude police detection. To rectify this, the *Herald* suggested that the "authorities would do well to keep a watchful eye on those parts of the city where evidences of the traffic would be likely to appear first."[83] The Halifax police followed this advice by concentrating their efforts at solving the city's drug problem on Chinatown. In August 1929, the police swooped down on a Chinese grocery store where they discovered an "opium den," replete with opium, pipes, lamps, and whisky. The owner of the store, Hem Key, faced charges of illegal possession of opium and of violating the Nova Scotia Temperance Act.[84] A few months later, in October, the police forced their way into a Chinese laundry and found an opium den "going full blast in the heart of the city." The police escorted three Chinese men to police headquarters, where they were charged with smoking opium and concealing poppy leaves used for the "repose of those who went into the land of opium dreams." This raid netted one of the largest seizures of opium to date in Halifax.[85] Not to be outdone, Special Officer Thomas Kennedy, at the end of November 1929, made "one of the most successful lone-handed raids ever to be staged on Halifax's Chinatown in many years." Kennedy, while on patrol, noticed a Chinese man rush into a grocery store on Granville Street, which immediately made him suspicious. Kennedy entered the store and proceeded to the upstairs rooms, where he arrested fourteen Chinese men for smoking opium.[86] In police court, six of the accused pleaded guilty to breaching the Opium and Narcotic Drug Act and paid fines totalling $350.[87] These cases heightened the debate surrounding the "dope evil" in Halifax and placed the blame for this problem squarely on the Chinese. It seemed to the police, court officials, and the general public that to rid the city of this scourge, the Chinese, with their unlawful indulgences, would have to be brought to justice.

Many believed that, like opium use, gambling among the Chinese also thrived as a part of their culture. The illegality of this activity, coupled with its implied significance as a component of the Chinese character, marked another area in which the Halifax criminal justice system and white society viewed the Chinese as a criminally inspired "other." In 1919, 25 Sackville Street played host to a mass arrest of twenty-three "Celestials" for keeping and being present in a gaming house. Acting on a tip, the police stormed into this restaurant and caught these "natives of the Far East" playing "their favourite game" in the basement.[88] Henceforth, the police kept a close watch on this establishment, but with few facilities at their disposal for entertainment, Chinese men in Halifax continued to frequent 25 Sackville Street. Nightly gatherings there resulted in another raid in 1924. On this occasion, four Chinese men were arrested, Fong Sing for operating a gambling house and the others for playing "Fan Tan."[89] The vice of gambling was not the exclusive prerogative of the Chinese: gambling among whites also flourished throughout these years. Gambling usually took place behind closed doors in several hotels, including the Lord Nelson and the Hotel Novascotian, as well as in poolrooms in the North End. Although doctors, lawyers, businessmen, and politicians gambled, illegal gambling was associated predominately with the Chinese.[90] And try as they might, the Halifax police could not stamp out illegal gambling.

This did not, however, prevent them from voicing their determination to do so. In a 1930 conversation with the *Halifax Herald*, Chief Howard Palmer vowed: "I am going to make a thorough clean up of the gambling devices which are becoming common to the city." He gave his officers instructions to "seize all these gambling machines," prompting one paper to announce: "[the] round-up is on and slot machines are fair game for the police."[91] In one raid alone the police confiscated fifteen slot machines and five gaming tables. As Chief of Police Conrad stated: "If the machines are not removed, we will seize them all. We are determined to stamp them out." Sidney Mintz, Angelos Paros, Peter Poulis, Edward McIsaac,

William Gosine, and Leo Resk, the so-called "highups" in the gambling racket, were charged under section 235 of the *Criminal Code* for unlawfully leasing and hiring a "gambling, wagering or betting machine or device."[92] Regardless of the police attempts to curtail the gambling of whites and foreigners, the Chinese continued to be their primary focus. Peter S. Li emphasizes the importance of opium use and gambling as recreational outlets for Chinese men who lived in poverty and social isolation. They also served as one of the main sources of interaction among friends.[93] In the small Chinese enclave in Halifax, opium and gambling were key to the community's sense of solidarity. Yet the Chinese did not use these practices to define themselves or their place in Halifax. This was done by those residents of the city who chose to identify the Chinese and their lifestyle as immoral and criminal. Paralleling the situation in Vancouver, in Halifax many white residents saw the Chinese as born gamblers and opium smokers. These private vices, so most members of respectable Halifax society maintained, ran counter to their own law-abiding nature and, as such, had to be eradicated. Frequent police round-ups of Chinese men for opium use and gambling solidified this feeling and contributed to the construction of a deviant identity for Halifax's Celestials.[94]

The flashpoint of opposition to the Chinese and their so-called improprieties arose over their relationship with Halifax's white "girls." The booths in some Chinese cafes and restaurants became the centre of this controversy and a symbol of the social ills that afflicted modern Halifax. In one sense, these booths became signifiers of Asian duplicity in the moral corruption of young women and Halifax itself. They also denoted the otherness of the Chinese and the fact that their world, embodied by the "Orient," had to be strictly regulated.[95] In a 1923 interview with the *Evening Echo*, Halifax policewomen May Virtue and Bessie Egan condemned the scenes that occurred nightly in these booths, where women associated with men and indulged in consuming liquor. According to Virtue, "More than fifty per cent of the crime with which we have come in contact has had its origins in Chinese booths." Egan added that more young women had been led astray by being in these booths than by any other source of indiscretion in the city. Once women of "good character" had experienced their first taste of the "initiations of the booths," both policewomen agreed, they fell "easy prey to sin and crime."[96]

Halifax's police chief shared these sentiments. Frank Hanrahan told one reporter that the dangers posed by Chinese booths were a "grim reality." Their presence, Hanrahan said, hampered police initiatives to arrest immoral characters and combat vice. "Street-walkers" made their headquarters in Chinese cafe booths. Many of these young women hailed from small towns and villages across the province, having come to the city in search of employment. Once in Halifax, the "thoughtless or foolishly adventurous" among them were spellbound by the "delightfully cosy and attractively risky" appeal of the booths.[97] The booths' elimination, Hanrahan and an *Echo* editorial asserted, would reduce the number of "delinquent girls" roaming the streets and deprive Chinese men of a place to conceal their drinking and other immoral pursuits.[98]

The *Echo* placed the blame for these "recesses" on the Chinese and their ideas about Western women. Here the paper evoked images of the Chinese that depicted them as different from and in opposition to white society. The "Eastern point of view" with regard to the morality of women, the *Echo* insisted: "is centuries older than the Western and ineradicably established in the Asiatic consciousness. For this reason ... the conditions allowed to exist here should be most closely looked after. If efforts to save Halifax girls from following the path that means destruction are hampered by these booths, then it should be an easy matter to have them abolished." Their removal would certainly mean the "disappearance of a fruitful source of evil and [would] be hailed with delight by all reform workers."[99] In Halifax and other Canadian cities, the booths in Chinese restaurants and cafes were a source of concern for many social reform advocates and criminal justice officials. The booth was interpreted as a "threatening 'partition' because it obstructed the white dominant gaze. In circumventing this barrier, Canadians constructed a narrative about the evils that transpired behind the partition and within the hidden minds and souls of Chinese men."[100] The police thus had to root out this menace. In late December 1923, Halifax's Chinatown received a "rude jolt" as the police department raided two of the city's most frequented "resorts": the Canton Cafe and the Royal Cafe on Hollis Street. The police charged the owners, Chin Sinn (Canton) and Hong Han (Royal), with procuring, and six "girls," said to be "frequenters," with vagrancy.[101] These women had allegedly been lured into the cafes on the promise of free meals in exchange for their help in enticing male customers inside and making themselves available, at the patrons' request, for "roadhouse" parties.[102] Five of the six women pleaded guilty and each received a one-year suspended sentence and a warning from Magistrate Archibald, who told them that if he saw them in his courtroom again on the same charge he would send them to jail.[103] Chin Sin and Hong Han, on the other hand, escaped conviction. Two of the women arrested, Helen McKenzie and Elsie Johnson, testified for the Crown. They told the court of the "revolting" and "disgusting" scenes they had witnessed in the booths between men and women. Yet, regardless of their testimony, the Crown could not muster enough solid evidence to convict the accused of procuring. The blame for this rested with the police, who had laid the wrong charge. In the *Echo*'s opinion, any other charge would have produced a guilty verdict and struck a blow against this "evil which ha[d] disturbed all [of] Halifax."[104]

Despite this setback, the police received ample praise for their work. Thanks to their efforts, one newspaper boasted, the "unsavoury condition[s] under which they [the cafes] were being conducted ha[d] been dragged into the limelight."[105] Another felt that the police department should be "congratulated upon the prompt response to the campaign for cleaning out the booths in Chinese restaurants."[106] This state of affairs could not be allowed to continue, the *Echo* insisted, since it only tarnished the good name of the city. While this action may have persuaded some women who visited these "haunts" to leave the city, the *Echo* considered this to be only temporary. The real problem continued to be the Chinese and their persistence in operating these establishments. As one editorial argued: "The Oriental idea of the functions of a restaurant is based upon the similar resorts in the Orient, where girls are bred for such a fate. White girls are not less but more attractive to them as lures for customers and one such girl is quite sure to decoy several others into the same path as she is following."[107] The "clean up" campaign directed against Chinese cafe booths in the name of law, order, and morality included an anti-drug emphasis. Chief Hanrahan informed the public that the raids had been designed to stamp out vice and to prevent the drug habit from "catching on" in Halifax. But policewoman Virtue felt that it was already too late to save Halifax from the drug menace. It seemed to her that drug use had spread among white women in the city, especially those who patronized Chinese cafes.[108]

In addition to dealing with the modern problems of drugs and restaurant booths, the criminal justice system had to cope with an alleged Chinese prostitution ring. Some of the same women who spent their time in cafe booths, it was claimed, were also enticed into prostitution. As early as 1913, following a police assault on Chinese laundries, a "hue and cry" went up about the prevalence of prostitutes in Halifax. Yet to those engaged in "rescue" work in the city this "present[ed] absolutely nothing new" since Chinese involvement in the "street walking" trade had "been going on for years."[109] As the owners of these laundries and cafes, whose "objectionable surroundings" bred vice and immorality, the Chinese, according to the reformers, carried some of the blame for Halifax's ongoing struggle with prostitution.[110] In a move to overcome this obstacle to law and order, the police and legal authorities pursued and prosecuted Chinese men who owned or kept "bawdy houses." Charlie Soo learned first hand of this initiative. After a lengthy surveillance of the American Cafe on Hollis Street, the police decided in March 1921 to mount an assault on "an extensive scale." They arrested the owner, Soo, and two young women since no "good reason could be shown for their presence [there]." Charged with unlawfully keeping a bawdy house for the purpose of prostitution, Soo was convicted and sentenced to six months in the City Prison.[111] Other Chinese merchants met a similar fate. Charles Yip and Yip Kwi, co-owners of the Shanghai Cafe, were caught up in the police department's drive to "clean up" the city. In March 1923, a squad of officers arrested them for running a "disorderly house." Two years later, the police continued with their plans to rid Halifax of resorts of "doubtful character" when they arrested Sing Hee of the Halifax Cafe for allowing his business to be used for the purposes of prostitution. Apparently Hee ran the cafe under filthy conditions and it thus posed a "nuisance" to the public.[112] In Halifax, as in other major Canadian cities, racism and a fear of the immoral character of the other, both black and Chinese, motivated these police activities.[113]

The women found in these places also shared in the guilt. In addition to Sing Hee the police dragnet scooped up Gladys Fleet, Olive Wylde, and Katherine Singer for leading immoral lives. In police court Officer Kellogg told the magistrate that the American Cafe attracted the "lowest types of women" in the city.[114] In fact, white women who worked in or frequented Chinese cafes and restaurants proved to be an irritant to the legal and social reform communities. Alderman W.J. O'Toole, when told of a proposed bill designed to prohibit white women from being employed in Chinese restaurants, heartily endorsed the measure. He told those gathered at a Progressive Club luncheon that the "guardians of the race" had to be kept out of the clutches of the Chinese.[115] Thus, even women who worked for Chinese employers came under suspicion, partly because of the assumption espoused by various legal and social reformers that, because they associated with Chinese men, they must be prostitutes.[116] By working in or visiting Chinese businesses, these "girls" transgressed the boundaries of moral and social order in Halifax and thus fell into disrepute. At the same time, by their apparent collusion in the moral corruption of these women, Chinese men became a threat to the sexual purity of white women specifically and the sexual status quo of white society generally.[117]

In the eyes of many law enforcement personnel, the Chinese represented one of Halifax's most morally and socially corrupting influences. The notion that crime, vice, prostitution, moral debasement, and drug use all emanated from Chinese cafes echoed the views of such social reformers as Emily Murphy, whose *The Black Candle* stresses the need to stringently educate the Chinese in order to make them more appreciative of this country's laws and morals. According to Murphy, "[If] we ... allow the Chinamen to swarm in filthy hovels and to burrow like rats in cellars, what else can we expect but vice unspeakable? We have made these men to be pariahs and perpetual aliens and accordingly, they have become to us a body of death."[118] Like the booths themselves, the Chinese lived in a dark underworld that had to be redeemed by the light of reform. As Mariana Valverde argues, this crisis in Halifax shows how "social purity ideas about vice and sexuality were suffused by racism – and [how,] vice versa, ideas about race were partly shaped by ideas about the sexual practices of different groups."[119] As a central figure in the category of racial other in Halifax, the Chinese constantly faced forms of state-enforced discrimination and had little power to counteract the effects.

"Foreigners" and Halifax's "Opened Gambling Houses ... Booze, and Prostitution Dens"

"Foreigners" in Halifax, those of non-British or non-French heritage other than the blacks and Chinese, found themselves in a similar dilemma with regard to the criminal justice system. Scattered throughout the city, often living in boarding houses in the city's poorer districts, and usually working as unskilled and migratory labourers, these foreigners were rarely accepted by Halifax society and were often branded as potential threats to law and order. In 1919, the police department let it be known that some foreigners had no place in Halifax. Chief of Police Hanrahan and Chief Detective Kennedy said that all "disreputable characters" in Halifax would have to leave the city or be thrown in jail. Seventy-five percent of those who appeared in police court, Hanrahan asserted, were foreigners. They came from far and wide to savour Halifax's "opened gambling houses ...

booze, and prostitution dens." Hanrahan and Kennedy assured the public that these foreigners, most of whom were men, would be driven out of town.[120] But the suspicions the police had about foreigners' being possible law-breakers cannot be justified statistically. The reports of the Halifax Chief of Police from 1917 to 1922, for example, record the number of known male and female offenders as 12,014. Of this total, foreign – that is, non-British and non-French – offenders comprised 8.9 percent, or 1,068, of those arrested for crimes.[121] While to Chief Hanrahan the term "foreigners" may have referred to all non-residents of the city, thus validating somewhat his claim about foreign criminality, the number of non-British or non-francophone citizens captured for violating the criminal law in Halifax remained small. Nevertheless, local discourse often affixed the term "foreigner" to immigrants who, either because of their name or language, did not adjust to Halifax's dominant British social and cultural milieu.

For much of the 1920s and 1930s, xenophobia ran high in certain areas of Canada, including Halifax. Anxiety about modernization and economic depression heightened concerns about "aliens" who might randomly commit crimes.[122] In feeling distinct from and in potential opposition to aliens, those British Haligonians were in fact resisting one of the key facets of modernity: the new social and cultural heterogeneity of populations. Deportation became one state response to this crisis. The Immigration Act, 1906, contained a clause that stipulated that if, within two years of arrival, any immigrant had "committed a crime involving moral turpitude," or had become "an inmate of a jail or hospital or other charitable institution," he or she could be removed from the country. From April 1929 to March 1935, the federal government deported 28,097 immigrants, or 3.1 percent of the 900,000 who had arrived during this period. As well, the number of criminals deported increased by over 50 percent.[123] In Halifax, John Knabe, a foreigner, was one of these statistics. He was arrested in 1932 on a vagrancy charge, Magistrate Barnhill reviewed his case, and he was deported. For police departments, courts, and all levels of government, deportation was an easy way of dispensing with undesirables.[124]

But not all of the foreigners who appeared in Halifax's police court had to leave. Nor did they face such relatively mundane charges as vagrancy. Instead, so many assumed, the city's foreign populace turned to more sinister and notorious deeds, which seemed indicative of their nationalities and inferior mental abilities. A "black hand" case is one such example. In

September 1922, the police detained Evan Varbeff, a Bulgarian, in connection with an anonymous letter he supposedly sent to James Moir, president of Moirs Limited, a Halifax confectionary company. In the letter Varbeff threatened Moir's life unless he left $25,000 in Point Pleasant Park. It read, in part: "Be careful in making know[n] the attempted mystery – or fail to obey the said order – you will be ... Murdered." Moir obliged, and when Varbeff arrived to collect the money the police apprehended him.[125] The nature of this crime led the police to suspect that a foreigner had been behind this scheme. Investigators considered the extortion attempt to be "clumsy" since it relied too heavily upon intimidation for success. Any "Canadian," the police surmised, would immediately do as Moir had done and report this type of threat to the proper authorities. A foreigner, however, might well act differently; and a foreigner would probably assume that the "menace" of death would ensure secrecy. Hence the "circumstances ... among other things led the police to believe that the culprit was of foreign origin." Such a desperate act, in other words, could only be the handiwork of a non-Canadian like Varbeff.[126] Magistrate Fielding committed Varbeff to stand trial and denied him bail. In Fielding's opinion the "court must protect itself. One cannot tell who may receive such a letter."[127] Varbeff was found guilty, and, in sentencing him to five years in Dorchester Penitentiary, the judge intimated that, even though this crime was infrequent, when it did occur, in either Canada or the United States, foreigners were the guilty parties. Judge O'Hearn hoped that this sentence would serve as a warning to others and send a clear message to immigrants that, while this country welcomed them, once here they must learn to respect Canadian laws. Otherwise they would suffer the consequences of "British justice."[128]

Roma, or "Gypsies," appeared to many to be another minority that needed to be taught to abide by the rules of Canadian justice. Although the number of Roma in Halifax was minuscule – in 1929 only one small "band" had set up an encampment in a local field – their image remained one of a dirty and untrustworthy people.[129] As an employee at Clayton and Sons in the 1930s, Harry D. Smith was one day assigned the task of watching a "gypsy woman" who had entered the store in case she shoplifted. Dressed in colourful cottons, gathered at the waist, with a "bosomy blouse effect ... which was intended to be the receiving agent for the stolen goods," the woman hovered over a table of clothes. Smith "kept a beady eye on her, and scrutinized her every movement, her every gesture."

Much to his jubilation, Smith had "thwarted her efforts that morning."[130] Smith's portrayal of this woman, and the suspicious lens through which he viewed her actions, was characteristic of Halifax society. The fortune-telling practices of Roma also brought them into conflict with the law. For most Roma, fortune telling served as one of the few opportunities open to them to earn a living. Yet, as some complained, the state saw fit to outlaw this last vestige of income and community identity.[131] Captain Peter Thomas went into a house on Upper Water Street to have his fortune told and left eighty-five dollars poorer. Sensing something untoward, Thomas contacted the police, who dispatched Chief Inspector George Fox and Detective John Stevenson to the scene. After a brief investigation, they arrested Mary Lee and Pidgie Markovitch for theft.[132] Pidgie Markovitch, local "gypsy maiden," was to become a familiar face to the police. On 3 February 1930, just after a magistrate had dismissed a charge of theft against her, she was once again arrested as a suspected thief.[133] Her repeated arrests are quite likely indicative of the intense scrutiny under which Roma women lived in Halifax. It may be argued that, every day, many people perform acts that might, under a strict construction of the law, be seen as illegal. But such close surveillance of a targeted minority group could, and in some instances did, become a self-fulfilling prophecy: crimes proliferate where authorities are disposed, on the grounds of ideology, to look for them. The same could also be said for most of the city's blacks, Chinese, and foreigners. Despite the rather innocuous nature of the "crimes" committed by Roma women, the police felt determined to bring them to justice. In this case, their identity as both "Gypsies" (and therefore foreign) and women brought them to the attention of the police.

Conclusion

The ethnic dimensions of Halifax's criminal "underworld" struck a discordant note among the city's criminal justice officials and law-abiding citizens. Determined to maintain order and to keep crime in check, many people in Halifax looked upon all those who committed criminal acts with scorn. Those groups who differed ethnically and culturally from the city's largely British character bore the added burden of being perceived as the "other," as of lower status and intelligence, and thus as subject to suspicion. This perception of the other as representing a threat to society's beliefs and values, as well as safety, emerged at a time when racism, as an "oppressive and dogmatic ideology," was gaining a new currency throughout North America. Indeed, racism helped to make the law an instrument that privileged those Canadians of European origin who controlled it. In Halifax, as in Canada generally, there existed a "readiness to use the machinery of the state to regulate relations between 'races,'" with "race" being used by the dominant sectors of society to label as inferior those individuals who were viewed as different.[134] In Canada, as Angus McLaren writes, "eugenically based racial concerns were all-pervasive in interwar Canadian society ... advanced, not by conservatives, but by progressives and medical scientists."[135] As a social category, race divided people and encouraged discrimination. From 1845 onwards, Pachai asserts, a growing perception emerged in Nova Scotia and elsewhere in the country – a perception that quickly became a reality and that saw the province and the country as belonging solely to white people.[136] Halifax prided itself not only on being a modern city but also on being a city that was still very much white and respectable.[137] In this conception of the city, little room could be found for blacks, Chinese, and foreigners since most were considered to be deviant and criminal. "Race" had driven a wedge between white Halifax society and the other and had built an identity for whites "based on what one isn't and on whom one can hold back."[138] Similarly, it gave those Haligonians most concerned with law and order the systematic power to dominate the other and thus to depict them as potentially criminal.

In Halifax from 1918 to 1935, this racist impulse, which had existed before and lasted long after this period, was particularly powerful. As a result, many ethnic minorities, particularly those visibly distinct from most citizens of the city of order, notably blacks and Chinese, lived in a place opposed or at best indifferent to their presence. The mere fact that some minorities lived among themselves – in the case of blacks in the North End suburbs and Africville, in the case of the Chinese in "Chinatown" – only added to their isolation and to the aura of suspicion that shrouded their lives. By being classified as other, they became easy prey for opponents bent on reducing crime and making Halifax a safe city in which to live. In this way, Halifax's machinery of order pinned a disproportionate share of the blame for the city's crime problems upon blacks, Chinese, and foreigners. This tactic of externalizing crime provided a measure of comfort to a homogeneous majority who could feel confident that they did not foster criminality or behave like the other. For blacks, Chinese, and foreigners, though, it meant an ongoing and often losing battle with the police and a justice system intent on suppressing the criminal and immoral behaviour that they associated with these minorities.

CONCLUSION

The Supremacy of Law and Order in Halifax

J.B. Feilding, a prison reform advocate and chairman of the Halifax Prisoners' Welfare Association, best summed up Halifax's uneasy relationship with crime. In a speech at the annual convention of the Union of Nova Scotia Municipalities in 1924, Feilding denounced the province's treatment of prisoners and the entire penal regime. "Now do not let us forget," Feilding told his audience, "that our present methods of penal treatment are grossly wasteful of productive labour, of the tax-payers' money, and our own personal effects." Then, almost pleadingly, Feilding asked, "Can we not get together and check this loss of wealth, at least to some extent?" As a way of underlining the importance of this task, Feilding noted: "War we will always have, so also crime, but we can at least mitigate the evil of both to some extent."[1] So it was that some members of the Halifax community openly accepted the fact that crime had become a permanent fixture in this modern city. Similarly, Feilding's words in some ways signalled a "progressive retreat" in the face of a recalcitrant problem. Social disorder could be checked but not vanquished in this "city of order," and lawlessness and disorder were, reluctantly, considered to be "solidly entrenched feature[s] of the social landscape."[2] Nevertheless, most Haligonians were not prepared to allow crime and disorder to consume their city. Instead, they placed their faith in the power and the efficacy of the law to control the outbreak of crime and to maintain a strict sense of order. A modern city, many believed, could not function without the imposition of order.[3] Yet, at the same time, as Feilding acknowledged, the machinery of order could not eliminate crime, only minimize its occurrence.

Modernity and the rule of law formed the context for the pursuit of law and order in Halifax from 1918 to 1935. From the transformation of the city's economy and the concomitant problems of unemployment and poverty to general social dislocation, Halifax seemed to be a city in crisis. Many citizens blamed modernity for corrupting public morality and fostering crime.[4] In response, local authorities tried to modernize Halifax's crime-fighting techniques and its criminal justice system. Yet this proved to be a protracted and incomplete process. "Traditionalists" considered the justice system in its nineteenth-century form to be well suited to apprehending and punishing criminals, protecting private property, and instilling a general sense of order in early twentieth-century Halifax. "Progressives," on the other hand, had loftier goals in mind. In part, progressivism tried to build the "future good society" by revamping the existing order.[5] Ideally then, crime, in the minds of most progressives, could be controlled and reduced. Similarly, with the proper care and guidance, some criminals could be rehabilitated for the present and future benefit of society. Thus the purchasing of patrol cars, the hiring of policewomen, the introduction of a juvenile court, and the new emphasis upon "crime control" became key parts of the city's modern machinery of order. In this sense, along with cities such as Hamilton, Montreal, Toronto, and Vancouver, Halifax was at the forefront of efforts to modernize its approach to tackling crime. Moreover, like these cities, Halifax was following the lead set by Parliament in its attempt, both during the 1918 to 1935 period and afterwards, to reform the criminal justice and penal systems.[6] These innovations did not, however, mark the triumph of progressivism. On the contrary, while Halifax's criminal justice system contained a few modern elements, it remained tied to the more traditional concerns of punishing those offenders who many thought were irremediable. The continuing influence of the "traditional" strategy for pursuing order can be partly attributed to the city's worsening economic position and to the fact that progressive experiments, such as upgrading the city's prisons, were expensive. While Halifax's "disciplinary technologies" did not always operate in a rational or efficient manner, they constantly strove to combat crime and to monitor society in Nova Scotia's capital.[7]

The rule of law provided legitimacy for the machinery of order, with the responsibility for the "manufacture of order" and the protection of property ultimately resting with the state. With the power of the law and the criminal justice system at its disposal, the state can regulate social relations and achieve a semblance of the correct "disposition of things." The process of doing so, however, in Halifax as elsewhere, remains complex.[8] In other words, while law and order did not dominate Halifax society in the sense that it eradicated crime, it did enjoy supremacy as both a discourse and a guiding principle for civil society. In general, citizens of Halifax prided themselves on living in what they hoped was a "modern" city of order. To that end and to the best of its ability, Halifax's machinery of order performed its duties. But crime and criminals directly challenged the law and social order in Halifax. Histories of crime, Peter Linebaugh notes, have often become examinations of the law and the "machinery of justice" rather than of criminals themselves.[9] I try to avoid this tendency by delving into the world of crime and criminals as they existed in Halifax. I also focus on the factors that directly affected how the city dealt with crime and the lives of those who broke the law. Order is not simply defined by the absence of violence and lawlessness but also by a set of social relations characterized by the inequality and discrimination perpetuated by the criminal justice system.[10]

Most of the people who lived in Halifax opposed crime and its perpetrators. Not only did criminals defy the law but they also disrupted the city's social order. This feeling of opposition persisted despite the fact that Halifax, when statistically compared with Saint John and Hamilton, was not a crime-ridden city. As a result, little support surfaced for measures to rehabilitate criminals. This was in keeping with a traditionalist mindset regarding the genesis of criminality. The criminal, traditionalists believed, chose, according to her or his own volition and due to some inherent individual moral weakness, to break the law. As such, they did not deserve special treatment or attention, only punishment, as meted out by the courts. In fact, so traditionalists argued, the criminal was often beyond reform. Although not every resident of Halifax agreed with this pessimistic view, many viewed crime and criminals with scorn and contempt. Only juvenile delinquents warranted help. By preventing a wayward child from becoming an adult criminal, many felt, the future stability of society would be assured. Hence the emergence of a separate court for juveniles and the resolve of the city's reformatories and criminal justice officials to "save" delinquents. Part of this effort also led to some tight restrictions being placed on the lives of mainly poor, working-class children and their families in order to prevent delinquency. This represented the only significant breakthrough for the "progressive" interpretation of crime as a remediable social problem.

Class, gender, and ethnicity conditioned public attitudes towards criminals. These factors also helped to determine criminality and shaped the way the justice system dealt with offenders. Men like Lewis Bevis and "Spanish Harry" were apparently doomed to live a life of crime. Born and raised in depravity and immorality, they and other working-class and poverty-stricken men formed the core of the city's perceived "criminal class." By constructing a determinate number of causes for crime and an image of the consummate criminal, the media and the machinery of order could easily locate their culprits and affix blame for the city's seemingly never-ending battle against "crime waves." Once the accused was in custody the courts made certain that justice prevailed. But in this setting, in which many defendants received little in the way of equality, "justice" often meant a conviction.

Besides white male criminals in Halifax, women and ethnic minorities endured their own distinct pattern of opposition from the law. Halifax society did not expect women to be a source of criminality. Thus when they did face a criminal charge not only did most women receive a stiff sentence but they also lost their social respectability. The case of Amelia Murray, found guilty on two separate occasions of performing an "illegal operation," illustrates this. Moreover, according to contemporary thinking, some women, notably prostitutes and vagrants, could resort to crime without hesitation. Subsequently, they faced the wrath of civil society and the machinery of order for breaching the Criminal Code and the city's code of moral and social conduct. Women did not fare much better when they turned to the criminal law to settle their grievances. Some wives took their abusive or non-supporting husbands to court, generally as a last resort. A few did win their cases, but the majority lost. Standing before a judicial system determined to keep the conjugal family together, and that did not place women on an equal legal footing with men, only weakened women's chances of success. Women who were physically assaulted by men in Halifax shared this hardship. The local community felt a deep sense of shock and outrage over the brutal murder of Marie Thibeault, but her death sparked even greater trepidation about the social and moral conduct of young women in modern Halifax. Whether as offender, complainant, or victim, justice for women, it seems, had more than one meaning for women and the city's criminal justice system – a conclusion echoed by other studies on women and the law in cities across Canada.[11]

A similar situation faced Halifax's ethnic minorities. As criminals and as citizens of Halifax, blacks, Chinese, and foreigners encountered racial animosity from much of white society. Depicted and treated as the other, blacks, Chinese, and foreigners lived on the margins of Halifax society. Even though they derived some strength from living in close proximity to one another, blacks in the North End suburbs and the Chinese in

Chinatown also incurred the penalties of increased visibility and vulnerability. This tendency to separate these minorities from the mainstream of the community, part of what Kay Anderson refers to as "racialization," continued into the realm of crime.[12] "Othering" made it easy for many observers to see crime not as a product of white society but, rather, as a sign of the corrupt moral and cultural life of the "alien." For many in this city of order, these minorities epitomized some of the worst aspects of Halifax's criminal underworld. The machinery of order, and especially the media, attributed certain crimes to minorities. Blacks, it was thought, orchestrated part of the city's prostitution (white slavery) trade and were prone to acts of violence. Granville Hutchings fell under police suspicion for procuring because of his skin colour, and Louis Jones, executed for the shooting death of his wife, was referred to as a "half white" killer and a "nigger." The Chinese, on the other hand, supposedly acted as the sole purveyors of the "dope evil" and gambling in Halifax. They also allegedly corrupted the lives of young white women who frequented Chinese cafes and booths. In the opinion of some commentators, these "vices" constituted an integral part of Chinese culture. Meanwhile, foreigners could be counted on to attempt an array of fiendish deeds from blackmail to theft. In each instance, the other posed a threat to the social and moral order of Halifax. From this perspective, one sees that the machinery of order had to act swiftly and decisively to capture and prosecute these criminals and to ensure that their illegal ways did not contaminate society as a whole. Thus, it and the law disadvantaged the disadvantaged, to paraphrase Alan Hunt, and, by extension, dominated the dominated in interwar Halifax.[13]

Life in Halifax from 1918 to 1935 did not revolve around the problem of crime. Other issues vied for public attention and people even had time for a bit of revelry. At an assortment of "gay parties and dances" held throughout the city on New Year's Eve 1934, many Haligonians bade farewell to the old year and welcomed in the new. The *Halifax Herald* claimed that it was "one of the gayest New Year's Eve celebrations for some years." Hundreds attended a charity ball hosted by the Goodfellows at the Lord Nelson Hotel, while a dinner and dance at the Halifax Hotel drew a huge crowd. Others flocked to the midnight shows at the theatres, and the tramway extended its hours of service to accommodate the extra commuters. The entire city was a "merry scene" indeed.[14] At moments such as these, modernity must have seemed a pleasant, even exhilarating experience. Yet with it came a harrowing sense of alienation, doubt, and insecurity. Halifax, as the newspapers and other interested parties liked to boast, was a "modern" city. The latest in entertainment, public transportation, and fashion were on display that December night in 1934. But one thing was missing: the absence of a "prolonged social stability" haunted the modern society and its "traditional elites."[15] Since the turn of the twentieth century, Halifax had witnessed a stream of socio-economic changes that had disrupted the daily course of most peoples' lives. In the years from 1918 to 1935 crime became, in the eyes of many, the essence of the disorder that modernity and the "society of strangers" brought with them. Crime appeared to many to be a manifestation of the dark undercurrent of modernity. Both traditionalists and progressives cherished the same goal: keeping Halifax a city of order. However, they differed fundamentally over how to achieve this end. The tensions between these two ideologies helped to shape Halifax's response to modernity and its attitude towards and treatment of crime and criminals. While traditionalists may have commanded more influence than progressives, the attempt to control crime and to ensure order was ongoing. The "city of order," although very real as an ideal (and, as such, was a profound influence on thousands of lives), remained elusive.

APPENDIX 1

Data Relating to Religion, Ethnicity, and Unemployment in Halifax, 1921-41

Table A1.1 Major religious denominations in Halifax, 1921-41

	1921	1931	1941
Roman Catholic	23,140	24,108	29,003
Anglican	16,367	17,008	19,507
Baptist	4,570	4,300	4,928
Methodist	5,634	–	–
Presbyterian	6,628	2,607	2,583
United Church	–	8,919	11,329

Sources: Sixth Census of Canada, 1921, 1:612-13; *Seventh Census of Canada, 1931,* 2:330-31; *Eighth Census of Canada, 1941,* 2:644-47.

*Table A1.2 Major ethnic groups in Halifax, 1921-41**

	1921	1931	1941
English	30,902	31,216	32,389
Irish	10,985	10,761	12,697
Scots	8,245	8,000	11,288
French	3,000	3,643	5,883

* The figures in this table refer to the "origins" of these ethnic groups as designated by the census.

Sources: Sixth Census of Canada, 1921, 1:392-93; *Seventh Census of Canada, 1931,* 2:330-31; *Eighth Census of Canada, 1941,* 2:330-31.

*Table A1.3 Prominent ethnic minorities in Halifax, 1921-41**

	1921	1931	1941
Chinese	141	129	127
German	730	1,256	1,031
Italian	157	128	177
Jewish	578	576	756
Russian	97	91	74
Scandinavian	284	439	513

* The figures in this table refer to the "origins" of these ethnic groups as designated by the census.

Sources: Sixth Census of Canada, 1921, 1:392-93, 612-13; *Seventh Census of Canada, 1931,* 2:330-31, 494-95, 542-43; *Eighth Census of Canada, 1941,* 2:330-31.

*Table A1.4 Unemployment in Halifax, 1931**

Total wage earners	17,780
Unemployed males	2,632
Unemployed females	270
Total unemployed	2,902
Unemployment rate	16.3%

* Reliable unemployment figures for 1921 are not available.

Source: Seventh Census of Canada, 1931, 6:1268, 1280-81.

Table A1.5 Unemployment in Nova Scotia, 1921 and 1931

	1921	1931
Total wage earners	118,084	117,781
Unemployed males	14,064	21,365
Unemployed females	1,499	1,404
Total unemployed	15,563	22,769
Unemployment rate	13.2%	19.3%

Source: Seventh Census of Canada, 1931, 6:2, 1304.

Table A1.6 Unemployment in Canada, 1921 and 1931

	1921	1931
Total wage earners	1,972,089	2,570,097
Unemployed males	169,744	422,076
Unemployed females	24,020	47,882
Total unemployed	193,764	469,958
Unemployment rate	9.8%	18.3%

Source: Seventh Census of Canada, 1931, 6:2, 1304.

APPENDIX 2

A Statistical Profile of Crime in Halifax, Saint John, and Hamilton, 1918-35

Table A2.1 Number of convictions for indictable offences: Halifax, Nova Scotia, and Canada, 1918-35

	Halifax	Nova Scotia	Canada
1918	346	717	17,370
1919	402	767	18,396
1920	292	713	18,443
1921	343	861	19,396
1922	218	701	15,720
1923	106	400	15,188
1924	198	595	16,258
1925	234	624	17,219
1926	312	752	17,448
1927	277	680	18,836
1928	363	891	21,720
1929	414	869	24,097
1930	412	875	28,457
1931	626	1,184	31,542
1932	438	1,072	31,383
1933	546	1,160	32,942
1934	422	992	31,684
1935	389	1,002	33,531

Sources: Forty-Third to *Sixtieth Annual Reports of Criminal Statistics,* 1918-35.

Table A2.2 Number of Convictions for summary offences: Halifax, Nova Scotia, and Canada, 1918-35

	Halifax	Nova Scotia	Canada
1918	1,673	4,794	105,899
1919	2,457	5,533	111,623
1920	2,364	5,790	144,265
1921	1,774	4,711	157,704
1922	1,007	3,332	136,322
1923	679	3,033	137,493
1924	685	3,355	142,999
1925	818	2,790	151,825
1926	1,036	3,568	169,913
1927	1,079	4,362	193,240
1928	1,077	3,426	245,763
1929	1,567	6,231	290,043
1930	1,392	6,299	308,759
1931	2,199	5,324	327,778
1932	2,240	3,563	297,909
1933	1,360	3,922	292,673
1934	1,414	4,216	328,744
1935	1,483	4,818	362,642

Sources: Forty-Third to *Sixtieth Annual Reports of Criminal Statistics*, 1918-35.

Table A2.3 *Number of convictions for indictable offences: Saint John and Hamilton, 1918-35*

	Saint John	Hamilton		Saint John	Hamilton
1918	192	631	1927	140	486
1919	145	789	1928	144	509
1920	183	585	1929	118	543
1921	113	485	1930	124	810
1922	89	420	1931	157	949
1923	34	383	1932	183	1,007
1924	67	395	1933	49	1,194
1925	84	431	1934	195	777
1926	91	406	1935	196	1,011

Sources: Forty-Third to *Sixtieth Annual Reports of Criminal Statistics,* 1918-35.

Table A2.4 *Number of convictions for summary offences: Saint John and Hamilton, 1918-35*

	Saint John	Hamilton		Saint John	Hamilton
1918	664	2,530	1927	1,144	7,067
1919	983	3,045	1928	1,295	9,858
1920	1,270	3,005	1929	1,952	9,765
1921	883	3,442	1930	1,742	12,058
1922	996	3,534	1931	2,179	11,669
1923	823	4,270	1932	1,637	9,403
1924	1,096	4,426	1933	1,549	8,258
1925	1,138	4,371	1934	1,620	9,128
1926	1,173	5,145	1935	1,634	10,027

Sources: Forty-Third to *Sixtieth Annual Reports of Criminal Statistics,* 1918-35.

*Table A2.5 Number of convictions for indictable offences (per 1,000 of population): Halifax, Nova Scotia, and Canada, 1918-35**

	Halifax	Nova Scotia	Canada
1918	6.2	1.4	2.1
1919	7.1	1.5	2.2
1920	5.1	1.4	2.1
1921	5.8	1.6	2.2
1922	3.7	1.3	1.8
1923	2.0	0.75	1.7
1924	3.2	1.1	1.8
1925	3.8	1.2	1.8
1926	5.0	1.4	1.8
1927	4.3	1.2	1.9
1928	5.6	1.6	2.2
1929	6.3	1.6	2.4
1930	6.2	1.6	2.8
1931	10.6	2.3	3.0
1932	7.3	2.1	3.0
1933	8.9	2.2	3.1
1934	6.7	1.9	2.9
1935	6.1	1.9	3.1

* The population figures for the inter-censal years used to tabulate the percentages contained in Tables A2.5 to A2.8 are estimates. They were obtained by calculating the differences in population between 1911 and 1921, 1921 and 1931, and 1931 and 1941, dividing by ten, and then adding this number to each inter-censal year.

Sources: Fifth Census of Canada, 1911, 1:2; *Sixth Census of Canada, 1921,* 1:3; *Seventh Census of Canada, 1931,* 1:348; *Eighth Census of Canada,* 1941, 1:5; Carleton University History Collaborative, *Urban and Community Development in Atlantic Canada, 1867-1991,* 106-12; *Forty-Third* to *Sixtieth Annual Reports of Criminal Statistics,* 1918-35.

Table A2.6 Number of convictions for summary offences (per 1,000 of population): Halifax, Nova Scotia, and Canada, 1918-35

	Halifax	Nova Scotia	Canada
1918	30.4	9.3	12.8
1919	43.7	10.7	13.1
1920	41.2	11.1	16.7
1921	30.4	9.0	17.9
1922	17.0	6.3	15.2
1923	11.3	5.7	15.1
1924	11.2	6.3	15.4
1925	13.2	5.2	16.1
1926	16.5	6.6	17.7
1927	16.9	8.0	19.8
1928	16.7	6.3	24.8
1929	23.9	11.3	28.8
1930	20.9	11.4	30.2
1931	32.1	10.4	31.6
1932	37.1	6.9	28.4
1933	22.1	7.4	27.6
1934	22.6	7.9	30.7
1935	23.3	8.9	33.5

Sources: Fifth Census of Canada, 1911, 1:2; *Sixth Census of Canada, 1921,* 1:3; *Seventh Census of Canada, 1931,* 1:348; *Eighth Census of Canada, 1941,* 1:5; Carleton University History Collaborative, *Urban and Community Development in Atlantic Canada, 1867-1991,* 106-12; *Forty-Third* to *Sixtieth Annual Reports of Criminal Statistics,* 1918-35.

Table A2.7 *Number of convictions for indictable offences (per 1,000 of population): Saint John and Hamilton, 1918-35*

	Saint John	Hamilton		Saint John	Hamilton
1918	4.2	6.1	1927	2.9	3.5
1919	3.1	7.4	1928	3.0	3.6
1920	3.9	5.3	1929	2.5	3.7
1921	2.4	4.2	1930	2.6	5.4
1922	1.9	3.6	1931	3.3	6.1
1923	0.7	3.1	1932	3.8	6.5
1924	1.4	3.1	1933	1.0	7.6
1925	1.8	3.3	1934	4.0	4.9
1926	1.9	3.0	1935	4.0	6.4

Sources: Eighth Census of Canada, 1941, 2:9; Carleton University History Collaborative, *Urban and Community Development in Atlantic Canada, 1867-1991*, 106-12; *Forty-Third* to *Sixtieth Annual Reports of Criminal Statistics,* 1918-35.

Table A2.8 *Number of convictions for summary offences (per 1,000 of population): Saint John and Hamilton, 1918-35*

	Saint John	Hamilton		Saint John	Hamilton
1918	14.5	24.3	1927	24.2	51.2
1919	21.3	28.4	1928	27.3	49.4
1920	27.2	27.3	1929	41.2	66.4
1921	18.9	30.2	1930	36.8	79.8
1922	21.1	29.9	1931	45.9	75.3
1923	17.4	35.0	1932	34.2	60.3
1924	23.2	35.1	1933	32.1	52.6
1925	24.1	33.6	1934	33.3	57.8
1926	24.8	38.4	1935	33.3	63.1

Sources: Eighth Census of Canada, 1941, 2:9; Carleton University History Collaborative, *Urban and Community Development in Atlantic Canada, 1867-1991*, 106-12; *Forty-Third* to *Sixtieth Annual Reports of Criminal Statistics,* 1918-35.

Table A2.9 Number of convictions for indictable offences (per 1,000 of population): Halifax, Saint John, and Hamilton, 1921 and 1931

	Halifax	Saint John	Hamilton
1921	5.9	2.4	4.2
Population	58,372	47,166	114,151
1931	10.6	3.3	6.1
Population	59,275	47,514	155,547

Sources: Seventh Census of Canada, 1931, 2:157; *Eighth Census of Canada, 1941,* 2:9; Carleton University History Collaborative, *Urban and Community Development in Atlantic Canada, 1867-1991*, 106-12; *Forty-Third* to *Sixtieth Annual Reports of Criminal Statistics*, 1918-35.

Table A2.10 Number of convictions for summary offences (per 1,000 of population): Halifax, Saint John, and Hamilton, 1921 and 1931

	Halifax	Saint John	Hamilton
1921	30.4	18.8	30.2
Population	58,372	47,166	114,151
1931	37.1	45.9	75.3
Population	59,275	47,514	155,547

Sources: Seventh Census of Canada, 1931, 2:157; *Eighth Census of Canada, 1941,* 2:9; Carleton University History Collaborative, *Urban and Community Development in Atlantic Canada, 1867-1991*, 106-12; *Forty-Third* to *Sixtieth Annual Reports of Criminal Statistics*, 1918-35.

Table A2.11 Number of cases tried before the Halifax Police Court, 1910-20

	All cases	Drunkenness cases
1910-11	1,715	598
1911-12	2,015	866
1912-13	2,229	735
1913-14	2,974	1,462
1914-15	3,435	1,700
1915-16	3,045	1,576
1917-18	2,124	572
1918-19	2,414	1,020
1919-20	3,204	1,291
Total	23,155	9,820 (42.4%)

Source: Halifax Herald, 31 December 1921.

*Table A2.12 Number and types of offences in Halifax, 1917-20**

	1917-18	1918-19	1919-20
Abandoning Infant	–	1	1
Absent from Corps	26	23	–
Abusive Language	–	2	12
Administering Drugs	2	–	–
Affray	–	22	30
Arson	–	1	–
Assault, Common	116	205	290
Assault, G.B.H.	25	29	37
Assault, Indecent	2	7	2
Assault, Indecent (Attempt)	–	1	–
Attempt to Rape	–	1	–
Attempt Burglary	–	2	–
Attempt to Steal	–	1	–
Attempt to Allure Girl	–	1	–
Attempted Suicide	–	–	–
Bigamy	2	–	–
Breaking and Entering	–	9	10
Buggery	–	2	4
Burglary	–	4	5
Carrying Concealed Weapons	–	2	7
Committing Damage	–	35	40
Corrupting Witness	1	3	–
Cruelty to Animals	4	1	–
Desertion	–	3	–
Discharging Firearms	–	2	2
Disorderly House, Keeping	11	7	–
Disorderly House, Inmates	10	7	8
Disturbance	114	131	202
Drinking in Public Place	–	5	8
Drunk	572	1,020	1,291
Escape from Police	–	6	2
Escape from City Prison	3	1	2
False Pretences	2	4	1
Firearms, Carrying	3	1	–
Forgery	7	5	5
Fraudulently Obtain Food	2	1	–
Gaming (Onlooker)	2	6	30

▶

◄ *Table A2.12*	1917-18	1918-19	1919-20
House Breaking (Attempt)	2	3	–
House Breaking and Theft	–	1	–
Incapable	7	6	–
Indecent Act	6	14	–
Inflicting G.B.H.	–	12	–
Inmate Bawdy House	–	9	10
Inmate Gaming House	–	13	35
Keeper Bawdy House	–	9	–
Keeper Gaming House	–	8	–
Manslaughter	3	–	–
Mischief	34	30	46
Murder	1	–	1
Murder (Attempt)	–	1	–
Neglect to Provide	12	3	1
Night Walker	1	2	2
Obscene Language	–	7	10
Offensive Language	–	3	–
Offensive Weapons	–	3	4
Perjury	1	1	2
Police, Assaulting	9	4	9
Police, Obstructing	6	10	14
Procuring of Women for Prostitution	1	–	–
Profane Language	–	1	4
Prostitution	1	1	18
Rape	–	1	4
Receiving Stolen Goods	–	4	4
Resisting Police	22	22	32
Robbery	–	1	2
Robbery with Violence	4	7	5
Seaman Absenting Himself	4	2	–
Seaman Wilfully Disobedient	6	15	–
Selling Cigarettes to Minors	–	1	–
Shop Breaking	–	7	–
Shop Breaking and Theft	7	6	–
Shop Breaking (Attempt)	2	1	–
Stowaways	2	5	14
Theft	118	160	200
Theft from Person	–	1	–

►

◀ *Table A2.12*	1917-18	1918-19	1919-20
Trespass	3	5	8
Unlawful Assembly	–	1	–
Unlawfully Carnal Knowledge	1	–	–
Unlawfully Carrying Pistol	–	1	–
Unlawfully Pointing Pistol	–	2	–
Using Threats	2	10	14
Vagrancy	5	11	15
Violation Bicycle Act	2	–	–
Violation Building Act	–	2	3
Violation Chimney Sweep Regulation	9	–	3
Violation City Health Board Rules	8	10	12
Violation Common School Act	12	–	–
Violation Dog Ordinance	11	–	–
Violation Drug Act	–	1	2
Violation Early Closings	–	5	30
Violation Fire Rules	–	1	–
Violation Hack Ordinance	6	–	–
Violation Health Act	–	16	12
Violation Junk Dealers Regulation	5	–	–
Violation Lord's Day Act	–	6	–
Violation Military Service Act	–	2	–
Violation Motor Vehicle Act	42	119	146
Violation N.S. Temperance Act	128	246	290
Violation Orders in Council	–	53	–
Violation School Board Rules	–	10	19
Violation Street Ordinance	131	85	97
Violation Traffic Ordinance	–	100	–
Violation Truck Ordinance	6	–	–
Total	1,524	2,565	3,056

* These yearly designations cover the period from 1 May to 30 April.

Source: Annual Report of the Several Departments of the Civic Government of Halifax, Nova Scotia for the Civic Years 1917-20: Report Chief of Police.

Table A2.13 *Number and types of offences in Halifax, 1920-22**

	1920-21	1921-22
Abandoning Infant	–	–
Absent from Corps	–	–
Abusive Language	28	2
Administering Drugs	–	–
Affray	27	4
Arson	–	7
Assault, Common	130	139
Assault, G.B.H.	–	–
Assault, Indecent	6	2
Assault, Indecent (Attempt)	–	–
Attempt to Rape	–	1
Attempt Burglary	–	–
Attempt to Steal	–	–
Attempt to Allure Girl	1	–
Attempted Suicide	1	–
Bigamy	–	4
Breaking and Entering	12	23
Buggery	3	–
Burglary	11	19
Carrying Concealed Weapons	3	–
Committing Damage	23	–
Corrupting Witness	–	–
Cruelty to Animals	–	–
Desertion	–	–
Discharging Firearms	1	–
Disorderly House, Keeping	–	1
Disorderly House, Inmates	4	2
Disturbance	197	78
Drinking in Public Place	6	–
Drunk	1,164	451
Escape from Police	–	–
Escape from City Prison	1	–
False Pretences	4	13
Firearms, Carrying	–	–
Forgery	5	1
Fraudulently Obtain Food	–	–
Gaming (Onlooker)	7	1

►

◀ *Table A2.13*	1920-21	1921-22
House Breaking (Attempt)	–	–
House Breaking and Theft	–	–
Incapable	–	–
Indecent Act	13	7
Inflicting G.B.H.	26	25
Inmate Bawdy House	15	16
Inmate Gaming House	8	–
Keeper Bawdy House	14	6
Keeper Gaming House	–	1
Manslaughter	–	1
Mischief	26	22
Murder	–	–
Murder (Attempt)	1	1
Neglect to Provide	7	17
Night Walker	2	–
Obscene Language	23	12
Offensive Language	–	–
Offensive Weapons	5	–
Perjury	7	3
Police, Assaulting	15	9
Police, Obstructing	44	17
Procuring of Women for Prostitution	–	–
Profane Language	22	7
Prostitution	15	4
Rape	2	–
Receiving Stolen Goods	1	3
Resisting Police	47	30
Robbery	6	14
Robbery with Violence	1	–
Seamen Absenting Himself	–	–
Seamen Wilfully Disobedient	–	–
Selling Cigarettes to Minors	–	–
Shop Breaking	–	12
Shop Breaking and Theft	–	–
Shop Breaking (Attempt)	–	–
Stowaways	3	5
Theft	134	106
Theft from Person	–	–
Trespass	8	10

▶

◄ *Table A2.13*	1920-21	1921-22
Unlawful Assembly	–	–
Unlawfully Carnal Knowledge	–	1
Unlawfully Carrying Pistol	–	1
Unlawfully Pointing Pistol	–	–
Using Threats	6	3
Vagrancy	14	35
Violation Bicycle Act	–	–
Violation Building Act	3	–
Violation Chimney Sweep Regulation	–	–
Violation City Health Board Rules	2	–
Violation Common School Act	–	–
Violation Dog Ordinance	–	–
Violation Drug Act	2	5
Violation Early Closings	17	–
Violation Fire Rules	–	–
Violation Hack Ordinance	–	–
Violation Health Act	3	–
Violation Junk Dealers Regulation	–	–
Violation Lord's Day Act	–	–
Violation Military Service Act	–	–
Violation Motor Vehicle Act	359	160
Violation N.S. Temperance Act	125	97
Violation Orders in Council	–	–
Violation School Board Rules	5	–
Violation Street Ordinance	336	9
Violation Traffic Ordinance	229	351
Violation Truck Ordinance	–	–
Total	3,180	1,737

* These yearly designations cover the period from 1 May to 30 April.

Note: The total number of offences for the period 1917-22 was 12,062, an average of 2,412 offences per year.

Source: Annual Report of the Several Departments of the Civic Government of Halifax, Nova Scotia for the Civic Years 1920-1922: Report Chief of Police.

Table A2.14 Number of offences known to the police: Halifax, Saint John, and Hamilton, 1930-35

	Halifax	Saint John	Hamilton
1930	4,390	2,124	22,942
1931	5,048	2,698	2,677
1932	3,508	1,918	12,016
1933	2,837	1,804	10,428
1934	4,212	2,204	12,925
1935	3,452	3,666	13,267
Total	23,447	14,414	74,255
Average	3,908	2,402	12,375

Source: Fifty-Fifth to Sixtieth Annual Reports of Statistics of Criminal and Other Offences, 1930-35.

Table A2.15 Number of offences known to the police (per 1,000 of population): Halifax, Saint John, and Hamilton, 1930-35

	Halifax	Saint John	Hamilton
1930	66.1	44.8	151.9
1931	85.3	56.8	17.3
1932	58.2	40.0	77.0
1933	46.2	37.3	66.4
1934	67.4	45.2	81.8
1935	54.3	74.7	83.4
Average	62.9	49.8	79.6

Source: Fifty-Fifth to Sixtieth Annual Reports of Statistics of Criminal and Other Offences, 1930-35.

Table A2.16 Halifax Police Force roster, 1923

Department number	Name	Rank
1	F. Hanrahan	Chief
2	W. Palmer	Deputy-Chief
3	H. Kennedy	Chief Detective
4	C. Nickerson	City Marshall
5	J.H. Meehan	Inspector
6	D.J. McIsaac	Inspector
7	W.J. Spruin	Inspector
8	J. Miller	Inspector
9	J. Reyno	Detective
10	C. Aitkin	Detective
11	R. Young	Sergeant
12	W. Doyle	Sergeant
13	M. O'Halloran	Sergeant
14	J. Eisenhaur	Sergeant
15	J.J. Conrad	Sergeant
16	J. O'Leary	Sergeant
17	*	–
18	J. Crichton	Clerk
19	J. Simmons	Patrolman
20	J. Johnstone	Patrolman
21	E. Barrett	Patrolman
22	T.A. Gray	Patrolman
23	A.S. Horne	Patrolman
24	W. Mitchell	Patrolman
25	F. Elford	Patrolman
26	G. Malally	Patrolman
27	R. Mitchell	Patrolman
28	T. McDonald	Patrolman
29	J. Kellock	Patrolman
30	T. Phalen	Patrolman
31	J. Collins	Patrolman
32	J. McAdams	Patrolman
33	H. Perry	Patrolman
34	J. Maloney	Patrolman
35	J. Connors	Patrolman
36	J. Martin	Patrolman
37	M. McLean	Patrolman

▶

◀ *Table A2.16*

Department number	Name	Rank
38	G. Fox	Patrolman
39	H. Lawler	Patrolman
40	C. Johnson	Patrolman
41	J.L. Power	Patrolman
42	D. Beazeley	Patrolman
43	A. Woolaston	Patrolman
44	E.L. Price	Patrolman
45	A. McIsaac	Patrolman
46	A. McLellan	Patrolman
47	M. Lawless	Patrolman
48	G. Buckler	Patrolman
49	N. McAlder	Patrolman
50	A. Callaghan	Patrolman
51	P. Young	Patrolman
52	J. Stevenson	Patrolman
53	J.W. Whittemore	Patrolman
54	J. Wilkie	Patrolman
55	P. Ryan	Patrolman
56	J. Walsh	Patrolman
57	S. Kennedy	Patrolman
58	J. Buchanan	Patrolman
59	R. Butler	Patrolman
60	A. McDonald	Patrolman
61	H. McLeod	Patrolman
62	C. Fulton	Patrolman
63	C. Algee	Patrolman
64	D. Tillbury	Patrolman
65	C. Ettinger	Patrolman
66	H. Smith	Patrolman
67	S.P. Grimm	Patrolman
68	J. McIntyre	Patrolman
69	W. Brommit	Patrolman
70	W. Parker	Patrolman
71	H. Smith	Patrolman
72	F. Weaver	Patrolman
73	C. Judge	Patrolman
74	M. Grant	Patrolman
75	C. Ryan	Patrolman

▶

◀ *Table A2.16*

Department number	Name	Rank
76	A. Burges	Patrolman
77	J. Carrol	Patrolman
78	B. Egan	Policewoman
79	M. Virtue	Policewoman
80	M. Griffin	Patrolman

* On the original roster the following note appears: "Note that number 17 on the department number column is left vacant, through resignation of Sergeant White and the City Council's motion on Sergt. Ryan. Ryan's particulars are filed as 55 on the Dept. list, no number having been allotted to him. His old number now being held by Officer J. Carrol, No 17."

Source: Edward Morris Collection, Dr. Barry Moody, Department of History, Acadia University.

Table A2.17 Religious composition of the Halifax Police Department, 1923

Religion	Number	Percent
Roman Catholics	43	53.8
Protestants	37	46.2
Church of England	15	18.9
Baptist	3	3.8
Methodist	3	3.8
Presbyterian	16	20.3
Total (all religions)	80	

Source: Edward Morris Collection, Dr. Barry Moody, Department of History, Acadia University.

Table A2.18 *Number of offenders by gender in Halifax, 1917-22*

	Female	Male
1917-18	159	1,213
1918-19	141	2,431
1919-20	206	2,813
1920-21	103	3,077
1921-22	140	1,631
Total	749	11,165
Average	150	2,233

Source: Annual Report of the Several Departments of the Civic Government of Halifax, Nova Scotia for the Civic Years, 1917-22: Report Chief of Police.

Table A2.19 *Percentage of offenders by gender in Halifax, 1917-22*

	Female	Male
1917-18	11.6	88.4
1918-19	5.5	94.5
1919-20	9.8	90.2
1920-21	3.2	96.8
1921-22	7.9	92.1
Average	7.6	92.4

Source: Annual Report of the Several Departments of the Civic Government of Halifax, Nova Scotia for the Civic Years, 1917-22: Report Chief of Police.

Table A2.20 Incidence of juvenile delinquency in Halifax, 1930-35

	Before the Court	Dismissed	Adjourned	Punished
1930	174	16	71	87
1931	145	18	63	64
1932	157	1	81	75
1933	92	4	54	34
1934	148	18	59	71
1935	124	8	23	93

Notes: Average number of cases before the court annually: 140
Total number of boys and girls before the court: 840
Total number boys before the court: 761
Total percentage of boys before the court: 90.6%
Total number girls before the court: 79
Total percentage of girls before the court: 9.4%

Sources: Annual Report of Statistics of Criminal and Other Offences, 1930, 86-87; *Annual Report of Statistics of Criminal and Other Offences, 1933,* 107-8; *Sixtieth Annual Report of Statistics of Criminal and Other Offences, 1935,* 185-87.

Table A2.21 Incidence of juvenile delinquency in Saint John, 1930-35

	Before the Court	Dismissed	Adjourned	Punished
1930	228	3	–	225
1931	294	–	–	294
1932	208	–	–	208
1933	264	–	–	264
1934	234	–	–	234
1935	212	–	–	212

Notes: Average number of cases before the court annually: 240
Total number of boys and girls before the court: 1,440
Total number of boys before the court: 1,319
Total percentage of boys before the court: 91.6%
Total number of girls before the court: 121
Total percentage of girls before the court: 8.4%

Sources: Annual Report of Statistics of Criminal and Other Offences, 1930, 86-87; *Annual Report of Statistics of Criminal and Other Offences, 1933,* 107-8; *Sixtieth Annual Report of Statistics of Criminal and Other Offences, 1935,* 185-87.

Table A2.22 Incidence of juvenile delinquency in Hamilton, 1930-35

	Before the Court	Dismissed	Adjourned	Punished
1930	405	25	–	380
1931	327	20	6	301
1932	315	27	23	265
1933	310	9	1	300
1934	323	3	27	293
1935	473	28	25	400

Notes: Average number of cases before the court annually: 359
Total number of boys and girls before the court: 2,153
Total number of boys before the court: 1,954
Total percentage of boys before the court: 90.8%
Total number of girls before the court: 199
Total percentage of girls before the court: 9.2%

Sources: Annual Report of Statistics of Criminal and Other Offences, 1930, 86-87; *Annual Report of Statistics of Criminal and Other Offences, 1933,* 107-8; *Sixtieth Annual Report of Statistics of Criminal and Other Offences, 1935,* 185-87.

APPENDIX 3

Report of the Royal Commission Concerning Jails, Province of Nova Scotia, 1933

Findings and Recommendations in Respect to Custodial Requirements for the City and County of Halifax.

While the aforegoing report is applicable to all Nova Scotia, there is more than one reason for additional investigation in connection with the conditions which obtain in the City and County of Halifax. In the first place, because of the larger population of the area, the institutional requirements are manifold in comparison with other portions of the Province. The statistics for the year 1931, indicate 4,853 commitments in the Province of Nova Scotia. It is significant that the Halifax County Jail and the City Prison received a total of 1,833 or nearly 40 percent of the entire admissions in the Province. In the second place there has been for many years much public dissatisfaction with the accommodations and conditions which have been said to exist in these institutions. These conditions have been the subject of critical reports by two Grand Juries, and while improvements have been made from time to time, the severity of the criticism has continued. In the third place, recent proposals for an extensive enlargement of the Halifax County Jail, presented by the Halifax County Council, have failed to receive the endorsation of the Inspector of Penal Institutions, whose approval is required before remodeling or enlargement of the structure can be carried out. In the light of this complex of conditions, the Commission has given additional time and thought to bring about a clarification of the situation.

The Commission has held several sessions in connection with the Halifax problem, and in addition has conducted one public session and many private sessions with judges, officials and committees. It has also examined or heard numerous witnesses. The Commission has inspected the Dartmouth Town Lockup, Halifax City Lockup, the County Jail and the City Prison, and begs to report its findings as follows:

The City and County of Halifax are served by four places of custody.

Halifax Penal Institutions:

1 The Town Lockup. This consists of a single room on the street floor of a wooden structure in the Town of Dartmouth. There are four cells, two of which are in use.

2 The City Lockup. This serves as an over-night place of detention for arrests in the City of Halifax. It is situated in the basement of the City Hall, and has a cell capacity of 15.

3 The County Jail. This has a double use since it serves as a place of detention and also as a place for the serving of sentences. It is situated in an old brick and stone building at the rear of the Court House on Spring Garden Road, one of the main thoroughfares of Halifax. It has 18 single and four double cells.

4 The City Prison. This is located at Rockhead, a farm of 68 acres in the northern section of the Peninsula. It is used only for the serving of sentences, and contains a total of 82 cells.

The Town Lockup:

The Dartmouth Lockup is one of the crudest relics in the Province. It is both unsanitary and unsafe and should have been condemned long ago. The cells are narrow low-topped inflammable boxes without vents for light or air except for gratings in the upper portion of the doors. Plank seats and dilapidated night pails are the only accommodations. A coal stove burns in the place but the cells are cold. It appears incredible that this place should ever be used by a single soul instead of by over fifty persons in the course of a year. The detention of women here, which is not unknown, is quite unthinkable.

The City Lockup:

The City of Halifax Lockup was found to be in an unbelievably filthy condition and was unquestionably one of the worst and most disreputable places of detention which the Commission has viewed. In the women's quarters, four cells were found, each of a maximum width of 3 ½ feet, with no provision for ventilation. In one cell there was a broken cot, which occupied the full width of the cell. No mattresses were used, and no blankets provided. The toilet was in a disgraceful condition and had a broken top. The floor was made of cement, and had no covering save filth. The quarters showed no evidence of having been cleaned for a considerable period.

The men's quarters are divided into two sections of five and six cells respectively, separated by an iron picket door. The six inner cells have tight dungeon-like doors and the five outer ones, which are more frequently used, have picket doors exposed to the corridor. There was absolutely no sitting or sleeping accommodation in spite of the fact that arrests must remain therein over-night and sometimes over an entire week-end. The men must either stand or lie on the cold cement floor like animals in a stable. That they did so was evident from the human excreta still lying unremoved on the floor. A toilet in the corridor was broken, dirty and repulsive. A small sink was dirty and apparently unusable. The walls had not been lime-washed for a long period, and were covered with improper writing. There was no provision for ventilation, and the stench was nauseating. There was no evidence that care of any kind had been given to the cells. The Commission can find no words adequate to condemn the use of pens of this character for the detention of men and women, however guilty they may be, while to the innocent, such confinement is grossly unjust.[1]

In contrast reference may be made to lockups elsewhere in Nova Scotia. One, in particular, situated in New Glasgow, is marked by commendable accommodation and cleanliness. It is equipped with steel latticed cells, while each cell is provided with a removable cot, leather mattresses, blankets, good light and ventilation. Two clean wash-bowls and water faucets are accessible; toilets are properly provided; blankets are sent to the laundry regularly; towels are changed daily; and cells are disinfected, after every occupancy, with hypo fluid.

The responsibility for the condition which obtains in the Halifax City Lockup rests upon the City Council.

The County Jail:

The County Jail was examined by members of the Commission, who found the following conditions:

In respect to accommodation there are 18 single cells and four double ones. These are constructed of brick and cement walls, 16 to 18 inches thick. They have a width of four feet, a height of 8 feet, are 7 ½ feet in depth, and have doors of iron construction. The doors are secured individually with old-fashioned locks to release which takes time. The lives of the prisoners in case of emergency are thereby seriously endangered. This system is not any longer permitted in jails of this capacity.

The cells contain mattresses which lie directly upon the stone floor, the custom being for two prisoners to sleep in a single cell. This is a practice which is prohibited in well-regulated jails, where in times of congestion inmates are required to sleep in the corridors under proper supervision. The ventilation in all parts of the building is far from good, and the lower north corridor is dark, cold and gloomy. There is no adequate accommodation for religious services. There are no satisfactory facilities for caring for the sick or temporarily indisposed, and the section for women prisoners is inadequate.

The equipment is ill supplied. Sanitary facilities are insufficient and unsatisfactory. The toilets are of the crudest type and located in ill-lighted closets. One used by the male prisoners is directly beneath the female quarters, and it is

1 A small detention room was also noted. It was found in an unsatisfactory condition.

reported to the Commission that inmates of opposite sexes are able to communicate with one another. There are no bathing facilities on the ground floor. In the corridors, there is but one dipper. Thus the healthy drink from the same vessel as those suffering from communicable disease. There appeared to be no strict enforcement of cleanliness, with the result that towels, pillows and bedclothing were not satisfactorily clean. There is no visitors' wicket for properly supervised interviews. While prisoners are permitted to receive books and magazines from friends, none are supplied by the jail authorities. All meals are served and eaten in the cell block corridors.

The Commission cannot commend the system under which the jail is conducted. An outstanding defect is lack of segregation. Youths in their teens are mixed with older offenders, the diseased with the healthy, and those awaiting trial with convicted prisoners. Lack of accommodation cannot be held entirely responsible for this condition. The division of corridors admits of at least a threefold classification. The existing state of affairs must be attributable largely to laxity or incompetence of administration.

Another serious failure in the system of conducting the jail lies in the non-use of the prison yard for exercise. That men and women should never be given opportunity for exercise in the open air, though confined over a period of months, is a breach of the jail regulations for which no adequate reason can be advanced.

The authorities exhibit little concern or responsibility for the reformation of the prisoner, by the furnishing of either occupational, educational or other elevating influences. Officials seem animated solely by custodial conceptions of prison work.

The administration makes no arrangement for night supervision. Prisoners after being locked up are left to themselves till morning, with primitive provision for their needs. No prison of this size should be without a night guard regularly on duty.

It is not however necessary to specify in further detail the disabilities of the County Jail. The County Council, which is the body primarily responsible, in a published statement has acknowledged the existence of unsatisfactory and unsanitary conditions, and has proposed to remodel and enlarge the jail. It should be commended for taking this step toward remedying conditions, so far as the building is concerned. The Commission feels obligated, however, to make it clear that there is more than the structure at fault. The antiquated nature of the architecture is not alone to blame for present conditions.

The City Prison:

The City Prison is situated in the northern section of the city. The building is over three-quarters of a century old and is constructed of granite.

In accommodation it provides 82 vault-like cells in a series of corridors, one of which used for storage purposes, still retains the old-time dungeon doors with small grated apertures for light and air. It is an antiquated structure, without proper lighting or ventilation, and there is considerable danger in case of fire. The institution is also antiquated in its arrangements, though commendable attempts have been made to adapt it to better conditions. It is entirely unsuited, however, for the housing of its population of often a hundred or more human beings. The cells are small and dark, and are frequently used for two prisoners at night, a practice which should never be followed. Segregation is mainly limited to a division of the men from the women. There is no hospital accommodation. Those too ill to be about, were found lying in their cells. All cells are without toilet facilities with the exception of badly battered night buckets.

The Commissioners noted that there was no Medical Report Book containing entries as required by law. No physical or mental examination of prisoners on entrance was customary, and the physician was required to make no regular visits but to respond only in case of call. Those suffering from communicable disease were not properly separated from other inmates, and there was little to safeguard healthy prisoners from the spread of infections.

The Commissioners are cognizant of the difficulties under which the Prison Governor labours, and commend the high standards of cleanliness maintained in the old building. The same comment, cannot, however, be made in respect to the appearance of some of the prisoners. Cleanliness of person and attire are regarded as fundamental in modern prison treatment.

The seasonal employment of the prisoners on the farm and in the stone shed is noted. It is the opinion of the Commission that stone-breaking is carried on under questionable health conditions, and that while perhaps better than idleness, such work is not calculated to send the inmates out into society better men.

In this connection the report of the Royal Commission on Penitentiaries in Canada (1914) comments: "Not a word was spoken. But the monotonous raps of the hammers, and the sullen, whitened faces of the forms, half crouching over their unhealthy, unprofitable, degrading tasks, were a mute but powerful denunciation of the system that permitted or rendered necessary, such an outrage. Nothing has been said, nothing can be said, in defence of the twentieth century reproduction of the unceasing toil of the galley-slaves."

Educational efforts are noticeably absent and no recreational facilities exist. There is no usable library, only a stack of worn and uninviting books.

The women inmates seem to be better cared for. They have the use of a corridor in which to work at their sewing. Yet they have little, if any, opportunity for exercise in the open air, and no planned programme for their physical and moral welfare. Their moral reformation seems to be left to chance or depend upon the questionable effect of their loss of liberty for punishment. The Commissioners are unanimous in the opinion that the females should not be admitted to the City prison. With this opinion members of the Prison Committee of the City Council expressed agreement at one of the hearings.

There is no visitor's waiting room provided at the Prison. The Commission received complaints that relatives and friends of inmates were required to remain outside in inclement weather while waiting their turn at the visitor's wicket.

Recommendations

The Commissioners are of the opinion that the evils which prevail in the Halifax Penal institutions are largely the same as those found elsewhere in the Province, but aggravated because of the numbers of those who must of necessity be subjected to them.

The Town Lockup:

It is recommended that these quarters shall cease to be used as being unfit for human habitation, and that provision shall be made immediately by the Dartmouth Town Council for a properly constructed lockup.

The City Lockup:

The Commission believes that conditions in the City Lockup are such as to call for its closing as it is wholly unfit even for temporary detention. The Commission is apprised that the Civic Authorities are alive to the present unsatisfactory conditions, and have considered the erection of a new building for a Police Station and Lockup. We urge the construction of such a building at once, provided it is adequate in size and along modern lines. This structure should take care of all prisoners whose cases are to be finally decided in the Police Court, and would obviate the transfer of arrests to and from the County Jail as at present practiced. Pending the erection of such a building, we advise that the present quarters shall be no longer used, and that temporary accommodation be secured elsewhere.

The County Jail:

The foregoing recommendation for the closing of the City Lockup bears directly upon the well-being of the Jail. As the Jail and the City Court are a distance from each other, there is a constant shuttling of prisoners back and forth, and these must often be re-confined in the vermin-infested Lockup while awaiting call to the adjoining Court. Thus the Lockup is as a continual source of pollution to the Jail, adding to the difficulty of keeping the latter in a clean and verminless condition. It should be said that the Jailer has repeatedly inveighed against this practice in his report book.

There is also to be recognized the unfavorable nature of the structural arrangements in the Jail house. The Commission is, however, of the view as stated above that criticism may be advanced with justice in regard to the administrative method in vogue. These, if altered, would partly if not wholly correct some of the more objectionable features bearing upon the health and morals of the inmates. The acknowledged difficulties met with in observing the jail regulations, have apparently become an excuse for the failure to attempt to observe them.

In respect to the daily exercise of prisoners in the open air, the admission was frankly made in the course of the inquiry that the primary reason for such neglect was the fact that an additional guard would have to be employed. It is subsequently admitted that prisoners could be taken to the jail yard in small groups, even without the additional of an extra man. This was not, however, being done. It is recommended that the jail stipulations in this respect should be consistently carried out. The Commission was surprised to learn that while the Jailer was unable because of lack of assistance to fulfil the obligations of his position, he was at the same time being employed upon other duties in connection with the Sheriff's office. The Commission recommends that the Jailer's time should be fully released for the performance of his duties as such.

In connection with the health of the inmates, the segregation of the diseased and other safeguards of this character, the Commission is not convinced that all which might reasonably be expected under the circumstances is being done. The Commission notes that the Jail Physician has recorded strong protests against the continuance of unsanitary conditions.

The Commission recommends that the Sheriff, the Jail Committee and all who are by law answerable for conditions in the County Jail, shall give their responsibilities and duties more serious and adequate attention.

Under the direction of the Chief Justice, the Grand Jury has made an investigation of the Jail, and prepared certain recommendations in respect to the improvement of these conditions. The Commission has taken these recommendations under consideration, and has noted the proposals. These call for an addition to the present building, and the removal of all persons whose sentences are in excess of thirty days, or failing this, that some form of employment be developed at the County Jail. The Grand Jury, however, failed to indicate either what acceptable provision could be made for the prisoner under sentence of more than thirty days, or what form of employment was practicable on the present site. Other proposals of a varied character have come to the attention of the Commission, to which reference will not be made, as equally unfeasible.

But more important to be considered than all the recommendations of Grand Juries, welfare agencies, and citizens, there remains the outstanding and fundamental objection that the Halifax County Jail is being used for a purpose for which it is not in the least equipped, that is, as a place for the detention of prisoners under sentence. It is also the opinion of the Commission, that the County Jail cannot be reconstructed to provide satisfactory care and treatment of sentenced prisoners upon the present site.

The first remedy, then, for the local situation is that all prisoners under sentence in this institution shall be transferred elsewhere. Legislation already exists to permit this transfer, in respect to some classes of prisoners, to be effected within the County. This action would relieve the Jail of a considerable percentage of its inmates, and go a considerable distance towards the solution of the problem of over-crowding. For the further accomplishment of this purpose, the Commission recommends that legislation be obtained amending Chapter 89 R.S.N.S. 1923, in respect to courthouses, jails and lockup houses, to provide that where there is within a certain stipulated distance of any county jail a penal institution which makes provision for the exercise and employment of inmates, existing jails which lack these essentials shall be accorded the status of a lockup and shall be used exclusively for the detention of prisoners awaiting trial, or sentence, such detention being provided for within the Act.

The inevitable question now presents itself: where shall sentenced prisoners be confined under such conditions and with such facilities for their reformation as will meet the compulsory standards recommended in this report? The answer is two-fold. In the first place, all sentenced prisoners serving terms of more than a month's duration shall, according to the recommendations of the Commission, be committed to the proposed Provincial Reformatory of Nova Scotia. In respect to prisoners sentenced to a period of one month or less, these should be committed in all cases to a re-organized institution at Rockhead, developed on the basis of a district jail to serve for City, Town and County. Further reference, however will be made to this on a subsequent page of this report.

To revert to the matter of the County Jail. The changing of the County Jail to the status of a lockup for the custody of those awaiting either trial or sentence, will not solve the problem completely, either as to capacity or adaptability to the sanitary requirements of the law. The Commission therefore, examined the proposals and plans for alterations and enlargement which were submitted by the Municipality of the County, but which were rejected by the Department of Government concerned. It may be said that these plans were reported on by the Inspector of Penal Institutions as adequate for "an admirable building," but objection was taken to the site, it being understood that the remodelled jail was to be used for sentenced prisoners. This objection would seem to fall to the ground, when provision has been made of the removal of all sentenced prisoners as herein recommended.

The plans call for a complete alteration of the building and the addition of a new wing, which would add to the institution accommodation for 24 additional prisoners. The cost involved was estimated as upwards of $100,000, or at the rate of nearly $4,000 per each additional prisoner, as present cell space has a capacity for 26. In view of the fact that a modern building entirely satisfactory for the detention of prisoners awaiting trial or sentence, has been built at Truro to house 30 prisoners at a figure less than $35,000 it would seem that alterations in the County Jail should be able to be effected more economically than the plan submitted will make possible. In the course of the inquiry, members of the

County Council were heard in respect to the matter, and it was stated that attention had not been given by them to the desirability of certain alternative propositions.

The Commission has been at pains to become conversant with the views of experts as well as of citizens generally in respect to the requirements of a detention centre adjacent to a Court House. It has also considered the wisdom of erecting an expensive prison in the heart of the City, where facilities are not and never can be made available for the proper treatment of sentenced prisoners. Having done so, the Commission is satisfied that the renovation of the County Jail should be carried out under a different policy than the one at present under consideration.

After the study of detention centres elsewhere, and of the dimensions of the County Jail buildings, the Commission is convinced that by certain interior alterations and by the addition of a system of dormitories, steel cubicles and cells, the present building can be made adequate for the detention requirements of all prisoners awaiting trial and sentence.

The first question naturally is: what accommodation will be necessary? The jail population at the time of the visit of the Commission, consisted of 37 inmates, ten of whom were under sentence. The removal of the sentenced men would bring the number down to twenty-seven. With the establishment of the new police centre and lockup as recommended, there will be a still further reduction of cell space required in the County Jail, as those with cases disposable in the Police Court will be held in custody in the lockup adjacent to the City Magistrate's court. The Commission, however, is confronted by the fact that there has been for many years an annual increase in the admissions.

1925-26	427
1926-27	492
1927-28	623
1928-29	680
1929-30	710
1930-31	899

Note: The figures show that out of 881 persons committed to the Jail in 1931, a total of 419, or 48% issued from the City Court.

Looking to the future and times of emergency it would be the part of wisdom to provide accommodation for at least 50 persons, even with the sentenced group removed, or for the same number which has been proposed by the Municipality as adequate both for prisoners awaiting trial and for those under sentence as well. The Commission believes that the Municipality has underestimated the future requirements of this respect.

The recommendation of the Commission calls for two fundamental changes in the present constitution of the Jail, in addition to the removal of all sentenced prisoners. These are, in the first place, the vacating of the building occupied by the Jailer and his family, and second, the removal of all women prisoners from the jail.

For reasons previously enumerated in this report the living quarters of jailers should under no circumstances be within the immediate precincts of the jail or adjoin the jail itself. This view is in accordance with the best modern opinion and practice, and the Commission has embodied a recommendation in its report to this effect. The jailer should be given an adequate salary, enough to live on and make provision for his housing requirements apart from his official expenses.

The Commission has also laid down the further principle, that women offenders shall not be detained in jails mainly or partly occupied by men, and has so recommended in its report. The women's section in the Halifax County Jail should also be vacated.

The release of space by means of these two expedients will, the Commission has reason to believe, furnish the additional area required to bring the accommodation of the County Jail up to the estimated need of 50 beds.

The Commission does not feel itself obligated to go further into the matter than to indicate such basic standards in the erection of Provincial jails as are calculated to improve their condition in Nova Scotia. It calls attention, however, to the fact that the jailer's residence adjoining the Halifax County Jail occupies a ground space equal to 97% of that of the actual jail-house itself. This building in addition to the space released by the removal of the women, would provide within the walls now standing an area almost as great as would be provided by the building of the contemplated wing.

The Commission is able to state on authority that 45% of the type of jail population under consideration may be so classed as to be properly cared for by dormitory and cubicle accommodation. For the rest, individual steel cells ought to be provided.

From an examination of the site plans of the connected buildings at the County Jail, and after consultation, the Commission is satisfied that it is feasible to remodel the present jail house according to the design accepted by the Municipality for that section of the work. On the basis of the plan, this provides for 24 steel cells or nearly 50% cell accommodation. The Commission is further competently advised that the remaining 26 beds can readily be placed in dormitories and cubicles of steel lattice construction within the walls of the jailer's house as part of the general remodelling scheme.

The Commission is in entire agreement with the County Council in respect to the design submitted as to the remodelling of the present jail house. This embraces modern ideas of corridors, guard walks, gang locks and classification facilities. It, however, approves of corridor toilet facilities in lieu of individual cell basins only on the principle that the new quarters are used for remand prisoners exclusively and not for sentenced offenders. It believes that with the addition of dormitory and cubicle accommodation as proposed in place of the jailer's present quarters, the County will have an institution entirely adequate for the services required for some years to come. It is therefore recommended that the County Council should call for plans to remodel the jailer's house, and that the idea of a new wing should be relinquished.

The working out of the Commission's proposal will operate towards the securing of four desirable jail standards. It will separate the jailer's living accommodations from the jail; it will require the removal of women prisoners; it will preserve the present jail yard space, and it will be more economically and quickly done.

The Commission is advised that the expensive Ontario steel cells included in the estimate of $90,000 are entirely unnecessary, and that steel cells made in Nova Scotia such as those used in New Glasgow, will give the necessary service and will be obtainable at a small fraction of the cost of the others. The use of a dormitory of lattice steel construction for half the accommodation as proposed, will further reduce the expenses for the steel cell equipment, and cut considerably the estimated cost of a remodelled jail.

The County Jail question, as will be noted, is inextricably bound up with that of the City prison, as the latter in turn is bound up with the Provincial Reformatory to which reference has earlier been made. It is now necessary to take up the discussion of the City Prison.

The City Prison:

After most careful consideration and after securing the best available advice in the matter the Commission has reached the conclusion that the City Prison is not and cannot be made completely satisfactory for the requirements and purposes of a modern correctional institution. It represents the old fortress type now being abandoned or restricted for penitentiary use. Conversion of the City Prison to modern requirements is impossible upon this site, nor would it be desirable if possible. The small acreage is such as to render impracticable the establishment of a modern prison farm.

The City Prison was visited during the past summer by the Superintendent of one of the largest prison farms in the United States. When asked by a member of the Commission what he would do with the institution he stated decisively that it could not be refashioned to serve the purpose of a modern reformatory.

Nevertheless, as the policy presented in this report calls for a progressive scheme of penal reform, the Halifax City Prison must still serve its present purpose until such time as the Provincial Reformatory shall have been established.

If the Provincial Reformatory, moreover, is to receive only persons with sentences of a month or more, then it will be necessary that the City Prison shall be converted into a district jail suitable for the short sentence group for City, Town and County as indicated above.[2]

Attention therefore must be given to such alterations to the City Prison as will be acceptable in accordance with the standards to be set up by the Province. The Prison contains an unused corridor of cells of obsolete construction, which could be altered for occupation at a minimum of expense. The corridor should, the Commission believes, be pressed into service at once. If the recommendations in respect to female offenders be adopted, as indicated hereafter, the section of the prison now occupied by women's quarters could be released and much additional accommodation thereby provided for males. This removal of the women from the City Prison was recommended by the City Prison Committee in conference with the Commission and it was stated that this would provide 22 additional cells.

Should these alterations not suffice, there are two alternatives to be considered with regard to the immediate policy. The first is, the conversion of one of the floors of the institution into a dormitory section as carried out in many penal establishments. The second, and perhaps the more acceptable plan is the construction by inmate labour of an adequate single storey building within the walls and adjacent to the main building. As elsewhere, this dormitory should be devoted to a selected group of prisoners, the expiration of whose sentence is near at hand, and who will not consequently imperil their expectation of release by disorder or misconduct. This is a necessary expedient to bridge the interval until the gradual transfer of eligible prisoners to the Provincial Reformatory can be accomplished.

This work, however, should be proceeded with in such a way as to form an integral part in a progressive scheme looking toward the development of the proposed Halifax District Jail. To this end the Commission recommends that plans be drafted, and the labour of inmates directed toward the reconstruction of the Rockhead institution on modern principles. Steel cells and such other equipment as will accord with present day standards of district jails should be provided. If possible additional land should be acquired adjacent to the present site.

It is further recommended that the members of the Prison Committee of the City Council should at once consult with the Prison Governor and the Health Officer with a view to the immediate provision of adequate hospital accommodation and better health standards generally. Elementary educational facilities

---

2 In the three year period 1930-33 out of 1916 prisoners committed to the City prison a total of 1455, or 76%, served sentences of one month or under.

should be made available, and more attention paid to the employment of the inmates on the farm during the entire year. Employment, other than stone breaking, which should be retained for disciplinary purposes only, if at all, should be provided.

It should also be borne in mind that legislation will have to be provided to constitute the City Prison a common jail for all offences punishable in any court.

The aforegoing recommendations will, in the judgment of the Commission meet the custodial needs of the City and County of Halifax, and at the same time fulfil the requirements of a sound Provincial penal programme.

Notes

INTRODUCTION

1 *Halifax Herald*, 1 and 4 November 1922.
2 Ibid., 1 November 1922.
3 *Morning Chronicle* (Halifax), 1 November 1922.
4 Ibid., 1 November 1922.
5 Ibid., 3 November 1922.
6 *Halifax Herald*, 6 November 1922.
7 *Morning Chronicle*, 3 November 1922.
8 *Halifax Herald*, 1 November 1922.
9 Ibid., 2 November 1922.
10 *Morning Chronicle*, 2 November 1922.
11 *Halifax Herald*, 3 November 1922.
12 Ibid., 3 November 1922 and 18 November 1922.
13 Ibid., 18 January 1923.
14 Ibid., 18 January 1923; *Morning Chronicle*, 15 January 1923. The outcome of this case is discussed in Chapter 2.
15 Karen Dubinsky, *Improper Advances: Rape and Heterosexual Conflict in Ontario, 1880-1929* (Chicago: University of Chicago Press, 1993), 162.
16 *Halifax Chronicle*, 21 December 1927.
17 Ibid., 17 July 1929.
18 Ibid., 17 July 1929.
19 Ibid., 22 January 1929.
20 *Halifax Herald*, 1 January 1923.
21 Anthropologists have described this aspect of a legal environment as "law-ways," the different mechanisms employed by a society to resolve disputes. See Louis A. Knafla and Susan W.S. Binnie, "Introduction – Beyond the State: Law and Legal Pluralism in the Making of Modern Societies," in *Law, Society, and the State: Essays in Modern Legal History*, ed. Louis A. Knafla and Susan W.S. Binnie (Toronto: University of Toronto Press, 1995), 10.
22 *Halifax Herald*, 26 December 1924.
23 Ibid., 25 June 1920 (emphasis in original).

24 Marshall Berman, *All That Is Solid Melts into Air: The Experience of Modernity* (New York: Penguin Books, 1988), 13-16; Anthony Giddens, *The Consequences of Modernity* (Stanford: Stanford University Press, 1990), 11-12.

25 Giddens, *Consequences of Modernity*, 10, 36, 100, and 105.

26 Charles Taylor, *The Malaise of Modernity* (Concord, ON: Anansi, 1991), 5.

27 Alan Hunt, "Marxism, Law, Legal Theory and Jurisprudence," in *Dangerous Supplements: Resistance and Renewal in Jurisprudence,* ed. Peter Fitzpatrick (Durham: Duke University Press, 1991), 116. According to Michel Foucault, security, or law and order, became a dominant component of modern governmental rationality from the eighteenth century onwards. However, this society of security underwent successive periods of alteration and modernization to meet changing conditions and social environments. See Graham Burchell, Colin Gordon, and Peter Miller, eds., *The Foucault Effect: Studies in Governmentality* (London: Harvester Wheatsheaf, 1991), 2, 20, and 104.

28 Burchell et al., *Foucault Effect*, 94-95. For more on the threat that crime and "fundamental violence" poses to the "order of droit [law]," see Jacques Derrida, "Force of Law: The 'Mystical Foundation of Authority,'" in *Deconstruction and the Possibility of Justice,* ed. Drucilla Cornell, Michel Rosenfeld, and David Gray Carlson, 3-67 (New York: Routledge, 1992).

29 Lawrence M. Friedman, *Crime and Punishment in American History* (New York: Basic Books, 1993), 3-4.

30 David Sugarman, "Law, Economy, and the State in England, 1750-1914: Some Major Issues," in *Legality, Ideology, and the State,* ed. David Sugarman (London: Academic Press, 1983), 253.

31 Derek Sayer, *The Violence of Abstraction: The Analytic Foundations of Historical Materialism* (Oxford: Basil Blackwell, 1987), 107-10; E.P. Thompson, *The Poverty of Theory and Other Essays* (London: Merlin, 1978), 96.

32 Thompson, *Poverty of Theory*, 96; E.P. Thompson, *Whigs and Hunters: The Origin of the Black Act* (New York: Pantheon Books, 1975), 262; Bob Fine, *Democracy and the Rule of Law: Liberal Ideals and Marxist Critiques* (London: Pluto Press, 1984), 142.

33 Douglas Hay, "Property, Authority, and the Criminal Law," in *Albion's Fatal Tree: Crime and Society in Eighteenth-Century England,* ed. Douglas Hay, Peter Linebaugh, John G. Rule, E.P. Thompson, and Cal Winslow (London: Penguin Books, 1975), 26.

34 Eric Colvin, "Criminal Law and the Rule of Law," in *Crime, Justice, and Codification: Essays in Commemoration of Jacques Fortin,* ed. Patrick Fitzgerald (Toronto: Carswell, 1986), 127-29.

35 Ibid., 136; Hay, "Property," 33; Thompson, *Whigs and Hunters*, 263.

36 Amy Bartholomew and Susan Boyd, "Toward a Political Economy of Law," in *The New Canadian Political Economy,* ed. Wallace Clement and Glen Williams (Kingston and Montreal: McGill-Queen's University Press, 1989), 229.

37 R.S. Ratner, John L. McMullan, and Brian E. Burtch, "The Problem of Relative Autonomy and Criminal Justice in the Canadian State," in *State Control: Criminal Justice Politics in Canada,* ed. R.S. Ratner and John L. McMullan (Vancouver: UBC Press, 1987), 93.

38 Michel Foucault, *Discipline and Punish: The Birth of the Prison* (New York: Vintage Books, 1979), 89-90 and 99.

39 Feminist scholars who have examined the victimization of women helped to pioneer the notion of the "power to define" in terms of how the criminal justice system has dealt with women both as victims and as offenders. For a review of some of the initial literature on this subject, see Nicole Hahn Rafter, "The Social Construction of Crime and Crime Control," *Journal of Research in Crime and Delinquency* 27, 4 (1990): 376-89.

40 Greg Marquis, "Law, Society, and History: Whose Frontier?" *Acadiensis* 21, 2 (1992): 162. For earlier assessments of the writing of Canadian legal history, see David H. Flaherty, "Writing Canadian Legal History: An Introduction," in *Essays in the History of Canadian Law,* ed. David H. Flaherty (Toronto: University of Toronto Press, 1981), 1:3-42; André Morel, "Canadian Legal History: Retrospect and Prospect," *Osgoode Hall Law Journal* 21, 2 (1983): 159-64; Barry Wright, "Towards a New Canadian Legal History," *Osgoode Hall Law Journal* 22, 2 (1984): 349-74; D.G. Bell, "The Birth of Canadian Legal History," *UNB Law Journal* 33 (1984): 312-18; Brian Young, "Law 'in the Round,'" *Acadiensis* 16, 1 (1986): 155-65.

41 David Sugarman made this claim in the foreword to Knafla and Binnie, *Law, Society, and the State*, ix.

42 For examples of this trend, see Desmond H. Brown, *The Genesis of the Canadian Criminal Code* (Toronto: University of Toronto Press, 1989); D.J. Bercuson and L.A. Knafla, eds., *Law and Society in Historical Perspective* (Calgary: University of Calgary Press, 1979).

43 Knafla and Binnie, "Introduction," 4; Young, "Law 'in the Round,'" 159-60; Marquis, "Law, Society, and History," 174; Jim Phillips, "Crime and Punishment in the Dominion of the North: Canada from New France to the Present," in *Crime History and Histories of Crime: Studies in the Historiography of Crime and Criminal Justice in Modern History,* ed. Clive Emsley and Louis A. Knafla (Westport, CO: Greenwood Press, 1996), 180-81. More recent examinations of Canadian legal history are provided by R. Blake Brown, "A Taxonomy of Methodological Approaches in Recent Canadian Legal History," *Acadiensis* 34, 1 (2004): 145-55; and Jim Phillips, "Why Legal History Matters," Victoria University Wellington Law Review 41, 3 (2010): 293-316.

44 It has also been argued that "Canadian criminal justice history is inherently multi-disciplinary in nature." See Russell Smandych and Bryan Hogeveen, "On the Fragmentation of Canadian Criminal Justice History," *Canadian Journal of Criminology* 41, 2 (April 1999): 193.

45 On this point see, for example, John A. Dickinson, "Native Sovereignty and French Justice in Early Canada," in *Essays in the History of Canadian Law,* vol. 5, *Crime and Criminal Justice,* ed. Jim Phillips, Tina Loo, and Susan Lewthwaite (Toronto: University of Toronto Press, 1994), 17-40; and Carolyn Strange, "Patriarchy Modified: The Criminal Prosecution of Rape in York County, Ontario, 1880-1930," in Phillips et al., *Essays*, 5:207-51.

46 Jean-Marie Fecteau, "Between the Old Order and Modern Times: Poverty, Criminality, and Power in Quebec, 1791-1840," in Phillips et al., *Essays*, 5:293-323; and Susan Lewthwaite, "Violence, Law, and Community in Rural Upper Canada," in Phillips et al., *Essays*, 5:353-86.

47 In particular, see Rainer Baehre, "Prison as Factory, Convict as Worker: A Study of the Mid-Victorian St. John Penitentiary, 1841-1880," in Phillips et al., *Essays,*

5:439-77; and Peter Oliver, "'To Govern by Kindness': The First Two Decades of the Mercer Reformatory for Women," in Phillips et al., *Essays*, 5:516-71.

48 Some of the key works include Rainer Baehre, "From Bridewell to Federal Penitentiary: Prisons and Punishment in Nova Scotia before 1880," in *Essays in the History of Canadian Law*, vol. 3, *Nova Scotia*, ed. Philip Girard and Jim Phillips (Toronto: The Osgoode Society, 1990), 163-99; Peter Oliver, *"Terror to Evil-Doers": Prisons and Punishments in Nineteenth-Century Ontario* (Toronto: University of Toronto Press, 1998); Wendy Ruemper, "Locking Them Up: Incarcerating Women in Ontario, 1857-1931," in Knafla and Binnie, *Law, Society, and the State*, 351-78.

49 Greg Marquis, "Towards a Canadian Police Historiography," in Knafla and Binnie, *Law, Society, and the State*, 477-96; Greg Marquis, "'A Machine of Oppression under the Guise of the Law': The Saint John Police Establishment," *Acadiensis* 16, 1 (1986): 58-77; Tamara Myers, "Women Policing Women: A Patrol Woman in Montreal in the 1910s," *Journal of the Canadian Historical Association* (1993): 229-45; William M. Baker, "The Miners and the Mounties: The Royal North West Mounted Police and the 1906 Lethbridge Strike," *Labour/Le Travail* 27 (1991): 55-96.

50 Marquis, "Towards a Canadian Police Historiography," 490. Allan Greer has done important work on the origins of the police and state formation in nineteenth-century Canada. See Allan Greer, "The Birth of the Police in Canada," in *Colonial Leviathan: State Formation in Mid-Nineteenth Century Canada*, ed. Allan Greer and Ian Radforth, 17-49 (Toronto: University of Toronto Press, 1992).

51 D. Owen Carrigan, *Crime and Punishment in Canada: A History* (Toronto: McClelland and Stewart, 1991). Carrigan has also published a book on the history of juvenile delinquency in Canada. See D. Owen Carrigan, *Juvenile Delinquency in Canada: A History* (Toronto: Irwin, 1998).

52 It is important to note that a group of scholars, led by Jim Phillips, Philip Girard, and R. Blake Brown, has begun to research and write a multi-volume legal history of Canada.

53 John C. Weaver, *Crime, Constables, and Courts: Order and Transgression in a Canadian City, 1816-1970* (Montreal and Kingston: McGill-Queen's University Press, 1995), 10.

54 John W. Fierheller, "Approaches to the Study of Urban Crime: A Review Article," *Urban History Review* 8, 2 (1979): 104.

55 Ibid., 110.

56 James P. Huzel, "The Incidence of Crime in Vancouver during the Great Depression," in *Vancouver Past: Essays in Social History*, ed. Robert A.J. McDonald and Jean Barman, 211-48 (Vancouver: UBC Press, 1986).

57 Greg Marquis's chapter in volume 6 of *Essays in the History of Canadian Law* reveals how the police in Vancouver dealt with "vice" in the first few decades of the twentieth century. See Greg Marquis, "Vancouver Vice: The Police and the Negotiation of Morality, 1904-1935," in *Essays in the History of Canadian Law*, vol. 6, *British Columbia and the Yukon*, ed. Hamar Foster and John McLaren, 242-73 (Toronto: University of Toronto Press, 1995).

58 André Cellard, "Le petit Chicago: La 'criminalité' à Hull depuis le debut du XX siècle," *Revue d'histoire de l'Amerique francaise* 45, 4 (1992): 519-43.

59 Weaver, *Crimes, Constables, and Courts*, 5.

60 Ibid., 7-8, 13, and 16-17.

61 Dean Jobb, professor of journalism at University of King's College, Halifax, has written three books in which he pulls together facts and anecdotal tidbits to chronicle everything from murder to celebrated cases of libel in Nova Scotia. While Jobb should be commended for making these stories available to a wider audience, his work has barely scratched the surface with regard to addressing the relationship between crime and society. See Dean Jobb, *Shades of Justice: Seven Nova Scotia Murder Cases* (Halifax: Nimbus Publishing Ltd., 1989); *Crime Wave: Con Men, Rogues, and Scoundrels from Nova Scotia's Past* (Lawrencetown Beach, NS: Pottersfield Press, 1991); *Bluenose Justice: True Tales of Mischief, Mayhem, and Murder* (Lawrencetown Beach, NS: Pottersfield Press, 1993).

62 Peter McGahan, "Reconstructing Patterns of Crime in Halifax and Saint John: A Preliminary Historical Analysis," in *Dimensions of Communities: A Research Handbook,* ed. Dan A. Chekki, 179-226 (New York and London: Garland, 1989). McGahan also completed a number of occasional papers on the Halifax police for the Atlantic Institute of Criminology: "Crime and Policing in Late Nineteenth Century Halifax," Report 5 (1989); "Detective Nick Power and the Halifax Police Department, Early 1900s," Report 8 (1989); "The Police Commission and the Halifax 'Guardians,' 1925-1931," Report 10 (1989); and "Halifax Police Department, 1919-1924," Report 14 (1989). He has also written two popular histories of crime in the Maritimes. See Peter McGahan, *Crime and Policing in Maritime Canada: Chapters from the Urban Records* (Fredericton, NB: Goose Lane, 1988); and Peter McGahan, *Killers, Thieves, Tramps, and Sinners* (Fredericton, NB: Goose Lane, 1989).

63 Judith Fingard, *The Dark Side of Life in Victorian Halifax* (Porters Lake, NS: Pottersfield Press, 1989), 16.

64 B. Jane Price, "'Raised in Rockhead. Died in the Poorhouse': Female Petty Criminals in Halifax, 1864-1890," in Girard and Phillips, *Essays in the History of Canadian Law,* 3:200-31.

65 Jim Phillips, "Poverty, Unemployment, and the Administration of the Criminal Law: Vagrancy Laws in Halifax, 1864-1890," in Girard and Phillips, *Essays in the History of Canadian Law,* 3:128-62; Jim Phillips, "Women, Crime, and Criminal Justice in Early Halifax, 1750-1800," in Phillips et al., *Essays in the History of Canadian Law,* 5:174-206; Jim Phillips and Allyson N. May, "Female Criminality in 18th-Century Halifax," *Acadiensis* 31, 2 (2002): 71-96.

66 Jim Phillips, "'Securing Obedience to Necessary Laws': The Criminal Law in Eighteenth Century Nova Scotia," *Nova Scotia Historical Review* 12, 2 (1992): 87-124. For an exploration of the law in Nova Scotia's colonial era, see Peter Waite, Sandra Oxner, and Thomas Barnes, eds., *Law in a Colonial Society: The Nova Scotia Experience* (Toronto: Carswell, 1984).

CHAPTER 1: A CITY OF ORDER IN A TIME OF TURMOIL

1 *The Public Gardens of Halifax, Nova Scotia* (Halifax: ca. 1930), 6, Nova Scotia Legislative Library, NS917.1622P.

2 Ibid., 8 and 17.

3 Ian McKay, "The Discrete Charm of the Halifax Bourgeoisie," *New Maritimes* 4, 7 (1986): 14-15. For more on the lifestyles of the Victorian elite in Halifax, see P.B.

Waite, *The Man from Halifax: Sir John Thompson, Prime Minister* (Toronto: University of Toronto Press, 1985).

4 In the aftermath of this fire, the Poor Asylum was relocated to a parcel of land between Morris and South streets. See McKay, "Discrete Charm," 15.

5 *Halifax Herald*, 2 June 1930.

6 Agnes Heller, "Rights, Modernity, Democracy," in *Deconstruction and the Possibility of Justice*, ed. Drucilla Cornell, Michel Rosenfeld, and David Gray Carlson (New York: Routledge, 1992), 346-49.

7 "Warden of the North" is the title of Thomas H. Raddall's classic account of the historical development of Halifax. See Thomas H. Raddall, *Halifax: Warden of the North* (Halifax: Nimbus, 1993). For a recent reassessment of Raddall's work, see Ian McKay and Robin Bates, *In the Province of History: The Making of the Public Past in Twentieth-Century Nova Scotia* (Montreal and Kingston: McGill-Queen's University Press, 2010), 200-52.

8 The information for this paragraph has been culled from the Carleton University History Collaborative, *Urban and Community Development in Atlantic Canada, 1867-1991* (Hull, QC: Canadian Museum of Civilization, 1993), 18-19, 76-82, and 110; and John G. Reid, *Six Crucial Decades: Times of Change in the History of the Maritimes* (Halifax: Nimbus, 1987), 33 and 101-3.

9 Morton Keller, *Regulating a New Society: Public Policy and Social Change in America, 1900-1933* (Cambridge: Harvard University Press, 1994), 4 and 36.

10 Ian McKay, "The 1910s: The Stillborn Triumph of Progressive Reform," in *The Atlantic Provinces in Confederation*, ed. E.R. Forbes and D.A. Muise (Toronto: University of Toronto Press, 1993), 193-95.

11 *Halifax, Nova Scotia: A Report Indicating the Need of a Social Survey*, Nova Scotia Archives (hereafter NSA), MG 1, vol. 2898, no. 43.

12 McKay, "1910s," 228; and David Frank, "The 1920s: Class and Region, Resistance and Accommodation," in Forbes and Muise, *Atlantic Provinces*, 271.

13 David A. Sutherland, "Halifax Harbour, December 6, 1917: Setting the Scene," in *Ground Zero: A Reassessment of the 1917 Explosion in Halifax Harbour*, ed. Alan Ruffman and Colin D. Howell (Halifax: Nimbus, 1994), 7. For more on the background of middle-class formation in Halifax, see David A. Sutherland, "Voluntary Societies and the Process of Middle-Class Formation in Early Victorian Halifax, Nova Scotia," *Journal of the Canadian Historical Association* 5, 1 (1994): 237-63.

14 Giddens, *Consequences of Modernity*, 10; and Berman, *All That Is Solid*, 5. As Richard Hofstadter notes, at its heart progressivism "was an effort to realize familiar and traditional ideals under novel circumstances." See Richard Hofstadter, *The Age of Reform: From Bryan to F.D.R.* (New York: Vintage Books, 1955), 215.

15 For more on the notion of social fragmentation as a product of modernity, see Taylor, *Malaise of Modernity*.

16 *Labour Gazette* (January 1918), 15; and Samuel Henry Prince, *Catastrophe and Social Change* (New York: AMS Press, 1968), 75. For more on the socio-economic consequences of the explosion and the reconstruction efforts, see Ruffman and Howell, *Ground Zero*.

17 *Labour Gazette* (January 1918), 15.

18 Ibid.; and Prince, *Catastrophe and Social Change*, 29.

19 Prince, *Catastrophe and Social Change*, 50-51, 76, 102, and 141-42.

20 Ibid., 77-78, 102, 124-27, and 139.

21 McKay, "1910s," 223. Much of this expansion was a carry-over from the early 1890s to 1913, when Halifax experienced continuous growth as shipping and railway traffic rose due to increased immigration and exports. See Murray B. Hodgins, "A City Transformed? Urban Development and the Role of Canadian Railway Policy In Halifax, Nova Scotia, 1900-1920" (MA thesis, Dalhousie University, 1992), 32.

22 Henry Roper, "The Halifax Board of Control: The Failure of Municipal Reform, 1906-1919," *Acadiensis* 14, 2 (1985): 46.

23 *Halifax Herald*, 9 June 1920.

24 Ibid.

25 Frank, "1920s," 234.

26 This was one of Canada's largest single-industry strikes. Only a year earlier the Halifax construction and trades workers waged a successful strike to secure an increase in their wages and shorter hours. As well, in 1919, the Halifax Labour Council boasted eight thousand members, making it the fourth largest labour council in the country. But with the onset of recession after 1920, it watched helplessly as its membership slowly disintegrated either because workers could not afford to pay their dues or because they left the city in search of work elsewhere. See McKay, "1910s," 225-27.

27 T.W. Acheson, "The National Policy and the Industrialization of the Maritimes, 1880-1910," *Acadiensis* 1, 2 (1972): 3-18; Reid, *Six Crucial Decades*, 125-57; and Sutherland, "Voluntary Societies," 239.

28 Acheson, "National Policy," 5.

29 Catherine Ann Waite, "The Longshoremen of Halifax, 1900-1930: Their Living and Working Conditions" (MA thesis, Dalhousie University, 1977), 9.

30 *Halifax, Nova Scotia: A Report Indicating the Need of a Social Survey*, NSA, 4. In 1891, 1,257 women worked in the city's factories. Most were concentrated in cotton and woollen manufacturing, boot and shoe making, tobacco processing, and the sweated garment trades. See Sharon Myers, "'Not to Be Ranked as Women': Female Industrial Workers in Turn-of-the-Century Halifax," in *Separate Spheres: Women's Worlds in the 19th-Century Maritimes*, ed. Janet Guildford and Suzanne Morton (Fredericton, NB: Acadiensis Press, 1994), 165.

31 Ian McKay, "Capital and Labour in the Halifax Baking and Confectionary Industry during the Last Half of the Nineteenth Century," *Labour/Le Travailleur* 3 (1978): 63-108. Craftspeople and labourers on the Halifax waterfront also saw the pace and nature of their work transformed with the advent of steam ships. See Ian McKay, "Class Struggle and Merchant Capital: Craftsmen and Labourers on the Halifax Waterfront, 1850-1902," in *The Character of Class Struggle: Essays in Canadian Working-Class History, 1850-1985*, ed. Bryan D. Palmer, 17-36 (Toronto: McClelland and Stewart, 1986).

32 Kris Inwood and John Chamard, "Regional Industrial Growth during the 1890s: The Case of the Missing Artisans," *Acadiensis* 16, 1 (1986): 103; and Kris Inwood, "Maritime Industrialization from 1870 to 1910: A Review of the Evidence and Its Interpretation," *Acadiensis* 21, 1 (991): 132-55.

33 The sex breakdown of these employment figures are as follows: 1921, 2,034 men and 767 women; 1931, 1,991 men and 517 women. See Canada, *Sixth Census of*

Canada, 1921, vol. 4 (Ottawa: King's Printer, 1929), 382-88; and Canada, *Seventh Census of Canada, 1931,* vol. 7 (Ottawa: King's Printer, 1936), 48-49.

34 Several of these labourers came from rural Nova Scotia. They flooded Halifax's labour market in the summer or winter in search of work to supplement their incomes. Most came from small towns whose industries had begun to falter, especially after 1890, or from farming communities when harvesting had ended. In the Maritimes, this occupational pluralism has been described as "instinctive, a cultural trait, passed from one generation to another as a tradition of necessity." See L.D. McCann, "'Living a Double Life': Town and Country in the Industrialization of the Maritimes," in *Geographical Perspectives on the Maritime Provinces*, ed. Douglas Day, 93-113 (Halifax: Atlantic Nova Print, 1988).

35 Ian McKay, *The Craft Transformed: An Essay on the Carpenters of Halifax, 1885-1985* (Halifax: Holdfast Press, 1985), 30-32. From 1850 to 1900, forty-two strikes erupted in Halifax. See Ian McKay, "Strikes in the Maritimes, 1901-1914," *Acadiensis* 13, 1 (1983): 5 and 10.

36 McKay, *Craft Transformed*, 68-73. In 1935 Halifax had five "leading" hotels with 785 rooms. They included the Carleton, Halifax, Lord Nelson, Nova Scotian, and Queen. As well, the city had six theatres with a seating capacity of six thousand. See Halifax-Dartmouth, *Halifax-Dartmouth City Directories, 1935* (Halifax: Might Directories Atlantic Ltd., 1935), 7. For more on the growth and importance of tourism to Nova Scotia's economy, see Forbes and Muise, *Atlantic Provinces.*

37 Waite, "Longshoremen of Halifax," 79; McKay, *Craft Transformed*, 90-91; and E.R. Forbes, "The 1930s: Depression and Retrenchment," in Forbes and Muise, *Atlantic Provinces*, 273.

38 Nova Scotia, *Halifax-Dartmouth City Directories, 1933* (Halifax: Might Directories Atlantic Ltd., 1933), 8; and Nova Scotia, *Halifax-Dartmouth City Directories, 1935*, 8.

39 McKay, *Craft Transformed*, 90-91.

40 Frank, "1920s," 234; Canada, *Sixth Census of Canada, 1921,* vol. 1 (Ottawa: King's Printer, 1924), 234; and Canada, *Seventh Census of Canada, 1931,* vol. 1 (Ottawa: King's Printer, 1936), 8. In 1911 the population of Halifax stood at 46,619. See Canada, *Fifth Census of Canada, 1911,* vol. 1 (Ottawa: King's Printer, 1912), 66.

41 John Herd Thompson with Allen Seager, *Canada, 1922-1939: Decades of Discord* (Toronto: McClelland and Stewart, 1985), 97.

42 In 1931, for example, Jews numbered 576, Lutherans 334, and the Salvation Army 300. These were the three most populous sects next to the Catholics and Protestants. See Canada, *Seventh Census of Canada, 1931,* vol. 2 (Ottawa: King's Printer, 1933), 542-43.

43 In 1921, blacks represented 1.6 percent of the city's population, in 1931 they represented 1.3 percent. See *Sixth Census of Canada, 1921,* 1:392-93; Canada, *Seventh Census of Canada, 1931,* 2:494-95; and Donald H. Clairmont and Dennis William Magill, *Africville: The Life and Death of a Canadian Black Community*, rev. ed. (Toronto: Canadian Scholars' Press, 1987), 59.

44 Canada, *Seventh Census of Canada, 1931,* 2:330-31 and 2:494-95.

45 Paul A. Erickson, *Halifax's North End: An Anthropologist Looks at the City* (Hantsport, NS: Lancelot Press, 1987), 73.

46 The "North End" is situated at the northeast quarter of the peninsula and, then as now, is bounded on the south by Cogswell and Cunard streets, on the west by Robie Street, and on the north and east by Bedford Basin and Halifax Harbour. See Erickson, *Halifax's North End,* 11 and 73-74.

47 Hugh MacLennan, *Barometer Rising* (Toronto: McClelland and Stewart, 1941), 88-89.

48 *Halifax Herald*, 23 September 1899.

49 *Halifax, Nova Scotia: A Report Indicating the Need for a Social Survey*, NSA, 1.

50 W.B. Wallace, *The Housing Problem in Nova Scotia: An Evil, Its Growth and Its Remedy*, NSA, V/F, vol. 10, no. 25, p. 16.

51 In 1919, the federal government made a direct loan of $25 million to the provinces for home construction. By 1923, 6,244 dwellings had been built across the country. See Michael Doucet and John Weaver, *Housing the North American City* (Montreal and Kingston: McGill-Queen's University Press, 1991), 113; and John Bacher, "From Study to Reality: The Establishment of Public Housing in Halifax, 1930-1953," *Acadiensis* 18, 1 (1988): 120.

52 The absence of public housing construction in Halifax in the 1920s had much to do with the lack of initiative shown by civic politicians. For example, in 1919-20, Halifax City Council failed to respond to the federal government's offer of a twenty-year loan to start a low-cost municipal housing program. See Henry Roper, "The Strange Political Career of A.C. Hawkins, Mayor of Halifax, 1918-1919," *Collections of the Royal Nova Scotia Historical Society* 41 (1982): 158.

53 Jay White, "Working-Class Housing in Halifax, 1905-1939," paper written for Department of History, McMaster University, 1986, p. 8. My thanks to Jay White for allowing me to quote from his paper. Since 1925, $17 million was spent on the construction of new homes, mainly in middle- and upper-class portions of the city. See *Halifax Herald*, 15 August 1933; and Samuel Henry Prince, *Housing in Halifax: A Report* (Halifax: The Citizens Committee on Housing, 1932), 16.

54 White, "Working-Class Housing," 10.

55 In 1949, the Bayers Road housing project marked the return of public housing to Halifax. See Bacher, "From Study to Reality," 123-25 and 133-35.

56 White, "Working Class Housing," 7 and 15.

57 Prince, *Housing in Halifax*, 3.

58 Ibid., 58.

59 In addition, 370 families occupied 192 condemned homes in the city. See Prince, *Housing in Halifax,* 11-15.

60 According to the report, those families that could afford the twenty dollars lived in a few rooms and were "glad to get them." See Prince, *Housing in Halifax,* 15 and 71. For more on the practice of "doubling up" as part of the survival strategy for many working-class families, see Bettina Bradbury, *Working Families: Age, Gender, and Daily Survival in Industrializing Montreal* (Toronto: McClelland and Stewart, 1993); and Denise Baillargeon, *Making Do: Women, Family, and Home in Montreal during the Great Depression* (Waterloo, ON: Wilfrid Laurier University Press, 1999).

61 Rents varied from twenty-five dollars a month for a four-room flat to fifty dollars for a seven-room house. See Janet F. Kitz, *Shattered City: The Halifax Explosion and the Road to Recovery* (Halifax: Nimbus, 1989), 188-90.

62 Prince, *Catastrophe and Social Change*, 132; and *Halifax Herald*, 3 June 1920.

63 Kitz, *Shattered City*, 199-200. Initially, the commission owned the homes and rented them to the people who lived in the area before the explosion. Beginning in 1949, the commission sold most of the homes to the tenants. See Ernest Clarke, "The Hydrostone Phoenix: Garden City Planning and the Reconstruction of Halifax, 1917-21," in Ruffman and Howell, *Ground Zero*, 401 and 404-5.

64 As quoted in Garry Shutlak, "A Vision of Regeneration: Reconstruction after the Explosion, 1917-21," in Ruffman and Howell, *Ground Zero*, 425-26. For more on the socio-economic dimensions of the North End, prior to and during the 1920s, see Suzanne Morton, *Ideal Surroundings: Domestic Life in a Working-Class Suburb in the 1920s* (Toronto: University of Toronto Press, 1995).

65 Africville belonged to Ward Six. For a general overview of the history of Africville, and the racism that its residents endured, see Clairmont and Magill, *Africville;* and Jennifer J. Nelson, *Razing Africville: A Geography of Racism* (Toronto: University of Toronto Press, 2008). Suzanne Morton and Judith Fingard provide excellent assessments of the lives of black women and men in nineteenth- and early twentieth-century Halifax, respectively. See Suzanne Morton, "Separate Spheres in a Separate World: African-Nova Scotian Women in late 19th-Century Halifax County," *Acadiensis* 22, 2 (1993): 61-83; and Judith Fingard, "From Sea to Rail: Black Transportation Workers and Their Families in Halifax, c. 1870-1916," *Acadiensis* 24, 2 (1995): 49-64.

66 Erickson, *Halifax's North End*, 68.

67 For a recent study of Halifax's "upper streets" and the people who inhabited this area, see David Hood, *Down but Not Out: Community and the Upper Streets in Halifax, 1890-1914* (Halifax: Fernwood, 2010).

68 Harry D. Smith, *Through Dirty Windows: A Humorous Account of Shop and Factory Life in the Incredible 1930s* (Windsor, NS: Lancelot Press, 1976), 67.

69 Erickson, *Halifax's North End*, 67-68.

70 *Morning Chronicle*, 24 August 1923.

71 Christina Simmons, "'Helping the Poorer Sisters': The Women of the Jost Mission, Halifax, 1905-1945," *Acadiensis* 14, 1 (1984): 3-27.

72 The breakdown of these children by age group is as follows: 818 under one year, 181 between one and two years, sixty-nine between two and three years, and eighty-seven between three and five years. See Prince, *Housing in Halifax*, 64. In Halifax in 1921 there were 135 deaths per thousand live births; by 1929 this had declined to seventy-six. In Nova Scotia, infant deaths per thousand live births averaged 93.7 from 1921 to 1925 and 84.8 from 1926 to 1930. See Suzanne Morton, "'Never Handmaidens': The Victorian Order of Nurses and the Massachusetts-Halifax Health Commission," in Ruffman and Howell, *Ground Zero*, 204, 448n67. For more on some of the advancements made in medical care in Halifax during the 1920s and 1930s, see Colin D. Howell, *A Century of Care: A History of the Victoria General Hospital in Halifax, 1887-1987* (Halifax: Victoria General Hospital, 1988).

73 *Halifax Herald*, 29 September 1933. Infant deaths were not only a problem in Halifax. In 1933, across the country an increase of 421 infant deaths under the age of one year was reported. This represented a rise from 70.8 to 73.6 deaths per one thousand live births in Canada. See Cynthia R. Comacchio, "*Nations Are*

Built of Babies": Saving Ontario's Mothers and Children, 1900-1940 (Montreal and Kingston: McGill-Queen's University Press, 1993), 158.

74 While not a cause of cholera, milk was a carrier of infectious diseases. Moreover, in Halifax some felt that an insufficient supply of milk led to ill health, thus exposing infants to cholera. See *Halifax Herald*, 26 and 28 September 1933; and Comacchio, *"Nations Are Built,"* 233. In 1934, Nova Scotia passed a pasteurization law to improve the quality of milk sold to consumers. See Nova Scotia, *The Revised Statutes of Nova Scotia, 1934* (Halifax: King's Printer, 1934), 1:88.

75 The newspapers were the *Halifax Herald* and the *Halifax Mail*. See Nova Scotia, *Annual Report: Halifax Visiting Dispensary, Seventy-Seventh Annual Meeting, 1933* (Halifax: T.C. Allen and Co., 1934), 11.

76 For many Nova Scotians, leaving home was a natural part of the family lifecycle. See Alan A. Brookes, "Family, Youth, and Leaving Home in Late Nineteenth-Century Rural Nova Scotia: Canning and the Exodus, 1868-1893," in *Childhood and Family in Canadian History*, ed. Joy Parr, 93-108 (Toronto: McClelland and Stewart, 1988).

77 By June 1931 the unemployment rate in the Maritimes had reached 19 percent. See Forbes, "1930s," 274.

78 Those cities were Calgary, Windsor, and Toronto. See Waite, "Longshoremen of Halifax," 79; and Michael J. Piva, "Urban Working-Class Incomes and Real Incomes in 1921: A Comparative Analysis," *Historie sociale/Social History* 16, 31 (1983): 160.

79 *Citizen*, 15 September 1922.

80 *Labour Gazette,* October 1921, 1323.

81 Ibid., 1316-23. Rent in Halifax in 1931 also topped the national average. A six-room house with "modern conveniences" in Halifax cost between $32 and $45 a month, while nationally the price was $27. For a six-room house with "incomplete modern conveniences," the cost per month in Halifax was between $20 and $30, with a national average of $19. See *Labour Gazette,* October 1931, 1144-49.

82 *Labour Gazette,* March 1921, 453-58.

83 Frank, "1920s," 251.

84 McKay, *Craft Transformed*, 75 and 87.

85 Piva, "Urban Working-Class Incomes," 162-65. By 1933, the per capita income for the Maritimes dropped to $181, which was significantly below the national average of $262. See Forbes, "1930s," 274.

86 Minutes of the City Council of the City of Halifax, Nova Scotia, for the Civic Year 1933-34, Halifax Regional Municipality Archives (hereafter HRMA).

87 This figure can be broken down into two categories: Married Men (2,300) and Single Men (380). See Correspondence of the Halifax Direct Relief Department (1933), HRMA.

88 Ibid.

89 Judith Fingard, "The Winter's Tale: The Seasonal Contours of Pre-Industrial Poverty in British North America, 1815-1860," in *Interpreting Canada's Past,* vol. 1, *Before Confederation*, ed. J.M. Bumsted, 248-72 (Toronto: Oxford University Press, 1986); and Judith Fingard, "The Relief of the Unemployed Poor in Saint John, Halifax and Saint John's, 1815-1860," *Acadiensis* 5, 1 (1975): 32-53.

90 *Correspondence of the Halifax Direct Relief Department* (1934), HRMA.

91 McGahan, *Crime and Policing*, 154-55. In December 1932, 279 men were housed in this camp. See *Halifax Herald*, 2 December 1932.

92 *Labour Gazette*, September 1931, 1002.

93 *Halifax Herald*, 20 March 1934.

94 McAlpine, *McAlpine's Halifax City Directory, 1918* (Halifax: Royal Print and Litho Ltd., 1918), 51, 84, 111, and 120.

95 Hodgins, "City Transformed?," 26, 29-30, and 47.

96 Ibid., 140; and Halifax Board of Trade, *Halifax: The City by the Sea* (Halifax: Halifax Board of Trade, circa 1931), 8.

97 *Commercial News*, August 1931. The *Commercial News* was the official monthly organ of the Halifax Board of Trade. It commenced publication in 1921 under the editorship of E.A. Saunders and boasted an initial circulation of five hundred, which eventually doubled. See Gertrude E.N. Tratt, *A Survey and Listing of Nova Scotia Newspapers, 1752-1957* (Halifax: Dalhousie University School of Library Service, Occasional Paper 21, 1979), 53. According to the *Commercial News*, there was one car for every seven persons in Halifax in 1931. The arrival of the car in Halifax may be seen as a potent symbol of the presence of modernity. From 1930 to 1935, there was a total of 36,227 motor vehicle registrations (30,300 passenger and 5,927 commercial) in Halifax. This works out to a total yearly average of 6,038 registrations. See Nova Scotia, *Halifax-Dartmouth City Directories, 1931-1936* (Halifax: Might Directories Atlantic Ltd., 1931-36).

98 *Halifax Herald*, 15 August 1933.

99 Ibid.

100 Ibid., 30 April 1930.

101 Halifax's population for 1921 and 1931 was 58,372 and 59,275, respectively. For Saint John and Hamilton, the respective figures are: 47,166 (1921), 47,514 (1931); and 114, 151 (1921), 155,547 (1931). See Carleton University History Collaborative, *Urban and Community Development*, 108-10; Canada, *Sixth Census of Canada, 1921,* 2:80; and Canada, *Seventh Census of Canada, 1931,* 2:495. John C. Weaver's *Crime, Constables, and Courts*, provides a detailed account of crime and crime rates in Hamilton, thereby making this city an obvious choice for the purposes of comparison with Halifax.

102 J.A. Sharpe, "The History of Crime in Late Medieval and Early Modern England: A Review of the Field," *Social History* 7, 2 (1982): 190.

103 V.A.C. Gatrell and T.B. Hadden, "Criminal Statistics and Their Interpretation," in *Nineteenth Century Society: Essays in the Use of Quantitative Methods for the Study of Social Data*, ed. E.A. Wrigley (Cambridge: Cambridge University Press, 1972), 348-51 and 361. For more background on the use of quantitative analysis, see Roderick Floud, *An Introduction to Quantitative Methods for Historians* (Princeton: Princeton University Press, 1973).

104 This factor and its implications for a quantitative examination of crime is discussed in F.H. McClintock, "The Dark Figure of Crime," in *Crime and Justice,* vol. 1, *The Criminal in Society*, 2nd and rev. ed., ed. Sir Leon Radzinowicz and Marvin E. Wolfgang, 126-39 (New York: Basic Books, 1977).

105 The average number of convictions for indictable offences per one thousand population for Halifax, Nova Scotia, and Canada from 1918 to 1935 are: 5.8 percent, 1.6 percent, and 2.3 percent, respectively. The average number of convic-

tions per one thousand population for summary offences are: 24.2 percent, 8.3 percent, and 21.9 percent, respectively. See Appendix 2, Tables A2.5 and A2.6.

106 Canada, *Fifty-Fourth Annual Report of Statistics of Criminal and Other Offences, 1929* (Ottawa: King's Printer, 1930), xvii-xxi.

107 Drunkenness was also the most prevalent offence in Halifax in the late nineteenth and early twentieth centuries. See McGahan, "Reconstructing Patterns of Crime," 185.

108 The years 1917 to 1922, which cover the period 1 May to 30 April, were selected because they represent the only years for which the annual reports of the chief of police for the 1918-35 period are extant. The total number of offences "known" to the police in Saint John and Hamilton in 1920 were 1,786 and 5,886, respectively. See Canada, *Forty-Fifth Annual Report of Criminal Statistics, 1920* (Ottawa: King's Printer, 1921), 276.

109 McGahan, "Reconstructing Patterns of Crime," 190-98.

110 Canada, *Fifty-Fourth Annual Report of Statistics of Criminal and Other Offences, 1929*, xvii.

111 Ibid., 128-39.

112 For comparative purposes, the total number of committals to jails in Halifax (which included the City Lockup and the City Prison) rose steadily during the 1930 to 1935 period. In 1929-30, 271 men and 12 women (283 in total) were held in these facilities. The numbers for 1930-31 were 874 men and 55 women (934 total); for 1931-32: 527 men and 32 women (559 total); for 1932-33: 706 men and 54 women (760 total); and for 1933-34: 880 men and 67 women (947 total). Figures for 1934-35 did not appear in the report for this year. See Nova Scotia, *Annual Reports of Penal Institutions, Province of Nova Scotia* (Halifax: King's Printer, 1931, 1932, 1933, 1934, and 1935).

113 As John C. Weaver notes in a discussion of theft in Hamilton during the Depression, the economic hardships of the 1930s alone did not increase the number of thefts. Lean times, however, may have prompted more people to inform the police if their money, food, or clothing had been stolen. See Weaver, *Crime, Constables, and Courts*, 243-62.

CHAPTER 2: THE MACHINERY OF LAW AND ORDER

1 *Halifax Herald,* 16 January 1935. The first reported use of fingerprint technology by the Halifax police to capture a criminal was in July 1932, when this evidence helped detectives apprehend Earle Cooke, who had broken into Cabot's Dry Goods store on Barrington Street. See *Halifax Herald*, 14 July 1932.

2 Ibid., 6 October 1934.

3 Giddens, *Consequences of Modernity*, 57-58. As Allan Greer points out, one of the primary roles of professional police forces since their emergence in Canada during the middle of the nineteenth century was to bring order and safety to urban streets and to discipline those "on the margins of the law." See Greer, "Birth of the Police," 41.

4 Background for these two paragraphs is drawn from Morton Keller, *Regulating a New Society: Public Policy and Social Change in America, 1900-1933* (Cambridge, MA: Harvard University Press, 1974), 158 and 184-86.

5 Greg Marquis, "The History of Policing in the Maritime Provinces: Themes and Prospects," *Urban History Review* 19, 1 (1990): 86-88.

6 With the use of a night-watch, Halifax followed a pattern found in many American cities in the mid- to late nineteenth century. See Greg Marquis, *Policing Canada's Century: A History of the Canadian Association of Chiefs of Police* (Toronto: University of Toronto Press, 1993), 13, 27, and 32-33; and Marquis, "History of Policing," 88. For an outline of similar developments in nineteenth-century Hamilton, see Weaver, *Crime, Constables, and Courts.*

7 For an examination of crime and social disorder in nineteenth-century Halifax, see Fingard, *Dark Side*. David Hood challenges Fingard's portrayal of the women and men who haunted Halifax's "upper streets," asserting that a transient "underclass" did not exist in Edwardian Halifax. According to him, the upper streets were home to a community that was stable and whose residents cared for one another. See Hood, *Down but Not Out*, 92-93.

8 Weaver, *Crime, Constables, and Courts*, 172.

9 This adherence and devotion to the notion of "British justice" is explored further in Chapter 3. For more on the notion of British justice see Greg Marquis, "Doing Justice to 'British Justice': Law, Ideology and Canadian Historiography," in *Canadian Perspectives on Law and Society: Issues in Legal History*, ed. W. Wesley Pue and Barry Wright, 43-69 (Ottawa: Carleton University Press, 1988).

10 Friedman, *Crime and Punishment*, 152; and Marquis, "History of Policing," 88.

11 Weaver, *Crime, Constables, and Courts* 17; and Keller, *Regulating a New Society*, 164-65.

12 The estimated populations of Halifax and Hamilton in 1923 and 1935 are, respectively: 60,172 and 122,431; and 63,675 and 159,857. See Canada, *Forty-Eighth Annual Report of Criminal Statistics, 1923* (Ottawa: King's Printer, 1924), 320; and Canada, *Sixtieth Annual Report of Statistics of Criminal and Other Offences, 1935* (Ottawa: King's Printer, 1936), 200-2.

13 In terms of the actual number of cases involved, for 1923 the Halifax Police Department reported 1,003 prosecutions and 581 convictions, while the Hamilton force listed 5,692 prosecutions and 4,817 convictions. In 1935, the number of prosecutions and convictions in Halifax was 2,190 and 1,709, and for Hamilton it was 11,708 and 10,199. See Canada, *Forty-Eighth Annual Report of Criminal Statistics, 1923*, 320; and Canada, *Sixtieth Annual Report of Statistics of Criminal and Other Offences, 1935*, 200-2.

14 *Halifax Chronicle*, 12 and 22 February 1929.

15 *Halifax Herald*, 29 April 1924. In Halifax, the position of chief of police was created in 1893. See Marquis, *Policing Canada's Century*, 33. For more on the work of Chief Hanrahan, see Michael Boudreau, "Francis Hanrahan: Halifax Chief of Police," in *Dictionary of Canadian Biography*, vol. 15, *1921-1930*, 452-53 (Toronto: University of Toronto Press, 2005).

16 *Halifax Herald*, 14 and 17 February 1933. On 20 October 1933, Palmer succumbed to his illness. In reviewing his tenure as police chief, the *Herald* noted that Palmer's record was one of "probity and fidelity to duty." Ibid., 21 October 1933.

17 Interview with Inspector Vincent O'Brien, conducted by Catherine Trapnell in Halifax on 8 March 1988. A transcript of this interview is in the author's

possession. My thanks to Dr. Jim Morrison, Department of History, Saint Mary's University, for providing me with a copy of this interview.

18 The Police Commission also dealt with retirements, leaves of absence, resignations, and dismissals from the force. See McGahan, "The Police Commission and the Halifax 'Guardians', 1925-1931," 3; and Nova Scotia, *The Halifax City Charter, 1931* (Halifax: King's Printer, 1931), 83.

19 Police Rosters, Edward Morris Collection, Dr. Barry Moody, Department of History, Acadia University. My thanks to Dr. Moody for furnishing me with copies of these rosters. For a listing of the officers in the Halifax Police Department in 1923, see Appendix 2, Table A2.16. In 1933, the Halifax City Council unanimously approved the appointment of an assistant deputy chief of police. See *Halifax Herald*, 6 April and 16 June 1933.

20 Interview with Sergeant Donald Whittemore, conducted by Catherine Trapnell in Halifax on 11 March 1988. A transcript of this interview is in the author's possession. Whittemore's father served on the Halifax police force for twenty-seven years (1920 to 1947).

21 In 1931, for instance, of the seventy-one members of the force, thirty-six (50.7 percent) were Protestants and thirty-five (49.3 percent) were Roman Catholics. See Police Roster, July 1931, Edward Morris Collection.

22 Vancouver was the first city to appoint two policewomen to its staff in 1912. Toronto followed suit in 1913 and Winnipeg in 1917. In 1915, Montreal hired its first policewoman, Lilian Clearihue, although her powers were somewhat restricted in relation to her those of her counterparts in these other cities. By 1918, Ottawa, Kingston, and London had policewomen on their rosters. See Myers, "Women Policing Women," 234; and Marquis, *Policing Canada's Century*, 93. Greg Marquis also offers a closer look at policewomen in Toronto in "The Police as a Social Service in Early Twentieth Century Toronto," *Historie sociale/Social History* 25, 50 (1992): 335-58. A similar time frame for the British context is covered by Philippa Levine, "'Walking the Streets in a Way No Decent Woman Should': Women Police in World War I," *Journal of Modern History* 66 (1994): 34-78.

23 Dorothy M. Schulz, "The Police Matron Movement: Paving the Way for Policewomen," *Police Studies* 12, 3 (1987): 122.

24 Prior to joining the force, Egan served for twenty years as an agent of the Society for the Prevention of Cruelty (SPC). As "Honorary Inspector of Children," a position she assumed in the SPC in 1900, she performed "splendid work" in following up cases of neglected children and bringing offenders before the courts. See *Halifax Evening Echo*, 9 December 1922; and Papers and Submissions to the City Council, 1918-35, HRMA. This support was also evident when Egan retired in 1934. A group of citizens, led by Samuel Prince, Reverend Dr. L.J. Donaldson, Judge Murray, and Mrs. William Dennis, petitioned the Police Commission to award Egan a grant of $600 in recognition of her service to the police department and the city. City Council eventually decided to pay Egan the grant in monthly instalments. See *Halifax Herald*, 28 March 1934.

25 Interview with Inspector Vincent O'Brien.

26 Murray was also a prominent criminal lawyer who, in 1933, was appointed as a Halifax County Supreme Court judge. See Scrapbook of the Local Council of Women (1908-17), NSA, MG 20, no. 204. For more on the work that policewomen

conducted with "wayward girls and women," see Tamara Myers, *Caught: Montreal's Modern Girls and the Law, 1869-1945* (Toronto: University of Toronto Press, 2006).

27 *Morning Chronicle*, 15 November 1923.

28 *Halifax Chronicle*, 21 March 1927. In January 1927, the *Morning Chronicle* was superseded by the *Halifax Chronicle,* which billed itself as a "dependable newspaper." See Tratt, *Survey and Listing of Nova Scotia Newspapers,* 48-51.

29 *Police Women Occurrence Report,* 14 October 1931, NSA, RG 35-102, ser. 16H, vol. 3.

30 Nova Scotia, *Halifax City Charter, 1931*, 87-88. They could also be called out in the event of a riot or in the case of a "disturbance or disorder occurring at any public meeting, or assemblage of persons."

31 Ibid., 88-89.

32 *Halifax Herald*, 15 July 1925.

33 Ibid., 10 December 1932.

34 Nova Scotia, *Halifax City Charter, 1931*, 83.

35 *Halifax Herald*, 23 April 1926; and Nova Scotia, *Halifax City Directory, 1929* (Halifax: Might Directories Atlantic Ltd., 1929), 9.

36 During the police "man-hunt" for Lewis Bevis, who had shot and killed police officer Charles Fulton in 1924, some of the policemen used their own guns. See *Halifax Herald*, 16 July 1924. This case is discussed in detail in Chapter 4. One former Halifax police officer recalled that, in 1933, the year he joined the force, policemen carried firearms at their own discretion: "We didn't have to carry one," Vincent O'Brien said, "but if we wanted [to] we could carry one." Interview with Inspector Vincent O'Brien.

37 *Halifax Herald*, 16 July 1924.

38 In total, the department had five revolvers to be used in emergency cases. See Police Commission Minutes, 15 and 22 October and 3 November 1924, Halifax Police Museum Archives, pp. 121, 127, and 131. As late as 1951 weapons were scarce within the department. As each officer finished his or her shift he/she gave his/her gun to the succeeding officer on the beat. It would not be until the expansion of the force in the early 1970s that revolvers became standard issue. See Halifax Police Department, *The History of the Halifax Police Department* (Halifax: Halifax Police Department, circa 1990), 3-5.

39 *Halifax Chronicle*, 22 February 1929.

40 Ibid.

41 Interview with Inspector Vincent O'Brien.

42 *Halifax Herald*, 2 February 1918.

43 Ibid.; and Papers and Submissions to the City Council, 1918-35, HRMA.

44 McAlpine, *McAlpine's Halifax City Directory, 1923* (Halifax: Royal Print and Litho Ltd., 1923). The trend of police officers' living in the city's North End increased over the course of the 1920s. In 1920, one officer lived in the working-class suburb of Richmond Heights, eleven did so in 1925, and, by 1929, the number had grown to twenty-one. See Morton, *Ideal Surroundings*, 157-59.

45 *Halifax Herald*, 8 October 1918; and *Morning Chronicle*, 6 June 1924. Similar complaints were echoed in 1913 when eight to ten of the "very best men on the force" contemplated joining another city's police force because of the better pay. Said the *Herald:* "It is no use talking; the time has come when Halifax must come over

with more money if it expects to have an efficient police force." See *Halifax Herald*, 30 August 1913.

46 *Halifax Herald*, 9 January 1918.

47 *Morning Chronicle*, 2 May 1924. Available financial estimates for the fiscal year 1918-19 indicate that the City of Halifax planned to spend $59,640 on the police department. The bulk of this amount ($55,840) went to salaries and the remainder ($3,800) was allocated to such things as: telephone ($250), patrol wagon maintenance ($350), uniform clothing ($2,100), prisoners' meals ($700), new motorcycle ($425), and miscellaneous ($400). See Submissions to the Board of Control – Financial Estimates, 1918-19, HRMA.

48 *Halifax Herald*, 6 December 1915.

49 *Halifax Chronicle*, 8 and 15 January 1927. Police unions in Canada were founded by rank and file members. Patrolmen in Halifax followed the examples set by officers in London, Ontario, who organized in 1917, while Victoria, Vancouver, Edmonton, Calgary, Winnipeg, Windsor, Hamilton, Toronto, Ottawa, Montreal, Quebec City, and Saint John all witnessed acrimonious battles over the formation of police unions and associations. See Greg Marquis, "Police Unionism in Early Twentieth-Century Toronto," *Ontario History* 81, 2 (1989): 113. For more on the working-class nature of police officers, see Greg Marquis, "Working Men in Uniform: The Early Twentieth-Century Toronto Police," *Historie sociale/Social History* 20, 40 (1987): 259-78.

50 *Halifax Herald*, 18 November 1921.

51 Ibid. Even as early as 1898 then chief of police O'Sullivan had asked for an increase in the number of men under his command "owing to the demands for increased police protection in the suburbs." See *Acadian Recorder*, 2 November 1898.

52 *Morning Chronicle*, 9 September 1924.

53 Ibid., 8 May 1926.

54 *Halifax Chronicle*, 7 January 1927. Prior to the 1930s, patrolmen did not have any way of contacting headquarters to request assistance if they encountered a serious situation. This also meant that the sergeant on duty at the station would have to dispatch another officer, or go himself, to notify a patrolman of a reported crime in his area. After 1930, however, the force began to experiment with a signal-box, or telegraph, system, which allowed officers to phone the station from their standing point. The efficacy of this system was first mentioned in 1913, when "North End Observer" wrote that the "police telegraph system seems to have a mission in modern civic life, and it would appear that in Halifax it can fulfil its mission to very great advantage." The cost, estimated at $7,000, prevented the system from being implemented until the 1930s. See *Halifax Herald*, 30 August 1913.

55 *Halifax Herald*, 23 April 1932.

56 *Halifax Chronicle*, 7 January 1927.

57 At times this practice prompted a reprimand from patrolmen's superiors, who complained that some officers were in the habit of loafing around street corners and talking idly with passers-by. Chief Palmer warned police officers against engaging in such behaviour. See *Halifax Herald*, 19 May 1926.

58 Ibid., 30 December 1921 and 14 July 1934. In the 1940s, the radio patrol car was the main technological advancement sought by police administrators. In 1948,

urban Ontario had close to two hundred, but the Maritimes combined only had twenty-six and the Prairie provinces forty. See Marquis, *Policing Canada's Century*, 211-12. In 1912, the department purchased a motorcycle. This became the first piece of motorized equipment used by the Halifax police. See V.W. Mitchell, "Halifax Police Department: A Brief History of Canada's Oldest Constabulary." *RCMP Quarterly* 30 (1965): 7.

59 Mayor's Correspondence – Police Department (1932-37), NSA, RG 35-102, ser. 3, B.2, vol. 44.

60 John Phyne, "Prohibition's Legacy: The Emergence of Provincial Policing in Nova Scotia, 1921-1932," *Canadian Journal of Law and Society* 7, 2 (1992): 158 and 183.

61 *Halifax Herald*, 22 May 1930; and R.C. Toner and D.C. Perrier, "Nova Scotia Police," *RCMP Quarterly* 47, 3 (1982): 33. For a brief overview of provincial policing in the Maritimes, see Marquis, "History of Policing," 91-93.

62 Nova Scotia, *Report of the Nova Scotia Police for the Year Ended December 31, 1930* (Halifax: King's Printer, 1931), 6 and 11.

63 Phyne, "Prohibition's Legacy," 181.

64 *Morning Chronicle*, 9 November 1922.

65 *Halifax Herald*, 15 December 1932.

66 Ibid., 16 November 1931.

67 This admiration can be measured against the dismally low opinion many American citizens had of their police establishment. See Marquis, *Policing Canada's Century*, 10.

68 Philip Girard, "The Rise and Fall of Urban Justice in Halifax, 1815-1886," *Nova Scotia Historical Review* 8, 2 (1988): 57-71.

69 Halifax County Supreme Court, NSA, RG 39, ser. C, vol. 705 (1921-23), no. 130.

70 Ibid.

71 *Halifax Herald*, 4 April 1923.

72 *Morning Chronicle* and *Halifax Herald*, 7 April 1923.

73 *Halifax Herald*, 7 April 1923. It was also suggested that the police did not conduct a thorough investigation of this case and turned a blind eye to the prime suspect.

74 Girard, "Rise and Fall," 58-60. In 1934, one American observer of the Canadian judicial system described police courts as "courts of first instance." See Ernest Jerome Hopkins, "How Canada Curbs Crime," *The Rotarian* 45, 4 (October 1934): 50.

75 The court's jurisdiction extended to the City of Halifax proper as well as to Halifax Harbour, the South-East Passage, Bedford Basin, and "the wharves, slips, docks, and landings therein, and the lakes constituting the supply of the water service of the City." See Nova Scotia, *Halifax City Charter, 1931*, 76-77.

76 Hamilton, Saint John, and Kingston all appointed stipendiary magistrates in the late 1840s, then Toronto and Montreal did so in 1851-52, Halifax in 1867, and Charlottetown in 1875. See Marquis, *Policing Canada's Century*, 37. Until 1867, stipendiary magistrates were not lawyers but justices of the peace, or lay judges. See Roy Edward Kimball, "The Provincial Court of Nova Scotia: The Struggle for Excellence" (LLM thesis, Dalhousie University, 1987).

77 Ibid., 36-37. For assessments of the police courts in Halifax and Toronto during the nineteenth century, see Fingard, *Dark Side*; Paul Craven, "Law and Ideology:

The Toronto Police Court, 1850-1880," in *Essays in the History of Canadian Law,* ed. David H. Flaherty, (Toronto: University of Toronto Press, 1983), 2:248-307; Gene Howard Homel, "Denison's Law: Criminal Justice and the Police Court in Toronto, 1877-1921," *Ontario History* 73, 3 (1981): 171-86; and Chris Burr, "'Roping in the Wretched, the Reckless, and the Wronged': Narratives of the Late Nineteenth-Century Toronto Police Court," *Left History* 3, 1 (1995): 83-108. For twentieth-century accounts of the police court, see Thomas Thorner and Neil B. Watson, "Keeper of the King's Peace: Colonel G.E. Sanders and the Calgary Police Magistrate's Court, 1911-1932," *Urban History Review* 12, 3 (1984): 45-55; and Joan Sangster, "'Pardon Tales' from Magistrate's Court: Women, Crime, and the Court in Peterborough County, 1920-50," *Canadian Historical Review* 74, 2 (1993): 161-97.

78 Henry Pryor was the driving force behind the act that created the office of stipendiary magistrate. It is important to note that, prior to 1938, stipendiary magistrates were not required to be lawyers. See Marquis, *Policing Canada's Century,* 32-33; and Girard, "Rise and Fall," 61 and 66-67. The definitive study of Nova Scotia's courts is Judge Roy Edward Kimball's *The Bench: The History of Nova Scotia's Provincial Courts* (Halifax: Nova Scotia Department of Government Services, 1989).

79 For two contemporary accounts of the rules and procedures governing the office of stipendiary magistrate, see S.A. Chesley, "The Office of the Stipendiary Magistrate as a Part of Municipal Government," in *Proceedings of the Twentieth Annual Convention of the Union of Nova Scotia Municipalities,* 1925, 73-78; and James Crankshaw, *Crankshaw's Magistrates' Manual: Being a Practical Guide to Police Magistrates and Justices of the Peace,* 3rd ed. (Toronto: Canada Law Book Company Ltd., 1921), 24.

80 The Constitution Act, chap. 6, sec. 91; and Girard, "Rise and Fall," 60.

81 The brother of Nova Scotia premier W.S. Fielding, G.H. Fielding, while practising law in various firms in Halifax, built a "sound reputation as an able solicitor and barrister." See *Halifax Herald* and *Halifax Chronicle,* 20 May 1932.

82 *Halifax Herald,* 17 September 1929. C.R. Chipman was an interim replacement for Cluney until 1931, when J.L. Barnhill assumed the position. Another member of the bench, W.J. O'Hearn, sat from 1918 to 1922 as deputy police magistrate, alternating with Fielding. Recognized as one of the leading authorities on criminal law in Canada, O'Hearn became Nova Scotia's attorney general in 1922, lectured on criminal law and procedure at the Dalhousie Law School from 1917 to 1923, and, in 1928, was made a judge of the County Court. While deputy stipendiary magistrate, O'Hearn established an "excellent" reputation in the exercise of judicial proceedings. He also had a "profound respect for the traditions of British Justice." See *Halifax Chronicle,* 26 April 1928; and *Halifax Herald,* 4 May 1933.

83 Nova Scotia Summary Convictions Act, c. 224, in Nova Scotia, *The Revised Statutes of Nova Scotia, 1923* (Halifax: King's Printer, 1923), 2:2074-75 and 2081.

84 Ibid., 2082.

85 Colonel J. Welsford MacDonald, "The Grand Jury in Nova Scotia," in *Proceedings of the Twentieth-ninth Annual Convention of the Union of Nova Scotia Municipalities,* 1934, 47.

86 This caution is contained in section 684 of the 1924 Criminal Code of Canada. See *Crankshaw's Criminal Code of Canada*, 5th ed. (Toronto: Carswell Co. Ltd., 1924), 780.

87 Most offenders were held in the Halifax County Jail during their preliminary hearing. See Halifax County Jail – Jailor's Reports, 20 January 1923, NSA, RG 35-312, ser. J.76. According to section 696 of the Criminal Code, the purpose of committing someone to prison before trial was to "ensure the appearance of the accused at the time and place when and where he [she] is to be tried." See *Crankshaw's Criminal Code of Canada*, 808.

88 Nova Scotia Summary Convictions Act, 2083.

89 The Supreme Court had two regular sittings to hear criminal cases: the first commenced on the third Tuesday of March and the second on the first Tuesday of October. Each sitting ran until the Court's docket had been cleared. See Nova Scotia, *The Judicature Act* (Halifax: King's Printer, 1920), 12-17. The rules and regulations of the Supreme Court of Nova Scotia are contained in this statute.

90 For a complete listing of contemporary indictable offences, see Crankshaw, *Crankshaw's Magistrate's Manual*, 254-80.

91 The Summary Convictions Act stipulated that in hearing an appeal the Supreme Court: "[shall] affirm, reverse, or modify the conviction, order, or determination in respect to which the case has been stated." See Nova Scotia Summary Convictions Act, 2088 and 2094.

92 MacDonald, "Grand Jury in Nova Scotia," 47. These exceptions, as outlined in section 825 of the Criminal Code, included "treason and certain offences against the government, judicial, municipal and other corruption, murder, and attempts, threats, conspiracies and being accessory after the fact of murder, manslaughter, rape, defamatory libel, combinations in restraint of trade, and bribery and other indictable offences under the Dominion Elections Act." See *Crankshaw's Criminal Code of Canada*, 974-75. The "Speedy Trials of Indictable Offences" comprised part 18 of the 1924 Criminal Code.

93 MacDonald, "Grand Jury in Nova Scotia," 47.

94 The Speedy Trials Act applied to all federally appointed judges across the country. See Nova Scotia, *The Statutes of Nova Scotia, 1889* (Halifax: Queen's Printer, 1889), chap. 11, p. 56; J. Murray Beck, *The Government of Nova Scotia* (Toronto: University of Toronto Press, 1957), 291-92; and R. Blake Brown, *A Trying Question: The Jury in Nineteenth-Century Canada* (Toronto: University of Toronto Press, 2009), 176-77. The rules and regulations governing the procedure of Nova Scotia's county courts are contained in Nova Scotia, *The Revised Statutes of Nova Scotia, 1923* (Halifax: King's Printer, 1923), vol. 2, chap. 215, sec. 22, pp. 1934-52.

95 Those supporters of the Grand Jury continued their struggle to have it preserved in Nova Scotia despite the fact that Britain and Manitoba (1923) had abolished their grand juries after the First World War. Moreover, Saskatchewan and Alberta never had a Grand Jury system. In 1923, Nova Scotia attorney general W.J. O'Hearn introduced a resolution in the Assembly calling for the abolition of the Grand Jury. O'Hearn felt: "[The Grand Jury is] a farce and a useless expenditure of money, and takes busy men from their vocation in life to attend this affair of state which is now not necessary." Although O'Hearn did not push his

resolution to a vote, the debate as to the efficacy of the Grand Jury continued to swirl within some judicial circles across the province. Colonel J. Welsford MacDonald, author of the address from which some of the information for this section has been culled, was a strong proponent of the Grand Jury as a safeguard of people's liberties. MacDonald's arguments, it should be noted, were steeped in notions of paternalism and a deep loyalty to all things British. See MacDonald, "Grand Jury in Nova Scotia," 43-45 and 48-53. For a more scholarly account of the history of juries in Canada, see Brown, *Trying Question*.

96 MacDonald, "Grand Jury in Nova Scotia," 44. In 1898, the government of Nova Scotia reduced the number of grand jurors to twelve, seven of whom were needed to find a "true bill." See Brown, *Trying Question*, 190.

97 Hopkins, "How Canada Curbs Crime," 50.

98 The provisions outlining the procedures and jurisdiction of the Grand Jury are contained in sections 873a to 878 of the Criminal Code. See *Crankshaw's Criminal Code of Canada*, 1024-30.

99 If the Grand Jury found "no bill" against the accused, usually because of insufficient or inconclusive evidence, the case would be dismissed and, if in custody, the accused would be released immediately. See MacDonald, "Grand Jury in Nova Scotia," 47-48.

100 Nova Scotia abolished the Grand Jury system in 1979, but the legislation was not promulgated until 1984. See Brown, *Trying Question*, 190 and 223.

101 Ibid., 48.

102 The provisions for summary convictions are contained in part 15 of the Criminal Code. See *Crankshaw's Criminal Code of Canada*, 817-926.

103 *Morning Chronicle*, 30 January 1924.

104 *Halifax Herald*, 9 August 1932.

105 Ibid., 3 December 1926.

106 Ibid., 1 November 1926.

107 Ibid., 10 November 1926. For a comprehensive listing of the charges filed before the Halifax Police Court, see Halifax City Magistrate's Court, 1917-34, NSA, RG 42, ser. C, vols. 10-22.

108 *Halifax Herald*, 23 July 1926.

109 *Morning Chronicle*, 23 April 1921. The absence of legal aid was lamented by A.E. Popple, who, in 1921, writing in the *Canadian Law Times*, stressed the need for a legal aid society to provide legal counsel on a voluntary basis for each "deserving case." See A.E. Popple, "Police Court Systems," *Canadian Law Times* 41 (1921): 523-24.

110 Nova Scotia, *Revised Statutes of Nova Scotia, 1923*, 1457. During the 1918 to 1935 period, the Halifax Juvenile Court occupied four different offices. From its founding in 1911 until 1929, the juvenile court resided in the former Poor Association building on the west side of Argyle Street. In 1929, it moved to the Dillon Building on the corner of Sackville and Market streets until 1931, when it relocated to a room in the Metropole Building on Hollis Street. In 1933, when this building was demolished to make way for the Provincial Building, the court moved to the court house on Spring Garden Road. See Margaret Godfrey, "The Development of the Juvenile Court in Halifax," Maritime School of Social Work (1948), 5-6, NSA, Welfare Council of Halifax and Dartmouth, MG 20, vol. 408, no. 8.13.

111 Winnipeg was the first city in Canada to establish a juvenile court (1909). Before 1929, the only other juvenile court in Nova Scotia was in Pictou County. Late in 1929, presumably after the government allocated sufficient funding, Cape Breton, Colchester, Hants, and Kings counties received juvenile courts. See Nova Scotia, *Annual Report of the Director of Child Welfare for the Province of Nova Scotia, 1930* (Halifax: King's Printer, 1931), 91-92.

112 Godfrey, "Development of the Juvenile Court," 4-6. Judge W.B. Wallace was the first judge appointed to the Juvenile Court in 1911 and gave close to eight years of "faithful and gratuitous service." Wallace had also served as a County Court judge for Halifax County since 1901. His replacement, Dr. J.J. Hunt, brought to the court a "well founded reputation for a deep interest in children, a scholarly and matured mind and a pleasing personality." See Nova Scotia, *Annual Report of the Superintendent of Neglected and Delinquent Children for the Province of Nova Scotia, 1918* (Halifax: King's Printer, 1920), 20. E.H. Blois had also served as the provincial superintendent of neglected and dependent children. Moreover, Blois was the only judge of the Juvenile Court who was not a lawyer. See Reneé Lafferty, "Modernity and the Denominational Imperative: The Children's Aid Society of Halifax, 1905-1925." *Journal of the Canadian Historical Association* 13, 1 (2002), 96.

113 Rose Henderson, "The Juvenile Court," *Canadian Municipal Journal* 12 (1916), 84. While Henderson's comments were made in direct reference to the Montreal Juvenile Court, they were intended for a broader audience and as a template for other juvenile courts that were being created across the country.

114 J.E. Hudson, who was a lawyer, succeeded W.W. Walsh as judge of the Halifax Juvenile Court. See Nova Scotia, *Annual Report of the Director of Child Welfare for the Province of Nova Scotia, 1930*, 95-97. For more on the theme of probation officers' monitoring children's activities, see Lorna F. Hurl and David J. Tucker, "The Michigan County Agents and the Development of Juvenile Probation, 1873-1900," *Journal of Social History* 30, 4 (1997): 905-35; and Myers, *Caught*.

115 Nova Scotia, *The Statutes of Nova Scotia* (Halifax: Queen's Printer, 1890), 47.

116 Keller, *Regulating a New Society*, 169.

117 Myers, *Caught*, 255.

118 *Halifax Herald*, 29 November 1905.

119 Winifred M. Ross, "Child Rescue: The Nova Scotia Society for the Prevention of Cruelty, 1880-1920" (MA thesis, Dalhousie University, 1975), 112 and 128-29. For more on the founding and work of the society, see Fingard, *Dark Side*, chap. 8.

120 *Halifax Herald*, 27 February 1918.

121 Ibid.

122 Nova Scotia, *Annual Report of the Superintendent of Neglected and Delinquent Children for the Province of Nova Scotia, 1918*, 22.

123 Ernest Blois was Nova Scotia's first superintendent of neglected and delinquent children. See Nova Scotia, *Annual Report of the Director of Child Welfare for the Province of Nova Scotia, 1930*, 97.

124 If parents could afford to do so, the court could order them to pay for their child's stay in a reformatory. See ibid., 97-98; and Nova Scotia, *Annual Report of the Superintendent of Neglected and Delinquent Children for the Province of Nova Scotia, 1918*, 22. For an examination of how juvenile and family courts tried to regulate

the lives of parents and their children, see Dorothy E. Chunn, *From Punishment to Doing Good: Family Courts and Socialized Justice in Ontario, 1880-1940* (Toronto: University of Toronto Press, 1992).

125 Godfrey, "Development of the Juvenile Court," 9; and Nova Scotia, *Annual Report of the Superintendent of Neglected and Delinquent Children for the Province of Nova Scotia, 1918*, 22.

126 Elizabeth J. Clapp, *Mothers of All Children: Women Reformers and the Rise of Juvenile Courts in Progressive Era America* (Pennsylvania: Pennsylvania State University Press, 1998), 131.

127 This theme is explored in the Nova Scotia context by Baehre, "From Bridewell to Federal Penitentiary," 163-99. For an insightful account of the changes in penal reform ideology, see Michael Ignatieff, *A Just Measure of Pain: The Penitentiary in the Industrial Revolution, 1750-1850* (London: Penguin Books, 1978).

128 Appointed in December 1931 and chaired by Alexander Campbell, KC, of Truro; Samuel H. Prince of Halifax; Reverend Charles Curran of Halifax; Samuel Williamson, MD, of Yarmouth; and A.D. Campbell, LLB, of Sydney, their mandate was to "inquire fully into and concerning the condition of the various jails in the Province, the administration of said jails and matters in relation thereto and what, if any, improvements can be made in the present system of constituting and administering jails." See Nova Scotia, *Report of the Royal Commission Concerning Jails* (Halifax: King's Printer, 1933), 5-6.

129 Morton Keller notes that, while progressives in the United States managed to secure a few modest improvements in the country's penal system, major reforms could not be attained due to lack of widespread public support. See Keller, *Regulating a New Society*, 170-74.

130 Nova Scotia, *Report of the Royal Commission Concerning Jails*, 99.

131 Ibid., 100. Earlier complaints about the unsanitary conditions of the City Lockup were also made by the County Jail Committee, which, in 1925, passed a resolution asking the city to clean up its cells. The committee drafted this resolution after it discovered that prisoners "from the station [were] frequently brought to the county jail infested with vermin." See *Halifax Herald*, 29 May 1925 and 30 November 1927.

132 Nova Scotia, *Report of the Royal Commission Concerning Jails*, 100 and 104. The commissioners also noted that a small detention room was "found in an unsatisfactory condition."

133 Ibid., 101; and Baehre, "From Bridewell to Federal Penitentiary," 184.

134 For more background on Roe, see his obituary in the *United Churchman*, 2 March 1949.

135 *Evening Mail*, 22 March 1924.

136 Ibid.

137 *Halifax Herald*, 25 March 1924.

138 Ibid., 27 March 1924.

139 It is important to note that the Grand Jury was independent of city and municipal government; hence, it could, in theory, conduct an objective investigation into the conditions in the County Jail. See *Daily Echo*, 14 April 1924.

140 *Halifax Herald*, 14 October 1927.

141 Ibid., 2 March 1929.

142 Ibid., 26 February 1932; and Nova Scotia, *Penal Institutions: Thirty-First Annual Report, 1930-1931* (Halifax: King's Printer, 1932), 9.

143 Ibid., 8 March 1932.

144 Nova Scotia, *Report of the Royal Commission Concerning Jails*, 101-2 and 106-7. The poor state of lockups and jails in Halifax and Nova Scotia, along with the 1933 royal commission, received some national attention when C.W. Topping, who had conducted a fairly thorough investigation of Canada's prisons, cited the commissioners' findings to support his argument that local jails had "outlived [their] usefulness and ... should be liquidated at the earliest possible moment." See C.W. Topping, *Canadian Penal Institutions* rev. ed. (Toronto: Ryerson Press, 1943), 129.

145 *Halifax Herald*, 26 and 28 February and 1 March 1935.

146 The County Jail also had a working relationship with Dorchester Penitentiary in New Brunswick. Halifax did not have a federally run institution in which to incarcerate those men and women who received sentences of two years or more. The men and women destined for Dorchester stayed in the County Jail long enough to have their files processed before being escorted by a police officer to the penitentiary. Some women remained in Dorchester until 1923, when the government decided to close the last female ward and transferred these women to Kingston Penitentiary. The Prison for Women in Kingston did not open until 1934. See Baehre, "From Bridewell to Federal Penitentiary," 163; and Sheelagh Cooper, "The Evolution of the Federal Women's Prison," in *In Conflict with the Law: Women and the Canadian Justice System*, ed. Ellen Adelberg and Claudia Currie, 33-49 (Vancouver: Press Gang, 1993). For the 1918 to 1935 period, only three women from Halifax served their sentences in Kingston: Edith Wolgast and Fannie Reiley, both sentenced to two years each for theft; and Amelia Murray, twice convicted of performing an "illegal operation." See Kingston Penitentiary, Convict Register and Description Book, Correctional Service of Canada Museum; and Dorchester Penitentiary, Convicts' Register, Miscellaneous P, 1905-36, NSA, microfilm copy of the original register (which is held at Library and Archives Canada [hereafter LAC]). The "History Sheet" on Fannie Reiley and Amelia Murray may be found in LAC, RG 73, acc. 1985-86/163, vols. 16, 17, and 22, files 465, 554, and 3250. My request for access to the file of Edith Wolgast was denied.

147 McAlpine, *McAlpine's Halifax City Directory, 1923*, 100.

148 Nova Scotia, *Report of the Royal Commission Concerning Jails*, 102.

149 Halifax City Prison Committee, Minute Book, 8 March 1934, NSA, RG 35-102, ser. 18 A; and Nova Scotia, *Annual Report of the Several Departments of the Civic Government of Halifax, Nova Scotia for the Civic Year 1918-1919: City Prison Report* (Halifax: T.C. Allen and Co., 1920), 115.

150 Canadian National Committee for Mental Hygiene, *Mental Hygiene Survey of the Province of Nova Scotia, 1920*, Nova Scotia Legislative Assembly, Halifax, 98. A condensed version of this report may be found in the *Canadian Journal of Mental Hygiene* 3, 1 (1921): 3-48. The survey committee included Dr. C.K. Clarke, dean of the medical faculty at the University of Toronto; Dr. C.M. Hincks; and Marjorie Keyes. See *Halifax Herald*, 17 August 1920. Established by Clarke and Hincks in 1918, the Canadian National Committee for Mental Hygiene launched

a campaign against crime, prostitution, and unemployment. See Angus McLaren, *Our Own Master Race: Eugenics in Canada, 1885-1945* (Toronto: McClelland and Stewart, 1990), 59.

151 Halifax City Prison Committee, Minute Book, 8 March 1934, NSA.

152 Baehre, "From Bridewell to Federal Penitentiary," 182.

153 Nova Scotia, *Halifax City Charter, 1931*, 82. In terms of expenditures on the City Prison, available figures indicate that, for the fiscal year 1918-19, Halifax spent $103,054 on "Charities and Corrections." For the following year, this increased to $157,772. Although a breakdown of these amounts is not given, one can assume, on the basis of the descriptions of the Police Lockup and the City Prison, that a small percentage of this money was allocated to the maintenance of these institutions. See Canada, *The Canada Year Book, 1920* (Ottawa: King's Printer, 1921), 576-77; and Canada, *The Canada Year Book, 1921* (Ottawa: King's Printer, 1922), 694-95.

154 Halifax City Prison, Day Book, 24 June 1920 and 19 April 1921, NSA, RG 35-102, ser. 18 D.7 and D.8.

155 Nova Scotia, *Penal Institutions: Twenty-Second Annual Report, 1921-1922* (Halifax: King's Printer, 1923), 6; and Halifax City Prison Committee, Minute Book, 8 March 1934, NSA. Created at the turn of the century, the office of provincial penal inspector may also be seen as an attempt by Nova Scotia to modernize the operation of its penitentiaries. In 1970, Rockhead was demolished. See John Hartlen, "Rockhead Prison," *Atlantic Advocate* 69, 12 (1979): 45.

156 Nova Scotia, *Report of the Royal Commission Concerning Jails*, 102 and 111.

157 Joan Sangster, "Creating Social and Moral Citizens: Defining and Treating Delinquent Boys and Girls in English Canada, 1920-65," in *Contesting Canadian Citizenship: Historical Readings*, ed. Robert Adamoski, Dorothy E. Chunn, and Robert Menzies (Peterborough: Broadview Press, 2002), 337.

158 *Halifax Chronicle*, 5 January 1929.

159 Sangster, "Creating Social and Moral Citizens," 338.

160 Nova Scotia, *Annual Report of the Director of Child Welfare for the Province of Nova Scotia, 1929*, 88; and Nova Scotia, *Halifax City Charter, 1914*, 76-77.

161 Nova Scotia, *Annual Report of the Halifax Industrial School, 1929* (Halifax: John Bowes Printing Co. Ltd., 1929), 3. For the act incorporating the Industrial School, see Nova Scotia, *The Statutes of Nova Scotia, 1865* (Halifax: Queen's Printer, 1865), 128-29.

162 Nova Scotia, *Annual Report of the Halifax Industrial School, 1935* (Halifax: John Bowes Printing Co. Ltd., 1935), 7.

163 Ibid., 6.

164 Ibid. (emphasis in original).

165 *Halifax Morning Chronicle*, 2 February 1885; and Fingard, *Dark Side*, 127.

166 Fingard, *Dark Side*, 127.

167 Ibid., 145-47; Nova Scotia, *Report of the Royal Commission Concerning Jails*, 114; and Canadian National Committee for Mental Hygiene, *Mental Hygiene Survey of the Province of Nova Scotia, 1920*, 125.

168 *The Annual Report of the Twelfth Year of Work of the Department of Temperance and Moral Reform, Methodist Church, Canada, 1913-1914*, United Church of Canada Maritime Conference Archives, Sackville, New Brunswick, box M-29, p. 16. For

more on the Maritime Home for Girls, see Caroline Caverhill Mann, "'It Pays to Be Good': An Exploration of the Maritime Home for Girls and the Interprovincial Home for Young Women, 1914-1931" (MA thesis, Dalhousie University, 2007).

169 Michael Boudreau, "The Emergence of the Social Gospel in Nova Scotia: The Presbyterian, Methodist and Baptist Churches and the Working Class, 1880-1914" (MA thesis, Queen's University, 1991), 152-53.

170 Canadian National Committee for Mental Hygiene, *Mental Hygiene Survey of the Province of Nova Scotia, 1920*, 118-19. It is important to note that the Sisters of the Good Shepherd also maintained an adult female reformatory until 1970.

171 The first newspaper reference located for the association appeared in 1927, which indicates that it had been in existence for at least a few years prior to this date. See *Halifax Herald*, 26 January 1927 and 20 April 1928; and John Kidman, *The Canadian Prison: The Story of Tragedy* (Toronto: The Ryerson Press, 1947), 31.

172 The objectives and aims of the CPWA included an intention to "help the man, woman, or child indicted by the law, whether in the courts, in jail, or after discharge therefrom; to ameliorate the conditions of prisoners and the treatment of delinquents generally by the introduction of more humane principles of penology; [and] to abolish the death penalty throughout the Dominion of Canada." Nellie McClung sat for a time on the CPWA's Board of Officers and Directors. See C.W. Topping, *Canadian Penal Institutions* (Chicago: University of Chicago Press, 1930), 113-14. The Prisoners' Aid Association of Canada, the nineteenth-century forerunner to the CPWA, emerged in 1878. The association helped ex-prisoners find work, operated a home for those released from jail, conducted evangelical work in local prisons, and lobbied for reform in prison management. See Carrigan, *Crime and Punishment*, 357.

173 Maritime School of Social Work, Canadian Penal Congress, Dalhousie University Archives and Special Collections (hereafter DUASC), MS-1-22, box 4, and MS-1-3, file 336; and *Halifax Chronicle Herald*, 23 November 1959.

174 *Halifax Mail Star*, 20 October 1960; and Leonard F. Hatfield, *Sammy the Prince: The Story of Samuel Henry Prince, One of Canada's Pioneering Sociologists* (Hantsport, NS: Lancelot Press, 1990), 129, 138, and 162.

175 *Halifax Mail Star*, 2 April 1964; and *Halifax Chronicle Herald*, 12 March 1982.

176 *Halifax Herald*, 3 February 1931; and *Halifax Chronicle Herald*, 22 September 1964.

177 Halifax-Dartmouth United Way, Minute Book, 26 September 1928, NSA, MG 20, vol. 1713. My thanks to Dr. Shirley Tillotson, Department of History, Dalhousie University, for providing me with this reference.

178 Canada, *Report of the Royal Commission to Investigate the Penal System of Canada* (Ottawa: King's Printer, 1938), 17.

179 Ibid.

180 Weaver, *Crime, Constables, and Courts*, 178.

CHAPTER 3: THE SOCIAL PERCEPTIONS OF CRIME AND CRIMINALS

1 *Halifax Herald*, 12 December 1918.

2 Marshall Berman, *All That Is Solid: Melts into Air: The Experience of Modernity* (New York: Penguin Books, 1988), 235.

3 *Halifax Herald*, 10 March 1925.

4 For more on the tension between modernity and tradition, see Giddens, *The Consequences of Modernity*, 36.

5 As Wayne Morrison argues, central to the idea of modernity "is an emphasis upon control and the reduction of the world to a collection of phenomena to be analyzed and mastered." Some Halifax progressives certainly viewed modernity from this perspective. See Wayne Morrison, *Theoretical Criminology: From Modernity to Post-Modernism* (London: Cavendish, 1995), 28.

6 Tina Loo and Lorna R. McLean, eds. *Historical Perspectives on Law and Society in Canada* (Toronto: Copp Clark Longman, 1994), 2.

7 Ibid.

8 This argument draws upon J.A. Sharpe's point that, in order to contextualize the history of crime, criminal behaviour must be defined in the terms in which contemporaries understood it. See Sharpe, "History of Crime," 188-89.

9 Martin J. Wiener, *Reconstructing the Criminal: Culture, Law, and Policy in England, 1830-1914* (Cambridge: Cambridge University Press, 1990), 11.

10 For more on how these factors influence social perceptions of crime and criminals, see Rafter, "Social Construction of Crime," 376-89.

11 R.C. Macleod, ed., *Lawful Authority: Readings on the History of Criminal Justice in Canada* (Toronto: Copp Clark Pitman Ltd., 1988), 3. Greg Marquis argues that the concepts of "British justice" and "British liberty" became enshrined in Canadian popular culture in the mid-nineteenth century. Marquis, "Doing Justice," 60.

12 *Halifax Chronicle*, 22 January 1929.

13 David Ray Papke, *Framing the Criminal: Crime, Cultural Work, and the Loss of Critical Perspective, 1830-1900* (Hamden CT: Archon Books, 1987), 19.

14 Marquis, "Doing Justice," 45-47.

15 John L. McMullan argues, in the context of early modern England, that definitions of certain behaviours as criminal "are the result of hegemonic and ideological struggles by magistrates, lawyers, local elites, moral entrepreneurs, and law and order political figures." See John L. McMullan, "Crime, Law, and Order in Early Modern England," *British Journal of Criminology* 27, 3 (1987): 268.

16 Keller, *Regulating a New Society*, 162 and 171.

17 *Halifax Herald*, 5 and 6 April and 3 May 1920.

18 Chris McCormick, ed. *Constructing Danger: The Mis/representation of Crime in the News* (Halifax: Fernwood, 1995), 4-5.

19 Steven Chermak, "Crime in the News Media: A Refined Understanding of How Crime Becomes News," in *Media, Process, and the Social Construction of Crime: Studies in Newsmaking Criminology*, ed. Gregg Barak (New York and London: Garland, 1994), 97.

20 The *Herald* was a staunch supporter of the provincial Conservative Party, while the *Chronicle* championed the cause of the Liberals. From 1918 to 1935, the *Herald* had a yearly average circulation of 19,750 copies and the *Chronicle* had 12,416. See William March, *Red Line: The Chronicle-Herald and the Mail-Star, 1875-1954* (Halifax: Chebucto Agencies Ltd., 1986), vi, 116, 203-04, 310, and 396-98.

21 *Halifax Herald*, 6 June 1918.

22 Ibid., 7 and 13 June 1918.

23 Ibid., 14 June 1918. This assertion seemed to be supported by Jos. Hughes, manager of the Williams' Standard Shows. In an interview with the *Halifax Mail* in

September 1918, Hughes said that he was forced to close down his shows after four evenings because of the rowdiness and vandalism caused by hundreds of boys. "For down right lawlessness," he commented, "Halifax leads all cities on the continent." See *Halifax Herald*, 20 September 1918.

24 Ibid., 14 June 1918 (emphasis in original).

25 Ibid., 29 October and 5 November 1919. The "Black Hand" was often known as the Mafia and was closely associated, rather stereotypically, with Italians and their alleged penchant for violence in the 1910s and 1920s in major American cities. See Jeffrey S. Adler, *First in Violence, Deepest in Dirt: Homicide in Chicago, 1875-1920* (Cambridge: Harvard University Press, 2006), 180-99.

26 *Halifax Herald*, 29 October 1919 (emphasis in original).

27 *Morning Chronicle*, 8 January 1925.

28 *Halifax Herald*, 8 August 1934.

29 *Morning Chronicle*, 1 November 1922.

30 Nova Scotia, *Report of the Royal Commission Concerning Jails*, 17.

31 *Halifax Herald*, 24 December 1920.

32 Ibid. (emphasis in original).

33 Ibid., 15 February 1921 (emphasis in original).

34 Ibid.

35 Nova Scotia, *Annual Report of the Several Departments of the Civic Government of Halifax, Nova Scotia, for the Civic Year 1917-1918: Report Chief of Police* (Halifax: T.C. Allen and Co., 1919), 149.

36 Ibid., 195.

37 *Halifax Herald*, 2 September 1922 (emphasis in original).

38 Ibid.

39 Ibid.

40 Ibid., 28 August 1931.

41 Ibid., 28 and 29 August, 1 September, and 12 October 1931. Chipman Smith and Richard Morse were charged with robbery with violence, while G. LeRoy Dickson, an employee of the bank, was taken into custody as an accomplice.

42 *Halifax Herald*, 29 August 1931.

43 Ibid., 2 November 1931. The actual number of "gangster" films banned was not specified, but of the 1,632 "moving pictures" viewed by the Nova Scotia Board of Censors, 1,522 were approved, sixty-five were approved with certain deletions, and forty-five were rejected. This was the highest number of films that the board had "condemned" to date.

44 For more on this theme see Elliott Leyton, William O'Grady, and James Overton, *Violence and Public Anxiety: A Canadian Case* (St. John's: Institute of Social and Economic Research, Memorial University of Newfoundland, 1992), xiii-xxvii.

45 Jim Phillips, "The History of Canadian Criminal Justice, 1750-1920," in *Criminology: A Reader's Guide*, ed. Jane Gladstone, Richard V. Ericson, and Clifford D. Shearing (Toronto: Centre of Criminology, University of Toronto, 1991), 88.

46 *Halifax Herald*, 7 January 1901. Wallace, a Roman Catholic, was also a staunch supporter of the Sisters of the Good Shepherd and their reformatory work for juvenile delinquents and "fallen women" (i.e., prostitutes).

47 Wallace, *Housing Problem*, NSA, 17-19.

48 *Morning Chronicle*, 5 April 1923.

49 *Halifax Herald*, 27 August 1924.
50 Ibid.
51 Ibid.
52 Ibid., 1 February 1926; and *Morning Chronicle*, 1 February 1926.
53 *Morning Chronicle*, 1 February 1926.
54 Ibid.; and *Halifax Herald*, 1 February 1926.
55 *Halifax Herald*, 8 October 1924. Justice Chisholm presided at Allister Munroe's murder trial.
56 Ibid., 9 October 1924.
57 Ibid.
58 Hatfield, *Sammy the Prince*, 38.
59 Ibid., 164.
60 Ibid., 123 and 138. Prince served as a member of the 1933 royal commission on jails in Nova Scotia.
61 *Halifax Herald*, 10 March 1925.
62 Hatfield, *Sammy the Prince*, 138.
63 *Halifax Herald*, 10 March 1925.
64 Ibid., 24 October 1930.
65 Ibid., 31 January 1934. Near the end of 1934, Murray, now a County Court judge, told a gathering of the WCTU that Halifax needed a "domestic relations" court that could handle all of the cases dealing with family quarrels. This court, Murray argued, would aid the "aim [of] social justice" in Halifax. Thus, at a fairly senior level there existed a "progressive," if not a visionary, drive to overhaul the city's judicial system to make it more proactive and social in its orientation. Murray may have had the Toronto Women's Court, which was created in 1913, in mind when he made these comments. See *Halifax Herald*, 14 December 1934. For more on Toronto's Women's Court, see Amanda Glasbeek, *Feminized Justice: The Toronto Women's Court, 1913-1934* (Vancouver: UBC Press, 2009).
66 *Morning Chronicle*, 5 April 1923. Nova Scotia's penal inspector shared this line of thought. Inspector T. Ives Byrne condemned idleness and feared jails had become "colleges of crime, with the most experienced faculties." In 1924, Inspector A.C. Jost commented on the rise of a "much more generally adopted attitude" among some officials "that law breaking [was] not so much the result of intent as it [was] the evidence of social maladjustment, and in many cases, [could] be better attacked by measures which [were] not wholly punitive." He went on to add that the "connection between crime and a limited mental outlook [was] better appreciated and [that] this ha[d] resulted in a great change in the treatment of criminals as a class." See Nova Scotia, *Penal Institutions: Thirty-First Annual Report, 1930-1931*, 7; and Nova Scotia, *Penal Institutions: Twenty-Fourth Annual Report, 1923-1924* (Halifax: King's Printer, 1925), 7.
67 J.B. Feilding, "Prison Reform in Nova Scotia," *Proceedings of the Nineteenth Annual Convention of the Union of Nova Scotia Municipalities*, 1924, 98-99 and 106.
68 Ibid., 100-1.
69 Ibid., 110.
70 Ibid., 110-11.
71 *Halifax Herald*, 20 and 21 December 1926.
72 Ibid., 30 July 1932.

73 Ibid., 15 January 1923.

74 Ibid., 21 and 22 July 1931.

75 Nova Scotia, *Report of the Royal Commission Concerning Jails*, 47.

76 Feilding, "Prison Reform in Nova Scotia," 105 and 109.

77 *Halifax Chronicle*, 14 February 1928. The same eugenicist views were sounded by a committee, appointed by the province in 1916, to investigate the "feebleminded" in Nova Scotia. The report concluded: "[feeblemindedness] is responsible for a very considerable share of the pauperism, illegitimacy, vice and crime which exist in our Province." As a result, "a strong effort should be made to limit the multiplication of this unfortunate class." See Nova Scotia, *Report on Feeble Minded in Nova Scotia* (Halifax: King's Printer, 1918), 8. The investigating committee consisted of: A.H. MacKay, the superintendent of education; E.H. Blois, the superintendent of neglected and delinquent children and later a judge of the Halifax Juvenile Court (1925-33); and W.H. Hattie, the provincial health officer.

78 Jennifer Stephen, "The 'Incorrigible,' the 'Bad,' and the 'Immoral': Toronto's 'Factory Girls' and the Work of the Toronto Psychiatric Clinic," in Knafla and Binnie, *Law, Society, and the State*, 432; and Ruth Harris, *Murder and Madness: Medicine, Law, and Society in the Fin de Siècle* (New York: Oxford University Press, 1989). Some members of the Nova Scotia League for the Care and Protection of Feebleminded Persons, and the eugenics movement in Canada, also supported the sterilization of the feebleminded. For more on these organizations, see McLaren, *Our Own Master Race*.

79 Phillips, "Poverty, Unemployment, and the Administration of the Criminal Law," in Girard and Phillips, *Essays in the History of Canadian Law*, 3:128 and 148.

80 Ibid., 129; and Richard Quinney, *The Social Reality of Crime* (Boston: Little, Brown and Company, 1970), 94-95. In eighteenth-century England, according to J.A. Sharpe, this process was tantamount to the "'criminalization' of the poor," whom the elite identified as a problem because of the expense involved in supporting them and their apparent proclivity for crime and disorder. See Sharpe, "History of Crime," 194.

81 The commissioners borrowed this quote from an un-named source and applied it to the situation in Nova Scotia. See Nova Scotia, *Report of the Royal Commission Concerning Jails*, 24. Similar public perceptions of vagrants as drunkards, labour radicals, and generally undesirable appeared in early twentieth-century Calgary. See David Bright, "Loafers Are Not Going to Subsist upon Public Credulence: Vagrancy and the Law in Calgary, 1900-1914," *Labour/Le Travail* 36 (1995): 37-58.

82 *Halifax Herald*, 24 August 1925.

83 *Crankshaw's Criminal Code of Canada*, 270-71.

84 John Kidman and C.H. Mercer, *Report on County Jails of Nova Scotia*, Canadian Prisoners' Welfare Association, 1934, 5 (Charles H. Mercer Papers, DUASC, MS 2 no. 659).

85 For 1935, Halifax secured sixty (fifty-four men and six women) convictions for vagrancy. See Canada, *Fifty-Fifth to Sixtieth Annual Reports of Statistics of Criminal and Other Offences, 1930-1935* (Ottawa: King's Printer, 1931-36).

86 Smith, *Through Dirty Windows*, 66.

87 *Halifax Herald*, 6 February 1933.

88 Marquis, "Police as a Social Service," 345-46.
89 *Halifax Herald*, 12 October and 3 November 1932.
90 Ibid., 8 November 1932.
91 Ibid., 10 November 1932.
92 Even Nova Scotia's Royal Commission on penal institutions recommended that the vagrancy law be administered to ensure that those people whose only fault was unemployment would not be classified as vagrants and thus subject to imprisonment. See Nova Scotia, *Report of the Royal Commission Concerning Jails*, 95.

CHAPTER 4: "MISCREANTS" AND "DESPERADOES"

1 *Halifax Herald*, 30 November 1925.
2 Ibid., 25 July 1932.
3 Interview with Inspector Vincent O'Brien.
4 Ibid.
5 *Halifax Herald*, 24 January 1927.
6 *Halifax Chronicle*, 9 April 1929.
7 Simon received a thirty-day sentence in the County Jail. See Halifax Magistrate's Court, 1930, NSA, RG 42, ser. C, vol. 16, no. 682.
8 *Halifax Herald*, 16 August 1922.
9 Ibid., 24 November 1924.
10 This point is taken in part from Louis Chevalier, who argues that, in the first half of the nineteenth century, the Parisian middle class saw the "dangerous classes" as a group of people isolated by their customs, speech, and general lifestyle. As such, they were often prone to crime. See Louis Chevalier, *Laboring Classes and Dangerous Classes in Paris during the First Half of the Nineteenth Century* (New York: Howard Fertig, 1973), 72-73.
11 Due to the destruction of the Halifax Juvenile Court records, this chapter is unable to offer a comprehensive study of how the court dealt with juveniles. Nevertheless, by utilizing the extant sources – notably the annual reports of the superintendent of neglected and delinquent children, the director of child welfare, and the reformatories, along with the truant officer's reports – many of the dimensions of juvenile crime in interwar Halifax can be explored.
12 Peter King and Joan Noel, "The Origins of 'The Problem of Juvenile Delinquency': The Growth of Juvenile Prosecutions in London in the Late Eighteenth and Early Nineteenth Centuries," *Criminal Justice History* 14 (1993): 17-41; and Sangster, "Creating Social and Moral Citizens."
13 Victor Bailey, "The Fabrication of Deviance: 'Dangerous Classes' and 'Criminal Classes' in Victorian England," in *Protest and Survival: The Historical Experience – Essays for E.P. Thompson*, ed. John Rule and Robert Malcolmson (London: Merlin Press, 1993), 239-40.
14 Ibid., 244. Middle-class residents of London in the 1840s looked upon the "dangerous classes" as the foci of crime. See Gareth Stedman Jones, *Outcast London: A Study in the Relationship between the Classes in Victorian Society* (London: Penguin Books, 1984), 167.
15 Eric H. Monkkonen, *The Dangerous Class: Crime and Poverty in Columbus, Ohio, 1860-1885* (Cambridge, MA: Harvard University Press, 1975), 72-73.

16 Chevalier, *Labouring Classes*, 364.

17 Fingard, *Dark Side*, esp. chap. 2.

18 Phyne, "Prohibition's Legacy," 160.

19 This point draws upon the seminal work of E.P. Thompson, *The Making of the English Working Class* (London: Penguin Group, 1980), 8-11.

20 For a discussion of the "criminal class" during the period of early industrial capitalism in Hamilton, Ontario, see Michael B. Katz, Michael J. Doucet, and Mark J. Stern, *The Social Organization of Early Industrial Capitalism* (Cambridge, MA: Harvard University Press, 1982), 219.

21 In the context of London in the second half of the nineteenth century, Jennifer S. Davis argues that some sections of the working class, especially the labouring poor, were more liable than others to feel the "disciplinary power of the state." See Jennifer S. Davis, "Prosecutions and Their Context: The Use of the Criminal Law in Later Nineteenth-Century London," in *Policing and Prosecution in Britain, 1750-1850*, ed. Douglas Hay and Francis Snyder (Oxford: Clarendon Press, 1989), 425.

22 Jennifer S. Davis, "Law Breaking and Law Enforcement: The Creation of a Criminal Class in Mid-Victorian London" (PhD diss., Boston College, 1984), 240-41.

23 McKay, "1910s," 222.

24 The racial motivations of the 1919 riots and the concomitant remarks concerning the city's Chinese community are examined in Chapter 6.

25 *Morning Chronicle*, 27 and 28 May 1918; and *An Enquiry Respecting the Riots in Halifax during May 1918 and February 1919*, held by the Grand Jury at Halifax, 21 March 1919, in Halifax County Supreme Court, 1918-19, NSA, RG 39, ser. C, vol. 702, no. 394.

26 *Morning Chronicle*, 27 May 1918.

27 *Enquiry Respecting the Riots*, 35.

28 Ibid.; and *Morning Chronicle*, 27 May 1918.

29 *Enquiry Respecting the Riots*, 47. Halifax has never been immune to public violence. As a temporary home for military and naval units throughout the nineteenth and early twentieth centuries, Halifax had seen its share of confrontations between and among men in uniform and civilians. For instance, in 1838, 1847, 1848, and 1850, military personnel rioted in the streets of Halifax to exact revenge for one of their own who had been cheated, injured, or killed in a brothel. See Michael S. Cross, "'The Laws Are Like Cobwebs': Popular Resistance to Authority in Mid-Nineteenth Century British North America," in Waite et al., *Law in a Colonial Society*, 118-19. In addition to these skirmishes, on VE Day (7 May 1945), thousands of civilians and ex-servicemen, caught up in the drunken euphoria of the war's end, pillaged downtown Halifax. About 564 businesses were damaged and close to $5 million worth of property wrecked. See Carman Miller, "The 1940s: War and Rehabilitation," in Forbes and Muise, *Atlantic Provinces*, 318-21. For an overview of some of the other public riots involving military personnel in Halifax, and Canada generally, see Judy M. Torrance, *Public Violence in Canada* (Kingston and Montreal: McGill-Queen's University Press, 1986).

30 *Morning Chronicle*, 27 May 1918.

31 Ibid.

32 *Halifax Herald*, 28 May 1918 (emphasis in original).
33 *Morning Chronicle*, 28 May 1918.
34 *Halifax Herald*, 19 February 1919.
35 Ibid.
36 *Enquiry Respecting the Riots*, 41.
37 When asked at the inquiry about the incident, Mayor Hawkins replied, "I think the explanation of that is they ... took her for a foreigner." See Ibid., 14.
38 *Halifax Herald*, 20 February 1919.
39 Ibid.
40 Ibid., 22 February 1919.
41 Ibid., 20 February 1919.
42 James Overton suggests that a violent, or riotous, act stirs those anxious about law and order into action. See James Overton, "Riots, Raids and Relief, Police, Prisons and Parsimony: The Political Economy of Public Order in Newfoundland in the 1930s," in Leyton et al., *Violence and Public Anxiety*, 254.
43 *Halifax Herald*, 22 February 1919.
44 McKay, "1910s," 222.
45 E.P. Thompson, *Customs in Common: Studies in Traditional Popular Culture* (New York: The New Press, 1991), 264-65.
46 George Rude, *The Crowd in History: A Study of Popular Disturbances in France and England, 1730-1848* (New York: John Willey and Sons, 1964), 6-8. For more on the social and cultural significance of mobs and riots, see E.J. Hobsbawm, *Primitive Rebels: Studies in Archaic Forms of Social Movement in the 19th and 20th Centuries* (New York: W.W. Norton and Company, 1959); and Scott See, *Riots in New Brunswick: Orange Nativism and Social Violence in the 1840s* (Toronto: University of Toronto Press, 1993).
47 "Chief Justice's Charge to the Grand Jury Regarding Riots, City of Halifax, 1919," Halifax County Supreme Court, 1920-21, NSA, RG 39, ser. C, vol. 704, no. 163a.
48 Halifax County Supreme Court, 1918-19, NSA, RG 39, ser. C, vol. 702, no. 394. It is, perhaps, curious that the Grand Jury, rather than a royal commission, was called upon to investigate the causes of this riot. However, in light of the fact that the Grand Jury was independent of government, it may have been felt that it was adequate to the task at hand. It may also be argued that the city, and the province, in an effort to avoid further embarrassment over this riot, chose not to appoint a royal commission, which would have attracted a great deal of public attention to the riot for an extended period of time.
49 Rude, *Crowd in History*, 242; and Torrance, *Public Violence in Canada*, 42.
50 Bevis's father also abused his mother. See *Halifax Herald*, 15 July 1924; and the Capital Case Files, LAC, RG 13, ser. B, vol. 1532, file 742, pt. 1. It should be noted that, in some records, Bevis's first name is spelled "Louis." However, the more commonly used "Lewis" is utilized in this chapter.
51 The three people with Bevis were Wilfred Slaughenwhite, age twenty-one, "pal and accomplice"; Ethel Slaughenwhite, the fourteen-year-old sister of Wilfred; and Muriel Bevis, Lewis's sixteen-year-old sister. See *Halifax Herald*, 15 July 1924; and Halifax County Supreme Court, 1924-25, NSA, RG 39, ser. C, vol. 707, no. 213.

52 *Halifax Herald*, 15 July 1924.
53 Halifax County Supreme Court, 1924-25, NSA, RG 39, ser. C, vol. 707, no. 213.
54 *Halifax Herald*, 15 July 1924.
55 *Morning Chronicle*, 15 July 1924.
56 *Halifax Herald*, 16 July 1924.
57 Ibid., 17 July 1924; and Halifax County Jail, Jailor's Reports, 1916-26, NSA, RG 35-312, ser. J.76.
58 Madden had a long career as a criminal lawyer. See *Halifax Herald*, 15 October 1924. Bevis enlisted in the Canadian Expeditionary Force when he was seventeen. For a more detailed, if somewhat melodramatic, account of Bevis's case, see the chapter on Bevis in Edward Butts, *The Desperate Ones: Forgotten Canadian Outlaws* (Toronto: Dundurn Press, 2006), 189-201. My thanks to one of the UBC Press readers for this reference.
59 *Halifax Herald*, 15 October 1924.
60 Ibid., 16 October 1924. This "hung" jury may indicate the reluctance of some members of the jury to condemn Bevis to death due to the fact that, as a veteran of the First World War, he had already suffered a great deal. It may also suggest a division of opinion within the community generally about the legitimacy of capital punishment.
61 *Halifax Herald*, 24 November 1924. At the second trial the Crown was able to introduce into evidence bullet fragments from officer Fulton's body that allegedly came from Bevis's revolver. See Butts, *Desperate Ones*, 200-1.
62 Madden based his appeal on the grounds that the police had used excessive force in apprehending Bevis. He argued that it would have been possible for the officers to capture Bevis using less violent means. As a result, Madden proposed, Bevis had been justified in repelling force with force, thereby reducing the offence from murder to justifiable homicide. The Nova Scotia Supreme Court, however, disagreed. In a unanimous decision it dismissed Bevis's appeal. In speaking for the court, Chief Justice Robert Harris said he believed that the "circumstances were undoubtedly such as to justify the police in shooting the prisoner to prevent his escape ... There is no evidence whatever that the shooting of the deceased was in self-defense." Harris also felt that Bevis "was a menace to society and was endeavouring to shoot his way to escape." See *The Nova Scotia Reports* (Toronto: Carswell, 1925), 57:513-21; and *Morning Chronicle*, 4 December 1924 and 20 January 1925.
63 Bevis listed "Church of England" as his religious denomination on his First World War enlistment form, 27 November 1916. See Soldiers of the First World War – CEF, Associated Images, LAC, available at www.lac-bac.gc.ca. According to the Great War Veterans' Association, if Lapointe had granted a fourteen-day reprieve for Bevis, they would have produced a petition with fifty thousand names demanding clemency. This file also contains an unsigned letter to Lapointe, which reads: "When the great judgement day comes may almighty God be more merciful to you than you were when you pronounced capital punishment upon poor unfortunate Lewis Bevis. You sent him into the next world when you could have prevented it." See Capital Case Files, LAC, RG 13, ser B, vol. 1532, file 742, pt. 1.
64 *Morning Chronicle*, 11 February 1925.

65 *Halifax Herald*, 11 February 1925. Hundreds of people, many of whom were no doubt still fascinated by this case and possibly opposed to hanging as a means of execution, attended Bevis's funeral.

66 For more on this theme, and the implementation of capital punishment, see Carolyn Strange, "The Lottery of Death: Capital Punishment, 1867-1976," *Manitoba Law Journal* 23 (1995): 594-619; Carolyn Strange, "The Undercurrents of Penal Culture: Punishment of the Body in Mid-Twentieth-Century Canada," *Law and History Review* 19, 2 (2001): 343-85; Kimberley White, *Negotiating Responsibility: Law, Murder, and States of Mind* (Vancouver: UBC Press, 2008); and Ken Leyton-Brown, *The Practice of Execution in Canada* (Vancouver: UBC Press, 2010). Bevis, at the age of twenty-five, belonged to an age category (twenty-one to thirty) whose male members experienced an execution rate of 76 percent. Many of these men were working class, with little formal education. See Kenneth L. Avio, "The Quality of Mercy: Exercise of the Royal Prerogative in Canada," *Canadian Public Policy* 13, 3 (1987): 368.

67 Katz et al., *Social Organization*, 214.

68 Fingard, *Dark Side*, 39-52.

69 *Halifax Chronicle*, 6 January 1927; and Halifax County Court, 1927, NSA, RG 38, vol. 335, no. 168.

70 *Halifax Chronicle*, 22 August, 19 October, and 3 November 1927.

71 Judith Fingard and David Hood outline some of the main characteristics of this undesirable class. See Fingard, *Dark Side*, 50-52; and Hood, *Down but Not Out*, 63-111.

72 *Halifax Chronicle*, 23 August 1927.

73 As quoted in McKay, "1910s," 222.

74 For more on the problems of demobilization and veterans' fight for adequate benefits and medical services, see Desmond Morton and Glenn Wright, *Winning the Second Battle: Canadian Veterans and the Return to Civilian Life, 1915-1930* (Toronto: University of Toronto Press, 1987).

75 Nova Scotia, *Report of the Nova Scotia Returned Solider Commission* (Halifax: King's Printer, 1921), 5, 7, and 9-11.

76 A year later things did not seem to be any better. Pope reported that one ex-serviceman, a shoemaker by trade, who had been out of work for several months and had sold most of his furniture to feed his five children, told him that he would be willing to do any sort of work. See *Halifax Herald*, 3 December 1920 and 9 May 1921.

77 *Morning Chronicle*, 3 August 1918; *Halifax Herald*, 1 April 1920; and Halifax County Supreme Court, 1918-19, NSA, RG 39, ser. C, vol. 702, no. 384.

78 *Morning Chronicle*, 31 December 1919.

79 Ibid., 26 March 1920.

80 At least for one soldier, even coping became too much of a burden. At the end of 1919, John Dowing tried to commit suicide by cutting his throat with a razor in his boarding house. He had been back in Halifax for seven months and was undergoing treatment at the Camp Hill military hospital for the side effects produced by a bout of malaria he had contracted in Salonica. He told the "mistress" of his boarding house that his health had not improved and that he did not want

to be sent to the asylum. Dowing was thirty-two years old, single, and had served four years with a medical unit. Apparently, he had been one of the first eligible citizens of Halifax to answer the call to arms in 1914. See *Morning Chronicle*, 30 December 1919.

81 Some of the main texts that deal with these issues include Victor Bailey, *Delinquency and Citizenship: Reclaiming the Young Offender, 1914-1948* (Oxford: Oxford University Press, 1987); Commacchio, *Nations Are Built*; Jacques Donzelot, *The Policing of Families* (London: Hutchinson, 1977); Myers, *Caught*; Anthony M. Platt, *The Child Savers: The Invention of Delinquency*, 2nd ed. (Chicago: University of Chicago Press, 1977); and Steven L. Schlossman, *Love and the American Delinquent: The Theory and Practice of "Progressive" Juvenile Justice, 1825-1920* (Chicago: University of Chicago Press, 1977).

82 Susan Magarey, "The Invention of Juvenile Delinquency in Early Nineteenth-Century England," *Labour History* 34 (1978): 20-25. For a more detailed exploration of the attitudes towards and the treatment of juvenile delinquents in Britain and the strategies developed to regulate childhood, see, Linda Mahood, *Policing Gender, Class, and Family: Britain, 1850-1940* (London: UCL Press, 1995).

83 As cited in Emily Jaquays, "What Is Our Mental Attitude to the Delinquent Girl?" *Social Welfare* 9, 6 (1927): 378.

84 Neil Sutherland, *Children in English-Canadian Society: Framing the Twentieth-Century Consensus* (Toronto: University of Toronto Press, 1976), 91, 123-25.

85 The idea of the separateness of children from adults emerged in a number of legal and social structures in nineteenth-century England. See Deborah Gorham, "The 'Maiden Tribute of Modern Babylon' Re-Examined: Child Prostitution and the Idea of Childhood in Late Victorian England," *Victorian Studies* 21, 3 (1978): 363.

86 *Crankshaw's Criminal Code of Canada*, 1414-15 and 1418; and Susan E. Houston, "Victorian Origins of Juvenile Delinquency: A Canadian Experience," *History of Education Quarterly* 12, 3 (1972): 266-70. In North America at the turn of the century, in both secular and religious quarters, a new appreciation of childhood as a specialized time of life emerged. See Commacchio, *Nations Are Built,"* 17; and Susan E. Houston, "The Role of the Criminal Law in Redefining 'Youth' in Mid-Nineteenth-Century Upper Canada," *Historical Studies in Education* 6, 3 (1994): 39. The belief that delinquent children could be made into better citizens continued into the post-Second-World-War era. See Brian T. Thorn, "'Healthy Activity and Worthwhile Ideas': Left- and Right-Wing Women Confront Juvenile Delinquency in Post-World-War II Canada," *Histoire Sociale/Social History* 42, 84 (2009): 359.

87 *Halifax, Nova Scotia – A Report Indicating the Need of a Social Survey*, NSA, 4.

88 *United Churchman*, 12 December 1934.

89 Nova Scotia, *Annual Report of the Several Departments of the Civic Government of Halifax, Nova Scotia for the Civic Year 1921-1922: Report Chief of Police* (Halifax: T.C. Allen and Company, 1923), 211-12. Parts of this section on Halifax's "juvenile delinquent class" are taken from Michael Boudreau, "'Delinquents Often Become Criminals': Juvenile Delinquency in Halifax, 1918-1935," *Acadiensis* 39, 1 (2010): 108-32.

90 The high percentage of adjournments in the Halifax Juvenile Court does appear to be anomalous when compared, statistically, with those of Saint John and Hamilton. For the 1930 to 1935 period, the juvenile court in Saint John meted out punishments to all but three of the 1,440 cases before it (Appendix 2, Table A2.21). In Hamilton, a similar pattern appeared. The Hamilton Juvenile Court passed sentence on 90.3 percent of the cases it heard during these years, dismissed 5.8 percent, and adjourned 3.9 percent (Appendix 2, Table A2.22). For more on how juvenile and family courts tried to regulate the lives of mothers and their children, see Donzelot, *Policing of Families*; Chunn, *From Punishment to Doing Good*; and Myers, *Caught*.

91 Canada, *Forty-Seventh Annual Report of Criminal Statistics, 1922* (Ottawa: King's Printer, 1924), 262, 266-67, and 276; and *Halifax Herald*, 17 November 1922.

92 *Annual Report of the Superintendent of Neglected and Delinquent Children for the Province of Nova Scotia, 1920* (Halifax: King's Printer, 1921), 87.

93 Halifax made attendance at school compulsory in 1915. Halifax's Compulsory Attendance at School Act is contained in Nova Scotia, *Halifax City Charter, 1914*, 272-80; and Nova Scotia, *Annual Report of the Superintendent of Education for Nova Scotia, 1920* (Halifax: King's Printer, 1921), xvi.

94 The Truant Officer's Reports are published in Nova Scotia, *Report of the Board of School Commissioners for the City of Halifax, Nova Scotia* (Halifax: Weeks Printing Co. Ltd./MacNab Print/Royal Print and Litho Ltd./Ross Print Ltd., 1919-37). R.J. Anderson served as truant officer for thirty-five years until his retirement in 1933. In that year, the School Board appointed H.R. Archard as Anderson's replacement. See *Halifax Herald*, 3 February 1933. Truancy was a problem across Canada for much of the twentieth century. See Neil Sutherland, *Growing Up: Childhood in English Canada from the Great War to the Age of Television* (Toronto: University of Toronto Press, 1997).

95 Nova Scotia, *Annual Report of the Superintendent of Education for Nova Scotia, 1921* (Halifax: King's Printer, 1922), 60.

96 In 1922-23, forty boys and fourteen girls received permits allowing them to leave school to work. See Nova Scotia, *Report of the Board of School Commissioners for the City of Halifax, 1921-1922 and 1922-1923* (Halifax: MacNab Print, 1922 and 1923), 26-27 and 25. The law did sanction this practice. Section 913, subsection 2.b and c, of the Compulsory Attendance at School Act states: "[any child] over fourteen years of age, if necessity requires such a child to work, and who shows that fact to the satisfaction of the board and obtains the written permission of the secretary of the board for such employment" and any child "between the ages of fourteen and sixteen who passes a satisfactory examination in grade seven of common school work and is actually at work [is exempt from full-time attendance]." See Nova Scotia, *Halifax City Charter, 1914*, 273.

97 As early as the 1870s, children roamed the streets of Halifax begging. See Waite, *Man from Halifax*, 36. For more on the nineteenth- and twentieth-century contexts of child labour and the opposition that it encountered from civic officials and child welfare agents, see John Bullen, "Hidden Workers: Child Labour and the Family Economy in Late Nineteenth-Century Urban Ontario," *Labour/Le Travail* 18 (1986): 163-87; and Neil Sutherland, "'We Always Had Things to Do':

The Paid and Unpaid Work of Anglophone Children between the 1920s and the 1960s," *Labour/Le Travail* 25 (1990): 105-41.

98 *Halifax Herald*, 9 August 1923 and 17 October 1927; and Nova Scotia, *Annual Report of the Director of Child Welfare for the Province of Nova Scotia, 1927* (Halifax: King's Printer, 1928), 87-89.

99 Nova Scotia, *Annual Report of the Director of Child Welfare for the Province of Nova Scotia, 1926* (Halifax: King's Printer, 1927), 73.

100 Tamara Myers, "Embodying Delinquency: Boys' Bodies, Sexuality, and Juvenile Justice in Early Twentieth-Century Quebec," *Journal of the History of Sexuality* 14, 4 (2005): 391.

101 Nova Scotia, *Report of the Board of School Commissioners for the City of Halifax, Nova Scotia, 1919* (Halifax: Weeks Printing Co. Ltd., 1920), 28.

102 *Morning Chronicle*, 13 January 1922. In June 1922, a father told the judge that, on his salary of thirteen dollars a week, he could not feed and clothe his seven children. If he could, he would gladly send his fifteen-year-old son to class, but under the circumstances he had little choice in the matter. Given this, the judge decided not to convict him, but he ensured that this father and every other parent before him received a warning about the perils of truancy. See ibid., 24 June 1922.

103 Nova Scotia, *Halifax City Charter, 1914*, 277.

104 Laws and Privileges Committee, Minute Book, 12 November 1931 and 29 January, 30 March, and 31 May 1932, NSA, RG 35-102, ser. 13 A.4; and Laws and Privileges Committee, Correspondence, 1931-33, NSA, RG 35-102, series 13 B.1.

105 Peter C. Baldwin, "'Nocturnal Habits and Dark Wisdom': The American Response to Children in the Streets at Night, 1880-1930," *Journal of Social History* 35, 3 (2002): 602.

106 *Halifax Herald*, 25 May 1923.

107 *Morning Chronicle*, 28 January 1924.

108 *Halifax Herald*, 10 and 11 September 1924.

109 Ibid., 15 July 1921; and Nova Scotia, *Annual Report of the Superintendent of Neglected and Delinquent Children for the Province of Nova Scotia, 1918*, 23-25.

110 The *Halifax Herald* also supported playgrounds as a "great ... influence for healthy moral development." See Nova Scotia, *Annual Report of the Superintendent of Neglected and Delinquent Children for the Province of Nova Scotia, 1918*, 15; and *Halifax Herald*, 31 July 1923. At the turn of the century, the drive for supervised playgrounds, supported by doctors and social reformers, was an attempt to cultivate the physical and moral child, while keeping her/him away from criminal activity. See Michael J. Smith, "Dampness, Darkness, Dirt, Disease: Physicians and the Promotion of Sanitary Science in Public Schools," in *Profiles of Science and Society in the Maritimes prior to 1914*, ed. Paul A. Bogaard (Fredericton, NB: Acadiensis Press, 1990), 212. Halifax built a few playgrounds following the 1917 explosion, and at least one commentator claimed that this helped to control delinquency. See Prince, *Catastrophe and Social Change*, 138; and Kitz, *Shattered City*, 141.

111 *Halifax Herald*, 18 August 1922.

112 See, for example, Myers, *Caught;* and Jean Trepanier, "Juvenile Delinquency and Youth Protection: The Historical Foundations of the Canadian Juvenile Delinquents Act of 1908," *European Journal of Crime, Criminal Law, and Criminal*

Justice 7, 1 (1999): 41-62. Susan E. Houston demonstrates how legal authorities and the social elite in mid-nineteenth-century Upper Canada viewed petty crimes committed by juveniles as "omens" of societal disorder. See Houston, "Role of the Criminal Law," 44-45.

113 *Halifax Chronicle*, 21 December 1927; and Cynthia Comacchio, "Dancing to Perdition: Adolescence and Leisure in Interwar English Canada," *Journal of Canadian Studies* 32, 3 (1997): 5-35.

114 *Halifax Chronicle*, 27 September 1934.

115 John C. Schneider, *Detroit and the Problem of Order, 1830-1880: A Geography of Crime, Riot, and Policing* (Lincoln: University of Nebraska Press, 1980), 83-84.

116 For more on the paternalistic nature of juvenile and family courts, see Chunn, *From Punishment to Doing Good*; Donzelot, *Policing of Families*; Myers, *Caught*; and Joan Sangster, *Girl Trouble: Female Delinquency in Canada* (Toronto: Between the Lines, 2002).

CHAPTER 5: WOMEN, CRIME, AND THE LAW

1 *Halifax Mail*, 29 September 1932. Although in a few newspaper reports Ms. Thibeault's first name appears as "Mary," the more frequently cited "Marie" is used here.

2 Douglas "Red" MacDonald was charged with the murder of Marie Thibeault, but after a two-day trial in March 1934, the jury found him not guilty. MacDonald's defence lawyer, Lionel Ryan, managed to undermine the credibility of some of the Crown's key witnesses. Ryan, a bi-racial West Indian lawyer, also participated in the deportation case of the Doukhobor leader Peter Verigin. See Halifax County Supreme Court, 1934, NSA, RG 39, ser. C, vol. 722, no. 1026; and *Halifax Herald*, 28 March 1934.

3 *Halifax Mail*, 30 September 1932.

4 Carolyn Strange, *Toronto's Girl Problem: The Perils and Pleasures of the City, 1880-1930* (Toronto: University of Toronto Press, 1995), 5 and 11.

5 *Halifax Mail*, 30 September 1932.

6 *Halifax Herald*, 27 December 1922.

7 During this same period, a total of 4,916 men were committed to the Halifax City Prison and 4,874 to the Halifax County Jail, representing 93.8 percent and 95.2 percent, respectively, of the total commitments. See Nova Scotia, *Penal Institutions: Thirtieth to Thirty-Sixth Annual Reports, 1929-1936* (Halifax: King's Printer, 1931-37).

8 Phillips, "Women, Crime, and Criminal Justice," 174-206; Phillips and May, "Female Criminality"; Jane B. Price, "'Raised in Rockhead. Died in the Poor-house': Female Petty Criminals in Halifax, 1864-1890," in Girard and Phillips, *Essays in the History of Canadian Law*, 3:200-31; and Fingard, *Dark Side*, esp. chap. 1.

9 Phillips, "Women, Crime, and Criminal Justice," 174.

10 Pat Carlen describes this response as "individualistic remedies to the social inequities stemming from class exploitation, sexism, and racism." See Pat Carlen, *Women, Crime, and Poverty* (Philadelphia: Open University Press, 1988), 17.

11 Morton, *Ideal Surroundings*, 37.

12 Ibid., 37-38.

13 For more on the attainment of respectability for blacks in Halifax, see Judith Fingard, "Race and Respectability in Victorian Halifax," *Journal of Imperial and Commonwealth History* 20, 2 (1992): 169-95.

14 For more on this theme, see Dubinsky, *Improper Advances*; Amanda Glasbeek, *Feminized Justice*; and Ann-Louise Shapiro, *Breaking the Codes: Female Criminality in Fin-de-Siècle Paris* (Stanford: Stanford University Press, 1996). Meda Chesney-Lind argues that the criminal justice system played a part in the enforcement of traditional "sex-role expectations" – epitomized by marriage, economic dependency, and respectability – by ensuring that women did not commit "unfeminine" offences. Once they did, however, the courts felt justified in punishing them accordingly. See Meda Chesney-Lind, "Women and Crime: The Female Offender," *Signs* 12, 1 (1986): 92.

15 In 1921, Halifax contained 30,015 women to 28,357 men; for 1931, the figures increased slightly to 30,669 and 28,606, respectively. See Canada, *Seventh Census of Canada, 1931*, 2:157.

16 For examples of families being separated because of male relations leaving home to find work, see Morton, *Ideal Surroundings*, 63-64, 68-69, and 92-93.

17 Ibid., 131-35.

18 Ibid.; and D.A. Muise, "The Industrial Context of Inequality: Female Participation in Nova Scotia's Paid Labour Force, 1871-1921," *Acadiensis* 20, 2 (1991): 13-16 and 23. Some women also managed to enter such traditionally male-dominated professions as the law. The first woman lawyer in Nova Scotia was Frances Fish, who was called to the bar in September 1918. For more on the history of female lawyers in Nova Scotia, see Barry Cahill, "Legislated Privilege or Common-Law Right? Provincial State Intervention and the First Women Lawyers in Nova Scotia," in *Making Up the State: Women in 20th-Century Atlantic Canada*, ed. Janet Guildford and Suzanne Morton, 79-92 (Fredericton, NB: Acadiensis Press, 2010).

19 Carolyn Strange explores a similar trend in Strange, *Toronto's Girl Problem*.

20 Welfare Council of Halifax and Dartmouth, *Report on Unemployed Women, 1933*, NSA, MG 20, vol. 416(A), no. 1. In 1933, the *Halifax Herald* reported that nearly nine hundred young women and "girls" were unemployed in the city, some of whom did not have a place to live. See *Halifax Herald*, 22 November 1933.

21 *Halifax Chronicle*, 22 November 1929.

22 Muise, "Industrial Context of Inequality," 16; Suzanne Morton, "Women on Their Own: Single Mothers in Working-Class Halifax in the 1920s," *Acadiensis* 21, 2 (1992): 90-107; and Morton, *Ideal Surroundings*, 79.

23 *Halifax Herald*, 6 April 1920 and 6, and 10 March 1933; and *Halifax Chronicle*, 15 September 1929. This offence was covered under section 150 of the Criminal Code: "Retail sale of liquor prohibited." The maximum penalty, under summary conviction, was a fine of $200 and court costs or, in default of payment, three months imprisonment. See *Crankshaw's Criminal Code of Canada*, 156-57.

24 *Halifax Herald*, 26 January 1929 and 27 June 1933.

25 By 1930, Eaton's had forty-seven stores and a nationwide catalogue network in place. It had also secured a 7 percent share of the country's retail sales. See Cynthia Wright, "'Feminine Trifles of Vast Importance': Writing Gender into the History of Consumption," in *Constructing Modern Canada: Readings in Post-Confederation History*, ed. Chad Gaffield (Toronto: Copp Clark Longman Ltd.,

1994), 289-98. For more on the rise of retail stores and consumer culture in twentieth-century Canada, see Donica Belisle, *Retail Nation: Department Stores and the Making of Modern Canada* (Vancouver: UBC Press, 2011).

26 Elaine S. Abelson, *When Ladies Go A-Thieving: Middle-Class Shoplifters in the Victorian Department Store* (New York: Oxford University Press, 1989), 4-5, 31, 151, and 164-65; and Glasbeek, *Feminized Justice*, 108.

27 *Police Women Occurrence Report,* 11 and 12 September 1931, NSA.

28 Halifax Magistrate's Court, miscellaneous minutes and evidence, 1930s, NSA, RG 42, ser. E, vol. 1; and Abelson, *When Ladies Go A-Thieving*, 66. Amanda Glasbeek notes that, in early-twentieth-century Toronto, most women who were arrested for theft were given short-term jail sentences rather than fines. Moreover, women who stole from their employers rarely received lenient treatment from the Toronto Women's Court. See Glasbeek, *Feminized Justice*, 108-16.

29 Sangster, "Pardon Tales," 165-67.

30 Price, "Raised in Rockhead," 204.

31 *Morning Chronicle*, 20 November 1923.

32 *Crankshaw's Criminal Code of Canada*, 270.

33 *Morning Chronicle*, 26 December 1924.

34 Grove wept as she made her way out of the courtroom. See ibid., 3 July 1925.

35 *Morning Chronicle,* 15 April 1926. Amanda Glasbeek shows that vagrancy was a "highly gendered crime." While women in Toronto accounted for few of the total arrests (on average 105 annually from 1913 to 1934), they represented almost 25 percent of all arrests for vagrancy in the same period. See Glasbeek, *Feminized Justice*, 96-97. Mary Anne Poutanen discovered similar themes about the treatment of female vagrants in early nineteenth-century Montreal. See Mary Anne Poutanen, "The Homeless, the Whore, the Drunkard, and the Disorderly: Contours of Female Vagrancy in the Montreal Courts, 1810-1842," in *Gendered Pasts: Historical Essays in Femininity and Masculinity in Canada*, ed. Kathryn McPherson, Cecilia Morgan, and Nancy M. Forestell, 29-47 (Toronto: Oxford University Press, 1999).

36 *Police Women Occurrence Report,* 19 November 1931, NSA.

37 *Morning Chronicle*, 3 August and 3 September 1926.

38 Morton, "Separate Spheres," 61, 67-69, and 83.

39 Ibid., 75; and *Morning Chronicle*, 28 October 1918. This attention to detail was typical of the press coverage of black women in Halifax and Toronto. See Glasbeek, *Feminized Justice*, 76.

40 A sampling of the historical literature that discusses the economic motivations behind prostitution includes Andree Levesque, *Making and Breaking the Rules: Women in Quebec, 1919-1939* (Toronto: McClelland and Stewart, 1994), especially chap. 3; Judy Bedford, "Prostitution in Calgary, 1905-1914," *Alberta History* 29, 2 (1981): 1-11; Judith R. Walkowitz, *Prostitution and Victorian Society: Women, Class, and the State* (Cambridge: Cambridge University Press, 1980); and Barbara Meil Hobson, *Uneasy Virtue: The Politics of Prostitution and the American Reform Tradition* (New York: Basic Books, 1987). For an assessment of the reasons that contemporary women choose to become sex workers, see Leslie Ann Jeffrey and Gayle MacDonald, *Talk Back: Sex Workers in the Maritimes* (Vancouver: UBC Press, 2006).

41 A breakdown of these offences is as follows: thirty-nine for "prostitution"; fifty for being an "inmate of a bawdy house"; ten for being a "keeper of a bawdy

house"; thirty-one for being an "inmate of a disorderly house"; nineteen for being a "keeper of a disorderly house"; seven for being a "night walker"; one for the "procuring of women for prostitution"; and two for attempting to "allure [a] girl." The total number of offences for the 1917 to 1922 period was 12,062. See Appendix 2, Tables A2.12 and A2.13. These offences fell under sections 216, 225, 228, and 238 of the 1924 Criminal Code. See *Crankshaw's Criminal Code of Canada*, 224-25, 235, and 271.

42 Philippa Levine, "Rough Usage: Prostitution, Law, and the Social Historian," in *Rethinking Social History: English Society, 1570-1920, and Its interpretation*, ed. Adrian Wilson (Manchester: Manchester University Press, 1993), 279 and 285; and Philippa Levine, "Women and Prostitution: Myth, Reality, History," *Canadian Journal of History* 28 (1993): 494.

43 Walkowitz, *Prostitution and Victorian Society*, 24-25; and Levine, "Women and Prostitution," 492.

44 George Nicol Gordon, *Halifax: "Its Sins and Sorrows"* (Halifax: Conference Job Printing Office, 1862), 3 and 22-26. Gordon, who came to Halifax as a theological student, was instrumental in establishing the Halifax City Mission in 1852 and became Halifax's first city missionary. See Fingard, *Dark Side*, 119; and George N. Gordon, *The Lost Martyrs of Eromanga: Being a Memoir of the Rev. George N. Gordon and Ellen Catherine Powell, His Wife* (Halifax: MacNab and Scaffer, 1863), 28-37.

45 A glimpse of this trend is contained in Carrigan, *Crime and Punishment*, 265.

46 *Halifax Herald*, 18 December 1907. For more on the social gospel in Nova Scotia, see Michael Boudreau, "Strikes, Rural Decay, and Socialism: The Presbyterian Church in Nova Scotia Grapples with Social Realities, 1880-1914," in *The Contribution of Presbyterianism to the Maritime Provinces of Canada*, ed. Charles H.H. Scobie and G.A. Rawlyk, 144-59 (Montreal and Kingston: McGill-Queen's University Press, 1997); Michael Boudreau, "'There Is ... No Pernicious Dualism between Sacred and Secular': Nova Scotia Baptists and the Social Gospel, 1880-1914," *Nova Scotia Historical Review* 16, 1 (1996): 109-31; and Nancy Christie and Michael Gauvreau, *A Full-Orbed Christianity: The Protestant Churches and Social Welfare in Canada, 1900-1940* (Montreal and Kingston: McGill-Queen's University Press, 1996).

47 *Halifax Herald*, 19 December 1907.

48 *Evening Mail*, 17 October 1912 (emphasis in original).

49 *Halifax Herald*, 19 October 1912.

50 Ibid., 8 and 9 November 1912.

51 Ibid., 1 February 1918.

52 Ibid., 13 March 1918 (emphasis in original).

53 Ibid., 13 January 1908 (emphasis in original). In the late nineteenth and early twentieth centuries, the Halifax Local Council of Women expressed its concern that young working women, by engaging in the public life of the street, placed themselves in sexual danger. The council argued in 1896 that "protection should be extended to *all* women in dependent positions, such as shop girls, domestic servants ... and not limited as in the present to women in factories, mills and workshops." See Myers, "Not to Be Ranked as Women,'" 180 (emphasis in original).

54 Ernest A. Bell, *War on the White Slave Trade* (Toronto: Coles, 1980), 345. Originally published in 1911. For more on the white slavery panic in Canada and the United States, see Mariana Valverde, *The Age of Light, Soap, and Water: Moral Reform in English Canada, 1885-1925* (Toronto: McClelland and Stewart, 1991), chap. 4; and Marlene D. Beckman, "The White Slave Traffic Act: The Historical Impact of a Criminal Law Policy on Women," *Georgetown Law Journal* 72 (1984): 1111-42.

55 *Halifax Herald*, 7 January 1918.

56 Valverde, *Age of Light*, 89-99.

57 Fingard, *Dark Side*, 136.

58 *Presbyterian Witness*, 20 November 1869.

59 Emily F. Murphy, *The Black Candle* (Toronto: Coles, 1973), 306-7 (originally published by Thomas Allen in 1922).

60 Janice Newton, *The Feminist Challenge to the Canadian Left, 1900-1918* (Montreal and Kingston: McGill-Queen's University Press, 1995), chaps. 5 and 6.

61 *Citizen*, 1 April 1927 (emphasis in original).

62 John McLaren documents similar strategies adopted by police forces across the country to cope with prostitution. See John Mclaren, "Chasing the Social Evil: Moral Fervour and the Evolution of Canada's Prostitution Laws, 1867-1917," *Canadian Journal of Law and Society* 1 (1986): 125-65. John McLaren and John Lowman argued that, since 1920, the primary discourse in characterizing and dealing with prostitution as a social problem has been "public order." See John McLaren and John Lowman, "Enforcing Canada's Prostitution Laws, 1892-1920: Rhetoric and Practice," in *Securing Compliance: Seven Case Studies,* ed. M.L. Friedland (Toronto: University of Toronto Press, 1990), 66.

63 *Crankshaw's Criminal Code of Canada*, 235.

64 Myers, "Women Policing Women," 229-45; and *Crankshaw's Criminal Code of Canada*, 270-71.

65 Halifax Magistrate's Court, Miscellaneous Minutes and Evidence, 1930s, NSA, RG 42, ser. E, vol. 1.

66 Ibid.

67 Halifax County Court, 1934, NSA, RG 38, ser. C, vol. 30, no. 3871; and Halifax Magistrate's Court, 1934, NSA, RG 42, ser. C, vol. 20, no. 142.

68 Halifax Magistrate's Court, 1925, NSA, RG 42, ser. C, vol. 10, no. 459.

69 *Morning Chronicle*, 17 January 1920.

70 As E. Nick Larsen argues, courts across Canada have been reluctant to convict men (when they were even charged) for procuring the services of a prostitute and/or frequenting a bawdy house. See E. Nick Larsen, "Canadian Prostitution Control between 1914 and 1970: An Exercise in Chauvinist Reasoning," *Canadian Journal of Law and Society* 7, 2 (1992): 147-48.

71 *Morning Chronicle*, 17 June 1924. According to the *Chronicle*, this was the first charge of its kind laid against the owner of a building. The Temperance Hotel was on Duke Street in downtown Halifax. See McAlpine, *McAlpine's Halifax City Directory, 1924* (Halifax: Royal Print and Litho Ltd., 1924), 465.

72 *R. v. Mamie Barrett*, Halifax County Court, 1918-20, NSA, RG 39, ser. C, vol. 703, no. 40. No further reference to this case could be found in either the Halifax County Criminal Proceedings Book, 1917-32, NSA, acc. no. 1998-019/148, or

the Halifax County Criminal Evidence Book, 1917-20, NSA, acc. no. 1998-019/141.

73 *Halifax Herald*, 20 March 1918.

74 For more on the motives and lifestyles of other prostitutes in Canada, see Lori Rotenberg, "The Wayward Worker: Toronto's Prostitute at the Turn of the Century," in *Women at Work: Ontario, 1850-1930*, ed. Janice Acton, Penny Goldsmith, and Bonnie Shepard, 33-69 (Toronto: Women's Press, 1974); Patrick A. Dunae, "Geographies of Sexual Commerce and the Production of Prostitutional Space: Victoria, British Columbia, 1860-1914, *Journal of the Canadian Historical Association* 19, 1 (2008): 115-42; and Deborah Nilsen, "The 'Social Evil': Prostitution in Vancouver, 1900-1920," in *In Her Own Right: Selected Essays on Women's History in BC*, ed. Barbara Latham and Cathy Kess, 205-28 (Victoria: Camosun College, 1980). Nilsen notes that the possibility of fines and/or imprisonment "did not deter prostitution let alone eliminate it" – an assessment that generally holds true for early twentieth-century Halifax.

75 John D'Emilio and Estelle B. Freedman, *Intimate Matters: A History of Sexuality in America* (New York: Harper and Row, 1988), 233-35 and 253-54; and Carroll Smith-Rosenberg, *Disorderly Conduct: Visions of Gender in Victorian America* (New York: Alfred A. Knopf, 1985), 217-18.

76 Constance Backhouse, "Prosecution of Abortions under Canadian Law, 1900-1950," in Phillips et al. *Essays in the History of Canadian Law*, 5:252-53.

77 For a detailed account of the use of death-bed confessions to charge abortionists in British Columbia and Chicago, see Susanne Klausen, "Doctors and Dying Declarations: The Role of the State in Abortion Regulation in British Columbia, 1917-37," *Canadian Bulletin of Medical History* 13 (1996): 53-81; and Leslie J. Reagan, "'About to Meet Her Maker': Women, Doctors, Dying Declarations, and the State's Investigation of Abortion, Chicago, 1867-1940," *Journal of American History* 77, 4 (1991): 1240-64.

78 Reagan, "About to Meet Her Maker," 1263; and Dubinsky, *Improper Advances*, 94-95.

79 Annie Hadley was twenty-six years of age, white, and a "Total Abstainer." George Hadley was "colored," age thirty-one, a miner, and a "Total Abstainer." See *R. v. Annie Hadley and George Hadley* (14 February and 18 and 25 March 1925), Minute Book, Nova Scotia County Court, Cape Breton, 1924-28, NSA, acc. no. 1991-067/36.

80 *R. v. Amelia Murray*, Halifax County Supreme Court, 1925-26 and 1932-33, NSA, RG 39, series C, vols. 708 and 717, nos. 315 and 917; Canada, *Forty-Ninth Annual Report of Criminal Statistics, 1925* (Ottawa: King's Printer, 1926), 6; Canada, *Fifty-Second Annual Report of Statistics of Criminal and Other Offences, 1927* (Ottawa: King's Printer, 1929), 6-7; and Canada, *Fifty-Ninth Annual Report of Statistics of Criminal and Other Offences, 1934* (Ottawa: King's Printer, 1936), 14-15.

81 This figure of 104 does not include the years 1926 and 1927, for which data are unavailable. For 1918 to 1920, deaths caused by abortion were not listed in Nova Scotia's vital statistics; instead, the category "Accidents of Pregnancy" appeared, of which there were thirty for these years. For the entire 1918 to 1935 period, the number of deaths in Nova Scotia due to "Accidents of Pregnancy" totalled eighty-five. Abortions no doubt accounted for some of these deaths, but it is

impossible to determine the exact number from this listing. See Nova Scotia, *Vital Statistics: Journals and Proceedings of the House of Assembly of the Province of Nova Scotia, 1919-1937* (Halifax: King's Printer, 1920-37).

82 Angus McLaren and Arlene Tigar McLaren, *The Bedroom and the State: The Changing Practices and Politics of Contraception and Abortion in Canada, 1880-1980* (Toronto: McClelland and Stewart, 1986), 51; and Angus McLaren and Arlene Tigar McLaren, "Discoveries and Dissimulations: The Impact of Abortion Deaths on Maternal Mortality in British Columbia," *BC Studies* 64 (1984-85): 3-26. Given the degree of inaccuracy involved with the compilation of vital statistics and the various categories of abortion-related deaths, such estimates should be approached cautiously. George Emery takes the McLarens to task on this point. See George Emery, "British Columbia's Criminal Abortion History, 1922-1949: A Critique of the Evidence and Methods in the Work of Angus and Arlene Tigar McLaren," *BC Studies* 82 (1989): 39-60. The McLarens respond in "'The Forest and the Trees': A Response to George Emery," *BC Studies* 82 (1989): 61-64.

83 Backhouse, "Prosecution of Abortions," 254-55; McLaren and McLaren, *Bedroom and the State*, 13 and 34-39; and Angus McLaren, "Illegal Operations: Women, Doctors, and Abortion, 1886-1939," *Journal of Social History* 26, 24 (1993): 801-8. For more on one community's response to the need for birth control, see Dianne Dodd, "Women's Involvement in the Canadian Birth Control Movement of the 1930s: The Hamilton Birth Control Clinic," in *Delivering Motherhood: Maternal Ideologies and Practices in the 19th and 20th Centuries*, ed. Katherine Arnup, Andree Levesque, and Ruth Roach Pierson, 150-72 (London: Routledge, 1990). For a counter-point to Dodd's article, see Catherine Annau, "Eager Eugenicists: A Reappraisal of the Birth Control Society of Hamilton," *Histoire sociale/Social History* 27, 53 (1994): 111-33. Andrea Tone discusses the public accessibility and commercialization of contraceptives in the United States during the 1930s. See Andrea Tone, "Contraceptive Consumers: Gender and the Political Economy of Birth Control in the 1930s," *Journal of Social History* 29, 3 (1996): 485-506.

84 *News and Sentinel*, 25 June 1926.

85 *Halifax Herald*, 24 June 1926. Doctors could legally perform an abortion if they felt it necessary to save the life of the mother. Abortionists and midwives, in the eyes of some physicians, undermined their ability to make such decisions and their profession in general. Women like Amelia Murray also provided stiff competition for doctors, which they wanted eliminated. See McLaren, "Illegal Operations," 798 and 805.

86 Wendy Mitchinson, *The Nature of Their Bodies: Women and Their Doctors in Victorian Canada* (Toronto: University of Toronto Press, 1991), 360; Wendy Mitchinson, *Giving Birth in Canada, 1900-1950* (Toronto: University of Toronto Press, 2002), 274-75; Colin D. Howell, "Reform and the Monopolistic Impulse: The Professionalization of Medicine in the Maritimes," *Acadiensis* 11, 1 (1981): 21-22; and Colin D. Howell, "Medical Professionalization and the Social Transformation of the Maritimes, 1850-1950," *Journal of Canadian Studies* 27, 1 (1992): 5-20.

87 O.A. Cannon, "Septic Abortion," *Canadian Medical Association Journal* 12 (1922): 164.

88 Ibid., 166.

89 *Halifax Herald* and *Evening Mail*, 24 June 1926. One year prior to the death of Flossie Joyce, Ruby Houghton of 33 Birmingham Street died in the Victoria General Hospital on 12 July 1925. The medical examiner wrote that her death "was the result of general peritonitis and the contributing causes, infection and forcible dilatation of the cervix uteri" – symptoms that usually occurred after a botched attempt to abort a foetus. An investigation into Houghton's death found insufficient evidence to lay charges. See Medical Examiner's Reports, Halifax County, 1925, NSA, RG 41, ser. D, vol. 84. This case may have placed the city's law enforcement officials and the medical examiner on alert for any more abortion-related deaths and drawn their attention to Amelia Murray. As well, on 25 November 1926, a few months after Joyce's death, Gladys Leahy of Halifax County died from a "criminal abortion." Although little mention was made of this in the local media, in some circles it probably fuelled suspicions of the growing menace of abortionists in Halifax. See Medical Examiner's Reports, Halifax County, 1926, NSA.

90 *Evening Mail*, 24 June 1926. In the early nineteenth century in the United States, abortionists – like Ann Lehman, alias Madame Restell, of New York – were portrayed as servants of evil women. However, as the nineteenth century progressed, in the minds of many observers, abortionists went from abetting immoral behaviour to harming "misguided women." See A. Cheree Carlson, *The Crimes of Womanhood: Defining Femininity in a Court of Law* (Urbana and Chicago: University of Illinois Press, 2009), 111-35.

91 *Halifax Herald*, 24 and 25 June 1926; and *Amherst Daily News*, 25 June 1926. For more on the demand of most doctors in North America to see abortionists prosecuted in order to protect their reputations and the prestige of their profession, see Angus McLaren, *A Prescription for Murder: The Victorian Serial Killings of Dr. Thomas Neill Cream* (Chicago and London: University of Chicago Press, 1993), 78-79; Mitchinson, *Nature of Their Bodies*, 133-35; and Tracey Penny, "'Getting Rid of My Trouble': A Social History of Abortion in Ontario, 1880-1929" (MA thesis, Laurentian University, 1995).

92 Section 303 reads: "Every one is guilty of an indictable offence and liable to imprisonment for life who, with intent to procure the miscarriage of any woman, whether she is or is not with child, unlawfully administers to her or causes to be taken by her any drug or other noxious thing, or unlawfully uses on her any instrument or any means whatsoever with the like intent." See *Crankshaw's Criminal Code of Canada*, 362; and *R. v. Amelia Murray,* Halifax County Supreme Court, 1925-26, NSA, RG 39, ser. C, vol. 708, no. 315.

93 *Oxford Journal*, 17 June 1926; and *Amherst Daily News*, 25 June 1926.

94 A "practical nurse," or "licensed practical nurse," was someone who possessed a licence to perform basic nursing tasks under the direction of a doctor or a registered nurse. See *The Canadian Oxford Dictionary* (Don Mills: Oxford University Press, 1998). This type of nursing was formalized in the second half of the twentieth century. My sincere thanks to Dr. Linda Kealey for her insights into this subject.

95 *Halifax Herald*, 25 June 1926; and Kingston Penitentiary, Convict Register and Description Book, Correctional Service of Canada Museum. Backhouse claims that female abortionists in Canada received an average fee of thirty-five dollars. See Backhouse, "Prosecution of Abortions," 266 and 269.

96 *R. v. Amelia Murray,* Halifax County Supreme Court, 1925-26, NSA, RG 39, ser. C, vol. 708, no. 315; *Halifax Chronicle*, 28 July 1926; and *Halifax Herald*, 21 October 1926.

97 All that is contained in the Supreme Court file is the information laid before the magistrate and an appeal Murray made to the Supreme Court for bail. See Halifax County Supreme Court, 1925-26, NSA, RG 39, ser. C, vol. 708, no. 315. Additional personal information on Murray may be found in LAC, RG 73, acc. 1985-86/163, vols. 17 and 22, files 554 and 3250. One newspaper condemned this practice of "snuffing" the press out of the case. See *Halifax Herald*, 24 March 1927.

98 Ibid.; and *Morning Chronicle*, 1 July 1926.

99 The original sentence was for five years, which included time already served. Murray was initially sent to Kingston Penitentiary, but within a few days she was transferred to Dorchester. She was granted parole on 24 December 1928. See Kingston Penitentiary, Convict Register and Description Book, Correctional Service of Canada Museum; Halifax County Supreme Court, 1925-26, NSA, RG 39, ser. C, vol. 708, no. 315; and *Halifax Herald*, 7 April 1927.

100 *R. v. Amelia Murray*, Halifax County Supreme Court, 1932-33, NSA, RG 39, ser. C, vol. 717, no. 917.

101 *Halifax Herald*, 2 September 1932.

102 Ibid., 22 October 1932, 29 March, 17 October, and 13 November 1933; and Dorchester Penitentiary, Convicts' Register, 1905-1936, NSA and Kingston Penitentiary, Convict Register and Description Book, the Correctional Service of Canada Museum.

103 McLaren, "Illegal Operations," 810.

104 Carlson, *Crimes of Womanhood*, 112.

105 For the 1918 to 1935 period, only one actual "Infanticide" death was registered for Nova Scotia, this occurring in 1924. The "Accidents of Pregnancy" category, noted above in the discussion of abortion, may have included some of the province's, and the city's, infanticide deaths. See Nova Scotia, *Vital Statistics: Journals and Proceedings of the House of Assembly of the Province of Nova Scotia, 1926* (Halifax: King's Printer, 1926), 79.

106 Section 272 of the 1924 Criminal Code states: "Every one is guilty of an indictable offence and liable to two years imprisonment, who disposes of the dead body of any child in any manner, with intent to conceal the fact that its mother was delivered of it, whether the child died before, or during, or after birth." See *Crankshaw's Criminal Code of Canada*, 330-31. See also Constance Backhouse, "Involuntary Motherhood: Abortion, Birth Control and the Law in Nineteenth Century Canada," *Windsor Yearbook of Access to Justice* 3 (1983): 79-81; and Constance Backhouse, *Petticoats and Prejudice: Women and Law in Nineteenth-Century Canada* (Canada: The Osgoode Society, 1991), chap. 4. In eighteenth-century Canada, penalties for infanticide were harsh, ranging from branding and banishment to flogging and death. See Andre Lachance, "Women and Crime in Canada in the Early Eighteenth Century, 1712-1759," in Macleod, *Lawful Authority*, 12-13.

107 When a guilty verdict was rendered, it was usually accompanied by a strong recommendation for mercy. In 1948, Parliament made infanticide a non-capital offence, thereby eliminating the death penalty for this crime. The new penalty for

infanticide, an indictable offence, was three years of imprisonment. See An Act to Amend the Criminal Code, S.C. 1948, c. 39; Carolyn Strange, "Mercy for Murderers? A Historical Perspective on the Royal Prerogative of Mercy," *Saskatchewan Law Review* 64, 2 (2001): 562-67.

108 Mary Ellen Wright, "Unnatural Mothers: Infanticide in Halifax, 1850-1875," *Nova Scotia Historical Review* 7, 2 (1987): 23 and 27. For more on the incidence of infanticide and its treatment by the law and society, see Kirsten Johnson Kramar, *Unwilling Mothers, Unwanted Babies: Infanticide in Canada* (Vancouver: UBC Press, 2005). A lenient approach towards women who had committed infanticide was also practised by many courts in the United States. See Adler, *First in Violence,* chap. 6.

109 *Morning Chronicle*, 19, 20, and 21 August 1924. In a similar case from 1917, a young domestic charged with infanticide also felt intimidated by the police and the prospect of facing the criminal justice system. When the police took her into custody, she asked, "Will they hang me?" See *Halifax Herald*, 26 June 1917.

110 Halifax County Supreme Court, 1924-25, NSA, RG 39, ser. C, vol. 707, no. 222.

111 Halifax Magistrate's Court, Miscellaneous Minutes and Evidence, NSA, RG 42, ser. E, vol. 2.

112 *Halifax Herald*, 17 January 1925; and *Halifax Chronicle*, 20 June 1929. This practice of leaving infant's bodies in public places also occurred throughout much of the nineteenth century in Halifax. See Wright, "Unnatural Mothers," 17-18.

113 *Halifax Chronicle*, 28 and 30 July 1928.

114 Ibid., 30 July 1928.

115 Halifax County Supreme Court, 1927-28, NSA, RG 39, ser. C, vol. 710, no. 454. In a similar context, Karen Dubinsky shows that, under some circumstances, courts dealt leniently with women who murdered in defence of their "honour." See Dubinsky, *Improper Advances*, 19. For a case in Ontario with similar themes, see Karen Dubinsky and Franca Iacovetta, "Murder, Womanly Virtue, and Motherhood: The Case of Angelina Napolitano, 1911-1922," *Canadian Historical Review* 72, 4 (1991): 505-31.

116 *Halifax Herald*, 24 November 1930; and Halifax County Supreme Court, 1929-31, NSA, RG 39, ser. C, vol. 712, no. 652.

117 Ibid.

118 *Halifax Herald*, 28 March 1931. Carolyn Strange discusses this transformation from killers to sympathetic victims that women like Gormley underwent in the courtroom. See Strange, *Toronto's Girl Problem*, 77-78.

119 *Halifax Herald*, 30 October 1920.

120 *Morning Chronicle*, 31 July and 10 October 1922.

121 Dubinsky, *Improper Advances*, 101. For more on the idea of the "stranger" (who in some cases was "dark" or allegedly a member of an ethnic minority) preying upon women, see Lesley Erickson, "Murdered Women and Mythic Villains: The Criminal Case and the Imaginary Criminal in the Canadian West, 1886-1930," in *People and Place: Historical Influences on Legal Culture*, ed. Jonathan Swainger and Constance Backhouse, 95-119 (Vancouver: UBC Press, 2003); and Lesley Erickson, *Westward Bound: Sex, Violence, the Law, and the Making of a Settler Society* (Vancouver: UBC Press and the Osgoode Society for Canadian Legal History, 2011).

122 *Halifax Herald*, 27 and 28 February 1931.

123 In the context of nineteenth-century Philadelphia, women often launched private prosecutions against their abusive husbands in the hopes of scaring them. Because of their economic dependency, however, most wives did not want their husbands thrown in jail. See Allen Steinburg, *The Transformation of Criminal Justice: Philadelphia, 1800-1880* (Chapel Hill: University of North Carolina Press, 1989), 47 and 69.

124 Terry L. Chapman, "'Til Death Do Us Part': Wife Beating in Alberta, 1905-1920," *Alberta History* 36, 4 (1986): 13-22; and Kathryn Harvey, "Amazons and Victims: Resisting Wife Abuse in Working-Class Montreal, 1869-1879," *Journal of the Canadian Historical Association* 2, 1 (1991): 131-48. Women were also vulnerable to abuse in eighteenth-century Nova Scotia. See Judith A. Norton, "The Dark Side of Planter Life: Reported Cases of Domestic Violence," in *Intimate Relations: Family and Community in Planter Nova Scotia, 1759-1800*, ed. Margaret Conrad, 182-89 (Fredericton, NB: Acadiensis Press, 1995).

125 Harvey, "Amazons and Victims," 143. Charges for wife abuse usually fell under section 292(c) of the Criminal Code, which states: "Every one is guilty of an indictable offence and liable to two years imprisonment, and to be whipped, who ... assaults and beats his wife or any other female and thereby occasions her actual bodily harm." See *Crankshaw's Criminal Code of Canada*, 347.

126 *Evening Mail*, 8 November 1922.

127 Even though Nova Scotia had comparatively liberal divorce laws, few divorces occurred in the province during the eighteenth and nineteenth centuries. According to Kimberley Maynard, this was due primarily to societal attitudes, which frowned upon marital break-ups. See Kimberley Smith Maynard, "Divorce in Nova Scotia, 1750-1890," in Girard and Phillips, *Essays in the History of Canadian Law*, 3:232-72; and Judith Fingard, "The Prevention of Cruelty, Marriage Breakdown and the Rights of Wives in Nova Scotia, 1880-1900," *Acadiensis* 22, 2 (1993): 85-88 and 96-100.

128 As James G. Snell notes, R.H. Graham, who in 1925 was appointed judge in equity and ex officio judge of the Court for Divorce and Matrimonial Causes, "placed a greater value on the maintenance of general marital order and stability than on the prevention of individual spousal suffering." See James G. Snell, "Marital Cruelty: Women and the Nova Scotia Divorce Court, 1900-1939," *Acadiensis* 18, 1 (1988): 4-5, 19, and 25-26.

129 Ibid., 27. When granting divorces, courts often gave precedence to adultery rather than to spousal abuse. For more on the general context of divorce law in Canada, see James G. Snell, *In the Shadow of the Law: Divorce in Canada, 1900-1939* (Toronto: University of Toronto Press, 1991).

130 Chapman, "'Til Death Do Us Part," 18-20; and Snell, "Marital Cruelty," 32. In their efforts to create moral order, several secular and religious social reform organizations in Victorian and Edwardian society placed much of their hope on the family. To them, the family "was assumed to be the core of social organization, the cornerstone of civilization, and the foundation of national life." See Neil Semple, *The Lord's Dominion: The History of Canadian Methodism* (Montreal and Kingston: McGill-Queen's University Press, 1996), 340-41.

131 *Halifax Chronicle*, 15 September 1928.

132 *Halifax Herald*, 15 June 1928.

133 Annalee E. Golz, "'If a Man's Wife Does Not Obey Him, What Can He Do?': Marital Breakdown and Wife Abuse in Late Nineteenth-Century and Early Twentieth-Century Ontario," in Knafla and Binnie, *Law, Society, and the State*, 343. Judith Fingard makes this point for late nineteenth-century Nova Scotia. As this evidence suggests, little had changed with the dawn of a new century. See Fingard, "Prevention of Cruelty," 100.

134 Morton, *Ideal Surroundings*, 101-5; and Nova Scotia, *Annual Report of the Superintendent of Neglected and Delinquent Children for the Province of Nova Scotia, 1920*, 82. One woman, who was deserted by her husband after his war-time service had ended, and who had no resources and a six-month-old baby to support, turned to the Nova Scotia Returned Soldier Commission for aid. The commission did all that it could to locate her husband, even to the point of contacting the Philadelphia Police Department after receiving word that he was in that city, but to no avail. As a result, the commission paid her passage home to Manchester, England. See Nova Scotia, *Report of the Returned Soldier Commission*, 14.

135 Nova Scotia passed An Act to Provide for the Maintenance of Deserted Wives and Children in 1941. See S.N.S., 1941, c. 8, Wives' and Children's Maintenance Act; and Nova Scotia, *Annual Report of the Superintendent of Neglected and Delinquent Children of the Province of Nova Scotia, 1920*, 82. See also Snell, "Marital Cruelty," 31-32.

136 Bradbury, *Working Families*, 103-4, 183, and 192-95; and Golz, "If a Man's Wife," 323-50.

137 Nova Scotia Society for the Prevention of Cruelty, Scrapbook, 1921-26, NSA, MG 20, vol. 519, no. 3. Section 24(a) of the Criminal Code – "Neglect to provide for wife, children or ward" – provided for a $500 fine and/or one year imprisonment for a husband or "head of family" who "neglect[ed] or refuse[d]s to provide ... necessaries for his wife or any child under sixteen years of age." See *Crankshaw's Criminal Code of Canada*, 282.

138 *Morning Chronicle*, 22 May 1926.

139 Ibid., 14 June 1926.

140 *Halifax Herald*, 15 June 1933.

141 Halifax City Court Record Book, January 1919-December 1923, NSA, RG 42, ser. B, vol. 45. The City Court, presided over by a magistrate, had jurisdiction over cases involving fines of up to $100. It met twice a month in the police court. See McAlpine, *McAlpine's Halifax City Directory, 1923*, 627.

142 For more on the relationship between women's economic hardships and their criminality, see M. Elizabeth Langdon, "Female Crime in Calgary, 1914-1941," in *Law and Justice in a New Land: Essays in Western Canadian Legal History*, ed. Louis A. Knafla, 293-312 (Toronto: Carswell, 1986); and Holly Johnson and Karen Rodgers, "A Statistical Overview of Women and Crime in Canada," in *In Conflict with the Law: Women and the Canadian Justice System*, ed. Ellen Adelberg and Claudia Currie, 95-116 (Vancouver: Press Gang, 1993).

143 This point draws upon the work of Lucia Zedner, who has explored the contradictory views of women with regard to their criminality and their treatment in nineteenth-century Britain and North America. See Lucia Zedner, "Women, Crime, and Penal Responses: A Historical Account," in *Crime and Justice: A Review*

of Research, ed. Michael Tonry, 14:307-62 (Chicago: The University of Chicago Press, 1991).

144 This point in explored in greater depth by Constance Backhouse, *Carnal Crimes: Sexual Assault Law in Canada, 1900-1975* (Toronto: Irwin Law, 2008).

CHAPTER 6: THE ETHNIC DIMENSIONS OF CRIME AND CRIMINALS

1 E.R. Forbes, "The 1930s: Depression and Retrenchment," in *The Atlantic Provinces in Confederation,* ed. E.R. Forbes and D.A. Muise (Toronto: University of Toronto Press, 1993), 283.

2 D. Owen Carrigan, "The Immigrant Experience in Halifax, 1881-1931," *Canadian Ethnic Studies* 20, 3 (1988): 29 and 39.

3 *Morning Chronicle*, 25 February 1924.

4 Halifax's population in 1931 was 59,275. See Canada, *Sixth Census of Canada, 1921,* 1:392-93; and Canada, *Seventh Census of Canada, 1931,* 2:330-31. For more on the city's population figures, see Chapter 1.

5 For a numerical breakdown of some of Halifax's ethnic minorities, see Appendix 1, Table A1.3. See also Canada, *Sixth Census of Canada, 1921,* 2:392-93; and Canada, *Seventh Census of Canada, 1931,* 2:300 and 494-95.

6 Peter S. Li notes that, in 1931, the majority of Chinese residents in Canada (58 percent) lived in British Columbia, followed by Ontario (15 percent), Alberta (8 percent), Saskatchewan (8 percent), Quebec (6 percent), Manitoba (4 percent), and the Maritimes and Territories combined (1 percent). See Peter S. Li, *The Chinese in Canada* (Toronto: Oxford University Press, 1988), 51.

7 Canada, *Sixth Census of Canada, 1921,* 2:456.

8 Li, *Chinese In Canada*, 3, 18, and 30-31; and Harry Con, Ronald J. Con, Graham Johnson, Edgar Wickberg, and William E. Willmott, *From China to Canada: A History of the Chinese Communities in Canada* (Toronto: McClelland and Stewart, 1982), 270.

9 Fingard, "Race and Respectability," 190. The confrontations that some black women had with the forces of law and order in Halifax are discussed in Chapter 5.

10 James W. St. G. Walker, "Black History in the Maritimes: Major Themes and Teaching Strategies," in *Teaching Maritime Studies*, ed. Phillip Buckner (Fredericton, NB: Acadiensis Press, 1986), 100. Although the African Episcopal Methodist Church also played an important role in the early years, the Baptist Church became the cornerstone of Halifax's black community. That the Baptist Church became such a central part of the Halifax black community is due in large part to the efforts of William Andrew White, pastor of the Cornwallis Street Baptist Church, 1919-36. For more on the importance of the Baptist Church and social activities among Nova Scotian blacks, see Robin W. Winks, *The Blacks in Canada: A History* (Montreal and Kingston: McGill-Queen's University Press, 1971), 345-52; and Bridgal Pachai, *Beneath the Clouds of the Promised Land: The Survival of Nova Scotia's Blacks,* vol. 2, *1800-1989* (Halifax: The Black Educators Association, 1990).

11 The Freemasons Society was located on 31 Granville Street, the Nationalist League was situated at 161 Hollis Street, while the Chinese Club could be found

on Grafton Street. See Nova Scotia, *The Halifax City Directory, 1927* (Halifax: Might Directories Atlantic Ltd., 1927), 87.

12 *Morning Chronicle*, 31 December 1926.

13 *Morning Chronicle*, 18 May 1921. A similar episode occurred in 1928 when several of Tom Kee's friends posted his bail after the police charged him with assaulting a man following an altercation in Kee's B and C Cafe on Upper Water Street. See *Halifax Herald*, 1 December 1928.

14 David A. Sutherland notes that, in mid-Victorian Halifax, the press often depicted blacks as sinister. See David A. Sutherland, "Race Relations in Halifax, Nova Scotia, during the Mid-Victorian Quest for Reform," *Journal of the Canadian Historical Association* 7, 1 (1996): 51. This view of the Chinese is consistent with a tendency across Canada, from 1900 to the 1930s, to see the Chinese as a "menace," immoral heathens, opium smokers, thieves, and gamblers. See Gunter Baureiss, "Chinese Immigration, Chinese Stereotypes, and Chinese Labour," *Canadian Ethnic Studies* 19, 3 (1987): 23-25; and Madge Pon, "Like a Chinese Puzzle: The Construction of Chinese Masculinity in Jack Canuck," in *Gender and History in Canada*, ed. Joy Parr and Mark Rosenfeld, 88-100 (Toronto: Copp Clark, 1996). In Hamilton, many police officers, sharing popular assumptions, believed that certain racial groups were inclined towards criminal behaviour. One view equated Chinese laundries and cafes with opium smoking, prostitution, and white slavery, while "foreigners" were perceived to be the purveyors of illegal liquor. See Weaver, *Crime, Constables, and Courts*, 115-17.

15 David R. Roediger, *Towards the Abolition of Whiteness: Essays on Race, Politics, and Working-Class History* (London: Verso, 1994), 2; and John Gabriel and Gideon Ben-Tovim, "Marxism and the Concept of Racism," *Economy and Society* 7, 2 (1978): 120.

16 Kay J. Anderson, *Vancouver's Chinatown: Racial Discourse in Canada, 1875-1980* (Montreal and Kingston: McGill-Queen's University Press, 1991), 6 and 18.

17 This tendency was evident in Toronto and Vancouver. Clayton James Mosher, *Discrimination and Denial: Systemic Racism in Ontario's Legal and Criminal Justice Systems, 1892-1961* (Toronto: University of Toronto Press, 1998); John McLaren, "Race and the Criminal Justice System in British Columbia, 1892-1920: Constructing Chinese Crimes," in *Essays in the History of Canadian Law*, vol. 3: *In Honour of R.C B. Risk*, ed. G. Blaine Baker and Jim Phillips, 398-442 (Toronto: University of Toronto Press, 1999); and Constance Backhouse, *Colour-Coded: A History of Legal Racism in Canada, 1900-1950* (Toronto: University of Toronto Press, 1999).

18 In the British context, a similar theme is explored by Geoffrey Pearson regarding the origins of "hooliganism." Pearson argues that a dominant theme in British political culture has been the invoking of "racial" metaphors of social disruption "according to which violence and disorder have been repeatedly disowned as an alien intrusion into the peaceful ancestry of the 'British way of life.'" See Geoffrey Pearson, *Hooligan: A History of Respectable Fears* (New York: Schocken Books, 1984), 225-26.

19 Another version of this story claimed that the "negro" had assaulted a returned soldier. After the police departed, the rioters looted several of the concession stands at Williams' vaudeville show, stealing cigarettes, confections, and "anything else they could conveniently carry away." Later they attacked a Chinese laundry on Agricola Street. See *Morning Chronicle* and *Evening Mail*, 16 September 1918.

20 Ibid. A similar incident occurred in 1937 in Trenton, Nova Scotia, when a group of four hundred whites destroyed the home of a black family that had chosen to live in an all-white neighbourhood. Afterwards, the police arrested a black man accused of assaulting a white woman during the confrontation. See Forbes, "1930s," 283. For a discussion of the social and cultural significance of lynchings in the American south between 1874 and 1947, when at least three thousand Blacks were murdered by white gangs, see E.M. Beck and Stewart E. Tolnay, "Violence toward African Americans in the Era of the White Lynch Mob," in *Ethnicity, Race, and Crime: Perspectives across Time and Place*, ed. Darnell F. Hawkins, 121-44 (Albany: State University of New York Press, 1995); and Michael J. Pfeifer, *Rough Justice: Lynching and American Society, 1874-1947* (Urbana: University of Illinois Press, 2006). Reports of lynchings of southern blacks were often recounted in lurid detail in several Halifax newspapers.

21 Those restaurants damaged included the Crown Cafe, the Busy Bee, the Nova Scotia Cafe, the Allies Cafe, the Victory Cafe, and the Frisco Cafe, all located in the city's downtown core. See *Halifax Herald*, 19 February 1919.

22 Ibid., 20 February 1919.

23 Ibid., 21 February 1919.

24 Nova Scotia, *An Enquiry Respecting the Riots in Halifax during May 1918 and February 1919*, NSA, RG 39 ser. C vol. 702, 1918-19, Halifax County Supreme Court, no. 394, 55.

25 *Halifax Herald* and *Morning Chronicle*, 28 February 1919. In October 1919, the city solicitor advised Halifax City Council that the city could not be held liable for the damages caused by the riot. See Papers and Submissions to the City Council and City of Halifax, Board of Control, Minute Book, 27 February and 13 March 1919, HRMA.

26 Two other unprovoked attacks on Chinese restaurateurs took place in January 1919 and August 1920. On the latter occasion, Angus MacDonald of Cape Breton allegedly "smote a celestial keeper" of the Nova Scotia Restaurant on Gottingen Street over the amount of his bill. See *Morning Chronicle*, 6 December 1919 and 27 August 1920; and Halifax County Supreme Court, 1918-19, NSA, RG 39, ser. C, vol. 702, no. 404.

27 Those responsible for this destruction fled before the police could arrest them. See *Morning Chronicle*, 1 November 1921.

28 One of the men, James Lee, received a swollen jaw. See *Halifax Herald*, 4 August 1928. For other examples of beatings inflicted upon Chinese men, see *Morning Chronicle*, 29 December 1924; and *Halifax Herald*, 19 June 1933.

29 Pon, "Like a Chinese Puzzle," 89.

30 Clairmont and Magill, *Africville*, 51, 54, and 56. It has also been argued that Africville was an embarrassment to many of Halifax's black residents who wished to cultivate, and maintain, a respectable image for themselves. For more on the tensions that existed in Halifax's black community, especially over the murder of prominent lawyer James R. Johnston, who was a vocal advocate for justice and equality for blacks in the city and the province, see Barry Cahill, "The 'Colored Barrister': The Short Life and Tragic Death of James Robinson Johnston, 1876-1915," *Dalhousie Law Journal* 15, 2 (1992): 336-79.

31 Papers and Submissions to the City Council, HRMA. The following people signed the petition: William Carvery, Alex Carvery, Edward Dixon, Rachel

Roan, George Carvery, Fanny Carvery, Mrs. Bryers, Arthur Luey, John Byers, Alexander Carvery, J. Dixon, and Fred Carvery. Inadequate police protection for Africville had been a long-standing complaint among residents. See Clairmont and Magill, *Africville*, 52.

32 Papers and Submissions to the City Council, HRMA.

33 *Halifax Herald*, 11 July 1919. In January 1930, a few residents of Africville requested city council to extend the city's street lighting system into their district. Upon investigation, the city engineer agreed that the northern parts of Barrington and Gottingen streets needed better lighting "for the convenience of the general public travelling over this route" and to replace "police protection, which, with the present limited force, [could not] be obtained in this district." City council adopted the engineer's report and did install a few new street-lights. See Minutes of the City Council of the City of Halifax, Nova Scotia, for the Civic Year 1929-30, HRMA.

34 Jennifer J. Nelson, "'Panthers or Thieves': Racialized Knowledge and the Regulation of Africville," *Journal of Canadian Studies* 45, 1 (2011): 127-28 and 133.

35 Clairmont and Magill, *Africville*, 113; and Nelson, *Razing Africville*, 33.

36 Valverde, *Age of Light*, 89-99.

37 There may be a kernel of truth to the belief that prostitutes from Montreal were brought to Halifax. However, it is more likely that they came of their own volition. For reports of prostitutes coming from Montreal to Halifax, see *Morning Chronicle*, 18 January and 15 April 1919; and *Halifax Herald*, 20 January 1919. For more on the city's efforts to combat prostitution, see the discussion in Chapter 5.

38 *Morning Chronicle*, 1 February 1919. The police could arrest Hutchings as a result of a 1913 amendment to the Criminal Code, which made it an indictable offence, subject to ten years imprisonment, for anyone to "procure[ ] or attempt[ ] to procure any woman or girl to become, either within or without Canada, a common prostitute," or to "live[ ] wholly or in part on the earnings of prostitution." See McLaren, "Chasing the Social Evil," 149. These laws are contained in section 216, subsections (d) and (l) of the 1924 Criminal Code. See *Crankshaw's Criminal Code of Canada*, 224-25.

39 Section 216 of *Crankshaw's Criminal Code of Canada*. See Halifax County Supreme Court, 1918-19, NSA, RG 39, ser. C, vol. 702, no. 396. In Vancouver during this period, the police often suspected black men who arrived from the United States of being "pimps" or drug addicts who preyed on white women. See Marquis, "Vancouver Vice," 254.

40 Halifax County Supreme Court, 1918-19, NSA, RG 39, ser. C, vol. 702, no. 396.

41 Ibid.; and *Morning Chronicle*, 4 February 1919.

42 The Grand Jury did not indict Forge, but it did recommend that she be placed in the care of a local benevolent society before being sent home to her family in Scotland. See Halifax County Supreme Court, 1918-19, NSA, RG 39, ser. C, vol. 702, no. 397.

43 For more on this point, see Valverde, *Age of Light*, chap. 4.

44 Dubinsky, *Improper Advances*, 35-36.

45 *Halifax Chronicle*, 17 September 1929.

46 *Halifax Herald*, 2 and 4 January 1929. William Walsh, who was white, had five brothers and sisters. Their mother cared for them alone since their father had gone to Detroit to work. Walsh later recovered from his injury.

47 *Halifax Chronicle*, 4 January 1929; and *Halifax Herald*, 3, 4, and 5 January 1929.

48 The trial transcripts for the Sampson case may be found in the following collections: Halifax County Supreme Court, 1933-34, NSA, RG 39, ser. C, vol. 722, no. 1033; Capital Case Files, LAC, RG 13, ser. B, vol. 1587, file cc412, pt. 1; and Capital Case Files, LAC, RG 13, ser. B, vol. 1593, file cc423, pt. 1. In the period from the late eighteenth century to the start of the First World War, many white Americans, especially in the south, constructed images of black men as potentially violent criminals. In response to this perceived threat, some whites turned to lynchings as a means of "informal social control." See Martha A. Myers, "The New South's 'New' Black Criminal: Rape and Punishment in Georgia, 1870-1940," in Hawkins, *Ethnicity, Race, and Crime*, 145-66.

49 Halifax County Supreme Court, 1926-27, NSA, RG 39, ser. C, vol. 709, no. 387.

50 *Halifax Herald*, 14 September 1927.

51 Ibid., 13 September 1927; and Capital Case Files, LAC, RG 13, ser. B, vol. 1545, file cc267, pt. 1. When the assault case against Louis Jones came to court, Alice Jones refused to press charges and Louis Jones was subsequently released. See *Halifax Chronicle*, 13 September 1927.

52 John Mahoney was a conservative member of the Nova Scotia Legislature. The few black lawyers in Halifax would not have taken Jones's case for fear that it would tarnish their hard-fought, yet fragile, respectability within the legal profession and parts of Halifax's white, middle-class community. See *Halifax Herald*, 26 and 27 October 1927; and Capital Case Files, LAC, file cc267.

53 Capital Case Files, LAC, file cc267.

54 *Halifax Herald*, 13 September 1927.

55 The phrase "half white" is attributed to Jones' lawyer, John F. Mahoney, indicating yet another aspect of Halifax's racial discourse. See Capital Case Files, LAC, file cc267.

56 *Halifax Herald*, 27 October 1927.

57 Ibid., 7 December 1927. As Carolyn Strange and Tina Loo argue, jury trials often draw upon and help to define community values and identity. The feelings of some white residents of Halifax about blacks certainly surfaced during the trial of Louis Jones. See Carolyn Strange and Tina Loo, "Spectacular Justice: The Circus on Trial, and the Trial as Circus, Picton, 1903," *Canadian Historical Review* 77, 2 (1996): 159-84.

58 White, *Negotiating Responsibility*, 91-93.

59 Capital Case Files, LAC, file cc267.

60 Ibid.

61 Ibid.

62 Ibid.

63 Jones's fate was sealed on 17 January 1928 by a telegram from Thomas Mulvey, under-secretary of state, which read: "I am commanded to inform you that His Excellency the Governor General is unable to order any interference with the sentence of the court with the capital case of Louis Jones." See *Halifax Herald*, 18 and 19 January 1928; and *Halifax Chronicle*, 19 January 1928.

64 *Maritime Merchant* 27, 1 (11 July 1918), 28. Established in 1892, the *Merchant* was published "every other Thursday" in Halifax. See Tratt, *Survey and Listing*, 60-61. "John Chinaman" was one of the more prominent names given to Chinese immigrants by nineteenth-century North Americans. See W. Peter Ward, *White*

Canada Forever: Popular Attitudes and Public Policy toward Orientals in British Columbia (Montreal and Kingston: McGill-Queen's University Press, 1978), 3.

65 *Maritime Merchant* 27, 1 (11 July 1918), 28. For more on Canada's restrictions on Chinese immigration from 1885 to 1947, see Li, *Chinese in Canada*, 30-31. The Chinese in New Brunswick were also considered to belong to an inferior race. Indeed, discrimination was a fact of life for the Chinese in New Brunswick generally and in Saint John specifically. According to one Saint John resident: "Unlike other minorities [in the early part of the twentieth century] they were willfully isolated ... The Irish, French and Lebanese suffered much, but the Chinese were way down at the bottom ... small in number they were dismissed as quite unimportant." See William Seto and Larry N. Shyu, *The Chinese Experience in New Brunswick: A Historical Perspective* (Fredericton, NB: Chinese Cultural Association of New Brunswick, 1986), 79-80.

66 This relationship of dominance also existed for women, Aboriginal peoples, and "foreigners" generally with regard to white patriarchal society. See Tina Loo, *Making Law, Order, and Authority in British Columbia, 1821-1871* (Toronto: University of Toronto Press, 1994), 160.

67 Interview with Chuck Lee, 1984, NSA, MG 100, vol. 59, no. 2. Across the Maritimes during this period a majority of Chinese residents either owned or worked in laundries, restaurants, cafes, and retail stores. See Con et al., *From China to Canada*, 310. For a visual sense of where "Chinatown" was situated, see the map of Halifax's downtown core on page xiii. Saint John, New Brunswick, also had a Chinese community, but a Chinatown never developed in the city. As of 1921, eighty-three Chinese, most of whom were men, lived in Saint John. Many opened laundries, cafes, and restaurants, which also doubled as their homes. See Seto and Shyu, *Chinese Experience in New Brunswick*, 26-27, 30, 38-39, and 43.

68 Interview with Chuck Lee. Charlie Hong, who came to Halifax in 1923, remembered his father teaching him a trade because, "choice of jobs was limited, you either worked in a laundry or a restaurant." See *Halifax Mail Star*, 23 November 1978.

69 As D. Owen Carrigan comments, the Chinese in Halifax remained "unobtrusive and outside the social mainstream of life." See Carrigan, "Immigrant Experience," 38. For more on the benefits and drawbacks of "ghettos" for immigrants, see the "Little Italies" discussion in Robert F. Harney, "Ambiente and Social Class in North American Little Italies," *Canadian Review of Studies in Nationalism* 2, 2 (1975): 208-24; Franca Iacovetta, *Such Hardworking People: Italian Immigrants in Postwar Toronto* (Montreal and Kingston: McGill-Queen's University Press, 1992); and John E. Zucchi, *Italians in Toronto: Development of a National Identity, 1875-1935* (Kingston and Montreal: McGill-Queen's University Press, 1988).

70 Anderson, *Vancouver's Chinatown*, 92, 99, and 104. In the United States, during the nineteenth and early twentieth centuries, many whites associated the Chinese with vice, opium, and gambling. They were also treated with contempt by the justice system. See Friedman, *Crime and Punishment*, 99 and 137. By the mid-1920s, Chinese merchants in Chinatowns across the United States began to renovate their shops and clean up the streets of "Chinatown" in the hopes of cashing in on the lucrative tourist trade. See Ivan Light, "From Vice District to Tourist

Attraction: The Moral Career of American Chinatowns, 1880-1940," in *Crime and Justice in American History,* vol. 8: *Prostitution, Drugs, Gambling and Organized Crime,* pt. 2, ed. Eric H. Monkkonen, 550-77 (Munich: K.G. Saur, 1992).

71 *Halifax Herald*, 6 July 1918.

72 On this topic, see Elizabeth Comack, "'We Will Get Some Good out of This Riot Yet': The Canadian State, Drug Legislation, and Class Conflict," in *The Social Basis of Law: Critical Readings in the Sociology of Law,* 2nd ed., ed. Elizabeth Comack and Stephen Brickey (Halifax: Garamond Press, 1991), 49 and 63; Neil Boyd, "The Origins of Canadian Narcotics Legislation: The Process of Criminalization in Historical Context," in Macleod, *Lawful Authority*, 203-4; Pon, "Like a Chinese Puzzle," 95-96; and Catherine Carstairs, *Jailed for Possession: Illegal Drug Use, Regulation, and Power in Canada, 1920-1961* (Toronto: University of Toronto Press, 2005).

73 *Halifax Herald*, 2 April 1923. In July 1921, the Halifax Police Commission urged city council to endorse a resolution passed by the Vancouver City Council, calling for amendments to the Opium and Drug Act to toughen the penalties for offenders, including five years imprisonment for a second offence and the right of the police to search for drugs without a warrant. See Papers and Submissions to the City Council, HRMA.

74 Murphy was a police court magistrate and judge of the juvenile court in Edmonton. See Murphy, *Black Candle*, 32. *Black Candle* "used all the puritanical linguistic imagery to reinforce the racial stereotypes which had been circulating ... for years, and brought these stereotypes to the centre stage of public attention." See Howard Palmer, *Patterns of Prejudice: A History of Nativism in Alberta* (Toronto: McClelland and Stewart, 1982), 84-85.

75 Murphy, *Black Candle*, 183 and 187-88.

76 *Halifax Herald*, 3 August 1922.

77 Ibid., 19 August 1922. The police curtailed a portion of this smuggling operation when they arrested Tom Jim in 1926 and Ah Tom in 1927 for illegal possession of opium. Both were taken into custody at the train station after their arrival from Montreal. Ah Tom, who had $1,000 worth of opium with him at the time of his capture, was fined $504 and given six months imprisonment (or, in default of payment, an additional three months in jail). Reportedly, the only white person arrested under suspicion of smuggling opium was Frank Moore, a well-dressed, "clean cut, fine looking fellow" from Montreal, who arrived in Halifax in 1921. See *Morning Chronicle*, 25 November 1921 and 14 October 1926; and *Halifax Chronicle*, 7 and 12 March 1927.

78 *Halifax Herald*, 3 August 1922.

79 For instance, Wong and Charlie Lee were convicted of illegal possession of opium and fined $200 or sentenced to three months in the county jail. They opted for the former penalty after they lost an appeal. See Ibid., 30 August 1922.

80 In 1922, 1,117, or 60.1 percent, of the 1,858 convictions under the Opium and Narcotic Drug Act were against the Chinese. See Canada, *Forty-Seventh Annual Report of Criminal Statistics, 1922*, xix and 312-13. This high conviction rate for the Chinese was also evident in Vancouver and Victoria. See McLaren, "Race and the Criminal Justice System." The Saint John Police Department also conducted a

series of raids on Chinese businesses to rid the city of the twin evils of gambling and opium use. The press in Saint John labelled many Chinese merchants as "gamblers" and "drug addicts." See Seto and Shyu, *Chinese Experience in New Brunswick*, 85-87.

81 In 1930, the Chinese comprised 63 percent, or 281, of the total convictions (446) in Canada. In Halifax, the corresponding figures are 80 percent and 10, respectively. See Canada, *Fifty-Fifth Annual Report of Statistics of Criminal and Other Offences, 1930* (Ottawa: King's Printer, 1931), xxiv-xxv and 110-11. R. Solomon and M. Green have attributed this decline in convictions for opium offences in Canada to the dying out of an older generation of opium smokers, the restrictions placed on Chinese immigration, and the deportation of over five hundred convicted Chinese offenders. See R. Solomon and M. Green, "The First Century: The History of Nonmedical Opiate Use and Control Policies in Canada, 1870-1970," *University of Western Ontario Law Review* 20, 2 (1982): 324.

82 *Halifax Chronicle*, 27 February 1929.

83 *Halifax Herald*, 2 April 1929.

84 *Halifax Chronicle*, 3 August 1929. A similar incident occurred at 25 1/2 Sackville Street in 1922, when about fifty Chinese "devotees of the poppy weed" had their "pipes dreams" interrupted by the police who broke down the door and took four of them into custody. Two were fined twenty-five dollars and court costs, the third was fined fifteen dollars and court costs, and the fourth had his charge dismissed. See *Morning Chronicle*, 2 and 6 October 1922.

85 *Halifax Chronicle*, 7 and 14 October 1929.

86 *Halifax Herald*, 30 November 1929.

87 The prosecution offered no evidence against the other eight, resulting in their release. See *Halifax Chronicle*, 3 December 1929. Clayton James Mosher notes that, during the 1892 to 1950 period, the police in Ontario made a "considerable" effort to uncover and arrest Chinese gamblers and their gambling dens. See Mosher, *Discrimination and Denial*, 170.

88 *Morning Chronicle*, 25 August 1919.

89 *Halifax Chronicle* and *Halifax Herald*, 15 December 1924. "Fan Tan" is a game in which the betters predict the number of buttons, shells, or beans that will remain when groups of four are removed from a randomly selected pile. See Con et al., *From China to Canada*, 288. Two other cases in the early 1920s involving Fan Tan, in which Lee You and Fong Man Lee were charged with unlawfully keeping a "gaming house," may be found in Halifax County Supreme Court, 1918-20, NSA, RG 39, ser. C, vol. 703, no. 131; and Halifax County Supreme Court, 1920-21, NSA, RG 39, ser. C. vol. 704, no. 197.

90 The Lord Nelson Hotel opened in 1928 and the Hotel Novascotian in 1931. See Steve Kimber, "The Halifax Gambling Scene Isn't What It Used to Be," *4th Estate,* 22 June 1972. While this account provides a rather idealized version of the history of gambling in Halifax, it does highlight the fact that most residents of Halifax in the 1920s and 1930s linked the criminal aspects of gambling directly to the Chinese. For more on the history of gambling in Canada, see Suzanne Morton, *At Odds: Gambling and Canadians, 1919-1969* (Toronto: University of Toronto Press, 2003).

91 *Halifax Herald*, 21 January 1930.

92 Ibid., 14 December 1933 and 26 January 1934. This offence carried a penalty of one year imprisonment and a fine "not exceeding one thousand dollars." See *Crankshaw's Criminal Code of Canada*, 259. Angelos Paros, who owned a confectionary store, was convicted in 1932 of operating a gambling machine on his premises. See *Halifax Herald*, 5 September 1932. For two other cases tried during the early 1930s police clampdown on gambling in Halifax, see Halifax Magistrate's Court, 1934, NSA, RG 42, ser. C, vol. 18, no. 20; Halifax Magistrate's Court, 1934, NSA, RG 42, ser. C, vol. 21, no. 205.

93 Li, *Chinese in Canada*, 81. Seto and Shyu make similar arguments for the Chinese in New Brunswick. Seto and Shyu, *Chinese Experience in New Brunswick*, 43.

94 Similar sentiments emerged in Saint John, where the Chinese played fantan and mahjong. Many newspapers in Saint John claimed that gambling among the Chinese was widespread in the city. See Seto and Shyu, *Chinese Experience in New Brunswick*, 88. Throughout the early part of the twentieth century in Vancouver, Chinese men formed a disproportionately large share of those arrested in gambling raids. See Marquis, "Vancouver Vice," 246-50.

95 Edward W. Said, *Orientalism* (New York: Vintage Books, 1979), 301. Since these booths provided some concealment from public view, they afforded users an opportunity for urban anonymity. In the minds of some, this privacy contributed to the loss of a "premodern" sense of "community."

96 *Evening Echo*, 14 December 1923. May Virtue helped to apprehend one such woman in January 1932. When Virtue received word on 11 January that twenty-one-year-old Helen West had been out all night "in [and] around" Chinese cafes, she notified an officer to take West into custody. Five days later, on 16 January, Virtue appeared in police court with West, who pleaded guilty to being a vagrant. She was sentenced to four months in the City Prison. See *Police Women Occurrence Report,* 11 and 16 January 1932, NSA.

97 *Evening Echo*, 15 December 1923.

98 Ibid.

99 Ibid.; and Anderson, *Vancouver's Chinatown*, 24-26. For more on the West's perception and construction of the "Orient," see Said, *Orientalism*.

100 Pon, "Like a Chinese Puzzle," 96.

101 In this case, according to section 216 of the 1924 Criminal Code, "procuring" could mean: "inveigles or entices any woman or girl not being a common prostitute or of known immoral character to a common bawdy or assignation house for the purpose of illicit intercourse or prostitution" or "knowingly conceals any woman or girl in any common bawdy or assignation house." See *Crankshaw's Criminal Code of Canada*, 224.

102 *Halifax Herald* and *Morning Chronicle*, 17 December 1923.

103 *Evening Echo*, 21 December 1923.

104 Ibid., 22 December 1923.

105 *Halifax Herald*, 17 December 1923.

106 *Evening Echo*, 18 December 1923.

107 Ibid.

108 *Morning Chronicle*, 6 March 1924.

109 *Halifax Herald*, 12 and 22 November 1913.

110 As quoted in Murray B. Hodgins, "City Transformed," 129. Next to their selling of and addiction to opium, the most serious moral charge that was brought against Chinese men across the country had to do with their indulgence in prostitution. See John A. Munro, "British Columbia and the 'Chinese Evil': Canada's First Anti-Asiatic Immigration Law," *Journal of Canadian Studies* 6, 4 (1971): 47.

111 Police Charge Book, 10 March 1921, NSA, RG 35-102, ser. 16A, vol. 81; *Halifax Herald*, 11 March and 11 April 1921; and Nova Scotia, *The Nova Scotia Reports* (Toronto: Carswell Co. Ltd., 1922), 54:439-42. A little over a month later, a young woman was before the police court on a charge of engaging in prostitution. She claimed that at the time of her arrest she had been lured into the establishment by the Chinese owner. See *Morning Chronicle*, 27 May 1921.

112 *Halifax Herald*, 17 March 1925; and *Morning Chronicle*, 16 March 1923 and 17 March 1925.

113 Strange, *Toronto's Girl Problem*, 156; Dubinsky, *Improper Advances*, 139; and Baureiss, "Chinese Immigration," 26-30.

114 Fleet and Singer were granted bail, but, because of her suspended sentence from a previous conviction, Wylde was not. See *Halifax Herald* and *Halifax Chronicle*, 17 March 1925.

115 O'Toole felt that better employment options, and satisfactory working conditions, also needed to be found for white "girls" in order to keep them from working in Chinese-owned businesses. See *Halifax Chronicle*, 10 April 1929. Harry Con et al. claim that the Nova Scotia government responded to complaints in the late 1920s and early 1930s about white women working in Chinese restaurants by passing a law restricting their employment in Chinese-owned businesses. They also note that, in Halifax, the enforcement of this law was "spotty." See Con et al., *From China to Canada*, 152. However, I have found no such law either in the Nova Scotia statutes or in the journals of the Nova Scotia Assembly. Similarly, there is no reference in the minutes of city council to such a by-law's being either proposed or passed in Halifax. However, in other parts of the country, legal action was taken. Legislation forbidding Chinese merchants from hiring white women ("white women's labour law") was enacted by Saskatchewan in 1912, Manitoba in 1913, British Columbia in 1919, and Ontario in 1920. Ontario drafted its law in 1914, but it did not come into effect until 1920. Manitoba repealed its law in 1940, followed by Ontario in 1947, British Columbia in 1968, and Saskatchewan in 1969. See *Labour Gazette* 29, 10 (1929): 1129. See also Constance Backhouse, "White Female Help and Chinese-Canadian Employers: Race, Class, Gender and Law in the Case of Yee Clun, 1924," *Canadian Ethnic Studies* 26, 3 (1994): 34-52; Backhouse, *Colour-Coded*, chap. 5; and James W. St. G. Walker, *"Race," Rights, and the Law in the Supreme Court of Canada: Historical Case Studies* (Waterloo: Wilfrid Laurier University Press, 1997), 66-72. Seto and Shyu note that, beginning in the 1930s and continuing into the 1940s, white women were hired as waitresses in Chinese cafes and restaurants in Saint John and elsewhere in New Brunswick. They contend that this was a sign of the Chinese being accepted into New Brunswick, and Canadian, society. See Seto and Shyu, *Chinese Experience in New Brunswick*, 56.

116 Sangster, "Pardon Tales," 182.

117 Similar themes are explored in Strange, *Toronto's Girl Problem;* Marquis, "Vancouver Vice"; and Pon, "Like a Chinese Puzzle," 95.

118 Murphy, *Black Candle*, 108-9.

119 Valverde, *Age of Light,* 112.

120 *Halifax Herald*, 17 April 1919.

121 This figure of 1,068 includes seventy-three Chinese offenders. Without the Chinese, the number of "foreign" offenders dips to 995, or 8.3 percent, of Halifax's known criminals from 1917 to 1922. See Nova Scotia, *Annual Reports of the Several Departments of the Civil Government of Halifax, Nova Scotia, for the Civic Years 1917-1922: Report of Chief of Police* (Halifax: T.C. Allen and Co., 1919-23).

122 Carrigan, "Immigrant Experience," 28. The RCMP responded to and enhanced this fear by improving and widening their security screening techniques, especially fingerprinting, in these decades. See Larry Hannant, *The Infernal Machine: Investigating the Loyalty of Canada's Citizens* (Toronto: University of Toronto Press, 1995), chap. 3; and Greg Marquis, "The Technology of Professionalism: The Identification of Criminals in Early Twentieth-Century Canada," *Criminal Justice History* 15 (1994): 165-88.

123 Deportation "was an expedient solution to the problem of inadequate social services" in Canada. See Henry F. Drystek, "'The Simplest and Cheapest Mode of Dealing with Them': Deportation from Canada before World War II," *Histoire sociale/Social History* 15, 30 (1982): 414, 427-28, and 441.

124 *Halifax Herald*, 30 August 1932. Vagrancy was a common charge laid against "radical" immigrants as an excuse to deport them from Canada. See Barbara Roberts, "Shovelling Out the 'Mutinous': Political Deportation from Canada Before 1936," *Labour/Le Travail* 18 (1986): 97. Moreover, these "undesirables" included "radicals," notably members of the Communist Party of Canada, which, in 1931, under section 98 of the Criminal Code, was declared illegal. And, under section 98, anyone who was deemed to be a member of an "unlawful association" could be deported. By the fall of 1931, the federal government had intensified its efforts to deport "undesirables" and "radicals," including the "Halifax Ten." The "Halifax Ten" were ten men who, in 1931, had been rounded up by the RCMP from across the country for their alleged subversive activities and sent to Halifax, where their deportation hearings were held. After a legal challenge launched by the Canadian Labour Defence League, which argued that these men's habeas corpus rights had been violated, was defeated, and they were deported from Canada in 1932. The RCMP barracks in Halifax were used to house most of the "radicals" who were due to be deported from the country. See Barbara Roberts, *Whence They Came: Deportation from Canada, 1900-1935* (Ottawa: University of Ottawa Press, 1988), 126, 129, and 145-51.

125 *Halifax Herald*, 18 and 21 September 1922.

126 Ibid., 18 September 1922. These types of crimes were often attributed to Italian immigrants, who, in American cities such as Chicago, belonged to the Mafia. See Adler, *First in Violence,* 180-99. Anonymous threatening letters, what E.P. Thompson describes as part of the "counter-theatre of the poor," are a "characteristic form of social protest" in societies in which "individuals who can be identified as

the organizers of protest are liable to immediate victimization." Varbeff fit this bill. See Thompson, *Customs in Common*, 67; and Thompson, "Crime of Anonymity," 255. Varbeff's actions also contain hints of what some scholars have called "social crime." Its main characteristics include: an act directed against an individual or social group, an element of social protest, and strong communal support. In this case, the first two criteria do apply, although somewhat arbitrarily. For more on the concept of "social crime," see Michael Freeman, "Plebs or Predators? Deer-Stealing in Whichwood Forest, Oxfordshire, in the Eighteenth and Nineteenth Centuries," *Social History* 21, 1 (1996): 1-21.

127 *Halifax Herald*, 21 September 1922.

128 *Morning Chronicle*, 28 November 1922. Section 415 of the Criminal Code – "Letters demanding property, with menaces" – stipulated: "Every one is guilty of an indictable offence and liable to fourteen years imprisonment who sends, delivers or utters, or directly or indirectly causes to be received, knowing the contents thereof, any letter or writing demanding of any person with menaces, and without any reasonable or probable cause, any property, chattel, money, valuable security or other valuable thing." See *Crankshaw's Criminal Code of Canada*, 549. Varbeff was discharged from Dorchester Penitentiary on 24 March 1926, more than a year prior to the expiration of his five-year sentence. See Dorchester Penitentiary, Convicts' Register, NSA. Some magistrates and judges even felt that "foreigners" were not worthy of "British justice" since they did not understand British traditions of jurisprudence. See Marquis, "Doing Justice," 58.

129 *Halifax Chronicle*, 29 July 1929. One autobiographical account of Gypsy life maintains that all Gypsies were usually "castigated" and "held responsible" for the criminal actions of one of their compatriots. See Ronald Lee, *Goddam Gypsy: An Autobiographical Novel* (Montreal: Tundra Books, 1971), 131. Another perspective on Gypsies may be found in Tanya Gogan, "'A Picturesque Lot': The Gypsies in Peterborough," *Beaver* 78, 5 (1998): 25-30.

130 Smith, *Through Dirty Windows*, 63-64.

131 Lee, *Goddam Gypsy*, 81 and 109.

132 *Halifax Chronicle*, 24 December 1929. Two more Gypsy women, Kathleen and Cecilia Markovitch, were charged in 1930 with fortune telling, or "phrenology," an offence covered under section 443 of the *Criminal Code* – "Pretending to use witchcraft." The law stated: "[anyone] is guilty of an indictable offence and liable to one year's imprisonment who pretends to exercise or use any kind of witchcraft, sorcery, enchantment or conjuration, or undertakes to tell fortunes, or pretends from his skill or knowledge in any occult or crafty science, to discover where or in what manner any goods or chattels supposed to have been stolen or lost may be found." See *Halifax Herald*, 6 February 1930; and *Crankshaw's Criminal Code of Canada*, 533-34.

133 *Halifax Herald*, 4 February 1930.

134 Walker, *"Race," Rights, and the Law*, ix-x and 302; Elazar Barkan, *The Retreat of Scientific Racism: Changing Concepts of Race in Britain and the United States between the World Wars* (Cambridge: Cambridge University Press, 1992), xi and 3-4; and Keller, *Regulating a New Society*, 251-81.

135 McLaren, *Our Own Master Race*, 91.

136 Pachai, *Beneath the Clouds*, 129. For more on how British Columbia applied this ideology towards the Chinese, see Ward, *White Canada Forever;* and Patricia Roy,

A White Man's Province: British Columbian Politicians and Chinese and Japanese Immigrants, 1858-1914 (Vancouver: UBC Press, 1989); and Patricia Roy, *The Oriental Question: Consolidating a White Man's Province, 1914-1941* (Vancouver: UBC Press, 2003).

137 Carrigan, "Immigrant Experience," 35.

138 Roediger, *Towards the Abolition of Whiteness*, 13-14.

CONCLUSION

1 Feilding, "Prison Reform in Nova Scotia," 105.

2 Pearson, *Hooligan*, 242.

3 A similar point is made by John C. Weaver regarding the citizens of Hamilton, who "essentially and uncritically" supported their city's institutions of law and order and the constant need for social order. See Weaver, *Crime, Constables, and Courts*, 21-22.

4 For an exploration of this point with regard to women and criminality in Toronto, see Strange, *Toronto's Girl Problem;* and Glasbeek, *Feminized Justice*.

5 Morrison, *Theoretical Criminology*, 28.

6 See the relevant work by Weaver, *Crime, Constables, and Courts*; Myers, *Caught*; Glasbeek, *Feminized Justice*; and Marquis, "Vancouver Vice." Such federal initiatives included in Canada, *Report of the Royal Commission to Investigate the Penal System of Canada*; *Report on the State and Management of the Female Prison at the Kingston Penitentiary, 1921*, LAC, RG 73, vol. 105; and Nova Scotia, *Report of the Royal Commission Concerning Jails, 1933*.

7 Sean Watson explores the state's need for "disciplinary technologies" to "manage" civil society. See Sean Watson, "Symbolic Antagonism, Police Paranoia, and the Possibility of Social Diversity," in *The Lesser Evil and the Greater Good: The Theory and Politics of Social Diversity*, ed. Jeffrey Weeks, 100-22 (London: Rivers Oram Press, 1994).

8 Elizabeth Comack, "A Marxian Theory of Law and Crime under Capitalism: The Canadian State, Class Conflict and Drug Legislation", PhD diss., University of Alberta, 1984, 102; Fine, *Democracy and the Rule of Law*, 142; Hugh Collins, *Marxism and Law* (Oxford: Oxford University Press, 1984), 43 and 95; Watson, "Symbolic Antagonism, 114-15; and Phillips et al., *Essays in the History of Canadian Law*, 5:12.

9 Peter Linebaugh, *The London Hanged: Crime and Civil Society in the Eighteenth Century* (London: Allen Lane, 1991), xviii-xix.

10 Loo, *Making Law*, 5.

11 For example, Backhouse, *Petticoats and Prejudice;* Backhouse, *Carnal Crimes*; Glasbeek, *Feminized Justice*; and Joan Sangster, *Regulating Girls and Women: Sexuality, Family, and the Law in Ontario, 1920-1960* (Don Mills: Oxford University Press, 2001).

12 Anderson, Vancouver's Chinatown, 8-33.

13 Hunt, "Marxism," 125.

14 *Halifax Herald*, 1 January 1935.

15 Berman, *All That Is Solid*, 95.

Bibliography

PRIMARY SOURCES

Archives

Correctional Service of Canada Museum, Kingston, Ontario.
Dalhousie University Archives and Special Collections (DUASC), Halifax, Nova Scotia.
Halifax Police Museum Archives (HPMA), Halifax, Nova Scotia.
Halifax Regional Municipality Archives (HRMA), Halifax, Nova Scotia.
Library and Archives Canada (LAC), Ottawa, Ontario.
United Church of Canada Maritime Conference Archives, Sackville, New Brunswick.
Nova Scotia Archives (NSA), Halifax, Nova Scotia.
Nova Scotia Legislative Library, Halifax, Nova Scotia.
Queen's University Archives, Kingston, Ontario.

PRINTED PRIMARY MATERIALS

Canada. *Annual Reports of Criminal Statistics, 1918-1935*. Ottawa: King's Printer, 1919-36.

Chesley, S.A. "The Office of the Stipendiary Magistrate as a Part of Municipal Government." In *Proceedings of the Twentieth Annual Convention of the Union of Nova Scotia Municipalities*, 1925, 73-78.

Belcher's Farmers' Almanac for the Maritime Provinces, 1918-1930. Halifax: Royal Print and Litho Ltd., 1917-1930.

Canada. *The Canada Year Book, 1920*. Ottawa: King's Printer, 1921.

–. *The Canada Year Book, 1921*. Ottawa: King's Printer, 1922.

–. *Fifth Census of Canada, 1911*, vol. 1 Ottawa: King's Printer, 1912.

–. *Fifth Census of Canada, 1911*, vol. 2. Ottawa: King's Printer, 1913.

–. *Eighth Census of Canada, 1941*, vol. 1. Ottawa: King's Printer, 1950.

–. *Eighth Census of Canada, 1941*, vol. 2. Ottawa: King's Printer, 1944.

–. *Report of the Department of Militia and Defence, 1920*. Ottawa: King's Printer, 1921.

–. *Report of the Department of National Defence, 1925-1929*. Ottawa: King's Printer, 1925-29.

–. *Report of the Militia Council, 1918-1919*. Ottawa: King's Printer, 1919-20.

–. *Report of the Royal Commission to Investigate the Penal System of Canada*. Ottawa: King's Printer, 1938.

–. *The Revised Statutes of Canada, 1927*, vol. 2 Ottawa: King's Printer, 1927.

–. *Seventh Census of Canada, 1931*, vol. 1. Ottawa: King's Printer, 1936.

–. *Seventh Census of Canada, 1931*, vol. 2 Ottawa: King's Printer, 1933.

–. *Seventh Census of Canada, 1931*, vol. 6. Ottawa: King's Printer, 1934.

–. *Seventh Census of Canada, 1931*, vol. 7. Ottawa: King's Printer, 1936.

–. *Seventh Census of Canada, 1931*, vol. 9. Ottawa: King's Printer, 1935.

–. *Sixth Census of Canada, 1921*, vol. 1. Ottawa: King's Printer, 1924.

–. *Sixth Census of Canada, 1921*, vol. 2. Ottawa: King's Printer, 1925.

–. *Sixth Census of Canada, 1921*, vol. 4. Ottawa: King's Printer, 1929.

Crankshaw, James. *Crankshaw's Magistrates' Manual: Being a Practical Guide to Police Magistrates and Justices of the Peace*, 3rd ed. Toronto: Canada Law Book Company Ltd., 1921.

Crankshaw's Criminal Code of Canada, 5th ed. Toronto: Carswell Co. Ltd., 1924.

Feilding, J.B. "Prison Reform in Nova Scotia." In *Proceedings of the Nineteenth Annual Convention of the Union of Nova Scotia Municipalities*, 1924, 97-113.

Godfrey, Margaret. "The Development of the Juvenile Court in Halifax." Unpublished paper, Maritime School of Social Work, 1948. NSA, Welfare Council of Halifax and Dartmouth, MG 20 vol. 408, no. 8.13.

Halifax Board of Trade. *Halifax: The City by the Sea*. Halifax: Halifax Board of Trade, ca. 1931.

Halifax Police Department. *The History of the Halifax Police Department*. Halifax: Halifax Police Department, ca. 1990.

Halifax: An Old City with a Brand New Future. Toronto: Rous and Mann Ltd., ca. 1913.

Halifax-Dartmouth. *Halifax City Directory, 1927*. Halifax: Might Directories Atlantic Ltd., 1927.

–. *Halifax City Directory, 1929*. Halifax: Might Directories Atlantic Ltd., 1929.

–. *Halifax-Dartmouth City Directories, 1931-1936*. Halifax: Might Directories Atlantic Ltd., 1931-36.

Kidman, John, and C.H. Mercer. *Report on County Jails of Nova Scotia*. Canadian Prisoners' Welfare Association, 1934. Charles H. Mercer Papers, DUASC, MS 2 no. 659.

McAlpine. *McAlpine's Halifax City Directory, 1918*. Halifax: Royal Print and Litho Ltd., 1918.

–. *McAlpine's Halifax City Directory, 1923*. Halifax: Royal Print and Litho Ltd., 1923.

–. *McAlpine's Halifax City Directory, 1924*. Halifax: Royal Print and Litho Ltd., 1924.

Nova Scotia. *Annual Report of the Several Departments of the Civic Government of Halifax, Nova Scotia for the Civic Years 1917-1922: Report Chief of Police*. Halifax: T.C. Allen and Co., 1919-23.

–. *Annual Report of the Several Departments of the Civic Government of Halifax, Nova Scotia: City Prison Reports, 1917-1935*. Halifax: T.C. Allen and Co., 1919-36.

–. *Annual Report of the Superintendent of Education for Nova Scotia, 1920*. Halifax: King's Printer, 1921.

–. *Annual Report of the Superintendent of Education for Nova Scotia, 1921*. Halifax: King's Printer, 1922.

–. *Annual Reports of the Director of Child Welfare for the Province of Nova Scotia, 1926-1935*. Halifax: King's Printer, 1927-36.
–. *Annual Reports of Penal Institutions for the Province of Nova Scotia, 1917-1935*. Halifax: King's Printer, 1918-36.
–. *Annual Reports of the Royal Canadian Mounted Police, "H" Division, 1932-1935*. Halifax: King's Printer, 1933-1936.
–. *Annual Reports of the Superintendent of Neglected and Delinquent Children for the Province of Nova Scotia, 1917-1925*. Halifax: King's Printer, 1919-26.
–. An Enquiry Respecting the Riots in Halifax during May 1918 and February 1919. NSA, RG 39 ser. C vol. 702, 1918-1919, Halifax County Supreme Court, no. 394.
–. *Fifty-Sixth to Seventy-Second Annual Report of the Halifax Industrial School, 1919-1935*. Halifax: John Bowes Printing Co. Ltd., 1919-35.
–. *The Halifax City Charter, 1914*. Halifax: King's Printer, 1914.
–. *The Halifax City Charter, 1931*. Halifax: King's Printer, 1931.
–. *The Judicature Act*. Halifax: King's Printer, 1920.
–. *The Nova Scotia Reports*, vol. 54. Toronto: Carswell, 1922.
–. *The Nova Scotia Reports*, vol. 57. Toronto: Carswell, 1925.
–. *The Nova Scotia Reports*, Vol. 59. Toronto: Carswell, 1928.
–. *The Public Gardens of Halifax, Nova Scotia*. Halifax: circa 1930. Nova Scotia Legislative Library, NS 917.1622P.
–. *Regulations for the Government and Management of the Common Jails in the Province of Nova Scotia, 1923*. Halifax: King's Printer, 1923.
–. *Report of the Board of School Commissioners for the City of Halifax, Nova Scotia, 1918-1936*. Halifax: Weeks Printing Co. Ltd./MacNab Print/Royal Print and Litho Ltd./Ross Print Ltd., 1919-37.
–. *Report on Feeble Minded in Nova Scotia*. Halifax: King's Printer, 1918.
–. *Report of the Returned Soldier Commission*. Halifax: King's Printer, 1921.
–. *Report of the Royal Commission Concerning Jails*. Halifax: King's Printer, 1933.
–. *Reports of the Nova Scotia Police, 1930-1932*. Halifax: King's Printer, 1931-33.
–. *The Revised Statutes of Nova Scotia, 1900*, vol. 2. Halifax: Queen's Printer, 1900.
–. *The Revised Statutes of Nova Scotia, 1923*, vol. 2. Halifax: King's Printer, 1923.
–. *The Revised Statutes of Nova Scotia, 1934*, vol. 1. Halifax: King's Printer, 1934.
–. *The Revised Statutes of Nova Scotia, 1954*, vol. 3. Halifax: Queen's Printer, 1954.
–. *Sixty-Fourth to Eightieth Annual Report of the Halifax Visiting Dispensary, 1920-1936*. Halifax: T.C. Allen and Co., 1921-37.
–. *The Statutes of Nova Scotia, 1865*. Halifax: Queen's Printer, 1865.
–. *The Statutes of Nova Scotia, 1889*. Halifax: Queen's Printer, 1889.
–. *The Statutes of Nova Scotia, 1890*. Halifax: Queen's Printer, 1890.
–. *The Statutes of Nova Scotia, 1892*. Halifax: Queen's Printer, 1892.
–. *The Statutes of Nova Scotia, 1899*. Halifax: Queen's Printer, 1899.
–. *The Statutes of Nova Scotia, 1902-8*. Halifax: King's Printer, 1902-8.
–. *The Statutes of Nova Scotia, 1918-35*. Halifax: King's Printer, 1918-35.
–. *The Statutes of Nova Scotia, 1948*. Halifax: King's Printer, 1948.
–. *Vital Statistics: Journals and Proceedings of the House of Assembly of the Province of Nova Scotia, 1919-1937*. Halifax: King's Printer, 1920-37.

Newspapers

Acadian Recorder (Halifax)
Amherst Daily News (Amherst, Nova Scotia)
Busy East (Sackville, New Brunswick)
The Citizen (Halifax)
Commercial News (Halifax)
Daily Echo (Halifax)
Evening Echo (Halifax)
Evening Mail (Halifax)
Globe and Mail (Toronto)
Halifax Chronicle
Halifax Chronicle Herald
Halifax Evening Echo
Halifax Herald
Halifax Mail
Halifax Mail Star
Labour Gazette (Ottawa)
Maritime Merchant (Halifax)
Morning Chronicle (Halifax)
Morning Journal (Halifax)
News and Sentinel (Amherst, Nova Scotia)
Oxford Journal (Oxford, Nova Scotia)
Presbyterian Witness (Halifax)
Unionist and Halifax Journal
United Churchman (Sackville, New Brunswick)

SECONDARY SOURCES

Abelson, Elaine S. *When Ladies Go A-Thieving: Middle-Class Shoplifters in the Victorian Department Store*. New York: Oxford University Press, 1989.

Abucar, Mohamed. *Struggle for Development: The Black Communities of North and East Preston and Cherry Brook, Nova Scotia, 1784-1987*. Dartmouth: Black Cultural Centre for Nova Scotia, 1988.

Acheson, T.W. "The National Policy and the Industrialization of the Maritimes, 1880-1910." *Acadiensis* 1, 2 (1972): 3-28.

Acton, Janice, Penny Goldsmith, and Bonnie Shepard, eds. *Women at Work: Ontario, 1850-1930*. Toronto: Canadian Women's Educational Press, 1974.

Adelberg, Ellen, and Claudia Currie, eds. *In Conflict with the Law: Women and the Canadian Justice System*. Vancouver: Press Gang, 1993.

Adler, Jeffrey S. *First in Violence, Deepest in Dirt: Homicide in Chicago, 1875-1920*. Cambridge: Harvard University Press, 2006.

Alexander, David. "Economic Growth in the Atlantic Region, 1880 to 1940." *Acadiensis* 8, 1 (1978): 47-76.

Anderson, Kay J. *Vancouver's Chinatown: Racial Discourse in Canada, 1875-1980*. Montreal and Kingston: McGill-Queen's University, 1991.

Annau, Catherine. "Eager Eugenicists: A Reappraisal of the Birth Control Society of Hamilton." *Histoire sociale/Social History* 27, 53 (1994): 111-33.

Arnup, Katherine, Andree Levesque, and Ruth Roach Pierson, eds. *Delivering Motherhood: Maternal Ideologies and Practices in the 19th and 20th Centuries*. London: Routledge, 1990.

Avio, Kenneth L. "The Quality of Mercy: Exercise of the Royal Prerogative in Canada." *Canadian Public Policy* 13, 3 (1987): 366-79.

Bacher, John. "From Study to Reality: The Establishment of Public Housing in Halifax, 1930-1953." *Acadiensis* 18, 1 (1988): 120-35.

Backhouse, Constance. *Carnal Crimes: Sexual Assault Law in Canada, 1900-1975*. Toronto: Irwin Law, 2008.

–. *Colour-Coded: A Legal History of Racism in Canada, 1900-1950*. Toronto: University of Toronto Press, 1999.

–. "Involuntary Motherhood: Abortion, Birth Control and the Law in Nineteenth Century Canada." *Windsor Yearbook of Access to Justice* 3 (1983): 61-130.

–. *Petticoats and Prejudice: Women and Law in Nineteenth-Century Canada*. Canada: The Osgoode Society, 1991.

–. "Prosecution of Abortions under Canadian Law, 1900-1950." In *Essays in the History of Canadian Law*. Vol. 5: *Crime and Criminal Justice*, ed. Jim Phillips, Tina Loo, and Susan Lewthwaite, 252-92. Toronto: University of Toronto Press, 1994.

–. "White Female Help and Chinese-Canadian Employers: Race, Class, Gender and Law in the Case of Yee Clun, 1924." *Canadian Ethnic Studies* 26, 3 (1994): 34-52.

Baehre, Rainer. "From Bridewell to Federal Penitentiary: Prisons and Punishment in Nova Scotia before 1880." In *Essays in the History of Canadian Law*. Vol. 3: *Nova Scotia*, ed. Philip Girard and Jim Phillips, 163-99. Toronto: The Osgoode Society, 1990.

–. "Prison as Factory, Convict as Worker: A Study of the Mid-Victorian St. John Penitentiary, 1841-1880." In *Essays in the History of Canadian Law*. Vol. 5: *Crime and Criminal Justice,* ed. Jim Phillips, Tina Loo, and Susan Lewthwaite, 439-77. Toronto: University of Toronto Press, 1994.

Bailey, Victor. *Delinquency and Citizenship: Reclaiming the Young Offender, 1914-1948*. Oxford: Oxford University Press, 1987.

–. "The Fabrication of Deviance: 'Dangerous Classes' and 'Criminal Classes' in Victorian England." In *Protest and Survival: The Historical Experience – Essays for E.P. Thompson*, ed. John Rule and Robert Malcolmson, 221-56. London: Merlin Press, 1993.

Baillargeon, Denise. *Making Do: Women, Family, and Home in Montreal during the Great Depression*. Waterloo: Wilfrid Laurier University Press, 1999.

Baker, G. Blaine, and Jim Phillips, eds. *Essays in the History of Canadian Law*. Vol. 8: *In Honour of R.C.B. Risk*. Toronto: University of Toronto Press, 1999.

Baker, William M. "The Miners and the Mounties: The Royal North West Mounted Police and the 1906 Lethbridge Strike," *Labour/Le Travail* 27 (1991): 55-96.

Baldwin, Peter C. "'Nocturnal Habits and Dark Wisdom': The American Response to Children in the Streets at Night, 1880-1930," *Journal of Social History* 35, 3 (2002): 593-611.

Barak, Gregg, ed. *Media, Process, and the Social Construction of Crime: Studies in Newsmaking Criminology*. New York and London: Garland, 1994.

Barkan, Elazar. *The Retreat of Scientific Racism: Changing Concepts of Race in Britain and the United States between the World Wars*. Cambridge: Cambridge University Press, 1992.

Bartholomew, Amy, and Susan Boyd. "Toward a Political Economy of Law." In *The New Canadian Political Economy*, ed. Wallace Clement and Glen Williams, 212-39. Kingston and Montreal: McGill-Queen's University Press, 1989.

Baureiss, Gunter. "Chinese Immigration, Chinese Stereotypes, and Chinese Labour." *Canadian Ethnic Studies* 19, 3 (1987): 15-34.

Beattie, J.M. *Crime and the Courts in England, 1660-1800*. New Jersey: Princeton University Press, 1986.

Beck, E.M., and Stewart E. Tolnay. "Violence toward African Americans in the Era of the White Lynch Mob." In *Ethnicity, Race, and Crime: Perspectives across Time and Place*, ed. Darnell F. Hawkins, 121-44. Albany: State University of New York Press, 1995.

Beck, J. Murray. *The Government of Nova Scotia*. Toronto: University of Toronto Press, 1957.

Beckman, Marlene D. "The White Slave Traffic Act: The Historical Impact of a Criminal Law Policy on Women." *Georgetown Law Journal* 72 (1984): 1111-42.

Bedford, Judy. "Prostitution in Calgary, 1905-1914." *Alberta History* 29, 2 (1981): 1-11.

Beirne, Piers, and Richard Quinney, eds. *Marxism and Law*. New York: John Wiley and Sons, 1982.

Belisle, Donica. *Retail Nation: Department Stores and the Making of Modern Canada*. Vancouver: UBC Press, 2011.

Bell, D.G. "The Birth of Canadian Legal History." *UNB Law Journal* 33 (1984): 312-18.

Bell, Ernest A. *War on the White Slave Trade*. Toronto: Coles, 1980 [1911].

Bennett, Paul W. "Taming the 'Bad Boys' of the 'Dangerous Class': Child Rescue and Restraint at the Victoria Industrial School, 1887-1935." *Histoire sociale/Social History* 21, 41 (1988): 71-96.

Bercuson, D.J., and L.A. Knafla, eds. *Law and Society in Canada in Historical Perspective*. Calgary: University of Calgary Press, 1979.

Berman, Marshall. *All That Is Solid Melts into Air: The Experience of Modernity*. New York: Penguin Books, 1988.

Binnie, Susan W.S. "The Blake Act of 1878: A Legislative Solution to Urban Violence in Post-Confederation Canada." In *Law, Society, and the State: Essays in Modern Legal History*, ed. Louis A. Knafla and Susan W.S. Binnie, 215-42. Toronto: University of Toronto Press, 1995.

–. "Explorations in the Use of Criminal Law in Canada, 1867-1892." PhD thesis, Carleton University, 1991.

Bogaard, Paul A., ed. *Profiles of Science and Society in the Maritimes prior to 1914*. Fredericton, NB: Acadiensis Press, 1990.

Bordua, David J., ed. *The Police: Six Sociological Essays*. New York: John Wiley and Sons, 1967.

Boritch, Helen, and John Hagan. "Crime and Changing Forms of Class Control: Policing Public Order in 'Toronto the Good,' 1859-1955." *Social Forces* 66, 2 (1987): 307-35.

Boudreau, Michael. "Crime and Society in Halifax, 1918-1935." *Collections of the Royal Nova Scotia Historical Society* 44 (1996): 95-103.

–. "'Delinquents Often Become Criminals': Juvenile Delinquency in Halifax, 1918-1935." *Acadiensis* 39, 1 (2010): 108-32.

–. "The Emergence of the Social Gospel in Nova Scotia: The Presbyterian, Methodist and Baptist Churches and the Working Class, 1880-1914." MA thesis, Queen's University, 1991.

–. "Francis Hanrahan: Halifax Chief of Police." In *Dictionary of Canadian Biography*. Vol. 15: *1921-1930*, 452-53. Toronto: University of Toronto Press, 2005.

–. "Strikes, Rural Decay, and Socialism: The Presbyterian Church in Nova Scotia Grapples with Social Realities, 1880-1914." In *The Contribution of Presbyterianism to the Maritime Provinces of Canada*, ed. Charles H.H. Scobie and G.A. Rawlyk, 144-59. Montreal and Kingston: McGill-Queen's University Press, 1997.

–. "'There Is ... No Pernicious Dualism between Sacred and Secular': Nova Scotia Baptists and the Social Gospel, 1880-1914." *Nova Scotia Historical Review* 16, 1 (1996): 109-31.

Boyd, Neil. "The Origins of Canadian Narcotics Legislation: The Process of Criminalization In Historical Context." In *Lawful Authority: Readings on the History of Criminal Justice in Canada*, ed. R.C. Macleod, 192-218. Toronto: Copp Clark Pitman Ltd., 1988.

Bradbury, Bettina. *Working Families: Age, Gender, and Daily Survival in Industrializing Montreal*. Toronto: McClelland and Stewart, 1993.

Bright, David. "Loafers Are Not Going to Subsist upon Public Credulence: Vagrancy and the Law in Calgary, 1900-1914." *Labour/Le Travail* 36 (1995): 367-58.

Brookes, Alan A. "Family, Youth, and Leaving Home in Late Nineteenth-Century Rural Nova Scotia: Canning and the Exodus, 1868-1893." In *Childhood and Family in Canadian History*, ed. Joy Parr, 93-108. Toronto: McClelland and Stewart, 1988.

Brown, Desmond H. *The Genesis of the Canadian Criminal Code*. Toronto: University of Toronto Press, 1989.

Brown, R. Blake. "A Taxonomy of Methodological Approaches in Recent Canadian Legal History." *Acadiensis* 34, 1 (2004): 145-55.

–. *A Trying Question: The Jury in Nineteenth-Century Canada*. Toronto: University of Toronto Press, 2009.

Buckner, Phillip, ed. *Teaching Maritime Studies*. Fredericton, NB: Acadiensis Press, 1986.

Bullen, John. "Hidden Workers: Child Labour and the Family Economy in Late Nineteenth-Century Urban Ontario." *Labour/Le Travail* 18 (1986): 163-87.

Bumsted, J.M., ed. *Interpreting Canada's Past*. Vol. 1: *Before Confederation*. Toronto: Oxford University Press, 1986.

Burchell, Graham, Colin Gordon, and Peter Miller, eds. *The Foucault Effect: Studies in Governmentality*. London: Harvester Wheatsheaf, 1991.

Burr, Chris. "'Roping in the Wretched, the Reckless, and the Wronged': Narratives of the Late Nineteenth-Century Toronto Police Court." *Left History* 3, 1 (1995): 83-108.

Burtch, Brian. *The Sociology of Law: Critical Approaches to Social Control*. Toronto: Harcourt Brace Jovanovich Canada, 1992.

Butts, Edward. *The Desperate Ones: Forgotten Canadian Outlaws*. Toronto: Dundurn Press, 2006.

Cahill, Barry. "The 'Colored Barrister': The Short Life and Tragic Death of James Robinson Johnston, 1876-1915." *Dalhousie Law Journal* 15, 2 (1992): 336-79.

–. "Legislated Privilege or Common-Law Right? Provincial State Intervention and the First Women Lawyers in Nova Scotia." In *Making Up the State: Women in 20th-Century Atlantic Canada*, ed. Janet Guildford and Suzanne Morton, 79-92. Fredericton, NB: Acadiensis Press, 2010.

–. "The Origin and Evolution of the Attorney and Solicitor in the Legal Profession of Nova Scotia." *Dalhousie Law Journal* 14, 2 (1991): 277-95.

Cain, Maureen, and Alan Hunt. *Marx and Engels on Law.* London: Academic Press, 1979.

Cannon, O.A. "Septic Abortion." *Canadian Medical Association Journal* 12 (1922): 163-68.

Carlen, Pat. *Women, Crime, and Poverty.* Philadelphia: Open University Press, 1988.

Carleton University History Collaborative. *Urban and Community Development in Atlantic Canada, 1867-1991.* Hull, QC: Canadian Museum of Civilization, 1993.

Carlson, A. Cheree. *The Crimes of Womanhood: Defining Femininity in a Court of Law.* Urbana and Chicago: University of Illinois Press, 2009.

Carrigan, D. Owen. *Crime and Punishment in Canada: A History.* Toronto: McClelland and Stewart, 1991.

–. "The Immigrant Experience in Halifax, 1881-1931." *Canadian Ethnic Studies* 20, 3 (1988): 28-41.

–. *Juvenile Delinquency in Canada: A History.* Toronto: Irwin, 1998.

Carstairs, Catherine. *Jailed for Possession: Illegal Drug Use, Regulation, and Power in Canada, 1920-1961.* Toronto: University of Toronto Press, 2005.

Cellard, Andre. "Le Petit Chicago: La 'Criminalite' a Hull depuis le debut du XX Siecle." *Revue d'histoire de l'Amerique francaise* 45, 4 (1992): 519-43.

Chapman, Terry L. "'Til Death Do Us Part': Wife Beating in Alberta, 1905-1920." *Alberta History* 36, 4 (1986): 13-22.

Chekki, Dan A., ed. *Dimensions of Communities: A Research Handbook.* New York and London: Garland, 1989.

Chermak, Steven. "Crime in the News Media: A Refined Understanding of How Crime Becomes News." In *Media, Process, and the Social Construction of Crime: Studies in Newsmaking Criminology,* ed. Gregg Barak, 95-129. New York and London: Garland, 1994.

Chesney-Lind, Meda. "Women and Crime: The Female Offender." *Signs* 12, 1 (1986): 78-96.

Chevalier, Louis. *Laboring Classes and Dangerous Classes in Paris during the First Half of the Nineteenth Century.* New York: Howard Fertig, 1973.

Christie, Nancy, and Michael Gauvreau. *A Full-Orbed Christianity: The Protestant Churches and Social Welfare in Canada, 1900-1940.* Montreal and Kingston: McGill-Queen's University Press, 1996.

Chunn, Dorothy E. *From Punishment to Doing Good: Family Courts and Socialized Justice in Ontario, 1880-1940.* Toronto: University of Toronto Press, 1992.

Clairmont, Donald H., and Dennis William Magill. *Africville: The Life and Death of a Canadian Black Community*, rev. ed. Toronto: Canadian Scholars' Press, 1987.

Clapp, Elizabeth J. *Mothers of All Children: Women Reformers and the Rise of Juvenile Courts in Progressive Era America.* Pennsylvania: Pennsylvania State University Press, 1998.

Clarke, C.K. "Juvenile Delinquency and Mental Defect." *Canadian Journal of Mental Hygiene* 2, 3 (1920): 228-32.

Clarke, Ernest. "The Hydrostone Phoenix: Garden City Planning and the Reconstruction of Halifax, 1917-21." In *Ground Zero: A Reassessment of the 1917 Explosion in Halifax Harbour*, ed. Alan Ruffman and Colin D. Howell, 389-408. Halifax: Nimbus, 1994.

Clement, Wallace, and Glen Williams, eds. *The New Canadian Political Economy*. Kingston and Montreal: McGill-Queen's University Press, 1989.

Collins, Hugh. *Marxism and Law*. Oxford: Oxford University Press, 1981.

Colvin, Eric. "Criminal Law and the Rule of Law." In *Crime, Justice, and Codification: Essays in Commemoration of Jacques Fortin*, ed. Patrick Fitzgerald, 125-52. Toronto: Carswell Co., 1986.

Comacchio, Cynthia. "Dancing to Perdition: Adolescence and Leisure in Interwar English Canada," *Journal of Canadian Studies* 32, 3 (1997): 5-35.

–. *"Nations Are Built of Babies": Saving Ontario's Mothers and Children, 1900-1940*. Montreal and Kingston: McGill-Queen's University Press, 1993.

Comack, Elizabeth. "A Marxian Theory of Law and Crime under Capitalism: The Canadian State, Class Conflict and Drug Legislation." PhD diss., University of Alberta, 1984.

–. "'We Will Get Some Good out of This Riot Yet': The Canadian State, Drug Legislation and Class Conflict." In *The Social Basis of Law: Critical Readings in the Sociology of Law*, 2nd ed., ed. Elizabeth Comack and Stephen Brickey, 48-70. Halifax: Garamond Press, 1991.

Comack, Elizabeth, and Stephen Brickey, eds. *The Social Basis of the Law: Critical Readings in the Sociology of Law*, 2nd ed. Halifax: Garamond, 1991.

Con, Harry, Ronald J. Con, Grahma Johnson, Edgar Wickberg, and William E. Willmott. *From China to Canada: A History of the Chinese Communities in Canada*. Toronto: McClelland and Stewart, 1982.

Connor, J.T.H. "'Larger Fish to Catch Here Than Midwives': Midwifery and the Medical Profession in Nineteenth-Century Ontario." In *Caring and Curing: Historical Perspectives on Women and Healing in Canada*, ed. Dianne Dodd and Deborah Gorham, 103-34. Ottawa: University of Ottawa Press, 1994.

Conrad, Margaret, ed. *Intimate Relations: Family and Community in Planter Nova Scotia, 1759-1800*. Fredericton, NB: Acadiensis Press, 1995.

Cooper, Sheelagh. "The Evolution of the Federal Women's Prison." In *In Conflict with the Law: Women and the Canadian Justice System*, ed. Ellen Adelberg and Claudia Currie, 33-49. Vancouver: Press Gang, 1993.

Copp, Terry. *The Anatomy of Poverty: The Condition of the Working Class in Montreal, 1897-1929*. Toronto: McClelland and Stewart, 1974.

Cornell, Drucilla, Michel Rosenfeld, and David Gray Carlson, eds. *Deconstruction and the Possibility of Justice*. New York: Routledge, 1992.

Coulter, Rebecca. "'Not to Punish but to Reform': Juvenile Delinquency and Children's Protection Act in Alberta, 1909-1929." In *Studies in Childhood: A Canadian Perspective*, ed. Patricia T. Rooke and R.S. Schnell, 167-84. Calgary: Detselig, 1982.

Craven, Paul. "Law and Ideology: The Toronto Police Court, 1850-1880." In *Essays in the History of Canadian Law*, Vol. 2, ed. David H. Flaherty, 248-307. Toronto: University of Toronto Press, 1983.

Cross, Michael S. "'The Laws Are Like Cobwebs': Popular Resistance to Authority in Mid-Nineteenth-Century British North America." In *Law in a Colonial Society: The*

Nova Scotia Experience, ed. Peter Waite, Sandra Oxner, and Thomas Barnes, 103-23. Toronto: Carswell, 1984.

D'Emilio, John, and Estelle B. Freedman. *Intimate Matters: A History of Sexuality in America*. New York: Harper and Row, 1988.

Dasgupta, Satadal, ed. *Studies on Atlantic Canada*. Charlottetown: University of Prince Edward Island, 1985.

Davis, Jennifer S. "Law Breaking and Law Enforcement: The Creation of a Criminal Class in Mid-Victorian London." PhD diss., Boston College, 1984.

–. "Prosecutions and Their Context: The Use of the Criminal Law in Later Nineteenth-Century London." In *Policing and Prosecution in Britain, 1750-1850*, ed. Douglas Hay and Francis Snyder, 397-426. Oxford: Clarendon Press, 1989.

Day, Douglas, ed. *Geographical Perspectives on the Maritime Provinces*. Halifax: Atlantic Nova Print, 1988.

Derrida, Jacques. "Force of Law: The 'Mystical Foundation of Authority.'" In *Deconstruction and the Possibility of Justice*, ed. Drucilla Cornell, Michel Rosenfeld, and David Gray Carlson, 3-67. New York: Routledge, 1992.

Dickinson, John A. "Native Sovereignty and French Justice in Early Canada." In *Essays in the History of Canadian Law*. Vol. 5: *Crime and Criminal Justice*, ed. Jim Phillips, Tina Loo, and Susan Lewthwaite, 17-40. Toronto: University of Toronto Press, 1994.

Dodd, Dianne. "Women's Involvement in the Canadian Birth Control Movement of the 1930s: The Hamilton Birth Control Clinic." In *Delivering Motherhood: Maternal Ideologies and Practices in the 19th and 20th Centuries*, ed. Katherine Arnup, Andree Levesque, and Ruth Roach Pierson, 150-72. London: Routledge, 1990.

Dodd, Dianne, and Deborah Gorham, eds. *Caring and Curing: Historical Perspectives on Women and Healing in Canada*. Canada: University of Ottawa Press, 1994.

Donzelot, Jacques. *The Policing of Families*. London: Hutchinson, 1977.

Doob, Anthony, and Edward L. Greenspan, eds. *Perspectives in Criminal Law: Essays in Honour of John L.J. Edwards*. Aurora: Canada Law Books, 1985.

Doucet, Michael, and John Weaver. *Housing the North American City*. Montreal and Kingston: McGill-Queen's University Press, 1991.

Downie, Ronald J., ed. *The Supreme Court of Nova Scotia and Its Judges, 1754-1978*. Halifax: The Nova Scotia Barristers' Society, 1978.

Drystek, Henry F. "'The Simplest and Cheapest Mode of Dealing with Them': Deportation from Canada before World War II." *Histoire sociale/Social History* 15, 30 (1982): 407-41.

Dubinsky, Karen. *Improper Advances: Rape and Heterosexual Conflict in Ontario, 1880-1929*. Chicago: University of Chicago Press, 1993.

Dubinsky, Karen, and Franca Iacovetta. "Murder, Womanly Virtue, and Motherhood: The Case of Angelina Napolitano, 1911-1922." *Canadian Historical Review* 72, 4 (1991): 505-31.

Dunae, Patrick A. "Geographies of Sexual Commerce and the Production of Prostitutional Space: Victoria, British Columbia, 1860-1914. *Journal of the Canadian Historical Association* 19, 1 (2008): 115-42.

Emery, George. "British Columbia's Criminal Abortion History, 1922-1949: A Critique of the Evidence and Methods in the Work of Angus and Arlene Tigar McLaren." *BC Studies* 82 (1989): 39-60.

Emsley, Clive. *Crime and Society in England, 1750-1900*. London: Longman Group Ltd., 1987.

Emsley, Clive, and Louis A. Knafla, eds. *Crime History and Histories of Crime: Studies in the Historiography of Crime and Criminal Justice in Modern History*. Westport, CT: Greenwood Press, 1996.

Erickson, Lesley. "Murdered Women and Mythic Villains: The Criminal Case and the Imaginary Criminal in the Canadian West, 1886-1930." In *People and Place: Historical Influences on Legal Culture*, ed. Jonathan Swainger and Constance Backhouse, 95-119. Vancouver: UBC Press, 2003.

–. *Westward Bound: Sex, Violence, the Law, and the Making of a Settler Society*. Vancouver: UBC Press and the Osgoode Society for Canadian Legal History, 2011.

Erickson, Paul A. *Halifax's North End: An Anthropologist Looks at the City*. Hantsport, NS: Lancelot Press, 1987.

Fecteau, Jean-Marie. "Between the Old Order and Modern Times: Poverty, Criminality, and Power in Quebec, 1791-1840." In *Essays in the History of Canadian Law*. Vol. 5: *Crime and Criminal Justice*, ed. Jim Phillips, Tina Loo, and Susan Lewthwaite, 293-323. Toronto: University of Toronto Press, 1994.

Fierheller, John W. "Approaches to the Study of Urban Crime: A Review Article." *Urban History Review* 8, 2 (1979): 104-12.

Fine, Bob. *Democracy and the Rule of Law: Liberal Ideals and Marxist Critiques*. London: Pluto Press, 1984.

Fingard, Judith. *The Dark Side of Life in Victorian Halifax*. Porters Lake, NS: Pottersfield Press, 1989.

–. "The Prevention of Cruelty, Marriage Breakdown and the Rights of Wives in Nova Scotia, 1880-1900." *Acadiensis* 22, 2 (1993): 84-101.

–. "Race and Respectability in Victorian Halifax." *Journal of Imperial and Commonwealth History* 20, 2 (1992): 169-95.

–. "The Relief of the Unemployed Poor in Saint John, Halifax and St. John's, 1815-1860." *Acadiensis* 5, 1 (1975): 32-53.

–. "From Sea to Rail: Black Transportation Workers and Their Families in Halifax, c. 1870-1916." *Acadiensis* 24, 2 (1995): 49-64.

–. "The Winter's Tale: The Seasonal Contours of Pre-Industrial Poverty in British North America, 1815-1860." In *Interpreting Canada's Past*. Vol. 1: *Before Confederation*, ed. J.M. Bumsted, 248-72. Toronto: Oxford University Press, 1986.

Fitzgerald, Mike, Gregor McLennan, and Jennie Pawson, eds. *Crime and Society: Readings in History and Theory*. London: The Open University Press, 1981.

Fitzpatrick, Peter, ed. *Dangerous Supplements: Resistance and Renewal in Jurisprudence*. Durham: Duke University Press, 1991.

Flaherty, David H., ed. *Essays in the History of Canadian Law*, vol. 1. Toronto: University of Toronto Press, 1981.

–, ed. *Essays in the History of Canadian Law*, vol. 2. Toronto: University of Toronto Press, 1983.

Fleming, Mona W. "The Halifax Visiting Dispensary – 100 Years Old." *The Nova Scotia Medical Bulletin* 36, 3 (March 1957): 106-9.

Floud, Roderick. *An Introduction to Quantitative Methods for Historians*. Princeton, NJ: Princeton University Press, 1973.

Forbes, E.R. "The 1930s: Depression and Retrenchment." In *The Atlantic Provinces in Confederation*, ed. E.R. Forbes and D.A. Muise, 272-305. Toronto: University of Toronto Press, 1993.

Forbes, E.R., and D.A. Muise, eds. *The Atlantic Provinces in Confederation*. Toronto: University of Toronto Press, 1993.

Foster, Deanna. *A History of Hangings in Nova Scotia*. Lawrencetown Beach, NS: Pottersfield Press, 2007.

Foster, Hamar, and John McLaren, eds. *Essays in the History of Canadian Law*. Vol. 6: *British Columbia and the Yukon*. Toronto: University of Toronto Press, 1995.

Foucault, Michel. *Discipline and Punish: The Birth of the Prison*. New York: Vintage Books, 1979.

Fox, Richard G. "The Treatment of Juveniles in Canadian Criminal Law." In *Perspectives in Criminal Law: Essays in Honour of John L.J. Edwards*, ed. Anthony Doob and Edward L. Greenspan, 149-85. Aurora: Canada Law Books, 1985.

Frank, David. "The 1920s: Class and Region, Resistance and Accommodation." In *The Atlantic Provinces In Confederation*, ed. E.R. Forbes and D.A. Muise, 233-71. Toronto: University of Toronto Press, 1993.

Frankenburg, Ruth. *White Women, Race Matters: The Social Construction of Whiteness*. Minneapolis: University of Minnesota Press, 1993.

Freeman, Michael. "Plebs or Predators? Deer-Stealing in Whichwood Forest, Oxfordshire, in the Eighteenth and Nineteenth Centuries." *Social History* 21, 1 (1996): 1-21.

Friedland, M.L., ed. *Securing Compliance: Seven Case Studies*. Toronto: University of Toronto Press, 1990.

Friedman, Lawrence M. *Crime and Punishment in American History*. New York: Basic Books, 1993.

Friedman, Lawrence M., and Robert V. Percival. *The Roots of Justice: Crime and Punishment in Alameda County, California, 1870-1910*. Chapel Hill: The University of North Carolina Press, 1981.

Fryer, Bob, Alan Hunt, Doreen McBarnet, and Bert Moorhouse, eds. *Law, State and Society*. London: Croom Helm, 1981.

Gabriel, John, and Gideon Ben-Tovim. "Marxism and the Concept of Racism." *Economy and Society* 7, 2 (1978): 118-54.

Gaffield, Chad, ed. *Constructing Modern Canada: Readings in Post-Confederation History*. Toronto: Copp Clark Longman, 1994.

Gatrell, V.A.C., and T. B. Hadden. "Criminal Statistics and Their Interpretation." In *Nineteenth-Century Society: Essays in the Use of Quantitative Methods for the Study of Social Data*, ed. E.A. Wrigley, 336-96. Cambridge: Cambridge University Press, 1972.

Gavigan, Shelley, A.M. "Women's Crime: New Perspectives and Old Theories." In *In Conflict with the Law: Women and the Canadian Justice System*, ed. Ellen Adelberg and Claudia Currie, 215-34. Vancouver: Press Gang, 1993.

Giddens, Anthony. *The Consequences of Modernity*. Stanford, California: Stanford University Press, 1990.

Girard, Philip. "The Rise and Fall of Urban Justice in Halifax, 1815-1886." *Nova Scotia Historical Review* 8, 2 (1988): 57-71.

–. "The Supreme Court of Nova Scotia, Responsible Government, and the Quest for Legitimacy, 1850-1920." *Dalhousie Law Journal* 17, 2 (1994): 430-57.

Girard, Philip, and Jim Phillips, eds. *Essays in the History of Canadian Law*. Vol. 3: *Nova Scotia*. Toronto: The Osgoode Society, 1990.

Gladstone, Jane, Richard Ericson, and Clifford Shearing, eds. *Criminology: A Reader's Guide*. Toronto: Centre of Criminology, University of Toronto, 1991.

Glasbeek, Amanda. *Feminized Justice: The Toronto's Women's Court, 1913-1934*. Vancouver: UBC Press, 2009.

Gogan, Tanya. "'A Picturesque Lot': The Gypsies in Peterborough." *Beaver* 78, 5 (1998): 25-30.

Golz, Annalee, E. "'If a Man's Wife Does Not Obey Him, What Can He Do?' Marital Breakdown and Wife Abuse in Late Nineteenth-Century and Early Twentieth-Century Ontario." In *Law, Society, and the State: Essays in Modern Legal History*, ed. Louis A. Knafla and Susan W.S. Binnie, 323-50. Toronto: University of Toronto Press, 1995.

Gordon, George Nicol. *Halifax: "Its Sins and Sorrows."* Halifax: Conference Job Printing Office, 1862.

–. *The Lost Martyrs of Eromanga: Being a Memoir of the Rev. George N. Gordon and Ellen Catherine Powell, His Wife*. Halifax: MacNab and Shaffer, 1863.

Gordon, Linda. "Family Violence, Feminism, and Social Control." In *Crime and Justice in American History*. Vol. 9: *Violence and Theft*, pt. 1, ed. Eric H. Monkkonen, 257-83. Munich: K.G. Saur, 1992.

Gorham, Deborah. "The 'Maiden Tribute of Modern Babylon' Re-Examined: Child Prostitution and the Idea of Childhood in Late Victorian England." *Victorian Studies* 21, 3 (1978): 353-79.

Gottfredson, Michael R., and Travis Hirschi. *A General Theory of Crime*. Stanford, CA: Stanford University Press, 1990.

Graff, Harvey J. "Crime and Punishment in the Nineteenth Century: A New Look at the Criminal." *Journal of Interdisciplinary History* 7, 3 (1977): 477-91.

Greenberg, David F. *Crime and Capitalism: Readings in Marxist Criminology*. California: Mayfield Publishing Company, 1981.

Greenwood, F. Murray, and Beverley Boissery. *Uncertain Justice: Canadian Women and Capital Punishment, 1754-1953*. Toronto: Dundurn Press, 2000.

Greer, Allan. "The Birth of the Police in Canada." In *Colonial Leviathan: State Formation in Mid-Nineteenth-Century Canada*, ed. Allan Greer and Ian Radforth, 17-49. Toronto: University of Toronto Press, 1992.

Greer, Allan, and Ian Radforth, eds. *Colonial Leviathan: State Formation in Mid-Nineteenth-Century Canada*. Toronto: University of Toronto Press, 1992.

Guildford, Janet, and Suzanne Morton, eds. *Separate Spheres: Women's Worlds in the 19th-Century Maritimes*. Fredericton, NB: Acadiensis Press, 1994.

Gurr, Ted Robert. *Rouges, Rebels, and Reformers: A Political History of Urban Crime and Conflict*. London: Sage, 1976.

Hall, Roger, William Westfall, and Laurel Sefton MacDowell, eds. *Patterns of the Past: Interpreting Ontario's History*. Toronto: Dundurn, 1988.

Hall, Stuart, Chas Critcher, Tony Jefferson, John N. Clarke, and Brian Roberts. *Policing the Crisis: Mugging, the State, and Law and Order*. New York: Holmes and Meier, 1978.

Hannant, Larry. *The Infernal Machine: Investigating the Loyalty of Canada's Citizens*. Toronto: University of Toronto Press, 1995.

Harney, Robert F. "Ambiente and Social Class in North American Little Italies." *Canadian Review of Studies in Nationalism* 2, 2 (1975): 208-24.

Harring, Sidney L. *Policing a Class Society: The Experience of American Cities, 1865-1915*. New Brunswick, NJ: Rutgers University Press, 1983.

Harris, Ruth. *Murder and Madness: Medicine, Law, and Society in the Fin de Siècle*. New York: Oxford University Press, 1989.

Hartlen, John. "Rockhead Prison." *Atlantic Advocate* 69, 12 (1979): 41-42 and 45.

Harvey, Kathryn. "Amazons and Victims: Resisting Wife Abuse in Working-Class Montreal, 1869-1879." *Journal of the Canadian Historical Association* 2, 1 (1991): 131-48.

Hatfield, Leonard F. *Sammy the Prince: The Story of Samuel Henry Prince, One of Canada's Pioneering Sociologists*. Hantsport, NS: Lancelot Press, 1990.

Hawkins, Darnell F., ed. *Ethnicity, Race, and Crime: Perspectives across Time and Place*. Albany: State University of New York Press, 1995.

Hay, Douglas. "Property, Authority and the Criminal Law." In *Albion's Fatal Tree: Crime and Society in Eighteenth-Century England*, ed. Douglas Hay, Peter Linebaugh, John G. Rule, E.P. Thompson, and Cal Winslow, 17-63. New York: Penguin Books, 1975.

Hay, Douglas, and Francis Snyder, eds. *Policing and Prosecution in Britain, 1750-1850*. Oxford: Clarendon Press, 1989.

Hay, Douglas, Peter Linebaugh, John G. Rule, E.P. Thompson, and Cal Winslow, eds. *Albion's Fatal Tree: Crime and Society in Eighteenth-Century England*. New York: Penguin Books, Ltd., 1975.

Heidensohn, Frances. *Crime and Society*. London: Macmillan Education Ltd., 1989.

Heller, Agnes. "Rights, Modernity, Democracy." In *Deconstruction and the Possibility of Justice*, ed. Drucilla Cornell, Michel Rosenfeld, and David Gray Carlson, 346-60. New York: Routledge, 1992.

Henderson, Rose. "The Juvenile Court." *Canadian Municipal Journal* 12 (1916): 84.

Henry, Frances. *Forgotten Canadians: The Blacks of Nova Scotia*. Don Mills: Longman Canada, 1973.

Hobsbawm, E.J. *Primitive Rebels: Studies in Archaic Forms of Social Movement in the 19th and 20th Centuries*. New York: W.W. Norton and Company, 1959.

Hobson, Barbara Meil. *Uneasy Virtue: The Politics of Prostitution and the American Reform Tradition*. New York: Basic Books, 1987.

Hodgins, Murray B. "A City Transformed? Urban Development and the Role of Canadian Railway Policy In Halifax, Nova Scotia, 1900-1920." MA thesis, Dalhousie University, 1992.

Hofstadter, Richard. *The Age of Reform: From Bryan to F.D.R.* New York: Vintage Books, 1955.

Homel, Gene Howard. "Denison's Law: Criminal Justice and the Police Court in Toronto, 1877-1921." *Ontario History* 73, 3 (1981): 171-86.

Hood, David. *Down but Not Out: Community and the Upper Streets in Halifax, 1890-1914*. Halifax: Fernwood, 2010.

Hopkins, Ernest Jerome. "How Canada Curbs Crime." *The Rotarian* 45, 4 (October 1934): 9-11 and 50-52.

Houston, Susan E. "The Role of the Criminal Law in Redefining 'Youth' in Mid-Nineteenth-Century Upper Canada." *Historical Studies in Education* 6, 3 (1994): 39-55.

–. "Victorian Origins of Juvenile Delinquency: A Canadian Experience." *History of Education Quarterly* 12, 3 (1972): 254-80.

Howell, Colin D. *A Century of Care: A History of the Victoria General Hospital in Halifax, 1887-1987*. Halifax: Victoria General Hospital, 1988.

–. "Medical Professionalization and the Social Transformation of the Maritimes, 1850-1950." *Journal of Canadian Studies* 27, 1 (1992): 5-20.

–. "Reform and the Monopolistic Impulse: The Professionalization of Medicine in the Maritimes." *Acadiensis* 11, 1 (1981): 3-22.

Hunt, Alan. "Marxism, Law, Legal Theory and Jurisprudence." In Peter Fitzpatrick, ed., *Dangerous Supplements: Resistance and Renewal in Jurisprudence*, 102-32. Durham: Duke University Press, 1991.

Hurl, Lorna F., and David J. Tucker. "The Michigan County Agents and the Development of Juvenile Probation, 1873-1900." *Journal of Social History* 30, 4 (1997): 905-35.

Huzel, James P. "The Incidence of Crime in Vancouver during the Great Depression." In *Vancouver Past: Essays in Social History*, ed. Robert A.J. McDonald and Jean Barman, 211-48. Vancouver: UBC Press, 1986.

Iacovetta, Franca. *Such Hardworking People: Italian Immigrants in Postwar Toronto*. Montreal and Kingston: McGill-Queen's University Press, 1992.

Ignatieff, Michael. *A Just Measure of Pain: The Penitentiary in the Industrial Revolution, 1750-1850*. London: Penguin Books, 1978.

–. "State, Civil Society and Total Institution: A Critique of Recent Social Histories of Punishment." In *Legality, Ideology, and the State*, ed. David Sugarman, 183-211. London: Academic Press, 1983.

Inglis, Judge R.E., and R.W. Kane. *Halifax Association for Improving the Conditions of the Poor*. Halifax: Halifax Association for Improving the Conditions of the Poor, 1981.

Innes, Joanna, and John Styles. "The Crime Wave: Recent Writing on Crime and Criminal Justice in Eighteenth-Century England." In *Rethinking Social History: English Society 1570-1920 and Its Interpretation*, ed. Adrian Wilson, 201-65. Manchester: Manchester University Press, 1993.

Inwood, Kris. "Maritime Industrialization from 1870 to 1910: A Review of the Evidence and Its Interpretation." *Acadiensis* 21, 1 (1991): 132-55.

Inwood, Kris, and John Chamard. "Regional Industrial Growth during the 1890s: The Case of the Missing Artisans." *Acadiensis* 16, 1 (1986): 101-17.

Jacobson, Miriam. *A Better Deal for Children: An Historical Study of the Children's Aid Society of Halifax*. Halifax: Department of Social Services, 1971.

Jaquays, Emily. "What Is Our Mental Attitude to the Delinquent Girl?" *Social Welfare* 9, 6 (1927): 378 and 384.

Jeffrey, Leslie Ann, and Gayle MacDonald. *Talk Back: Sex Workers in the Maritimes*. Vancouver: UBC Press, 2006.

Jobb, Dean. *Bluenose Justice: True Tales of Mischief, Mayhem, and Murder*. Lawrencetown Beach, NS: Pottersfield Press, 1993.

–. *Crime Wave: Con Men, Rogues, and Scoundrels from Nova Scotia's Past*. Lawrencetown Beach, NS: Pottersfield Press, 1991.

–. *Shades of Justice: Seven Nova Scotia Murder Cases*. Halifax: Nimbus, 1988.

Johnson, Holly, and Karen Rodgers. "A Statistical Overview of Women and Crime in Canada." In *In Conflict with the Law: Women and the Canadian Justice System*, ed. Ellen Adelberg and Claudia Currie, 95-116. Vancouver: Press Gang, 1993.

Jones, Andrew. "'Closing Penetanguishene Reformatory': An Attempt to Deinstitutionalize Treatment of Juvenile Offenders in Early Twentieth-Century Ontario." In *Lawful Authority: Readings on the History of Criminal Justice in Canada*, ed. R.C. Macleod, 277-92. Toronto: Copp Clark Pitman Ltd., 1988.

Jones, Gareth Stedman. *Outcast London: A Study in the Relationship between Classes in Victorian Society*. London: Penguin Books, 1984.

Katz, Michael B., Michael J. Doucet, and Mark J. Stern. *The Social Organization of Early Industrial Capitalism*. Cambridge, MA: Harvard University Press, 1982.

Keller, Morton. *Regulating a New Society: Public Policy and Social Change in America, 1900-1933*. Cambridge, MA: Harvard University Press, 1994.

Keshen, Jeffrey. "Wartime Jitters over Juveniles: Canada's Delinquency Scare and Its Consequences, 1939-1945." In *Age of Contention: Readings in Canadian Social History, 1900-1945*, ed. Jeffrey Keshen, 364-86. Toronto: Harcourt Brace, 1997.

Kidman, John. *The Canadian Prison: The Story of Tragedy*. Toronto: The Ryerson Press, 1947.

–. "Nova Scotia's Jails." *Social Welfare* 15, 3 (June 1934): 47 and 52.

–. "Nova Scotia's Jails." *Social Welfare* 15, 4 (September 1934): 67-68.

–. "Prison Farms." *Proceedings of the Twenty-Ninth Annual Convention of the Union of Nova Scotia Municipalities*, 1934, 68-79.

Kimball, Roy Edward. *The Bench: The History of Nova Scotia's Provincial Courts*. Halifax: Nova Scotia Department of Government Services, 1989.

–. "The Provincial Court of Nova Scotia: The Struggle for Excellence." LLM thesis, Dalhousie University, 1987.

Kimber, Steve. "The Halifax Gambling Scene Isn't What It Used to Be." *4th Estate*, 22 June 1972.

King, Peter, and Joan Noel. "The Origins of 'The Problem of Juvenile Delinquency': The Growth of Juvenile Prosecutions in London in the Late Eighteenth and Early Nineteenth Centuries." *Criminal Justice History* 14 (1993): 17-41.

Kitz, Janet F. *Shattered City: The Halifax Explosion and the Road to Recovery*. Halifax: Nimbus, 1989.

Klausen, Susanne. "Doctors and Dying Declarations: The Role of the State in Abortion Regulation in British Columbia, 1917-37." *Canadian Bulletin of Medical History* 13 (1996): 53-81.

Knafla, Louis A., ed. *Crime and Criminal Justice in Europe and Canada*. Waterloo: Wilfrid Laurier University Press, 1981.

–, ed. *Law and Justice in a New Land: Essays in Western Canadian Legal History*. Toronto: Carswell, 1986.

Knafla, Louis A., and Susan W.S. Binnie, eds. *Law, Society, and the State: Essays in Modern Legal History*. Toronto: University of Toronto Press, 1995.

Kramar, Kirsten Johnson. *Unwilling Mothers, Unwanted Babies: Infanticide in Canada*. Vancouver: UBC Press, 2005.

Kumar, Krishan. "Civil Society: An Inquiry into the Usefulness of an Historical Term." *British Journal of Sociology* 44, 3 (1993): 375-95.

Lachance, Andre. "Women and Crime in Canada in the Early Eighteenth Century, 1712-1759." In *Lawful Authority: Readings on the History of Criminal Justice in Canada*, ed. R.C. Macleod, 9-21. Toronto: Copp Clark Pitman Ltd., 1988.

Lafferty, Reneé. "Modernity and the Denominational Imperative: The Children's Aid Society of Halifax, 1905-1925." *Journal of the Canadian Historical Association* 13, 1 (2002), 95-118.

Lai, David Chuenyan. *Chinatowns: Towns within Cities in Canada*. Vancouver: UBC Press, 1988.

Langdon, M. Elizabeth. "Female Crime in Calgary, 1914-1941." In *Law and Justice in a New Land: Essays in Western Canadian Legal History*, ed. Louis A. Knafla, 293-312. Toronto: Carswell, 1986.

Larsen, E. Nick. "Canadian Prostitution Control between 1914 and 1970: An Exercise in Chauvinist Reasoning." *Canadian Journal of Law and Society* 7, 2 (1992): 137-56.

Latham, Barbara, and Cathy Kees, eds. *In Her Own Right: Selected Essays on Women's History in BC*. Victoria: Camosun College, 1980.

Lee, Ronald. *Goddam Gypsy: An Autobiographical Novel*. Montreal: Tundra Books, 1971.

Leslie, Genevieve. "Domestic Service in Canada, 1880-1920." In *Women at Work: Ontario, 1850-1930*, ed. Janice Acton, Penny Goldsmith, and Bonnie Shepard, 71-125. Toronto: Canadian Women's Educational Press, 1974.

Levesque, Andree. *Making and Breaking the Rules: Women in Quebec, 1919-1939*. Toronto: McClelland and Stewart, 1994.

Levine, Philippa. "Rough Usage: Prostitution, Law, and the Social Historian." In *Rethinking Social History: English Society, 1570-1920, and Its Interpretation*, ed. Adrian Wilson, 266-92. Manchester: Manchester University Press, 1993.

–. "'Walking the Streets in a Way No Decent Woman Should': Women Police in World War I." *Journal of Modern History* 66 (1994): 34-78.

–. "Women and Prostitution: Myth, Reality, History." *Canadian Journal of History* 28 (1993): 479-94.

Lewthwaite, Susan. "Violence, Law, and Community in Rural Upper Canada." In *Essays in the History of Canadian Law*. Vol. 5: *Crime and Criminal Justice*, ed. Jim Phillips, Tina Loo, and Susan Lewthwaite, 353-86. Toronto: University of Toronto Press, 1994.

Leyton, Elliott, William O'Grady, and James Overton. *Violence and Public Anxiety: A Canadian Case*. St. John's: Institute of Social and Economic Research, Memorial University of Newfoundland, 1992.

Leyton-Brown, Ken. *The Practice of Execution in Canada*. Vancouver: UBC Press, 2010.

Li, Peter S. *The Chinese In Canada*. Toronto: Oxford University Press, 1988.

Light, Ivan. "From Vice District to Tourist Attraction: The Moral Career of American Chinatowns, 1880-1940." In *Crime and Justice in American History*. Vol. 8: *Prostitution, Drugs, Gambling and Organized Crime*, pt. 2, ed. Eric Monkkonen, 550-77. Munich: K.G. Saur, 1992.

Linebaugh, Peter. *The London Hanged: Crime and Civil Society in the Eighteenth Century*. London: Allen Lane, 1991.

Loo, Tina. *Making Law, Order, and Authority in British Columbia, 1821-1871*. Toronto: University of Toronto Press, 1994.

Loo, Tina, and Lorna R. McLean, eds. *Historical Perspectives on Law and Society in Canada*. Toronto: Copp Clark Longman, 1994.

MacDonald, Colonel J. Welsford. "The Grand Jury in Nova Scotia." In *Proceedings of the Twenty-Ninth Annual Convention of the Union of Nova Scotia Municipalities, 1934*. Halifax: 1934.

MacLennan, Hugh. *Barometer Rising*. Toronto: McClelland and Stewart, 1941.

Macleod, R.C. "The Shaping of Canadian Criminal Law, 1892 to 1902." *Canadian Historical Association – Historical Papers* 13, 1 (1978): 64-75.

–, ed. *Lawful Authority: Readings on the History of Criminal Justice in Canada*. Toronto: Copp Clark Pitman, 1988.

Macleod, R.C., and David Schneiderman, eds. *Police Powers in Canada: The Evolution and Practice of Authority*. Toronto: University of Toronto Press, 1994.

Magarey, Susan. "The Invention of Juvenile Delinquency in Early Nineteenth-Century England." *Labour History* 34 (1978): 11-27.

Mahood, Linda. *Policing Gender, Class, and Family: Britain, 1850-1940*. London: UCL Press, 1995.

Mann, Caroline Caverhill. "'It Pays to Be Good': An Exploration of the Maritime Home for Girls and the Interprovincial Home for Young Women, 1914-1931." MA thesis, Dalhousie University, 2007.

March, William. *Red Line: The Chronicle-Herald and the Mail-Star, 1875-1954*. Halifax: Chebucto Agencies, 1986.

Marquis, Greg. "Doing Justice to 'British Justice': Law, Ideology and Canadian Historiography." In *Canadian Perspectives on Law and Society: Issues In Legal History*, ed. W. Wesley Pue and Barry Wright, 43-69. Ottawa: Carleton University Press, 1988.

–. "The History of Policing in the Maritime Provinces: Themes and Prospects." *Urban History Review* 19, 1 (1990), 84-99.

–. "Law, Society and History: Whose Frontier?" *Acadiensis* 21, 2 (1992): 162-74.

–. "'A Machine of Oppression under the Guise of the Law': The Saint John Police Establishment." *Acadiensis* 16, 1 (1986): 58-77.

–. "The Police as a Social Service in Early Twentieth-Century Toronto." *Histoire sociale/Social History* 25, 50 (1992): 335-58.

–. "Police Unionism in Early Twentieth-Century Toronto." *Ontario History* 81, 2 (1989): 109-28.

–. *Policing Canada's Century: A History of the Canadian Association of Chiefs of Police*. Toronto: University of Toronto Press, 1993.

–. "Power from the Street: The Canadian Municipal Police." In *Police Powers in Canada: The Evolution and Practice of Authority*, ed. R.C Macleod and David Schneiderman, 24-43. Toronto: University of Toronto Press, 1994.

–. "The Technology of Professionalism: The Identification of Criminals in Early Twentieth-Century Canada." *Criminal Justice History* 15 (1994): 165-88.

–. "Towards a Canadian Police Historiography." In *Law, Society, and the State: Essays in Modern Legal History*, ed. Louis A. Knafla and Susan W.S. Binnie, 477-96. Toronto: University of Toronto Press, 1995.

–. "Vancouver Vice: The Police and the Negotiation of Morality, 1904-1935." In *Essays in the History of Canadian Law*. Vol. 6: *British Columbia and the Yukon*, ed. Hamar Foster and John McLaren, 242-73. Toronto: University of Toronto Press, 1995.

–. "Working Men in Uniform: The Early Twentieth-Century Toronto Police." *Histoire sociale/Social History* 20, 40 (1987): 259-78.

Marx, Karl. *Theories of Surplus Value,* vol. 1. Moscow: Foreign Languages Publishing House, 1969.

Matters, Diane L. "The Boys' Industrial School: Education for Juvenile Offenders." In *Schooling and Society in Twentieth Century British Columbia*, ed. Donald Wilson and David C. Jones, 53-70. Calgary: Detselig, 1980.

Maynard, Kimberley Smith. "Divorce in Nova Scotia, 1750-1890." In *Essays in the History of Canadian Law.* Vol. 3: *Nova Scotia*, ed. Philip Girard and Jim Phillips, 232-72. Canada: The Osgoode Society, 1990.

Maynard, Steven. "Through a Hole in the Lavatory Wall: Homosexual Subcultures, Police Surveillance, and the Dialectics of Discovery, Toronto, 1890-1930." *Journal of the History of Sexuality* 5, 2 (1994): 207-42.

McCann, L.D. "'Living a Double Life': Town and Country in the Industrialization of the Maritimes." In *Geographical Perspectives on the Maritime Provinces,* ed. Douglas Day, 93-113. Halifax: Atlantic Nova Print, 1988.

McClintock, F.H. "The Dark Figure of Crime." In *Crime and Justice.* Vol. 1: *The Criminal in Society*, 2nd and rev. ed., ed. Sir Leon Radinowicz and Marvin E. Wolfgang, 126-39. New York: Basic Books, 1971.

McConville, Mike, Andrew Sanders, and Roger Leng. *The Case for the Prosecution.* London: Routledge, 1991.

McCormick, Chris, ed. *Constructing Danger: The Mis/representation of Crime in the News.* Halifax: Fernwood, 1995.

McDonald, Robert A.J., and Jean Barman, eds. *Vancouver Past: Essays in Social History.* Vancouver: UBC Press, 1986.

McGahan, Peter. "Crime and Policing in Late Nineteenth-Century Halifax." Atlantic Institute of Criminology, Report 5 (1989).

–. *Crime and Policing in Maritime Canada: Chapters from the Urban Records.* Fredericton, NB: Goose Lane, 1988.

–. "Detective Nick Power and the Halifax Police Department, Early 1900s." Atlantic Institute of Criminology, Report 8 (1989).

–. "Halifax Police Department, 1919-1924." Atlantic Institute of Criminology, Report 14 (1989).

–. *Killers, Thieves, Tramps and Sinners.* Fredericton, NB: Goose Lane, 1989.

–. "The Police Commission and the Halifax 'Guardians,' 1925-1931." Atlantic Institute of Criminology, Report 10 (1989).

–. "Reconstructing Patterns of Crime in Halifax and Saint John: A Preliminary Historical Analysis." In *Dimensions of Communities: A Research Handbook*, ed. Dan A. Chekki, 179-226. New York and London: Garland, 1989.

McKay, Ian. "The 1910s: The Stillborn Triumph of Progressive Reform." In *The Atlantic Provinces in Confederation*, ed. E.R. Forbes and D.A. Muise, 192-229. Toronto: University of Toronto Press, 1993.

–. "Capital and Labour in the Halifax Baking and Confectionary Industry during the Last Half of the Nineteenth Century." *Labour/Le Travailleur* 3 (1978): 63-108.

–. "Class Struggle and Merchant Capital: Craftsmen and Labourers on the Halifax Waterfront, 1850-1902." In *The Character of Class Struggle: Essays in Canadian Working-Class History, 1850-1985*, 17-36. Bryan D. Palmer, ed. Toronto: McClelland and Stewart, 1986.

–. *The Craft Transformed: An Essay on the Carpenters of Halifax, 1885-1985*. Halifax: Holdfast Press, 1985.

–. "The Discrete Charm of the Halifax Bourgeoisie." *New Maritimes* 4, 7 (1986): 14-15.

–. "Strikes in the Maritimes, 1901-1914." *Acadiensis* 13, 1 (1983): 3-46.

McKay, Ian, and Robin Bates. *In the Province of History: The Making of the Public Past in Twentieth-Century Nova Scotia*. Montreal and Kingston: McGill-Queen's University Press, 2010.

McLaren, Angus. "Illegal Operations: Women, Doctors, and Abortion, 1886-1939." *Journal of Social History* 26, 4 (1993): 797-816.

–. *Our Own Master Race: Eugenics in Canada, 1885-1945*. Toronto: McClelland and Stewart, 1990.

– . *A Prescription for Murder: The Victorian Serial Killings of Dr. Thomas Neill Cream*. Chicago and London: University of Chicago Press, 1993.

McLaren, Angus, and Arlene Tigar McLaren. *The Bedroom and the State: The Changing Practices and Politics of Contraception and Abortion in Canada, 1880-1980*. Toronto: McClelland and Stewart, 1986.

–. "Discoveries and Dissimulations: The Impact of Abortion Deaths on Maternal Morality in British Columbia." *BC Studies* 64 (1984-85): 3-26.

– . "'The Forest and the Trees': A Response to George Emery." *BC Studies* 82 (1989): 61-64.

McLaren, John. "Chasing the Social Evil: Moral Fervour and the Evolution of Canada's Prostitution Laws, 1867-1914." *Canadian Journal of Law and Society* 1 (1986): 125-65.

– . "Race and the Criminal Justice System in British Columbia, 1892-1920: Constructing Chinese Crimes." In *Essays in the History of Canadian Law*. Vol. 3: *In Honour of R.C.B. Risk*, ed. G. Blaine Baker and Jim Phillips, 398-442. Toronto: University of Toronto Press, 1999.

– . "White Slavers: The Reform of Canada's Prostitution Laws and Patterns of Enforcement, 1900-1920." *Criminal Justice History* 8 (1987): 53-119.

McLaren, John, and John Lowman. "Enforcing Canada's Prostitution Laws, 1892-1920: Rhetoric and Practice." In *Securing Compliance: Seven Case Studies*, ed. M.L. Friedland, 21-87. Toronto: University of Toronto Press, 1990.

McMullan, John L. "Crime, Law, and Order in Early Modern England." *British Journal of Criminology* 27, 3 (1987): 252-74.

–. "The 'Law and Order' Problem in Socialist Criminology." *Studies in Political Economy* 21 (1986): 175-92.

Mennel, Robert M. *Thorns and Thistles: Juvenile Delinquents in the United States, 1825-1940*. Hanover, NH: The University Press of New England, 1973.

Merrill, Maud A. "Feeble-Mindedness and Crime." *Dalhousie Review* 1, 4 (1922): 360-68.

Messerschmidt, James W. *Capitalism, Patriarchy, and Crime: Towards a Socialist Feminist Criminology*. Totowa, NJ: Rowman and Littlefield, 1986.

Mewett, Alan W. "The Criminal Law, 1867-1967." In *Lawful Authority: Readings on the History of Criminal Justice in Canada*, ed. R.C. Macleod, 155-66. Toronto: Copp Clark Pitman, 1988.

Miller, Carman. "The 1940s: War and Rehabilitation." In *The Atlantic Provinces in Confederation*, ed. E.R. Forbes and D.A. Muise, 306-45. Toronto: University of Toronto Press, 1993.

Miller, Janice H. "Halifax, Nova Scotia: A Study of the Effects of Disaster upon Urban Morphology." In *Ground Zero: A Reassessment of the 1917 Explosion in Halifax Harbour*, ed. Alan Ruffman and Colin D. Howell, 409-20. Halifax: Nimbus, 1994.

Mitchell, V.W. "Halifax Police Department: A Brief History of Canada's Oldest Constabulary." *RCMP Quarterly* 30, 4 (1965): 3-8.

Mitchinson, Wendy. *Giving Birth in Canada, 1900-1950*. Toronto: University of Toronto Press, 2002.

–. *The Nature of Their Bodies: Women and Their Doctors in Victorian Canada*. Toronto: University of Toronto Press, 1991.

Monkkonen, Eric H. *The Dangerous Class: Crime and Poverty in Columbus, Ohio, 1860-1885*. Cambridge, MA: Harvard University Press, 1975.

–, ed. *Crime and Justice in American History.* Vol. 8: *Prostitution, Drugs, Gambling and Organized Crime,* pt. 2. Munich: K.G. Saur, 1992.

–, ed. *Crime and Justice in American History:* Vol. 9: *Violence and Theft,* pt. 1. Munich: K.G. Saur, 1992.

Morel, Andre. "Canadian Legal History: Retrospect and Prospect." *Osgoode Hall Law Journal* 21, 2 (1983): 159-64.

Morrison, Wayne. *Theoretical Criminology: From Modernity to Post-Modernism*. London: Cavendish Publishing, 1995.

Morton, Desmond. "'Kicking and Complaining': Demobilization Riots in the Canadian Expeditionary Force, 1918-19." *Canadian Historical Review* 61, 3 (1980): 334-60.

Morton, Desmond, and Glenn Wright. *Winning the Second Battle: Canadian Veterans and the Return to Civilian Life, 1915-1930*. Toronto: University of Toronto Press, 1987.

Morton, Suzanne. *Ideal Surroundings: Domestic Life in a Working-Class Suburb in the 1920s*. Toronto: University of Toronto Press, 1995.

–. "'Never Handmaidens': The Victorian Order of Nurses and the Massachusetts-Halifax Health Commission." In *Ground Zero: A Reassessment of the 1917 Explosion in Halifax Harbour*, ed. Alan Ruffman and Colin D. Howell, 195-205. Halifax: Nimbus, 1994.

–. *At Odds: Gambling and Canadians, 1919-1969*. Toronto: University of Toronto Press, 2003.

– . "Separate Spheres in a Separate World: African-Nova Scotian Women in Late 19th-Century Halifax County." *Acadiensis* 22, 2 (1993): 61-83.

– . "Women on Their Own: Single Mothers in Working-Class Halifax in the 1920s." *Acadiensis* 21, 2 (1992): 90-107.

Mosher, Clayton James. *Discrimination and Denial: Systemic Racism in Ontario's Legal and Criminal Justice Systems, 1892-1961*. Toronto: University of Toronto Press, 1998.

Muise, D.A. "The Industrial Context of Inequality: Female Participation in Nova Scotia's Paid Labour Force, 1871-1921." *Acadiensis* 20, 2 (1991): 3-31.

Munro, John A. "British Columbia and the 'Chinese Evil': Canada's First Anti-Asiatic Immigration Law." *Journal of Canadian Studies* 6, 4 (1971): 42-51.

Murphy, Emily F. *The Black Candle*. Toronto: Coles, 1973 [Thomas Allen, 1922].

Murray, Glenn F. "Cocaine Use in the Era of Social Reform: The Natural History of a Social Problem in Canada, 1890-1911." *Canadian Journal of Law and Society* 2 (1987): 29-43.

Myers, Martha A. "The New South's 'New' Black Criminal: Rape and Punishment in Georgia, 1870-1940." In *Ethnicity, Race, and Crime: Perspectives across Time and Place*, ed. Darnell F. Hawkins, 145-66. Albany: State University of New York Press, 1995.

Myers, Sharon. "The Apocrypha of Minnie McGee: The Murderous Mother and the Multivocal State in 20th-Century Prince Edward Island." *Acadiensis* 38, 2 (Summer 2009): 5-28.

–. "'Not to Be Ranked as Women': Female Industrial Workers in Turn-of-the-Century Halifax." In *Separate Spheres: Women's Worlds in the 19th-Century Maritimes*, ed. Janet Guildford and Suzanne Morton, 161-83. Fredericton, NB: Acadiensis Press, 1994.

–. "Revenge and Revolt: The Boys' Industrial Home of East Saint John in the Inter-War Period." In *Children's Voices in Atlantic Literature and Culture: Essays on Childhood*, ed. Hilary Thompson, 104-13. Guelph: Canadian Children's Press, 1995.

Myers, Tamara. *Caught: Montreal's Modern Girls and the Law, 1869-1945*. Toronto: University of Toronto Press, 2006.

–. "Embodying Delinquency: Boys' Bodies, Sexuality, and Juvenile Justice in Early Twentieth-Century Quebec," *Journal of the History of Sexuality* 14, 4 (2005): 383-414.

–. "Women Policing Women: A Patrol Woman in Montreal in the 1910s." *Journal of the Canadian Historical Association* 4, 1 (1993): 229-45.

Nelson, Jennifer J. "'Panthers or Thieves': Racialized Knowledge and the Regulation of Africville." *Journal of Canadian Studies* 45, 1 (2011): 121-42.

–. *Razing Africville: A Geography of Racism*. Toronto: University of Toronto Press, 2008.

Newton, Janice. *The Feminist Challenge to the Canadian Left, 1900-1918*. Montreal and Kingston: McGill-Queen's University Press, 1995.

Nilsen, Deborah. "The 'Social Evil': Prostitution in Vancouver, 1900-1920." In *In Her Own Right: Selected Essays on Women's History in BC*, ed. Barbara Latham and Cathy Kess, 205-28. Victoria: Camosun College, 1980.

Norton, Judith A. "The Dark Side of Planter Life: Reported Cases of Domestic Violence." In *Intimate Relations: Family and Community in Planter Nova Scotia, 1759-1800*, ed. Margaret Conrad, 182-89. Fredericton, NB: Acadiensis Press, 1995.

Ogden, H.R. "Halifax Carries On." *Social Welfare* 13, 6 (1931): 124.

Oliver, Peter. "'To Govern by Kindness': The First Two Decades of the Mercer Reformatory for Women." In *Essays in the History of Canadian Law.* Vol. 5: *Crime and Criminal Justice,* ed. Jim Phillips, Tina Loo, and Susan Lewthwaite, 516-72. Toronto: University of Toronto Press, 1994.

–. *"Terror to Evil-Doers": Prisons and Punishments in Nineteenth-Century Ontario*. Toronto: University of Toronto Press, 1998.

Overton, James. "Riots, Raids and Relief, Police, Prisons and Parsimony: The Political Economy of Public Order in Newfoundland in the 1930s." In *Violence and Public Anxiety: A Canadian Case*, ed. Elliott Leyton, William O'Grady, and James Overton, 195-334. St. John's: Institute of Social and Economic Research, Memorial University of Newfoundland, 1992.

Pachai, Bridglal. *Beneath the Clouds of the Promised Land: The Survival of Nova Scotia's Blacks*. Vol. 2: *1800-1989*. Halifax: The Black Educators Association, 1990.

Palmer, Bryan D., ed. *The Character of Class Struggle: Essays in Canadian Working-Class History, 1850-1985*. Toronto: McClelland and Stewart, 1986.

Palmer, Howard. *Patterns of Prejudice: A History of Nativism in Alberta*. Toronto: McClelland and Stewart, 1982.

Papke, David Ray. *Framing the Criminal: Crime, Cultural Work, and the Loss of Critical Perspective, 1830-1900*. Hamden, CT: Archon Books, 1987.

Parker, Graham. "Canadian Legal Culture." In *Law and Justice in a New Land: Essays in Western Canadian Legal History*, ed, Louis A. Knafla, 3-29. Toronto: Carswell, 1986.

Parr, Joy, ed. *Childhood and Family in Canadian History*. Toronto: McClelland and Stewart, 1988.

Parr, Joy, and Mark Rosenfeld, eds. *Gender and History in Canada*. Toronto: Copp Clark, 1996.

Pearson, Geoffrey. *Hooligan: A History of Respectable Fears*. New York: Schocken Books, 1984.

Pedersen, Diana. "'Keeping Our Good Girls Good': The YWCA and the 'Girl Problem,' 1870-1930." *Canadian Woman Studies* 7, 4 (1986): 20-24.

Penny, Tracy. "'Getting Rid of My Trouble': A Social History of Abortion in Ontario, 1880-1929." MA thesis, Laurentian University, 1995.

Pfeifer, Michael J. *Rough Justice: Lynching and American Society, 1874-1947*. Urbana: University of Illinois Press, 2004.

Phillips, Jim. "Crime and Punishment in the Dominion of the North: Canada from New France to the Present." In *Crime History and Histories of Crime: Studies in the Historiography of Crime and Criminal Justice in Modern History*, ed. Clive Emsley and Louis A. Knafla, 163-99. Westport, CT: Greenwood Press, 1996.

–. "The History of Canadian Criminal Justice, 1750-1920." In *Criminology: A Reader's Guide*, ed. Jane Gladstone, Richard Ericson, and Clifford Shearing, 65-124. Toronto: Centre of Criminology, University of Toronto, 1991.

–. "Poverty, Unemployment, and the Administration of the Criminal Law: Vagrancy Laws in Halifax, 1864-1890." In *Essays in the History of Canadian Law*. Vol. 3: *Nova Scotia,* ed. Philip Girard and Jim Phillips, 128-62. Toronto: The Osgoode Society, 1990.

–. "'Securing Obedience to Necessary Laws': The Criminal Law in Eighteenth-Century Nova Scotia." *Nova Scotia Historical Review* 12, 2 (1992): 87-124.

–. "Why Legal History Matters." *Victoria University Wellington Law Review* 41, 3 (2010): 293-316.

–. "Women, Crime, and Criminal Justice in Early Halifax, 1750-1800." In *Essays in the History of Canadian Law*. Vol. 5: *Crime and Criminal Justice,* ed. Jim Phillips, Tina Loo, and Susan Lewthwaite, 174-206. Toronto: University of Toronto Press, 1995.

Phillips, Jim, and Allyson N. May, "Female Criminality in 18th-Century Halifax." *Acadiensis* 31, 2 (2002): 71-96.

Phillips, Jim, Tina Loo, and Susan Lewthwaite, eds. *Essays in the History of Canadian Law*. Vol. 5: *Crime and Criminal Justice*. Toronto: University of Toronto Press, 1994.

Phyne, John. "Prohibition's Legacy: The Emergence of Provincial Policing in Nova Scotia, 1921-1932." *Canadian Journal of Law and Society* 7, 2 (1992): 157-84.

Piva, Michael. *The Condition of the Working Class in Toronto, 1900-1921*. Ottawa: University of Ottawa Press, 1979.

–. "Urban Working-Class Incomes and Real Incomes in 1921: A Comparative Analysis." *Histoire sociale/Social History* 16, 31 (1983): 143-67.

Platt, Anthony M. *The Child Savers: The Invention of Delinquency*, 2nd ed. Chicago: University of Chicago Press, 1977.

Pon, Madge. "Like a Chinese Puzzle: The Construction of Chinese Masculinity in Jack Canuck." In *Gender and History in Canada*, ed. Joy Parr and Mark Rosenfeld, 88-100. Toronto: Copp Clark, 1996.

Popple, A.E. "Police Court Systems." *Canadian Law Times* 41 (1921): 523-24.

Poutanen, Mary Anne. "The Homeless, the Whore, the Drunkard, and the Disorderly: Contours of Female Vagrancy in the Montreal Courts, 1810-1842." In *Gendered Pasts: Historical Essays in Femininity and Masculinity in Canada*, ed. Kathryn McPherson, Cecilia Morgan, and Nancy M. Forestell, 29-47. Toronto: Oxford University Press, 1999.

Price, B. Jane. "'Raised in Rockhead. Died in the Poorhouse': Female Petty Criminals in Halifax, 1864-1890." In *Essays in the History of Canadian Law.* Vol. 3: *Nova Scotia*, ed. Philip Girard and Jim Phillips, 200-31. Toronto: The Osgoode Society, 1990.

Prince, Samuel Henry. *Catastrophe and Social Change*. New York: AMS Press, 1968 [Columbia University Press, 1920].

–. *Housing in Halifax: A Report*. Halifax: The Citizens' Committee on Housing, 1932.

Pue, W. Wesley, and Barry Wright, eds. *Canadian Perspectives on Law and Society: Issues in Legal History*. Ottawa: Carleton University Press, 1988.

Quinney, Richard. *The Social Reality of Crime*. Boston: Little, Brown and Company, 1970.

Raddall, Thomas H. *Halifax: Warden of the North*. Halifax: Nimbus, 1993.

Radzinowicz, Sir Leon, and Marvin E. Wolfgang, eds. *Crime and Justice*. Vol. 1: *The Criminal in Society*, 2nd and rev. ed. New York: Basic Books, 1971.

Rafter, Nicole Hahn. "The Social Construction of Crime and Crime Control." *Journal of Research in Crime and Delinquency* 27, 4 (1990): 376-89.

Ratner, R.S., and John L. McMullan, eds. *State Control: Criminal Justice Politics in Canada*. Vancouver: UBC Press, 1987.

Ratner, R.S., John L. McMullan, and Brian E. Burtch. "The Problem of Relative Autonomy and Criminal Justice in the Canadian State." In *State Control: Criminal Justice Politics in Canada*, ed. R.S. Ratner and John L. McMullan, 85-125. Vancouver: UBC Press, 1987.

Reagan, Leslie J. "'About to Meet Her Maker': Women, Doctors, Dying Declarations, and the State's Investigation of Abortion, Chicago, 1867-1940." *Journal of American History* 77, 4 (1991): 1240-64.

Reid, John G. *Six Crucial Decades: Times of Change in the History of the Maritimes*. Halifax: Nimbus, 1987.

Riegel, Robert E. "Changing American Attitudes toward Prostitution, 1800-1920." In Eric Monkkonen, ed., *Crime and Justice in American History*. Vol. 8: *Prostitution, Drugs, Gambling and Organized Crime*, pt. 2, 632-47. Munich: K.G. Saur, 1992.

Roberts, Barbara. "Shovelling Out the 'Mutinous': Political Deportation from Canada before 1936." *Labour/Le Travail* 18 (1986): 77-110.

–. *Whence They Came: Deportation from Canada, 1900-1935*. Ottawa: University of Ottawa Press, 1988.

Roediger, David R. *Towards the Abolition of Whiteness: Essays on Race, Politics, and Working-Class History*. London: Verso, 1994.

Rooke, Patricia T., and R.C. Schnell, eds. *Studies in Childhood History: A Canadian Perspective*. Calgary: Detselig, 1982.

Roper, Henry. "The Halifax Board of Control: The Failure of Municipal Reform, 1906-1919." *Acadiensis* 14, 2 (1985): 46-65.

–. "The Strange Political Career of A.C. Hawkins, Mayor of Halifax, 1918-1919." *Collections of the Royal Nova Scotia Historical Society* 41 (1982): 141-63.

Ross, Winifred M. "Child Rescue: The Nova Scotia Society for the Prevention of Cruelty, 1880-1920." MA thesis, Dalhousie University, 1975.

Rotenberg, Lori. "The Wayward Worker: Toronto's Prostitute at the Turn of the Century." In *Women at Work: Ontario, 1850-1930*, ed. Janice Acton, Penny Goldsmith, and Bonnie Shepard, 33-69. Toronto: Canadian Women's Educational Press, 1974.

Rothman, David J. *The Discovery of the Asylum: Social Order and Disorder in the New Republic*. Boston: Little, Brown and Company, 1971.

Roy, Patricia E. *The Oriental Question: Consolidating a White Man's Province, 1914-41*. Vancouver: UBC Press, 2003.

–. *A White Man's Province: British Columbia Politicians and Chinese and Japanese Immigrants, 1858-1914*. Vancouver: UBC Press, 1989.

Rude, George. *Criminal and Victim: Crime and Society in Early Nineteenth-Century England*. Oxford: Clarendon Press, 1985.

–. *The Crowd in History: A Study of Popular Disturbances in France and England, 1730-1848*. New York: John Wiley and Sons, 1964.

Ruemper, Wendy. "Locking Them Up: Incarcerating Women in Ontario, 1857-1931." In *Law, Society, and the State: Essays in Modern Legal History*, ed. Louis A. Knafla and Susan W.S. Binnie, 351-78. Toronto: University of Toronto Press, 1995.

Ruffman, Alan, and Colin D. Howell, eds. *Ground Zero: A Reassessment of the 1917 Explosion in Halifax Harbour*. Halifax: Nimbus, 1994.

Rule, John, and Robert Malcolmson, eds. *Protest and Survival: The Historical Experience – Essays for E.P. Thompson*. London: Merlin Press, 1993.

Said, Edward W. *Orientalism*. New York: Vintage Books, 1979.

Sangster, Joan. "Creating Social and Moral Citizens: Defining and Treating Delinquent Boys and Girls in English Canada, 1920-65." In *Contesting Canadian Citizenship: Historical Readings*, ed. Robert Adamoski, Dorothy E. Chunn, and Robert Menzies, 337-58. Peterborough: Broadview Press, 2002.

–. *Girl Trouble: Female Delinquency in English Canada*. Toronto: Between the Lines, 2002.

–. "'Pardon Tales' from Magistrate's Court: Women, Crime and the Court in Peterborough County, 1920-50." *Canadian Historical Review* 74, 2 (1993): 161-97.

–. *Regulating Girls and Women: Sexuality, Family, and the Law in Ontario, 1920-1960*. Don Mills: Oxford University Press, 2001.

Saunders, S.A. *The Economic History of the Maritime Provinces*. Fredericton, NB: Acadiensis Press, 1984.

Sayer, Derek. *The Violence of Abstraction: The Analytic Foundations of Historical Materialism*. Oxford: Basil Blackwell, 1987.

Schlossman, Steven L. *Love and the American Delinquent: The Theory and Practice of "Progressive" Juvenile Justice, 1825-1920*. Chicago: University of Chicago Press, 1977.

Schlossman, Steven, and Stephanie Wallach. "The Crime of Precocious Sexuality: Female Juvenile Delinquency in the Progressive Era." *Harvard Educational Review* 48, 1 (1978): 65-94.

Schneider, John C. *Detroit and the Problem of Order, 1830-1880: A Geography of Crime, Riot, and Policing*. Lincoln: University of Nebraska Press, 1980.

Schulz, Dorothy M. "The Police Matron Movement: Paving the Way for Policewomen." *Police Studies* 12, 3 (1987): 115-24.

See, Scott. *Riots in New Brunswick: Orange Nativism and Social Violence in the 1840s*. Toronto: University of Toronto Press, 1993.

Semple, Neil. *The Lord's Dominion: The History of Canadian Methodism*. Montreal and Kingston: McGill-Queen's University Press, 1996.

Seth, James. "Halifax Revisited." *Dalhousie Review* 1, 4 (1922): 333-39.

Seto, William, and Larry N. Shyu. *The Chinese Experience in New Brunswick: A Historical Perspective*. Fredericton, NB: Chinese Cultural Association of New Brunswick, 1986.

Shapiro, Ann-Louise. *Breaking the Codes: Female Criminality in Fin-de-Siècle Paris*. Stanford: Stanford University Press, 1996.

Sharpe, J.A. "The History of Crime in Late Medieval and Early Modern England: A Review of the Field." *Social History* 7, 2 (1982): 187-203.

Shaver, Frances M. "The Regulation of Prostitution: Avoiding the Morality Traps." *Canadian Journal of Law and Society* 9, 1 (1994): 123-45.

Shelley, Louise I. *Crime and Modernization: The Impact of Industrialization and Urbanization on Crime*. Carbondale and Edwardsville: Southern Illinois University Press, 1981.

Shore, Heather. "'Inventing' the Juvenile Delinquent in Nineteenth-Century Europe." In *Comparative Histories of Crime*, ed. Barry S. Godfrey, Clive Emsley, and Graeme Dunstall, 110-24. Devon: Willan Publishing, 2003.

Shutlak, Garry. "A Vision of Regeneration: Reconstruction after the Explosion, 1917-21." In *Ground Zero: A Reassessment of the 1917 Explosion in Halifax Harbour*, ed. Alan Ruffman and Colin D. Howell, 421-26. Halifax: Nimbus, 1994.

Silver, Allan. "The Demand for Order in Civil Society: A Review of Some Themes in the History of Urban Crime, Police and Riot." In *The Police: Six Sociological Essays*, ed. David J. Bordua, 1-24. New York: John Wiley and Sons, 1967.

Simmons, Christina. "'Helping the Poorer Sisters': The Women of the Jost Mission, Halifax, 1905-1945." *Acadiensis* 14, 1 (1984): 3-27.

Smandych, Russell, and Bryan Hogeveen. "On the Fragmentation of Canadian Criminal Justice History." *Canadian Journal of Criminology* 41, 2 (April 1999): 191-203.

Smart, Carol. *Women, Crime and Criminology: A Feminist Critique*. London: Routledge and Kegan Paul, 1977.

Smith, Harry D. *Through Dirty Windows: A Humorous Account of Shop and Factory Life in the Incredible 1930s*. Windsor, NS: Lancelot Press, 1976.

Smith, Michael J. "Dampness, Darkness, Dirt, Disease: Physicians and the Promotion of Sanitary Science in Public Schools." In *Profiles of Science and Society in the Maritimes prior to 1914*, ed. Paul A. Bogaard, 195-218. Fredericton, NB: Acadiensis Press, 1990.

Smith-Rosenberg, Carroll. *Disorderly Conduct: Visions of Gender in Victorian America*. New York: Alfred A. Knopf, 1985.

Snell, James. "Marital Cruelty: Women and the Nova Scotia Divorce Court, 1900-1939." *Acadiensis* 18, 1 (1988): 3-32.

–. *In the Shadow of the Law: Divorce in Canada, 1900-1930*. Toronto: University of Toronto Press, 1991.

Solomon, R., and M. Green. "The First Century: The History of Nonmedical Opiate Use and Control Policies in Canada, 1870-1970." *University of Western Ontario Law Review* 20, 2 (1982): 307-36.

Steinberg, Allen. *The Transformation of Criminal Justice: Philadelphia, 1800-1880*. Chapel Hill: The University of North Carolina Press, 1989.

Stephen, Jennifer. "The 'Incorrigible,' the 'Bad,' and the 'Immoral': Toronto's 'Factory Girls' and the Work of the Toronto Psychiatric Clinic." In *Law, Society, and the State: Essays in Modern Legal History*, ed. Louis A. Knafla and Susan W.S. Binnie, 405-39. Toronto: University of Toronto Press, 1995.

Strange, Carolyn. "The Lottery of Death: Capital Punishment, 1867-1976." *Manitoba Law Journal* 23 (1995): 594-619.

–. "Mercy for Murderers? A Historical Perspective on the Royal Prerogative of Mercy." *Saskatchewan Law Review* 64, 2 (2001): 559-72.

–. "Patriarchy Modified: The Criminal Prosecution of Rape in York County, Ontario, 1880-1930." In *Essays in the History of Canadian Law*. Vol. 5: *Crime and Criminal Justice*, ed. Jim Phillips, Tina Loo, and Susan Lewthwaite, 207-51. Toronto: University of Toronto Press, 1994.

–. *Toronto's Girl Problem: The Perils and Pleasures of the City, 1880-1930*. Toronto: University of Toronto Press, 1995.

–. "The Undercurrents of Penal Culture: Punishment of the Body in Mid-Twentieth-Century Canada." *Law and History Review* 19, 2 (2001): 343-85.

Strange, Carolyn, and Tina Loo. *Making Good: Law and Moral Regulation in Canada, 1867-1939*. Toronto: University of Toronto Press, 1997.

–. "Spectacular Justice: The Circus on Trial, and the Trial as Circus, Picton, 1903." *Canadian Historical Review* 77, 2 (1996): 159-84.

Sugarman, David. "Law, Economy, and the State in England, 1750-1914: Some Major Issues." In *Legality, Ideology, and the State*, ed. David Sugarman, 213-66. London: Academic Press, 1983.

–, ed. *Legality, Ideology, and the State*. London: Academic Press, 1983.

Sumner, Colin. *Reading Ideologies: An Investigation into the Marxist Theory of Ideology and Law*. London: Academic Press, 1979.

Sutherland, David A. "Halifax Harbour, December 6, 1917: Setting the Scene." In *Ground Zero: A Reassessment of the 1917 Explosion in Halifax Harbour*, ed. Allan Ruffman and Colin D. Howell, 3-8. Halifax: Nimbus, 1994.

–. "Race Relations in Halifax, Nova Scotia, during the Mid-Victorian Quest for Reform." *Journal of the Canadian Historical Association* 7, 1 (1996): 35-54.

–. "Voluntary Societies and the Process of Middle-Class Formation in Early Victorian Halifax, Nova Scotia." *Journal of the Canadian Historical Association* 5, 1 (1994): 237-63.

Sutherland, Neil. *Children in English-Canadian Society: Framing the Twentieth-Century Consensus*. Toronto: University of Toronto Press, 1976.

–. *Growing Up: Childhood in English Canada from the Great War to the Age of Television*. Toronto: University of Toronto Press, 1997.

–. "'We Always Had Things to Do': The Paid and Unpaid Work of Anglophone Children between the 1920s and the 1960s." *Labour/Le Travail* 25 (1990): 105-41.

Swainger, Jonathan, and Constance Backhouse, eds. *People and Place: Historical Influences on Legal Culture*. Vancouver: UBC Press, 2003.

Taylor, Charles. *The Malaise of Modernity*. Concord, ON: Anansi, 1991.

Taylor, Ian, Paul Watson, and Jock Young, eds. *Critical Criminology*. London: Routledge and Kegan Paul, 1975.

Thomas, Ernest. "Drinking, Drunkenness and Crime in Canada." *Social Welfare* 6, 4 (1924): 74-79.

Thompson, E.P. "The Crime of Anonymity." In *Albion's Fatal Tree: Crime and Society in Eighteenth-Century England,* ed. Douglas Hay, Peter Linebaugh, John G. Rule, E.P. Thompson, and Cal Winslow, 255-344. London: Penguin Books, 1975.

–. *Customs in Common: Studies in Traditional Popular Culture*. New York: The New Press, 1991.

–. *The Making of the English Working Class*. London: Penguin Group, 1980.

–. *The Poverty of Theory and Other Essays*. London: Merlin Press, 1978.

–. *Whigs and Hunters: The Origin of the Black Act*. New York: Pantheon Books, 1975.

Thompson, Hilary, ed. *Children's Voices in Atlantic Literature and Culture: Essays on Childhood*. Guelph: Canadian Children's Press, 1995.

Thompson, John Herd, with Allen Seager. *Canada, 1922-1939: Decades of Discord*. Toronto: McClelland and Stewart, 1985.

Thomson, Anthony. "The Development of the Penitentiary in Nova Scotia in the Nineteenth Century." In *Studies on Atlantic Canada*, ed. Satadal Dasgupta, 100-17. Charlottetown: University of Prince Edward Island, 1985.

Thorn, Brian T. "'Healthy Activity and Worthwhile Ideas': Left- and Right-Wing Women Confront Juvenile Delinquency in Post-World-War II Canada." *Histoire sociale/Social History* 42, 84 (2009): 327-59.

Thorner, Thomas, and Neil B. Watson. "Keeper of the King's Peace: Colonel G.E. Sanders and the Calgary Police Magistrate's Court, 1911-1932." *Urban History Review* 12, 3 (1984): 45-55.

Thornton, Patricia A. "The Problem of Out-Migration from Atlantic Canada, 1871-1921: A New Look." *Acadiensis* 15, 1 (1985): 3-34.

Tone, Andrea. "Contraceptive Consumers: Gender and the Political Economy of Birth Control in the 1930s." *Journal of Social History* 29, 3 (1996): 485-506.

Toner, R.C., and D.C. Perrier. "Nova Scotia Police." *RCMP Quarterly* 47, 3 (1982): 33-45.

Tonry, Michael, ed. *Crime and Justice: A Review of Research,* vol. 14. Chicago: The University of Chicago Press, 1991.

Topping, C.W. *Canadian Penal Institutions*. Chicago: University of Chicago Press, 1930.

–. *Canadian Penal Institutions,* rev. ed. Toronto: Ryerson Press, 1943.

Torrance, Judy M. *Public Violence in Canada, 1867-1982*. Kingston and Montreal: McGill-Queen's University Press, 1986.

Tratt, Gertrude E.N. *A Survey and Listing of Nova Scotia Newspapers, 1752-1957*. Halifax: Dalhousie University School of Library Service, Occasional Paper 21, 1979.

Trepanier, Jean. "Juvenile Delinquency and Youth Protection: The Historical Foundations of the Canadian Juvenile Delinquents Act of 1908." *European Journal of Crime, Criminal Law, and Criminal Justice* 7, 1 (1999): 41-62.

Valverde, Marianna. *The Age of Light, Soap, and Water: Moral Reform in English Canada, 1885-1925*. Toronto: McClelland and Stewart, 1991.

Veinott, Rebecca. "The Changing Legal Status of Women in Nova Scotia, 1850-1910." MA thesis, Dalhousie University, 1989.

Waite, Catherine Ann. "The Longshoremen of Halifax, 1900-1930: Their Living and Working Conditions." MA thesis, Dalhousie University, 1977.

Waite, P.B. *The Man from Halifax: Sir John Thompson, Prime Minister*. Toronto: University of Toronto Press, 1985.

Waite, Peter, Sandra Oxner, and Thomas Barnes, eds. *Law in a Colonial Society: The Nova Scotia Experience*. Toronto: Carswell, 1984.

Walker, James W. St. G. "Black History in the Maritimes: Major Themes and Teaching Strategies." In *Teaching Maritime Studies*, ed. Phillip Buckner, 96-107. Fredericton, NB: Acadiensis Press, 1986.

–. *"Race," Rights, and the Law in the Supreme Court of Canada: Historical Case Studies*. Waterloo: Wilfrid Laurier University Press, 1997.

Walkowitz, Judith R. *Prostitution and Victorian Society: Women, Class and the State*. Cambridge: Cambridge University Press, 1980.

Ward, W. Peter. *White Canada Forever: Popular Attitudes and Public Policy toward Orientals in British Columbia*. Montreal: McGill-Queen's University Press, 1978.

Watson, Sean. "Symbolic Antagonism, Police Paranoia, and the Possibility of Social Diversity." In *The Lesser Evil and the Greater Good: The Theory and Politics of Social Diversity*, ed. Jeffrey Weeks, 100-22. London: Rivers Oram Press, 1994.

Weaver, John C. *Crime, Constables, and Courts: Order and Transgression in a Canadian City, 1816-1970*. Montreal and Kingston: McGill-Queen's University Press, 1995.

Weeks, Jeffrey, ed. *The Lesser Evil and the Greater Good: The Theory and Politics of Social Diversity*. London: Rivers Oram Press, 1994.

White, Jay. "Working-Class Housing in Halifax, 1905-1939." Unpublished paper, Department of History, McMaster University, 1986.

White, Kimberley. *Negotiating Responsibility: Law, Murder, and States of Mind*. Vancouver: UBC Press, 2008.

Wiener, Martin J. *Reconstructing the Criminal: Culture, Law, and Policy in England, 1830-1914*. Cambridge: Cambridge University Press, 1990.

Wilson, Adrian, ed. *Rethinking Social History: English Society 1570-1920 and Its Interpretation*. Manchester: Manchester University Press, 1993.

Wilson, J. Donald, and David C. Jones, eds. *Schooling and Society in Twentieth-Century British Columbia*. Calgary: Detselig, 1980.

Winks, Robin W. *The Blacks in Canada: A History*. Montreal and Kingston: McGill-Queen's University Press, 1971.

Wolcott, David B. *Cops and Kids: Policing Juvenile Delinquency in Urban America, 1890-1940*. Columbus: Ohio University Press, 2005.

Wright, A. Jeffrey. "The Halifax Riot of April, 1863." *Nova Scotia Historical Quarterly* 4, 3 (1974): 299-310.

Wright, Barry. "Towards a New Canadian Legal History." *Osgoode Hall Law Journal* 22, 2 (1984): 349-74.

Wright, Cynthia. "'Feminine Trifles of Vast Importance': Writing Gender into the History of Consumption." In *Constructing Modern Canada: Readings in Post-Confederation History*, ed. Chad Gaffield, 288-310. Toronto: Copp Clark Longman Ltd., 1994.

Wright, Mary Ellen. "Unnatural Mothers: Infanticide in Halifax, 1850-1875." *Nova Scotia Historical Review* 7, 2 (1987): 13-29.

Wrigley, E.A., ed. *Nineteenth-Century Society: Essays in the Use of Quantitative Methods for the Study of Social Data.* Cambridge: Cambridge University Press, 1972.

Young, Brian. "Law 'in the Round.'" *Acadiensis* 16, 1 (1986): 155-65.

Zedner, Lucia. "Women, Crime, and Penal Responses: A Historical Account." In *Crime and Justice: A Review of Research*, ed. Michael Tonry, 14:307-62. Chicago: University of Chicago Press, 1991.

Zehr, Howard. *Crime and the Development of Modern Society: Patterns of Criminality in Nineteenth-Century Germany and France.* London: Croom Helm, 1976.

Zucchi, John E. *Italians in Toronto: Development of a National Identity, 1875-1935.* Kingston and Montreal: McGill-Queen's University Press, 1988.

Index

a = appendix f = figure n = note

Jacqueline D. Krikorian
International Trade Law and Domestic Policy: Canada, the United States, and the WTO (2012)

Michael Boudreau
City of Order: Crime and Society in Halifax, 1918-35 (2012)

Lesley Erickson
Westward Bound: Sex, Violence, the Law, and the Making of a Settler Society (2011)

David R. Boyd
The Environmental Rights Revolution: A Global Study of Constitutions, Human Rights, and the Environment (2011)

Elaine Craig
Troubling Sex: Towards a Legal Theory of Sexual Integrity (2011)

Laura DeVries
Conflict in Caledonia: Aboriginal Land Rights and the Rule of Law (2011)

Jocelyn Downie and Jennifer J. Llewellyn (eds.)
Being Relational: Reflections on Relational Theory and Health Law (2011)

Grace Li Xiu Woo
Ghost Dancing with Colonialism: Decolonization and Indigenous Rights at the Supreme Court of Canada (2011)

Fiona Kelly
Transforming Law's Family: The Legal Recognition of Planned Lesbian Motherhood (2011)

Colleen Bell
The Freedom of Security: Governing Canada in the Age of Counter-Terrorism (2011)

Andrew S. Thompson
In Defence of Principles: NGOs and Human Rights in Canada (2010)

Aaron Doyle and Dawn Moore (eds.)
Critical Criminology in Canada: New Voices, New Directions (2010)

Joanna R. Quinn
The Politics of Acknowledgement: Truth Commissions in Uganda and Haiti (2010)

Patrick James
Constitutional Politics in Canada after the Charter: Liberalism, Communitarianism, and Systemism (2010)

Louis A. Knafla and Haijo Westra (eds.)
Aboriginal Title and Indigenous Peoples: Canada, Australia, and New Zealand (2010)

Janet Mosher and Joan Brockman (eds.)
Constructing Crime: Contemporary Processes of Criminalization (2010)

Stephen Clarkson and Stepan Wood
A Perilous Imbalance: The Globalization of Canadian Law and Governance (2009)

Amanda Glasbeek
Feminized Justice: The Toronto Women's Court, 1913-34 (2009)

Kimb Brooks (ed.)
Justice Bertha Wilson: One Woman's Difference (2009)

Wayne V. McIntosh and Cynthia L. Cates
Multi-Party Litigation: The Strategic Context (2009)

Renisa Mawani
Colonial Proximities: Crossracial Encounters and Juridical Truths in British Columbia, 1871-1921 (2009)

James B. Kelly and Christopher P. Manfredi (eds.)
Contested Constitutionalism: Reflections on the Canadian Charter of Rights and Freedoms (2009)

Catherine Bell and Robert K. Paterson (eds.)
Protection of First Nations Cultural Heritage: Laws, Policy, and Reform (2008)

Hamar Foster, Benjamin L. Berger, and A.R. Buck (eds.)
The Grand Experiment: Law and Legal Culture in British Settler Societies (2008)

Richard J. Moon (ed.)
Law and Religious Pluralism in Canada (2008)

Catherine Bell and Val Napoleon (eds.)
First Nations Cultural Heritage and Law: Case Studies, Voices, and Perspectives (2008)

Douglas C. Harris
Landing Native Fisheries: Indian Reserves and Fishing Rights in British Columbia, 1849-1925 (2008)

Peggy J. Blair
Lament for a First Nation: The Williams Treaties of Southern Ontario (2008)

Lori G. Beaman
Defining Harm: Religious Freedom and the Limits of the Law (2007)

Stephen Tierney (ed.)
Multiculturalism and the Canadian Constitution (2007)

Julie Macfarlane
The New Lawyer: How Settlement Is Transforming the Practice of Law (2007)

Kimberley White
Negotiating Responsibility: Law, Murder, and States of Mind (2007)

Dawn Moore
Criminal Artefacts: Governing Drugs and Users (2007)

Hamar Foster, Heather Raven, and Jeremy Webber (eds.)
Let Right Be Done: Aboriginal Title, the Calder *Case, and the Future of Indigenous Rights* (2007)

Dorothy E. Chunn, Susan B. Boyd, and Hester Lessard (eds.)
Reaction and Resistance: Feminism, Law, and Social Change (2007)

Margot Young, Susan B. Boyd, Gwen Brodsky, and Shelagh Day (eds.)
Poverty: Rights, Social Citizenship, and Legal Activism (2007)

Rosanna L. Langer
Defining Rights and Wrongs: Bureaucracy, Human Rights, and Public Accountability (2007)

C.L. Ostberg and Matthew E. Wetstein
Attitudinal Decision Making in the Supreme Court of Canada (2007)

Chris Clarkson
Domestic Reforms: Political Visions and Family Regulation in British Columbia, 1862-1940 (2007)

Jean McKenzie Leiper
Bar Codes: Women in the Legal Profession (2006)

Gerald Baier
Courts and Federalism: Judicial Doctrine in the United States, Australia, and Canada (2006)

Avigail Eisenberg (ed.)
Diversity and Equality: The Changing Framework of Freedom in Canada (2006)

Randy K. Lippert
Sanctuary, Sovereignty, Sacrifice: Canadian Sanctuary Incidents, Power, and Law (2005)

James B. Kelly
Governing with the Charter: Legislative and Judicial Activism and Framers' Intent (2005)

Dianne Pothier and Richard Devlin (eds.)
Critical Disability Theory: Essays in Philosophy, Politics, Policy, and Law (2005)

Susan G. Drummond
Mapping Marriage Law in Spanish Gitano Communities (2005)

Louis A. Knafla and Jonathan Swainger (eds.)
Laws and Societies in the Canadian Prairie West, 1670-1940 (2005)

Ikechi Mgbeoji
Global Biopiracy: Patents, Plants, and Indigenous Knowledge (2005)

Florian Sauvageau, David Schneiderman, and David Taras,
with Ruth Klinkhammer and Pierre Trudel
The Last Word: Media Coverage of the Supreme Court of Canada (2005)

Gerald Kernerman
Multicultural Nationalism: Civilizing Difference, Constituting Community (2005)

Pamela A. Jordan
Defending Rights in Russia: Lawyers, the State, and Legal Reform in the Post-Soviet Era (2005)

Anna Pratt
Securing Borders: Detention and Deportation in Canada (2005)

Kirsten Johnson Kramar
Unwilling Mothers, Unwanted Babies: Infanticide in Canada (2005)

W.A. Bogart
Good Government? Good Citizens? Courts, Politics, and Markets in a Changing Canada (2005)

Catherine Dauvergne
Humanitarianism, Identity, and Nation: Migration Laws in Canada and Australia (2005)

Michael Lee Ross
First Nations Sacred Sites in Canada's Courts (2005)

Andrew Woolford
Between Justice and Certainty: Treaty Making in British Columbia (2005)

John McLaren, Andrew Buck, and Nancy Wright (eds.)
Despotic Dominion: Property Rights in British Settler Societies (2004)

Georges Campeau
From UI to EI: Waging War on the Welfare State (2004)

Alvin J. Esau
The Courts and the Colonies: The Litigation of Hutterite Church Disputes (2004)

Christopher N. Kendall
Gay Male Pornography: An Issue of Sex Discrimination (2004)

Roy B. Flemming
Tournament of Appeals: Granting Judicial Review in Canada (2004)

Constance Backhouse and Nancy L. Backhouse
The Heiress vs the Establishment: Mrs. Campbell's Campaign for Legal Justice (2004)

Christopher P. Manfredi
Feminist Activism in the Supreme Court: Legal Mobilization and the Women's Legal Education and Action Fund (2004)

Annalise Acorn
Compulsory Compassion: A Critique of Restorative Justice (2004)

Jonathan Swainger and Constance Backhouse (eds.)
People and Place: Historical Influences on Legal Culture (2003)

Jim Phillips and Rosemary Gartner
Murdering Holiness: The Trials of Franz Creffield and George Mitchell (2003)

David R. Boyd
Unnatural Law: Rethinking Canadian Environmental Law and Policy (2003)

Ikechi Mgbeoji
Collective Insecurity: The Liberian Crisis, Unilateralism, and Global Order (2003)

Rebecca Johnson
Taxing Choices: The Intersection of Class, Gender, Parenthood, and the Law (2002)

John McLaren, Robert Menzies, and Dorothy E. Chunn (eds.)
Regulating Lives: Historical Essays on the State, Society, the Individual, and the Law (2002)

Joan Brockman
Gender in the Legal Profession: Fitting or Breaking the Mould (2001)

Printed and bound in Canada by Friesens

Set in Perpetua and Minion Condensed by Artegraphica Design Co. Ltd.

Copy editor: Joanne Richardson

Proofreader and indexer: Dianne Tiefensee

Cartography: Eric Leinberger